SANDRA DAY
O'CONNOR

SANDRA DAY
O'CONNOR

How the First Woman on the Supreme Court

Became Its Most Influential Justice

JOAN BISKUPIC

An Imprint of HarperCollinsPublishers

HarperCollins books may be purchased for educational, business, or sales promotional use. For information, please write: Special Markets Department, HarperCollins Publishers, 10 East 53rd Street, New York, NY 10022.

FIRST EDITION

Designed by Joseph Rutt

Printed on acid-free paper

Library of Congress Cataloging-in-Publication Data
is available upon request.

ISBN-10: 0-06-059018-1
ISBN-13: 978-0-06-059018-5

05 06 07 08 09 10 DIX/RRD 10 9 8 7 6 5 4 3 2 1

For Clay and Elizabeth

"As you will recall, Sandra forced my hand by
threatening to lead the revolution. . . ."

—personal note
from
Justice William J. Brennan Jr.
to
Justice Thurgood Marshall,
June 7, 1990

CONTENTS

SANDRA DAY
O'CONNOR

PROLOGUE

As Sandra Day O'Connor celebrated her 51st birthday in suburban Phoenix on Thursday, March 26, 1981, Supreme Court Justice Potter Stewart and Attorney General William French Smith spoke confidentially in the solarium of Stewart's home in the lush Palisades neighborhood of northwest Washington, DC.[1]

The private meeting had been arranged by Stewart's old friend George H. W. Bush, then the vice president. Appointed to the bench by President Eisenhower, Stewart had decided to retire in June, at age 66, at the end of the Court's term. To give President Ronald Reagan time to pick a successor, Stewart needed to inform Smith now. But he wanted his decision kept quiet until June.

The next day, Smith asked an assistant to begin research on a list of potential Supreme Court nominees. Without mentioning his conversation with Stewart, Smith said the office should prepare for the possibility of a vacancy occurring in the summer. It had been six years since the last Supreme Court appointment, and all but two of the justices were over 65, so Smith's request was not extraordinary. Working with White House counsel Fred Fielding, Smith already had begun an informal short list of possible nominees. Smith scrawled his names on a pink telephone message slip in his office.

"Who's O'Connor?" asked the assistant, Ken Starr, when Smith handed him the slip. "All you've got here is a last name."

"That's Sandra Day O'Connor," Smith said. "She's an appeals court judge in Arizona." Smith knew little more about her, only that her name had been passed on by at least one person in his circle. A few other women's names made the list, along with a couple of men, including Robert Bork, a Yale University law professor and former U.S. solicitor general, a favorite of political conservatives.

Smith planned to inform President Reagan early the next week that he would soon have an appointment to make to the nation's highest court. But before Smith could arrange a private conversation, fate intervened. On Monday, March 30, Reagan was shot and wounded as he was leaving the Washington Hilton after a speech. The bullet hit the president under his left arm, narrowly missed a vital artery, and lodged in his left lung. Secret Service agents rushed him to a hospital, where he underwent emergency surgery.[2]

Reagan returned to the White House living quarters two weeks later, but it was not until April 21, nearly a month after Smith's conversation with Justice Stewart, that the attorney general thought the president was sufficiently recovered to hear of the impending Court vacancy. A long-time Reagan confidant distinguished by his silver hair and year-round tan, Smith disclosed the news as the two men talked in the president's private study on the third floor of the White House. As a candidate in 1980, Reagan had promised the nation a woman justice, and now he told Smith of his preference for a female nominee.[3]

Smith said that a search was already underway and that women were included on the list.

O'Connor's credentials did not make her an obvious candidate. She was not on a federal court or top state court, as many nominees in the recent past had been. Instead, she was a judge on a state intermediate court handling criminal and civil appeals. But she was also a former state senator with deep and well-maintained political connections to the Republican Party. In the fall of 1971, she had created a vast network to advance the Supreme Court nomination of William Rehnquist, her old Stanford Law School classmate. She had then become cochairman of Richard Nixon's 1972 reelection campaign in Arizona. She was also old friends with senator Barry Goldwater, an early apostle of the conservatism that Reagan had since brought to Washington. Strengthening her hand considerably was a bond she had developed with Chief Justice Warren

Burger after a vacation together. They had been guests of a mutual friend on a houseboat trip on scenic Lake Powell in Utah in 1979. Burger had appointed O'Connor to judicial commissions that gave her exposure in national and even international legal circles.[4]

O'Connor also stood out at a time when women, especially Republican women, were a rarity on state and federal courts. When Stewart announced his retirement on June 18, news reporters immediately focused on the few women judges with Republican connections, such as Cornelia Kennedy, a judge on the U.S. Court of Appeals for the Sixth Circuit, and Joan Dempsey Klein, a judge on the Los Angeles Superior Court.[5]

Starr, then 35 and Smith's chief lieutenant in screening the backgrounds of potential nominees, reviewed O'Connor's court rulings. The son of a Texas minister, Starr had gone to Duke Law School and landed a plum job as a law clerk to Chief Justice Burger, before settling into practice with Smith at the Los Angeles law firm of Gibson, Dunn and Crutcher. Starr then followed Smith into the Reagan administration.

The research on O'Connor in Arizona fell to another Justice Department lawyer, F. Henry "Hank" Habicht, a 28-year-old native of suburban Chicago. He flew to Phoenix to look up legislation O'Connor had sponsored and to interview her former colleagues in the Arizona legislature. Wearing a jacket and tie in defiance of the broiling Arizona sun, the Midwesterner did not go unnoticed, and word of Habicht's visit soon reached O'Connor.[6]

At the White House, the idea of a female nominee was gaining momentum, although *who* that would be was still an open question. "I think it is imperative that you appoint a woman to the Supreme Court," wrote Lyn Nofziger, Reagan's longtime political advisor who served as liaison to conservative groups. "It means you will live up to a commitment you made and have that behind you. It will go a long way toward solving the problem we have with the lack of women in this administration in high places. It will take off your back the impression, however unjustified, that you and your senior staffers are anti-women." The Reagan cabinet had no women, although the administration's most prominent female appointee, Jeane Kirkpatrick, U.S. ambassador to the United Nations, had cabinet status. As Nofziger and other Reagan advisors saw it, the search for a candidate was about politics as much as it was about legal qualifications—not a new development in Supreme Court selection.[7]

The next day, on June 23, Smith briefed Reagan on the leading candidates. The president was interested in O'Connor. Her childhood on the Lazy B ranch intrigued the man who had adopted California as his home, rode horses, and chopped wood for exercise. For Reagan—the self-styled nontraditional politician—O'Connor's turn as a legislator and her relative lack of judicial experience made her more attractive than conventional nominees.[8]

Another major asset was that she appeared to have sidestepped the political traps of the day: abortion and the Equal Rights Amendment. She had worked for women's rights, but not in the hard-line way that defined the more vocal elements of the movement. "I come to you tonight wearing my bra and my wedding ring," she used to tell local audiences. She had stuck with dresses and pearls as her female contemporaries moved into pantsuits.[9]

Two days later, on June 25, Smith called O'Connor for the first time. She had heard that the Justice Department was nosing around, so the call was not entirely unexpected. But the timing was inopportune: she was recuperating from a hysterectomy. Smith told her that she was being considered for a "federal position." She knew Smith's background at the law firm of Gibson, Dunn and Crutcher, and she immediately kidded, "It must be a secretarial position, is it not?" This remark alluded to an episode O'Connor had never forgotten: after she had graduated from Stanford Law School in 1952, his Los Angeles law firm offered her only a legal-secretary job. But on this June 1981 day, Smith ignored the allusion and told O'Connor that Starr and another aide would be flying out to interview her in two days. They wanted to meet at her house rather than a public place, so that they could keep the process confidential.[10]

At the time, Starr was surprised that the relatively unknown O'Connor had become such a focus of attention. "There was a certain oddity to her being in the mix at all," he said later. "Judge O'Connor was in Arizona, not on an impressive court, not in a key state. I was skeptical. She was a judicial unknown." But in the living room of her white adobe home, Starr found, "she had clearly prepared for us." She gave elaborate answers to their questions about constitutional law. When they took a break for lunch, she served them a salmon mousse salad she had fixed earlier.[11]

Starr left O'Connor's house ready to give Smith a glowing report and having no idea that she had recently been through the ordeal of a hysterectomy. Later that evening, after hearing from Starr, Smith called O'Connor. He asked if she could come to Washington, DC, to meet him as soon as possible. Because of her surgery, she told him, she would first have to obtain her doctor's permission to travel. She did, and on June 29, O'Connor met Smith and his wife, Jean, at the Jefferson Hotel, a sophisticated Beaux-Arts hotel and residence downtown, where the Smiths lived.

"Jean and I agreed that the judge was a highly intelligent, straightforward, and altogether charming person," Smith wrote later. "Perhaps it was the power of suggestion, or the example set for decades by her fellow Arizonan, Barry Goldwater, but it seemed to us that Sandra Day O'Connor, both in her looks and in her personality, had that same direct friendliness one associates with the wide-open territory where she lived."[12]

Smith arranged for O'Connor to have breakfast the next morning, June 30, with other men whose opinion would be important to her candidacy: Deputy Secretary of State and Reagan confidant William P. Clark (a former justice of the California Supreme Court, appointed by then-Governor Reagan) and Deputy Attorney General Edward C. Schmults. Later that afternoon, Smith introduced O'Connor to White House counsel Fred Fielding and the so-called Troika: Edwin Meese, counselor to the president; James Baker, chief of staff; and Michael Deaver, deputy chief of staff.[13]

One of those participants said later that O'Connor did not challenge anyone's idea of what the first woman on the Court should *look* like. "I know this sounds awful," he said, "but you don't want someone who looks like William Taft. She was very attractive and engaging." O'Connor understood the point. "When I first ran for the state legislature," she later recalled, "it was simply a matter of political reality that, in order to get elected, a woman had to appear and act 'feminine.' People gave up their traditional notions only grudgingly."[14]

By July 1, all that was left was for the candidate to meet the president of the United States. O'Connor's name was still under wraps, and Smith and Fielding wished to keep it that way. Neither of them wanted to accompany O'Connor into the White House, for fear of drawing attention from prying reporters. So, Smith's secretary, Myra Tankersley, arranged to get O'Connor as soon as word came down that the president was available to meet her.[15]

Shortly before 10 a.m. on July 1, O'Connor's phone rang. Tankersley said she would pick her up outside a drugstore on Dupont Circle near O'Connor's hotel. It was an overcast Wednesday morning in Washington, as O'Connor, dressed in a lavender suit, waited for her ride. And when she stepped into that car, she stepped onto the national scene, where she has remained for nearly a quarter of a century.

I

———◆◆◆———

PIONEER ROOTS

To ready herself for the birth of her first child, Ada Mae Day left her home on an Arizona ranch and her husband of three years. She traveled two hundred miles east, to her mother's place in El Paso, Texas, to be near a city hospital. After baby Sandra was born on March 26, 1930, at the Hotel Dieu Hospital, Harry Day came by train to see Ada Mae and his new daughter. "Although I cannot say that I feel any great parental love for Sandra yet," Harry wrote to his wife upon his return to the Lazy B, "I would like to see her and touch her again."[1]

Sandra was a mixed blessing for Harry. The deep passion he felt for Ada Mae was complicated by the infant, as was the burden of making a living from the dry expanse of the Lazy B. He could not abide separation from his young wife. "I wonder continually what you are doing, where you are, who you are with," he wrote to her a year after they married. "I wonder what you will be like when I see you again. Will you be changed? Somehow I am afraid you will be different."[2] Harry's insecurities were ratcheted up by the looming Depression. Even before the arrival of this new mouth to feed, life was defined by scarcity. Too little water. Too few hands for the work to be done.

Decades later, as a Supreme Court justice, Sandra Day O'Connor would write a nostalgically sweet memoir of her ranch childhood. In it, her father, Harry, is painted as a rugged American type, a self-taught man who would become the greatest single influence on her life. Yet, beneath the Gary Cooper of her portrayal, was a man who bequeathed a complex legacy to his children. Harry Day was harsh, demanding, and unpredictable. But Sandra left the Lazy B with a lesson in the virtues of hard work, a talent for maneuvering among tough characters, and a competitive drive that sustained her through a journey no woman had taken before.

HARRY DAY WAS THE fifth and last child of Henry Clay Day, who headed off from Vermont in the mid-1870s to make his fortune. The father, named for the Whig politician Henry Clay, had worked his family's farm in Coventry, Vermont, until 1865, when he turned 21. Then he moved west, first laboring in a general merchandise store on the Canadian border, and later opening his own building-supply business in Wichita, Kansas. There, when he was 35, he met and married Alice Edith Hilton, 18, the daughter of a rector in the Episcopal Church. With his angular New England visage, bushy mustache, and stone-faced demeanor, H. C. Day was marked by his Yankee heritage. But he also could not stay put. He constantly looked for fresh adventures and travel.

In 1880, Day sought acreage in the newly opened public lands of the New Mexico Territory for the grazing of livestock. Down in Mexico, he bought a herd of cattle and settled on a parcel of his new land south of the Gila River, on what would become the border between New Mexico and Arizona. The Mexican cattle had been branded on the left hip with a B lying down flat—a "lazy" B. So, he named his ranch for the brand, and it endured as the Lazy B through the generations. Joining the rush for open range, H. C. Day arrived just as cattle-grazing conditions were becoming harder for ranchers. Dry spells and overstocking were quickly destroying the arid and fragile land. Cattle prices were tumbling. The pioneers were being sorely tested.[3]

Day hired a foreman to manage operations at the Lazy B, began taking steps to move his family to the more pleasant environs of Pasadena, California, and continued his travels, now to England and Germany. The flinty New Englander wanted to be based in California, in a promising city where the orange trees blossomed year round, but Day soon discovered that the ranch foreman was stealing from him.[4] So, he brought his family back to the Gila River valley and the Lazy B, where he built a house and a one-room school for his children. The youngest of H. C.'s and Alice's children, Harry was born at that ranch house in 1898 and lived there until he was about 10 years old. H. C. Day, by then, had a foreman he trusted, and California continued to beckon. He moved his wife and children back to the sweetness of Pasadena. An athletic boy with an attractive smile, young Harry thrived in city schools. He won state swimming awards. So pleased was he to graduate in 1918 from Pasadena High School that he saved his fancy, typeset commencement program and high school picture until the day he died.[5] Harry wore the trappings of city life well. In photographs from these years, Harry looks the dashing young fellow in blazer and cap. He had hopes of college and travel to exotic places.

H. C. was preoccupied, as usual, with his business enterprises. As a father, he was more aloof than affectionate.[6] On the other hand, Harry's mother, Alice, doted on the boy. When he was away from home, she wrote him long, worried letters about whether he had enough clothes to keep warm and whether he was taking care of himself. "Be a good boy and don't lift heavy things or do anything else to injure yourself," she wrote at one point.[7] From both parents, Harry received a sense for business and handling financial affairs.

Harry's dream, born in his Pasadena years, was to attend Stanford University. But as he graduated from high school, Harry was drafted for World War I. The war, however, ended before he saw any action. Then, in 1919, H. C. Day's health slipped and, as he worried about the ranch's finances, he sent Harry, the second of his two sons, to check on its operation. Harry, then 21 years old, found the land a terrible place to live, and hoped to stay at the Lazy B only long enough to make some money and then find someone else to run it.

But when H. C. Day died in 1921, Harry, then 23, was the only one available to take over. "I think if you try your best that you will be able to make some money out of the place or else be able to sell it for a good price when the drouth is over," his mother, Alice, wrote in response to one of Harry's letters in which he was trying to extract himself from the obligation of living on the bleached-brown land and at the mercy of a wildly fluctuating cattle market.[8] Harry's mother and older brother, Courtland, wrote Harry continually from California about how he should handle the problems brought on by deals made before he took over. Harry alone shouldered the burden of being there. "I would be glad to help you in any way—should we retain the ranch—and would be glad to come there and spend what time was necessary," Courtland wrote at one point, "but I feel that the ranch must first be in a position so that it could pay me to do this. . . . Here is the situation in plain words. I am earning here $300 a month. . . . Now you see if I quit my job to go to the ranch, I would have no income besides what I got out of the ranch. I would still have to keep up my family expenses and I would not expect the cattle business to pay me anything near what I am getting here." At the end of Courtland's let-ter, written in elegant cursive, he struck a sympathetic note: "I know it must seem hard for you at times to have to stick there out in the hills all the time."[9]

Harry's desire to attend Stanford or return to Pasadena withered in the dusty struggle to make the ranch profitable.

But once, on a visit to El Paso, his luck was good. It was in the summer of 1927, while he was in town to buy some new bulls, that he was smitten by a cattleman's daughter. The attraction was mutual.

Ada Mae Wilkey had been born in Mexico in 1904, the first of three children of W. W. Wilkey and Mamie Scott Wilkey, who were living in Sonora at the time. Soon after Ada Mae was born, the family moved to Douglas, directly across the border in Arizona. In another move, W. W. Wilkey bought the Duncan Mercantile general store and acquired a cat-tle ranch north of the Gila River. Only about thirty miles from the Lazy B, the Wilkeys crossed paths with H. C. and Alice Day—and their chil-dren—when the Days were in the region of the ranch. But Harry was six years older than Ada Mae and, of course, paid no attention to the girl. A few years later, when Ada Mae was in high school, her parents sold the Duncan Mercantile. The Wilkeys moved with their three children to El Paso, where they bought a second cattle ranch, close to Fort Hancock.

Ada Mae's formative years, spent within an easy ride from the Lazy B, may have enhanced her attraction to Harry and the Day family ranch. And at age 23, when she met Harry again, the slender, charming Ada Mae was experienced enough not to be intimidated by Harry's hardened veneer. She had graduated from the University of Arizona (a rarity for a woman born at the turn of the century) and been married and divorced (also rare). She plunged into life with infinite energy and was not afraid of the isolated life of the Lazy B.

Mamie Wilkey, on the other hand, was worried: Harry was temperamental, had little money, no college education. The Lazy B had no running water or electricity. What kind of life would her daughter have there? It was not for Mamie Wilkey to answer. After a three-month, long-distance romance, Ada Mae and Harry eloped and were married by a Presbyterian minister in Las Cruces, New Mexico.[10] Harry sent a telegram to his sister Eleanor in Pasadena on September 19, 1927: "Hope you won't be too surprised to hear that I married today. Although I have never said anything to you, we have been engaged three months so I didn't take a leap in the dark. Planning for you to visit us as soon as we are settled. She is just the kind you would have picked for me."[11] Mamie Wilkey had a few last words when her daughter's move seemed inevitable: "Ada Mae, don't ever learn to milk the cow."[12]

Harry was one year shy of 30 at the time. He had accepted the family mandate to run the ranch, but he was making his own life with the hand he had been dealt.

THE GREAT DEPRESSION ARRIVED with their daughter Sandra. Banks closed. Hundreds of thousands of people lost their jobs. As markets collapsed, livestock in places like the Lazy B died on the hoof. Across the country, as historian David Kennedy wrote in *Freedom from Fear,* "haggard men in shabby overcoats, collars turned up against the chill wind, newspapers plugging the holes in their shoes, lined up glumly for handouts at soup kitchens."[13] Harry at least had food, a house, and some family money. ("I don't know what I would have done if I had not had an inheritance from my parents," Harry wrote in later years to his sister Eleanor.)[14] He might have to walk away from the ranch but he would never be destitute and he would not starve.

On the morning of Sandra's birth, March 26, 1930, the *Tucson Daily Citizen* and *Arizona Daily Star* reported on the sinking cattle market, plunging agriculture prices, and national unemployment figures. The *Arizona Star* happened to publish a piece about the doings of the U.S. Supreme Court (at the time, housed inside the Capitol). A syndicated

"Washington Bystander" column focused on the nation's newly appointed chief justice, Charles Evans Hughes, who had succeeded William Howard Taft: "Stroll by the Capitol any of these fine, bracing March mornings along about 9 a.m. and you are apt to see a sturdy, upright man in his late sixties come striding briskly up the hill and disappear into the Supreme Court area of the vast building. He wears, you will note, a neatly trimmed beard, now turned almost white, and sweeps along in vigorous fashion at a round pace, as though he had business in hand. Then you might say to yourself, 'Well, I have seen a sight. There goes Chief Justice Charles Evans Hughes, getting on the job early.' "[15]

The nation was still mourning the passing of Taft, who had died on March 8 at age 72. In a bizarre coincidence, the recently retired chief justice (and, of course, the nation's twenty-seventh president) had died on the same day as Justice Edward Terry Sanford, who was 64. As United Press International reported the dual deaths on March 8, "Death [for Taft] came unexpectedly at 5:15 p.m., only five hours after it had reached its tragic hand into the court over which Taft formerly presided and struck down apparently one of the most robust members. . . . [Sanford] collapsed in the dentist's chair and passed away soon afterward."[16]

Sandra was barely two years old when drought seared the ranch again. Harry could not afford to purchase feed for the cattle. He tried to find a buyer for a couple hundred thin cows. In the Lazy B memoir she coauthored with her brother, Alan, she wrote that the one man who even bothered to look at the cows was so disappointed by their withered condition that he said, "I wouldn't take that bunch of cows if you gave them to me. It wouldn't be worth the shipping charges."[17]

Harry was depressed. Compounding his troubles was a protracted lawsuit over ownership of portions of the Lazy B, brought on by H. C. Day's collaboration and subsequent falling out with a partner.[18] It was this legal struggle that caused Harry to despise lawyers and to want redress through his daughter's becoming one.

Sandra's early life was buoyed by the spirit and aspirations of her mother. Unlike Harry, who had drawn the short straw in the family and was stuck with the ranch, Ada Mae made the very deliberate choice to live there. "Harry, I want to give you laughter and courage, ambition and fulfillment, and in that way, I shall find my own," she had written to him shortly before they eloped in 1927.[19]

Even in hard times, Ada Mae, who washed diapers in buckets of water hauled up to the house by cowboys, wore dresses and stockings. Her aesthetic sensibility turned the small adobe house into an oasis. Meals were served on fine dinnerware. She delighted in playing love songs on the upright piano she brought from her childhood home.[20] Even in the desert, she cultivated a small flower garden. In time, she subscribed to *Vogue, House Beautiful,* and the *New Yorker.* When she was finished devouring the recent magazines, she stored them in closets and under beds, to read again.[21] Ada Mae enjoyed entertaining visitors. "You hardly ever saw her in an apron," her only son, Alan, recalled. "When company came, she would sit down and have a drink. She would get up occasionally, and pretty soon, she would say, 'Dinner's served.' and it would be a gourmet dinner. You'd wonder where that came from."[22]

With her way of dressing and keeping up her home, she promoted a certain status for herself that may have been incongruous but that was accepted by her family and the ranch hands. In the *Lazy B,* Ada Mae is painted with a dignity that recalls a portrait by Wallace Stegner (O'Connor's favorite author) of the early West protagonist in *Angle of Repose:* "The camps all but doffed their caps to Susan Ward, as if she had been a lady from a castle instead of from a cottage."[23]

Ada Mae tried to expose her oldest child to the best of ranch life. On long walks across the Lazy B, she pointed out unusual plants and insects and looked for Indian artifacts, obsidian arrowheads, pottery shards. She taught Sandra to read by age four. She instilled in her daughter a love of music and a gift for entertaining, along with a talent for cards and a spirit of adventure.

Harry skimped through the Depression. He made some money from a federal initiative that bought up cattle to feed the hungry. According to Harry's business records, he kept the number of cowboys low and paid modest wages, about $50 apiece per month. "I wish you could see the cattle now," Harry wrote to his brother, Courtland, in Pasadena in 1936. "They look better in flesh and also better in quality than I ever remember seeing them."[24] By the early 1940s and World War II, the ranch turned the corner. Beef prices soared, saving cattle ranchers everywhere.

President Roosevelt's New Deal helped in part to bail out the Lazy B, but Harry loathed the Democratic president. Harry Day was a man of individual initiative, and FDR's social welfare agenda rankled him. Alan said Harry would listen to the president's radio reports until "steam would come out of his ears." One often-told family story revolved around his father's anger that FDR reinstated Daylight Saving Time during the war. In Harry's mind, "now the son of a bitch is telling us when to get up and when to go to bed."[25]

Radio broadcasts also brought news of FDR's clash with the Supreme Court. The dire economic conditions had prompted Roosevelt to launch a set of initiatives with Congress to restore agricultural prices and industrial production. But the recovery programs designed to lift up workers meant the unparalleled expansion of federal power and restrictions on business. (Harry was not unwilling to take the benefits—perhaps he had no choice—but he was angered by the broader federal interference.)

The Supreme Court then was firmly on the side of individual enterprise and business, over the interests of workers. The era began with a 1905 decision, *Lochner v. New York,* invalidating a New York law setting maximum hours for bakery workers. The Court said that a "liberty to contract" was part of the liberty embodied in the due process clauses of the Fifth and Fourteenth Amendments. That meant that any laws interfering with the fundamental right to contract—for example, limiting hours of employment or requiring a minimum wage—would be struck down except in compelling circumstances. That view of the Constitution, shielding business from government interference, was invoked three decades later, as the Court vigorously disapproved of Roosevelt's penchant for experimenting with federal solutions to the nation's economic calamity.[26]

Two decisions in May 1935 helped set off a near-crisis in American constitutional law. First, the justices ruled that Congress violated the due process guarantee and overstepped its authority to regulate interstate commerce when it established a pension system for railroad workers. The Retirement Act of 1934, intended to help vast numbers of men survive in retirement, was a variation on Roosevelt's ambitious Social Security legislation then pending. Nineteen days later, the Court struck down the National Industrial Recovery Act, which established "codes of fair competition" for wages, prices, and trade practices, and made clear the right of labor to organize for collective bargaining. It was the heart of the recovery effort drafted in the famous "100 Days" of 1933. The Supreme Court said that in the NIRA, Congress exceeded its power to regulate interstate commerce and wrongly delegated its legislative authority to the president.[27]

Roosevelt was furious at the Supreme Court. "We have been relegated to the horse-and-buggy definition of interstate commerce," he declared to reporters at a news conference after the rulings were handed down.[28] At the time, the Court was filled by men born in the mid-nineteenth century. The majority were Republicans and four were staunch conservatives (known as the "Four Horsemen"), voting consistently against FDR's New Deal.[29]

The following year, 1936, after Roosevelt won reelection by a landslide, he set out to change things. He proposed that Congress pass a statute letting him appoint an additional member of the Supreme Court for each sitting justice over age 70. This plan would have enabled FDR immediately to name six new justices and likely be assured a majority to support his New Deal programs. In a March 9, 1937, radio address, the president declared, "We have . . . reached the point as a nation where we must take action to save the Constitution from the Court and the Court from itself.[30]

The plan backfired. As one FDR biographer, Ted Morgan, wrote, "He had violated his own method for making sure he had support before he went ahead. Court packing was the one great topic . . . and there were acres of editorials."[31] Roosevelt was criticized by fellow Democrats in Congress as well as in newspapers that had supported his reelection. It was a blunder of unusual magnitude for a president considered a master politician. There is little doubt that at the Lazy B, Harry had plenty to say about high-handed Roosevelt and the tempest over the Supreme Court.

Perhaps because of Roosevelt's pressure, or perhaps for a host of other reasons that have been speculated on through history, it soon became clear that the justices were ready to abandon their conservative approach and let the federal government take steps to spur economic recovery. On March 29, 1937, in a 5-4 decision, the Court upheld Washington State's minimum-wage law for women.[32] That decision effectively reversed a ruling a year earlier that had voided a New York State minimum-wage law. Justice Owen Roberts, who had voted to strike down the similar New York statute on the grounds that it interfered with the liberty to contract, cast his vote for the Washington law.

The turnabout by Roberts, who had succeeded Sanford in 1930, was popularly called "the switch in time that saved nine." Chief Justice Hughes, who had succeeded Taft, wrote the majority decision in the Washington State case, which put to rest the principle that the "liberty" embodied in the due-process guarantee protected a "liberty to contract" that prevented government regulation of business. The decision ushered the Court into a new constitutional era. Thus, the two justices appointed in the year of Sandra's birth helped create the ideological alignment that moved the nation through the Court-packing crisis of 1937. The rest of the New Deal stood.

LIFE ON THE RANGE SHAPED Sandra's early years, but so did her absence from it. At age 6, she was sent away to school in El Paso, the home of her maternal grandmother, Mamie Wilkey. As a child, Sandra could not shed the fear that her parents wanted her out of the house and might not welcome her back. It was a long and lonely existence, by all accounts. "The real trauma of living in a remote ranch area is the educational problem of children," she said years later. "You really have limited choices. It's kind of a poor choice whichever way you go."[33] Some ranch and farm mothers obtained materials to try to teach their children at home, as Ada Mae tried with Sandra one year. An alternative was for mother and children to move into town, where there were schools, as Ada Mae tried once with Sandra's younger sister, Ann, born in 1938, and brother, Alan, born in 1939. But in their early years of marriage, Ada Mae and Harry could not bear to be away from each other.

Sandra attended the Radford School for Girls, which was founded in 1910 in El Paso and known for its rigorous traditional education. In those years, many girls boarded, and when they returned home for vacations, it was to beautiful, well-appointed places that young Sandra could only envy. Rather than board at Radford, Sandra lived in a bungalow in El Paso with Grandma Wilkey, a determined woman whose temperament was often compared to her son-in-law Harry's. Sandra later described her grandmother as an excessively talkative woman who forced her granddaughter to learn to keep out distractions as she read and studied.[34]

At Christmas, at Easter, and during summer vacations, Sandra returned home. But each time these reunions ended, she felt torn again from her parents, nicknamed "MO" and "DA."[35] "I climbed on board and sat at a window waving at MO and DA as the train slowly moved along the track and out of sight of my parents and the town."[36] The lingering pain would be so great that Sandra would say in a 1980 interview that "I dislike El Paso to this day, largely because I was homesick."[37]

A school picture taken when she was about 10 years old bears out her unhappiness. There Sandra stands, sullen, alongside mostly smiling girls. Many have bows in their hair and a look of self-assurance in their stance. Sandra has neither. She also is much darker-complected than the others, no doubt the product of weeks on the sun-blazed Lazy B. For a girl so young, she looks unusually hardened.

For some of her years at Grandma Wilkey's and the Radford School, Sandra had a favorite cousin at her side. Flournoy, a year older, was the daughter of Ada Mae's sister, Evelyn. (Ada Mae and Evelyn had one brother, Scott.) During their years together, Sandra and Flournoy shared a room at their grandmother's, and activities at school. While Sandra was reserved as a child, Flournoy was a natural charmer. She was featured in local fashion shows and was a flower girl in El Paso society weddings.[38] Flournoy's father's family had long been business and political leaders in El Paso, which gave Sandra some exposure to the town's upper crust as she was growing up.[39]

A letter that Grandma Wilkey wrote to the two girls attested to their grandmother's attention as well as to the differences between Sandra and Flournoy. On each page of the six-page letter, Mamie Wilkey pasted charming cutout pictures of fashionable women, children, and animals. "Dear little cousins," she wrote on the first page. "This is a picture of a bride. When you all get to be big girls you will be brides, too. Flournoy, I want you to tell Sandra the difference between a bride's wedding *gown* and a wedding *dress*. You have seen both. Which do you like best?"[40]

Even with the companionship of Flournoy and Grandma Wilkey, Sandra was heartsick away from the Lazy B. An episode that occurred when she was 11 reveals her uncertainty about how she fit in: "One of my school friends said she knew something about me and my mother. 'Oh. What is that?' 'I'm not supposed to tell,' she said. 'Come on. You have to tell me!' 'Well, my mother says your mother was married to somebody else, not Harry Day.' . . . I was shocked and frightened. Had I been adopted? Is that why MO and DA sent me off to school in El Paso?[41] Sandra asked her grandmother Wilkey, who acknowledged that Ada Mae had a short-lived first marriage and that Sandra was indeed the child of Ada Mae and Harry.

The tale provided a glimpse into the psyche of a woman who kept her emotions under cover. As an adult, O'Connor did not dwell on deficits, and, in fact, became adept at accentuating what she had rather than what she did not. Rarely did she speak about life in El Paso, preferring to cast her life for the public in terms of the ranch rather than the considerably longer time away from it at Grandma Wilkey's and private school. Once, when the *New York Times* asked a number of prominent people to describe a piece of school artwork that had impressed them, O'Connor answered in a way that further revealed the disturbing impressions she retained from her El Paso years. "The artifact I remember best from my childhood was a death mask of Pancho Villa. It showed his face after death, complete with a bullet wound in the forehead. It was on display at Miss Radford's School for Girls . . . which I attended for some years. Just why it was there I never knew, but the horror of it is still part of my memory bank."[42]

When O'Connor returned to the school as a justice in 1987 and received a symbolic key to the school, she referred to the late principal as a "frightening" woman. She probably meant it as a joke—a news report of the day said she humorously remarked that she was not sure the principal would want her to have the key. But it was clear that the kind of upbeat tone she adopted about her ranch girlhood stopped when she described her substantial time away at school in El Paso. A former dean of girls at Radford recounted Sandra's unhappiness years later: "She loved riding horses and she got homesick for her family."[43]

Sandra's younger sister, Ann, had similar longings when she was eventually sent away. But she did not cope quite as well. "I used to say that I didn't have an identity until I was 40. Don't draw conclusions from me because Sandra was able to handle it. Sandra was always much more sure of herself, more at ease. . . . Why? She is who she is."[44] Ann repeatedly said, "Sandra had no choice. That's why she handled it." For Harry Day's eldest, there was an acceptance that life was not easy.

When Ann and Alan were sent to Mamie Wilkey's in El Paso, after Sandra already had graduated, they made enough of a fuss to end up back at the ranch. They attended local schools, although their parents believed the Duncan, Arizona, school district, thirty miles away, offered an inferior education. They also felt no kinship with the locals.

"They remained aloof from the community," Alan said. "They would never go in to the county fair. They didn't have their kids join the 4-H. . . . In a small town, the town revolves around the school. The town gets behind their football team. They never went to PTA meetings. They never came and met my teachers. They never watched me play football. They never came to my high school graduation."[45] Recalled Ann, "When I graduated from Duncan High School . . . he [Harry Day] came to my graduation. My mother did not. She was just not happy that her daughter was graduating from Duncan High School."[46]

Harry and Ada Mae lived their Arizona ranch life, even reveled in it as they grew old together. But they were not part of the greater ranching community. Too much of Pasadena and El Paso remained within them and held them apart from their neighbors.

For eighth grade, Sandra won a year in local school, after constantly begging her parents to let her stay at the ranch. They enrolled her in the Lordsburg, New Mexico, public school, across the Arizona border but only twenty miles away. Each morning before sunrise, either her mother or father would drive Sandra over eight miles of ranch road to a highway intersection where she would wait for a bus. The bus ride took an hour. She would not return until after sundown. By the end of the year, her parents decided the education was not worth the trouble of getting it.[47] Years later, grown up and appearing before senators at her Supreme Court confirmation hearing, Sandra referred to this as a life lesson against busing to achieve racial integration. She concentrated not on the societal goal of integration but on the cost to an individual child.[48] Back in the mid-1940s, she returned to Radford, then moved on to El Paso's Austin High School, from which she graduated at age 16.

Whatever else might be said of the justice's ranch life and school days, they certainly steeled her for other challenges. Said brother Alan, "Since she was a little girl, she was never afraid of work and never afraid of a challenge. She had gone through life, instead of fighting those things or getting worn out, allowing those things to take her places that other people wouldn't go."[49]

In the summer before her last year of high school, Sandra had an experience that left a lasting impression. Told in her usual blithe manner, the episode nonetheless revealed the emotional isolation of her childhood even when she was home at the Lazy B. On a July morning in 1945, at age

15, she climbed into an old truck, checked to make sure it had enough gas, and began driving the dirt roads to bring lunch to her father and the cowboys out branding calves. Heading south over an especially rugged area, she suddenly felt the truck wobble. The left rear tire was flat. Sandra knew how to change a tire. Since she was 8, she had been driving on the ranch. But after placing rocks by the truck's tires to keep it from rolling, and jacking it up, she discovered rusted lug nuts that would not budge. She had to figure another way. She jacked the truck down and tried to loosen the lug nuts by stomping her foot on the lug wrench. The nuts cracked loose. She jacked up the truck to finish the job. She was soaked with perspiration, her dark hair dripping.

When Sandra arrived at the camp, she was an hour past the crew's usual lunchtime. She was eager to tell her father about how she figured out how to change the tire. She wanted to win his praise. But her father ignored her.

When he finally spoke to her, he said, "You're late."

She explained the flat tire.

"You should have started earlier," he said. "You need to expect anything out here."[50]

As Harry told her to expect anything, he taught her to expect nothing. While his daughter's *Lazy B* tales exhibited an at-times incongruous cheeriness, she did allow that Harry "had periods of moodiness and depression. He was very critical of MO and Alan during these periods. He wanted things done his way, which he was certain was the best way."[51]

In her recounting, O'Connor provides no analysis of the emotional freight her childhood left her with. But stripped of its wistful gloss, her version of events reveals a series of episodes in which she tries desperately to prove herself. She would paint a screen door over and over until it was exactly to her father's specifications. Would these experiences with her father cause her to want to prove herself as an adult? Did she believe they prepared her to achieve in the male-dominated spheres she entered? She did not address those questions. Rather, she concluded, "As the first child, nine years older than the next, I received all the attention and love that DA had to give during those early years. . . . I developed a love for the land and for the way of life on the ranch that has stayed with me. Spending hours each day at the dinner table discussing ranching, politics, or economics is a treat that many young people don't experience."[52]

Alan recalled that his father was "on his best behavior when she was around, because Sandra would bring up stimulating subjects that he would want to talk about. And they would mentally head down the path together."

With Alan, Harry was quicker to anger. Alan recalled a time when he was a teenager handling cows in a corral with his father and other cowboys. "We're working cattle and I'm working a gate and paying attention, doing what I think is a good job. And all of a sudden he comes over and just gets on me and says, 'Why did you let that cow through?' I say, 'You didn't signal that the cow was coming this way.' And he said, 'You can't treat me like that. What the hell's the matter with you?' And I said, 'Look, I didn't hear you say shut the gate.' And he said, even louder, 'Yes you did. I said it plainly.' I didn't know what to say. He had me in a box and there was no way out. I was scared to death."[53]

Alan said he wanted to put the anecdote in the *Lazy B,* but his sister would not allow it. Still, Alan concluded about his father, "he made it happen on a tough piece of land while people around him were falling apart."[54] Most important, remembrances of Harry Day reveal how a powerful American woman took root in a place where little else could.

He died in 1984, three years after his daughter had joined the Supreme Court. Two years later, the family began selling the Lazy B. In the next generation of the Day family, there were no takers for the uncertain prospects of a cattle ranch. They opted to get out with their money rather than to hire someone to work the ranch for them. "It's hard to go back out there," said Ann. "It was like a death in the family."[55] Both Ann and Alan have taken trips back to the ranch. Justice O'Connor has not returned to the land.[56]

In effect, the penning of the *Lazy B* memoir was her way of going back, her way of preserving the ranch as she wanted it preserved. The effort was unusual because justices, especially sitting justices, rarely write memoirs.[57] She said she intended to capture a life that most Americans did not know firsthand. When Sandra returned to the house after the ordeal of the flat tire and told her mother of her father's reaction, Ada Mae said only, "He gets that way." Sandra learned from her mother's talent for making "a hard life look easy." And she would cloak her ambition and drive in the mantle of dutiful daughter, devoted wife, tireless public servant, and, finally, determined first woman justice.

2

"THE RULES OF THE GAME"

U pon graduation from high school in 1946, Sandra Day chose Stanford University, the school to which her father had aspired. Founded in 1891 by California senator Leland Stanford and his wife, Jane, the university occupied a lush green expanse that once was a horse farm in Santa Clara County, California. Its buildings, designed by American architect Henry Hobson Richardson, were modeled after the old San Juan Capistrano Mission. The campus offered natural abundance and the promise that was absent on the Lazy B. Here Sandra could prove herself and open doors that had long been closed to her father.

Harry and Ada Mae drove their eldest daughter to the Palo Alto campus in early September. In the postwar flush, Harry favored Chryslers and every year traded last year's four-door sedan for a newer model.[1] Sandra arrived with the university's largest enrollment to date, slightly more than seven thousand students, nearly twice the prewar classes of four thousand. According to the *Stanford Daily* newspaper, 3,900 of the students were veterans. For a late-1940s campus, there was also a significant female population. Sandra joined some two thousand female students.[2]

At 16, she was younger than most others, and she worried that she would not fit in. But her choice and timing were perfect. The girl who had dreaded El Paso had learned in that grief to turn life's shortfalls into challenges. In the optimistic postwar environment of Palo Alto, she blossomed. The university was also maturing from a high-quality regional institution into a national one.

Sandra was in a dormitory with other girls from rural areas, including Diane Cooley, who grew up on a prosperous ranch in Watsonville, California. Cooley remembered Sandra as a shy, insecure girl whose accent, a combination of Lazy B and the Radford School, was different.[3] She also remembered how quickly Sandra learned to navigate the girls' social rituals. After the first school dance, Cooley said, "she came back with this *cute* guy, Andy, a returning vet, who had a red convertible. We were blown away." As Sandra's status among the girls rose, her sense of social inferiority diminished. She also had a major advantage. "She had gorgeous clothes," said Cooley. "Her mother was very stylish, and her grandmother also saw to it that she had the right things." In photos, Sandra seems easily one of the girls, wearing fashionable sweaters and pearls or a scarf knotted at her neck.

She earned high grades. On the Lazy B, verbal skills were less valued than the ability to change a flat tire. But Sandra had a natural verbal facility, with grammar honed at the Radford School, and she spoke up in class. Based on her grades, she earned membership in the Cap and Gown, the senior women's society.[4] She also was an enthusiastic and adroit competitor who loved all manner of sports and games. Her worries about fitting in were dissolving into successes as she took advantage of the opportunities presented to her by Stanford.

Outwardly, she conformed and was very much the coed. Like many young women in that era, perhaps most, she might have seemed to be interested mainly in attracting a husband with potential and becoming the perfect housewife. Her classmates recalled that she never adopted an air of being smarter than other students. She simply outperformed most of them. She studied economics, learning the theoretical side of what she had witnessed firsthand as the Lazy B struggled to stay in the black. When she returned to the ranch for Christmas and summer vacations, she tangled heatedly with her father at the dinner table. "The Keynesian economic theories I was learning at Stanford were not consistent with [father's] pay-as-you-go economic theories," she wrote.[5] She was gaining intellectual independence, her ambitions stirred.

From a legendary economics professor, Harry Rathbun, Sandra

learned the notion of community—another concept in opposition to the ways of her father and mother, who had isolated themselves from some of the Gila River locals. Professor Rathbun's lectures on the roles individuals play in the evolution of the human spirit and in communities were popular on campus. He taught business classes from 1929 to 1959, and in 1950, not long after he met Sandra, he received the Stanford students' designation of "great teacher."[6]

Rathbun was the first major intellectual force in Sandra's life. He had been influenced by Henry Burton Sharman, a University of Chicago theologian who in the early 1900s developed a philosophy of individual responsibility based on the life of Jesus. Sharman considered what lessons from the Gospels were scientifically possible and used them as a model for individual ethics and behavior. He held seminars in the Canadian wilderness each summer, attended by Rathbun, who brought back to his own Stanford students what he had learned. Rathbun's approach was, by turns, spiritual and pragmatic.[7] Gazing inward did not come naturally to the people of the Lazy B, but the future justice was intrigued by the idea fostered by Rathbun that individuals could find their place and make a difference in the world.

Rathbun's view of the law also appealed to Sandra's competitive nature and belief in an orderly universe. "The law is the expression of the rules of the game which all men play—that of getting along together as members of an organized society," he wrote in a 1941 collection of essays on the law.[8]

The lesson Sandra took from Rathbun, she said in a later interview, was that an individual had a responsibility to the community. "I had never heard that before," she said. "He wanted to persuade us to go out into the world and do something. Because of that professor, I went to law school."[9] Her parents, having loathed their reliance on lawyers to settle their business problems at the ranch, realized the benefit of having one of their own in the family and agreed to pay for law school.[10] Rathbun himself admonished, "no layman ought ever to be led to believe it safe for him to rely on his own legal knowledge to the extent of acting as his own lawyer any more than to believe that he may safely be his own physician or surgeon. . . ."[11]

In 1946, the year Sandra entered as an undergraduate, Carl Spaeth, a former assistant U.S. secretary of state, had taken over the Stanford law school. He recruited new faculty, instituted a law review, and oversaw the development of a new law school building.[12] By the time Sandra was accepted in the program, Stanford was able to offer an education rivaling the well-established East Coast schools.

She impressed her classmates as unusually confident, particularly since she was a mere 19 when she finished her undergraduate work and entered law school. She was one of only five women in the class. A fellow student, William Rehnquist, who was detoured by World War II and entered law school at age 25, was impressed by her practice of asking any question without fear of ridicule, a trait she had developed with her father. She and Rehnquist became members of the law review.

She was smart but she also played a bit of the ingenue. Fellow law student Fred Steiner remembered noticing Sandra at a school dance. "Girls were in short supply. Sandra was one of the two beauties. I was lucky enough to have one dance with her, learning that she, too, came from Arizona. Beyond that, I learned little more—for she drew me out, learning all she could about me and letting me know, in the subtle ways women have, how lucky she felt to be with me in the same room, at the same school, and in the same class, sterling fellow that I was. When we parted, I was impressed with her, but even more with myself. I had somehow been infected and inflated with the idea I was a meld of Prince Charming and Socrates."[13]

Steiner said he "fell for it, hook, line, and sinker." Only later did he realize "that she was one of the leading lights of the law school." He said, "She never acted that way to you." They attended classes in the new law school building, dedicated by visiting Supreme Court Justice Robert Jackson in July 1950. Coincidentally, Jackson was introduced to Rehnquist during that event. When Rehnquist graduated in 1952, Jackson hired him to be a law clerk, putting Rehnquist on a path that would only beget other opportunities.

Sandra Day and Bill Rehnquist became friends beyond the classroom. A native of suburban Milwaukee and son of a paper salesman, Rehnquist had been in the Army Air Corps, then enrolled as an undergraduate at Stanford on the G.I. Bill. He obtained his B.A. in 1948, went off to Harvard for an M.A., then returned to the law school in 1950. He and Sandra dated briefly, went to a few movies together. Years later, she described Rehnquist as "always amusing, intelligent, with lots of interests outside of the law."[14] Steiner, who was friends with both Sandra and Bill, said no one would have predicted their future fates. "We were all young colts in a pasture, callow youths," Steiner said.[15]

Whatever romantic attraction Sandra might have felt for Rehnquist faded when she met John O'Connor III, another law student and the son of a San Francisco physician. In manner and breeding, he was very far from the Lazy B. "John was witty, charming, and very smooth," recalled Diane Cooley, Sandra's friend from her undergraduate days. "He always came to everything dressed for the country club. He was a new breed of cat for her."[16]

John's family had emigrated from County Kerry, Ireland. His grandfather came over with a younger brother, sent across the Atlantic on a steamship by a father determined to keep his spirited younger son out of local trouble. And the O'Connor boys made good. Joined by two other brothers, they became physicians and hospital administrators. As such, they helped to found St. Francis Hospital in San Francisco. John J. O'Connor III was born at the hospital on January 10, 1930, delivered by an uncle. John's mother, Sara Flynn, had grown up in St. Louis and Denver and was a swimmer who won statewide competitions. The O'Connor family was well off, and even in the Depression was able to keep hired help.[17]

By the time he arrived at Stanford, John was good-looking, with thick, dark hair and a broad smile. He enjoyed telling tales and playing jokes. But he also had drive, and, while in law school, wrote daily notes to himself about the importance of staying focused. He studied hard and after his first year became a member of the law review.

Sandra and John became better acquainted while proofreading and checking the citations in a law review article. After working on it at the library, John suggested they go to Dinah's Shack, a local diner. "Beware of proofreading over a glass of beer," Sandra quipped later. "It can result in unexpected alliances."[18] After their first encounter, Sandra said, neither of them dated anyone else. John later recounted to family that they went out forty-one nights in a row.[19]

On a spring break from classes, she took O'Connor home to meet her parents. "MO made me feel comfortable right away," John told family members. He said Sandra's father was another story. "You had to prove to Harry Day that you were the right kind of person before he would really open up. In addition, it was clear that Sandra was his treasure."[20]

What transpired at the first visit to the ranch has been told many times, including in the *Lazy B* memoir. But it is worth repeating here, for the rendering the story offers of Sandra's father and of the man she would marry—the rancher and the city boy, the domineering presence and the promising suitor.

"The branding irons were heating in the fire, and the crew were putting the calves through the branding chute one at a time," she wrote. "DA was branding them. Others were castrating them." Her father did not acknowledge Sandra and her beau until he went to the corral fence and took down a piece of baling wire that was hanging there. "He straightened it out and reached into a dirty-looking bucket and pulled out a couple of bloody testicles. DA trimmed them a bit with his pocketknife, then put them on the baling wire and placed them in the branding fire, where the 'mountain oysters,' as we called them, sizzled and cooked. DA turned them to cook all sides, then brought the baling-wire skewer over to John and said, 'Here, John, try some of these.' John gulped a bit and said, 'Sure, Mr. Day.' He plucked one of the oysters off the wire and popped it in his mouth. 'Umm, pretty good,' he said." John did not flinch. Sandra thought: "Welcome to the Lazy B."[21] And that is how she ended the tale. A reader cannot help but wonder about the psychological complexities that produced such a moment as father tested the city-bred beau who had been able to go to college and law school and faced a future of great promise.

"Of wide interest is the announcement of the engagement of Miss Sandra Day to John Jay O'Connor III," the *El Paso Times* reported on October 8, 1952.[22] They were married on December 20, 1952, at the ranch. As recorded separately by the *Lordsburg Liberal* (New Mexico) newspaper, Sandra emerged as no dusty rancher's daughter. She wore a gown of white nylon tulle with pleated bouffant skirt. She carried a bouquet of white camellias.[23] Hundreds of friends, family, and neighbors attended the wedding. The feast included meat from cows Harry had killed and slow-cooked over pits. Sandra and John flew to Acapulco for their honeymoon.

This was her first major commitment as an adult. John offered Sandra many obvious advantages, including status and a good financial future. But she must have known the deeper commitment she was winning from a 1950s husband: an appreciation of her independence and ambition and a willingness to sacrifice some of his own drive for hers.

The bride returned with her husband for his final semester of law school at Stanford. With her freshly minted 1952 diploma, she sought full-time legal work. She interviewed with several law firms in California, among them the Los Angeles–based firm of Gibson, Dunn and Crutcher. She had graduated in the top 10 percent of her law-school class and been on the board of editors of the *Stanford Law Review*.[24] But she received no offers from any of the law firms, and Gibson, Dunn offered her only a position as a legal secretary. "I declined that," she said.[25] She eventually found work as a deputy county attorney handling civil cases in the San Mateo County attorney's office, in an area just north of Stanford.

What happened to Sandra O'Connor was not an exceptional experience. Many female, black, and Hispanic lawyers were unwelcome in the corporate legal world. O'Connor was actually more fortunate than some other law graduates, because she did not have to support her family alone.[26]

After John graduated in 1953, he was drafted into the army, and Sandra accompanied him to Germany, where he worked in the Judge Advocate General Corps. Sandra obtained a job as a civilian attorney for the United States Quartermaster Corps in Frankfurt. That office arranged the sale of equipment and supplies the U.S. government had left over from World War II. On weekends and holidays, Sandra and John traveled throughout Europe and began the serious downhill skiing that would become a regular part of their family vacations. "After John had finished his army service, we decided to stay the winter until either the money or the snow ran out," she said later. "To be [safe], we bought our tickets home. Who could believe you could enjoy skiing every day for three months? Then our money and the snow ran out together and we came home."[27]

She really came home. It was 1957, and Sandra was expecting their first child. They decided to settle in Phoenix, the capital of Arizona, rather than in more populous California. "John and I felt that by living in Phoenix we would have an opportunity to be more actively involved with our community than might be the case if we were to return to California," she said.[28] They weighed the advantages of their contacts in the big city of San Francisco against the opportunities to be big fish in the smaller pond of Phoenix. Sandra also liked the idea of her children growing up within driving distance of the Lazy B. Harry and Ada Mae were in high spirits over their daughter's return to the state and looked forward to their first grandchild.

The O'Connors already had friends in Phoenix. Bill Rehnquist and his wife, Nan, and Fred Steiner and his wife, Jacque, had settled there. Thousands of people like them were flocking to the Sunbelt after the war. Between 1947 and 1957, Arizona's population and economy boomed. In Phoenix alone, the population rose from 156,000 in 1945 to 450,000 in 1959. Air-conditioning made the low desert areas comfortable and allowed business and industry to maintain year-round production schedules.[29] The new Arizona economy, shedding reliance on the traditional "three Cs"—cotton, cattle, and copper—was diversifying with light manufacturing and service sectors.[30]

John took a job at Fennemore Craig, one of the oldest and largest law firms in the Southwest. Sandra was unsure what kind of work she might find. She was certain, however, that she would part company with most of the women of her generation who settled for a housewife's existence. She plunged into tasks with high energy. She seemed always a woman with a mission, and often several at once. As she prepared for admittance to the Arizona bar in the summer of 1957, she planned for the birth of her first child.

John and Sandra rented a small apartment. One of the first items this competitive couple bought was a ping-pong table.[31] Their shared legal background drew the attention of the *Arizona Republic,* which published a feature story on the couple a week before they were to be jointly sworn in to the state bar at the Capitol. The story referred to their budding romance at the *Stanford Law Review* and noted that Sandra previously had worked for San Mateo County. "She probably was the youngest and, undoubtedly, the prettiest assistant DA to be found anywhere," the reporter wrote in a piece that would for years set the admiring tone of local coverage of O'Connor.[32]

Sandra and John were sworn into the Arizona bar on October 5, 1957. Their son Scott was born three days later.

Sandra did not wait long to return to the working world. After securing a babysitter for Scott, she found that the law firms still were not hiring women lawyers.[33] But she was master of her own fate. In spring of 1958, she set up a law firm with a University of Michigan law graduate whom she had met while studying for the bar exam. Her partner, Tom Tobin, had gone to Princeton before studying law at the University of Michigan. He had then traveled through Europe, the Soviet Union, and the Far East. O'Connor and Tobin rented space in a shopping center in Phoenix, alongside a grocery store, television repair shop, liquor store, and dry cleaners. It was a growing blue-collar area, Tobin recalled, and they both immediately joined as many local civic clubs as possible to get their names out in the community and drum up business.[34]

"We did everything that we could get," O'Connor said. "If there were local merchants who needed a lease prepared or some advice concerning a contract or commercial matter, we would handle that; if people in the . . . area had a marriage or divorce problem or had a landlord-tenant problem, we were available to handle that. And we also took criminal appointments because, in those days, we didn't have a public defender's office and if you were willing to accept appointment for a criminal case then you could go down to the courthouse and wait in the courtroom during the criminal arraignments and the judge would consider appointing you to do something, and then you were paid some grand sum like $25 for your services."[35]

Tobin recalled that the cases usually involved burglary or assault. "Most of the time you'd make a deal with the county attorney to get some of the charges dropped," Tobin said. "Or, you'd enter a plea of not guilty and arrange to go up and see [the defendant] in the courthouse jail." He and O'Connor split money from the cases.[36]

Perhaps inspired by Stanford professor Rathbun's notions of community, perhaps intuitively knowing where to seek power, perhaps both, O'Connor also became involved in politics. She campaigned on behalf of local Republican candidates and earned appointments to county boards and panels.

Recalling these years, Tobin said he has no memories of O'Connor showing up with her baby son in arms, or her being preoccupied by the demands of motherhood. She did not appear stretched thin, he said. From early on, she made it look easy—even if it was not. But when her second child, Brian, was born in 1960, O'Connor no longer could work miracles. Scott's babysitter moved to California and O'Connor could not find an adequate replacement, so, she said, "I then stayed home myself for about five years and took care of those two."[37]

She did not really stay home. She stepped up her political involvement. She became a precinct committeeman, then county vice chairman for the Republican Party. She kept her hand in the practice of law, too, writing wills and serving as a trustee for the Federal Bankruptcy Court in a number of cases that could be handled from home. In 1962, O'Connor had a third son, Jay. "Do marriage, families, and careers for women mix?" she asked years later in a speech to Arizona State University students. "It depends, of course, on the personalities of the husband and the wife and the special needs of the children. For me, the answer has been emphatically 'Yes!' . . . The ultimate happiness to me is the feeling of fulfillment which comes from doing constructive work for the good of society and mankind."[38]

"It helps to marry someone with the understanding and expectation of both partners that the wife intends to pursue her separate career," O'Connor added. "If this is clear at the outset, there is less likelihood of subsequent disappointment by the husband who experiences a greater share of responsibility for child care as a result." John, who was moving up on the Fennemore track, supported her many endeavors and did not seem nervous about his place in the world.[39]

Indeed, out of the shadow of the O'Connors who had prospered in San Francisco, John was making a name for himself. He joined the Young Republicans and Phoenix Rotary Club, and eventually became president of the Rotary. He was a member of the boards of the local United Way and, fittingly for his family background, the Maricopa County General Hospital. He cut a sophisticated figure in his tailored suits and was considered a raconteur. He also was known for his goofy sense of humor. When he was running for president of the Rotary Club, he listed his qualifications as: "Beautiful wife. Rich father-in-law. Pool hustler." He took to handing out mock business cards with ridiculous occupations.[40]

His wife, meanwhile, found a way to combine the roles of mother, spouse, and professional woman that few of her peers were able to manage. For many women, the demands of motherhood and the realities of a woman's place in the early 1960s proved insurmountable obstacles. But, by most accounts, Sandra O'Connor easily overcame these and not at the cost of her traditional views of wifehood and motherhood.

She put herself into the center of every undertaking and sought to be indispensable. She worked her way up in the Phoenix Junior League— the status organization for ambitious wives. She turned the white adobe-brick house she and John built in suburban Paradise Valley into a community hub, entertaining friends and holding election-night parties. She cooked the way her mother did: frequently, for many guests, and seemingly effortlessly.

Phoenix kept up with her. By 1960, the year the O'Connors moved into the adobe house on Denton Lane, Phoenix was the largest city in the Southwest. Light manufacturing, defense, and tourism played growing roles in Arizona's economy. Most important for O'Connor the politician, the population and economic growth turned Republican a state that had been staunchly Democratic from 1912 until World War II. The new young immigrants, many of them men like Rehnquist, were more individualistic, philosophical conservatives. An influx of senior citizens transforming the state into a retirement mecca also had strong Republican loyalties.[41]

The power of organized labor and Democrats' other traditional constituencies was declining. "We didn't have any damn Republicans in this state," one old Democrat grumbled, "until they invented air-conditioning."[42] The O'Connors mingled with the state's postwar elite, including publisher Eugene Pulliam, banker Sherman Hazeltine, and jeweler Harry Rosenzweig, who became state GOP chairman.

The optimism felt by the O'Connors was not shared by African-Americans, Native Americans, and other minorities who lived in the rundown sections of Phoenix. Bradford Luckingham, author of *Phoenix: Southwestern Metropolis,* wrote that Native Americans in the 1960s "remained poor and lived in the deteriorating downtown neighborhoods," while de facto segregation put African-Americans in the worst schools and jobs.[43] In a similar vein, Robert Alan Goldberg, a biographer of Republican senator Barry Goldwater, wrote, "A strict color line scarred Phoenix, dividing black and white worlds socially, economically, and residentially. While discrimination was mainly of a de facto nature, it proved as restrictive and humiliating to blacks as the system existing in the South. . . . Unlike southern states, Arizona granted blacks the vote, but whites tested this right on occasion."[44]

As Republican numbers swelled in Arizona, the U.S. Supreme Court also affected political power. The justices originally had turned down appeals to get involved in state redistricting, with Justice Felix Frankfurter saying memorably in 1946 that the Court should not enter the "political thicket."[45] But then, in 1962, the justices abandoned the view that they should stay out of legislative redistricting battles, and, two years later, imposed a "one person, one vote" rule on the states.[46] That required state legislatures to reapportion districts to represent an equal number of people—no more favoring of sprawling but sparsely populated rural areas at the expense of growing urban areas. In Arizona, the ruling suddenly meant that half the members of the state legislature—fifteen senators and thirty representatives—would be from Phoenix's Maricopa County. The reapportionment shifted control from the Democrats to the Republicans.[47]

SANDRA O'CONNOR'S FIRST EXPERIENCE with a statewide campaign had been the 1958 reelection bid of Barry Goldwater, the heir to a department-store fortune who became the patriarch of modern conservatism.[48] It was just a year after she had returned to Arizona and while she cared for her one-year-old son and tried to generate business at the law firm with Tobin.

When he first won in 1952, defeating then U.S. Senate Majority Leader Ernest McFarland, Goldwater broke the Democratic lock on the state. His stature increased as business boomed in Arizona. All economic indicators continued to rise: income, housing starts, bank deposits, federal contracts, and employment.[49] Goldwater's opposition to big government struck a chord with the new citizenry.

In his reelection bid, Goldwater won with 56 percent of the vote in 1958, a year that saw more losses among Republican senatorial candidates than victories. His clear victory enhanced his prominence nationally and generated a greater in-state following for his ultraconservative ideas. Goldwater advocated militancy in foreign affairs and opposed the budding civil-rights movement of the day. He ended up voting against the landmark 1964 Civil Rights Act. Goldwater also opposed the Senate censure of the red-baiting Wisconsin senator Joseph McCarthy, and became a hero to the John Birch Society, which was emerging in the late 1950s.

Goldwater insisted that his opposition to antibias laws, open housing ordinances, and forced desegregation did not mean he was racist. Rather, he said, it was "impossible to legislate moral conduct." "You cannot pass a law that will make me like you or you like me," he said. O'Connor did not appear troubled by his position on civil rights or a worldview of women that held they were better off at home raising children than alongside men on the job.[50]

In 1964, O'Connor vigorously supported Goldwater's presidential bid. He lost by a landslide to Lyndon B. Johnson, but her involvement in his campaign deepened her connections to GOP power brokers in the state. The following year, 1965, O'Connor went back to work full-time as an assistant state attorney general. "I had the three boys in a situation where I felt I could then find babysitters again and be somewhat active in the legal profession," she said, but then admitted: "Really, I needed to go back to work, because I had gotten so busy in civic and community affairs that I was desperate to go back to work so I wouldn't have so much to do and I'd have a good excuse."[51] She said she had liked working in the San Mateo County attorney's office after graduating from Stanford and thought the Arizona attorney general's office would provide a similar experience.

Assisted by her network of Republican insiders, she was hired by Republican attorney general Bob Pickrell. "I really wanted to work part-time rather than full-time, but there was no chance of getting a part-time job; that was unheard of," O'Connor said. Her desire to work part-time did not reflect her need to be home with her children. Rather, her election to president of the Phoenix Junior League "was a big commitment in terms of time, so I very much needed part-time employment at the Attorney General's office."[52]

As an assistant attorney general, O'Connor represented state agencies and boards—further widening her contacts. "I did the best I could in order that they would feel that I was indispensable," she said. "Then when I told them that I very much needed to work only part-time and asked them if they wouldn't work out an arrangement for me, they then agreed to do it because, by then, they decided that they needed me even on my terms."[53] Her moves demonstrated her ability to make herself central to the operation, as well as her skill at negotiating for what she wanted.

Somehow, she also managed to keep her strong hand in the household and the raising of her boys. "My mom was definitely the caretaker of the house," said Jay, her youngest son. "She organized everything. She had help, certainly, from a maid and a babysitter, but she ran the household and figured out all the meals and all the planning." After dinner, the boys did their homework or went off to a swim-meet or other sports activity. O'Connor turned to work she brought home from the office or played tennis. Recalled Jay, "My mom would rarely flop down on the couch."[54]

In 1969, her connections and industriousness paid off again. As newly elected President Richard Nixon was setting up his administration, he chose Isabel Burgess, an Arizona state senator, to be on the National Transportation Safety Board. O'Connor pursued her open seat. Clearly, O'Connor had laid the groundwork for political appointment. She was friendly with Burgess and knew the county board supervisors who would make the appointment (all of them Republican). Local press reports of the day said O'Connor actively sought the appointment in meetings with supervisors. Years later, however, O'Connor recounted her actions in this bland fashion: "I went to [the supervisors] and asked them if they would consider appointing me to the vacancy in the state Senate. There were several other people interested, but I was selected, and I filled the vacancy and then ran for the Senate thereafter at the next election and the election after that."[55]

With Republicans controlling the legislature, O'Connor quickly obtained the chairmanship of a legislative committee in the Senate—State, County and Municipal Affairs—and a seat on the Appropriations Committee and on the Judiciary Committee. "In the years when I started in the legislature," she recalled, "it was the beginning of the movement in the '60s where many women around the nation were claiming more in terms of their desire to be treated equally and to have equal opportunities at work. I was the beneficiary, really, of a lot of that sentiment in that people were more than willing to give me responsibility."[56]

They were willing, and O'Connor was ready. In barely twelve years, including the five that she ostensibly was home with her sons, she had worked her way into a position of considerable political clout. This Senate appointment moved her in from the fringes of influence—all her community activities—to the center. Her life until now had been a series of trade-offs and compensations: accepting the next-best job, volunteering without pay. The Senate appointment put her inside the corridors of power.

The following year, when O'Connor explained her interest in politics in a speech, she quoted anthropologist Margaret Mead: " 'If women want real power and change, they must run for public office and use the vote more intelligently' . . . I think Dr. Mead is absolutely right about this."[57] Years later, O'Connor elaborated, tying power to the well-learned lesson of hard work on the Lazy B: "Power [is] the ability to do. For both men and women, the first step in getting power is to become visible to others—and then to put on an impressive show."[58]

3

A SUPREME COURT
OPENING

Sandra O'Connor walked briskly into the basement auditorium of the
Phoenix City Hall on October 21, 1971, and took a seat in a folding
chair for a meeting of the Phoenix Historical and Museum Commission.
She and other community leaders were there to discuss the preservation
of the history of a city that had been founded a century earlier on the
ruins of a prehistoric farming civilization and named for the mythical
bird that burns itself on a pyre and arises from its own ashes. Before 1971,
the historical record of Phoenix's frontier days was piecemeal and disorganized. City leaders had decided that it was time to begin to document
and preserve the past. With the history of the Lazy B ranch running deep
in her bones, O'Connor was part of this pioneer heritage.[1]

As usual, O'Connor, a state senator, was juggling many obligations as
she made time for this inaugural meeting of the commission called by
Mayor John Driggs. In the Arizona Senate, she was busy with a special
session to redraw the state's legislative and congressional districts. After
nearly four weeks of negotiations, senators were within hours of finishing the plan—one that O'Connor had helped steer to favor Republican
incumbents.[2] There was O'Connor's family, too. Her boys were now ages
14, 11, and 9, and she made a point of being home to fix them dinner. As a

state senator, O'Connor enjoyed telling audiences that her husband, John, joked, "I think it is a tribute to American democracy when a cook who moonlights as a janitor can be elected to high public office."[3] When she turned 40, John and the boys had sent twenty-one long-stemmed red roses to her at the Capitol. The message read: "You will always be 21 to us."[4] As she had worked to gain power in the clubby world of the state legislature, O'Connor continued to flourish in the traditional woman's role.

With the historical commission meeting underway, one of Mayor Driggs's aides entered the room. He handed the mayor a note. As he glanced at it, Driggs's mouth fell open. "President Nixon is naming Bill Rehnquist to the Supreme Court," he announced.[5] O'Connor was surprised. The fellow Stanford Law graduate and longtime Phoenix friend had not been a reported candidate for the nomination. In the 1960s, Rehnquist had become a fixture in Arizona Republican politics. He had written speeches for U.S. senator Barry Goldwater's 1964 presidential campaign, and when Nixon was elected four year later, Rehnquist had gone to Washington to work with Arizonan Richard Kleindienst, deputy to Attorney General John Mitchell. Before leaving Phoenix, the Rehnquists had socialized regularly with the O'Connors. With a few other couples, they played charades or cards on weekends. Their families went out into the mountains for picnics. In the late 1960s, the Rehnquists took Ada Mae Day, O'Connor's mother, on a two-week pack trip along the Gila River. (The O'Connors were scheduled to go along, too, but when one of their boys became ill, Ada Mae joined the Rehnquists on her own. The two families were that comfortable together.)

Yet O'Connor's response to news of an old friend's nomination to the Supreme Court was tinged with one regret. Three weeks earlier, O'Connor had written to President Nixon to suggest he name a woman to one of two Supreme Court openings. The sudden vacancies were caused by the retirements of Justice Hugo Black, impaired by a stroke, and Justice John Marshall Harlan, who had cancer of the spine. In his presidency, Nixon already had filled two Supreme Court seats, appointing Warren Burger in 1969 to succeed the retiring Chief Justice Earl Warren, and Harry Blackmun in 1970 to succeed Justice Abe Fortas, who resigned under pressure in 1969 after a financial scandal. It was remarkable that a first-term president was about to make his third and fourth appointments to the Supreme Court, and the significance was increased by the fact that Nixon had campaigned in 1968 against the liberal Warren-led Court and vowed to remake it in his conservative image. It was a goal that O'Connor, a Nixon loyalist, embraced.

Still, O'Connor counted herself among the many women nationwide who believed it was time for a woman to be appointed. America's highest court had been a men-only institution for 182 years, and the agitation of the women's movement was in the air. Gloria Steinem was about to launch *Ms.* magazine. The American Civil Liberties Union was starting a women's rights project, led by a 38-year-old lawyer named Ruth Bader Ginsburg. The proposed Equal Rights Amendment was being debated in Congress and already roiling state legislatures, including Arizona's.[6] O'Connor had focused on women's rights since becoming a state senator in 1969. "Of the nation's entire roster of 8,750 judges, 300 are women," she took to saying in 1971. "Eight are judges of federal courts."[7]

Never one to upend the system, she worked within it to get what she wanted. To many of her constituents in appropriately named Paradise Valley just outside Phoenix, she was still Mrs. John O'Connor III. She could be counted on for any civic cause, from the Junior League to the historical commission. She rarely used her maiden name of Day. And the rancher's daughter wore dresses, not pants. Newspaper reporters mentioned in stories that the senator was "attractive," "feminine," even "lissome." One Senate colleague said at the time, "When you first meet Sandra, you think, 'What a pretty little thing.' Next you think, 'My, it's got a personality, too.' After listening a bit you begin to wonder how that quietly feminine voice can pack so much fact-power. From then on it's but a step to discovery that this pretty little thing carries a disconcerting load of expertise."[8] She was clever in a way that most men, in 1971, did not expect from their female counterparts. Still, at 41, she was relatively young, and when it came to the politics of the nation's capital, inexperienced and unsophisticated.

If O'Connor had known that Nixon's selection process was concentrated on old-boy insiders, she might not have bothered to write to him. But she believed in Nixon, his tough-on-crime inclination and his fiscal conservatism. From the platform of her state Senate office, she thought she had something to say. "I am confident that your selections will be well considered and wise. Chief Justice Warren Burger has already proven himself to the American people to have been a splendid choice," she wrote on October 1, 1971, to Nixon, as a prelude to her main order of business: "It is my belief that the citizens of this nation would warmly accept appointment of a woman to the Supreme Court." She told the president that in her own state of Arizona, the state supreme court had a long-serving woman on its bench. Lorna Lockwood, the daughter of a venerable state supreme court justice, was elected to the court in 1960 and was made chief justice in 1965. "The citizens of Arizona have demonstrated their high regard and affection for the distaff member of our court in many statewide elections," O'Connor wrote, then closed: "With every good wish for this and the other tasks which you are performing so well for our country. Sincerely, Sandra D. O'Connor, Arizona State Senator."

As the news of Rehnquist's nomination became the talk of the Historical and Museum Commission meeting, O'Connor voiced no objections to Nixon's passing up a woman.[9] Her qualms, if she had any, were characteristically kept to herself. She joined the others in expressing surprise at the announcement from Washington. Rehnquist's name had not been seriously raised in the press over the past month, as dozens of other names had. Little did O'Connor know that Rehnquist, the 47-year-old director of the obscure but powerful Justice Department's Office of Legal Counsel, actually had been Nixon's choice for only twenty-four hours. When Nixon's apparent preferences had been scuttled one by one by politics, the president's selection team had settled on the brainy assistant attorney general with unassailable law-and-order credentials.

O'Connor had been clipping news stories that speculated about the possibility of Nixon's choosing a woman. The president had forwarded the name of Mildred Lillie, a California state court of appeals judge, along with the names of five other potential nominees, to the American Bar Association for its traditional advisory review. Lillie, 56, of Los Angeles, was a registered Democrat, but Republicans had appointed her to court positions throughout her career, which began in 1947, when California governor Earl Warren named her to a municipal court. The White House let it leak that Lillie was at the top of Nixon's list. But a month earlier, just as O'Connor happened to be drafting her letter to the president, Nixon had confided to aides (in a conversation picked up by the taping system that would become infamous during Watergate) that he really did not want a woman justice: "I'm against it, frankly. . . . I don't want any of them around. Thank God we don't have any in the cabinet." Then, in characteristic Nixon style, the president added, "The cabinet's so lousy, we might as well have a woman, too."[10] Chief Justice Burger, 64, set in his ways, also was making his opposition to a woman nominee known. "Burger is totally against it," Nixon told his aides.[11]

Two days before Nixon announced his Supreme Court choices, the screening committee of the American Bar Association had leaked its "unqualified" rating of Lillie. Nixon, deft at defensive politics, quickly used the Lillie evaluation as an excuse to avoid a woman nominee. While he publicly denounced the ABA as biased against women, Nixon secretly felt "really off the hook on a woman." In a taped conversation with long-time aide John Connally, shortly after Nixon heard of the ABA screening committee's 11-to-1 vote against Lillie, the president said, "Of course, as you know, I am not keen on a woman anyway." The next day, he told his political advisor Richard Moore that the bar group "played right into our hands." He later remarked of Lillie and the other supposed candidates, "We were just playing around with those others. . . . They were just out as blocking backs. It was like a screen pass, basically."[12]

Nixon did not settle on Rehnquist for Harlan's seat until the day before his nationally televised October 21 announcement, the day O'Connor learned of his choice at the historical commission meeting. The front-runner until then was junior Tennessee senator Howard Baker, a Republican from the South who could help the president with an important voting bloc and a man who would pass Senate confirmation easily. But Baker was uncertain about leaving the push and shove of legislative politics for the isolation of the Court. As Baker vacillated, Nixon's political advisor Moore began pressing for Rehnquist, who had been first in his Stanford class of 1952 and a former law clerk to Justice Robert Jackson. "Who's going to argue with a guy who was Bob Jackson's clerk," the president said to Mitchell.[13] Nixon also knew Rehnquist was "on our side." Rehnquist, a tall, broad-shouldered man with clashing shirts and ties and a Midwestern bluntness, had been the voice of the administration against Vietnam War protesters. He was a critic of the Warren Court, which he believed was undermining law enforcement in its zeal for protecting defendants' rights. After getting Attorney General John Mitchell's endorsement, Nixon decided—essentially, on the spot—that Rehnquist should succeed Justice Harlan. "I think Rehnquist is just made to order on this," the president said, later telling Chief Justice Burger, "He isn't going to be moved by the Georgetown set."[14]

That same evening, Nixon announced his nomination of longtime Richmond lawyer and former American Bar Association president Lewis F. Powell Jr. to fill the other high court opening. Nixon's aides had been trying to persuade the highly respected Powell to be an appointee since 1969, when Nixon—looking for a successor to Fortas—wanted a southerner to help shore up this critical constituency. On that occasion, Powell, a descendant of one of the original Jamestown colonists, had asked, because of his age and declining eyesight, that his name not be considered. After losing Senate fights over two earlier nominees—U.S. appeals court judge Clement F. Haynsworth Jr. of South Carolina and U.S. appeals court judge G. Harold Carswell of Florida—in 1970, Nixon eventually settled on Harry Blackmun, a U.S. appeals court judge in Minnesota who had been best man at Burger's wedding. By 1971, Powell was even more concerned about his age, now 64, and his poor vision. But Nixon and Attorney General Mitchell convinced him to take the nomination. Powell's record—a Harvard graduate, decorated Army Air Corps officer, and longtime civic leader—made him a good political choice for an antagonistic Senate.

Far removed from the political machinations of Washington, O'Connor apparently put aside regrets that a woman had not been nominated as she left the historical commission meeting. She immediately threw her support to Nixon's choice. Taking the floor of the contemporary marble-and-walnut-paneled Arizona Senate chamber the day after Nixon's announcement, O'Connor described Rehnquist as "one of the most brilliant legal minds in the country." She told of how she and Rehnquist had been law school classmates. He "appeared to be head and shoulders above everyone else in the class in terms of pure legal ability," she said into the handheld microphone. O'Connor then added a prediction that might have seemed presumptuous, even outlandish, for a nominee who had come out of nowhere and was facing significant opposition. She declared on the Arizona Senate floor on October 22, 1971, that because of his young age, Rehnquist might one day become chief justice. But the possible appointment of a woman justice was not forgotten. Revealing that desire, she joked that she regretted that the nominee "doesn't wear a skirt."[15]

Rehnquist's legal and political work in Arizona was not without controversy, although O'Connor glossed over that. He had opposed a 1964 local antidiscrimination ordinance and testified against a 1967 school desegregation program. "We are no more dedicated to an 'integrated' society than we are to a 'segregated' society," Rehnquist had declared at a public meeting, rejecting the need for government remedies to end discrimination.[16]

Arizona was at the vanguard of a trend that eventually would affect the entire nation, and as Rehnquist articulated his opposition to government efforts to solve race discrimination, he foreshadowed the forty-eighth state's emergence as the heart of the conservative Sunbelt. "What has brought people to Phoenix and to Arizona?" he asked at a 1964 public hearing. "My guess is no better than anyone else's but I would say it's the idea of the lost frontier here in America. Free enterprise, and by that I mean not just free enterprise in the sense of a right to make a buck but the right to manage your own affairs as free as possible from the interference of government."[17]

Another piece of ammunition for Rehnquist critics was that he had been part of a Republican team that challenged Democrats at the polls, many of them black, to show that they were eligible to vote. One claim, unsubstantiated but a focal point of his opponents' complaints, was that Rehnquist had harassed blacks by demanding that they read the Constitution aloud before being allowed to vote. Once in Washington as an assistant attorney general in the Nixon Justice Department, Rehnquist had reinforced his reputation as a hard-line conservative by criticizing the civil rights movement, expressing disdain for Vietnam protesters, and becoming a vocal advocate for government to engage in wiretapping and other surveillance practices.[18]

In the Arizona Senate chamber, Cloves Campbell, the only member of the body who was African-American, had something to say about that. Campbell had tangled with Rehnquist on just about every civil rights controversy in Phoenix and was stunned by the nomination. "If the president of the United States is serious about this appointment," Campbell declared, "then all the good work that has been accomplished by the

Supreme Court might just as well be thrown out the window."[19] In the Arizona Senate, Campbell, unlike O'Connor, was an outsider. He had moved to Phoenix as a child in 1945, after a doctor recommended the dry climate for his father, a sawmill worker in Louisiana who was sick with tuberculosis. Within a few months, however, his father died. Three years later, his mother passed away. At 14, Campbell lived with a sister and brother-in-law and took up several odd jobs as he worked his way through high school. He attended Arizona State College on a football scholarship, became an activist on just about every cause for racial minorities, and eventually bought the state's leading black newspaper.[20] He won election to the state House in 1962, and in 1966 became the first African-American elected to the Arizona state Senate. Blacks were then and have remained a small percentage of Arizonans, about 3 percent.

A big, muscular man who liked to wear three-piece suits ("when I could afford them"), Campbell felt he had to "defend a people."[21] So the day after Nixon's televised announcement, when O'Connor took to the floor to endorse Rehnquist, Campbell stood up to denounce him. He said the nomination was a setback for civil rights and asserted that "Mr. Rehnquist has in the past demonstrated that [he believes that the] rights of minorities [are] something associated with the Communist cause."[22]

Taking the lead against the nominee in Washington were Democratic U.S. senators Birch Bayh, from Indiana, and Edward M. Kennedy, from Massachusetts, and civil rights leader Joseph Rauh, then counsel to the coalition group known as the Leadership Conference on Civil Rights. Bayh said Rehnquist's record "reveals a persistent distaste for governmental efforts to correct the injustices that racial discrimination has wrought." For his part, Rehnquist believed many antibias efforts were unnecessary and wrongly encroached on business and property rights.[23]

From her Senate desk in a building adjacent to the copper-domed Capitol, O'Connor began a campaign for Rehnquist on her own initiative and independent of the Nixon administration. On a yellow legal pad, she wrote the word "Assignments." She listed ten names, including her own, her husband's and Mayor Driggs's. She jotted down work for each, from calling lawyers and legislators to feeling out minority groups in search of support for Rehnquist. She had ideas for contacting church groups and ministers, and she made a note to consider seeking an "editorial comment on Campbell"—likely to oppose his views—from a local newspaper writer. O'Connor then sent a letter to the U.S. Senate Judiciary Committee Chairman James Eastland, praising Rehnquist and asking to testify before the committee on his behalf. While she continued to juggle her state Senate work—the special redistricting session was over but she was working on a school finance proposal—she gathered news clippings for Rehnquist from the *Arizona Republic* and *Phoenix Gazette* newspapers, sending them to him with a note that said, "I thought it might be useful for you to have a complete set. We are working as rapidly as possible in our attempts to spread a network of support for you throughout the country."[24]

Drawing heavily on the old-boys' network of Stanford University Law School, she contacted many of their classmates. O'Connor systematically began going through a roll of the law graduates to figure out whether she or someone better positioned should make contact on behalf of Rehnquist. She started a list of U.S. senators who, based on their records, might oppose Rehnquist, and kept track of senators' comments for or against Rehnquist.

But at this point in O'Connor's political education, she was not adroit at all the personal maneuverings that came with the political territory. She wrote a letter to Eugene Pulliam, the wealthy hands-on publisher of the *Arizona Republic* and *Indianapolis Star and News,* with the request that he try to counter Indiana Democrat Bayh's opposition to Rehnquist. She opened her letter to Pulliam with compliments for an extraordinary front-page editorial that had run in the *Arizona Republic* on October 24, 1971, with the banner headline "Will the Federal Bureaucracy Destroy Individual Freedom in America?" This editorial, lambasting the hand of the federal government in American life, written and signed by Pulliam, would be legendary in the history of the *Arizona Republic*.[25] It also would be so compelling to Harry and Ada Mae Day, Sandra's parents, that they would save it among their important papers and family albums at the ranch.[26]

"I am writing you directly in the hope that you will be in a position to at least tone down the attack against Mr. Rehnquist," O'Connor told Pulliam on October 27, urging him "to use your influence in Indiana to do whatever is possible to support the nominee."[27] She appeared oblivious to the possibility that Pulliam's intervention might very well rile Bayh even more.

A week after Rehnquist's nomination announcement, O'Connor used the occasion of a previously scheduled speech to the Camelback Kiwanis Club to complain about Senator Campbell and other local critics: "It is regrettable that the confirmation . . . is being opposed by a few citizens of this community on grounds which cannot be substantiated. . . . When Bill has expressed concern about any law or ordinance in the area of civil rights, it has been to express a concern for the preservation of individual liberties of which he is a staunch defender in the tradition of the late Justice Black." The comparison was jarring, given Rehnquist's complaints about criminal rights and civil liberties. Black, who died eight days after a stroke forced his retirement in September, around the time of Harlan's, had interpreted the Bill of Rights broadly. He authored the famous 1963 *Gideon v. Wainwright* decision that gave indigent people accused of serious crimes the right to a lawyer. It is difficult to know whether O'Connor's comments reflected a simple misunderstanding of the two men's records, an outright misrepresentation, or an attempt at a more subtle comparison not evident after the fact. In her speech to the Kiwanis, O'Connor also declared, "Bill Rehnquist . . . is neither a racist nor a bigot. He has the potential to become one of the great jurists of our highest court. Forgive the digression, but the confirmation of this man is so important to this nation that I could not resist talking about it." [28]

O'Connor surely knew Rehnquist's attitude. He was never one to sugarcoat his views. As the Vietnam War generated increasing protest in the streets, Rehnquist thought that law enforcement should have a freer hand for arrests, wiretapping, and other surveillance. O'Connor had sent him an old opinion column he had written for the *Phoenix Weekly Gazette,* in which Rehnquist made clear his feelings. Her note said: "[I]t would be just as well if this one did not come out, I think. So far, I don't believe it has been brought forth." In the piece, Rehnquist refers to the Supreme Court's "bleeding heart" toward criminal suspects and "the dangers of hair-splitting and ivory tower technicalities in the administration of criminal justice." [29] So, while she was not disturbed by his views, she was aware that they could get him in trouble.

Rehnquist's Senate Judiciary Committee hearings were set to begin on November 3, when O'Connor and her husband had been long scheduled to be in Puerto Vallarta, Mexico, for a vacation. But O'Connor told Rehnquist she would, if needed, make arrangements to fly to Washington. She wrote to him daily, letting him know of the contacts she had made on his behalf. Her network focused on law school deans, business leaders, lawyers, and—most important—U.S. senators. She kept home-state Senator Goldwater informed of her work.

O'Connor was not needed to testify. Rehnquist had Goldwater and Arizona's other senator, Republican Paul Fannin, there for him. She went with her husband to Puerto Vallarta, telling one friend, "It was the first time John and I did absolutely nothing for one week."[30] Once back in Arizona, O'Connor resumed her mission, whether needed or not. Rehnquist apparently began to realize the extent of her work. On November 10, he sent a note on Department of Justice stationery to the O'Connors: "Words are inadequate to convey my appreciation for what you have done for me in connection with the nomination to the Supreme Court. I feel that a very effective organization has somehow been suddenly called into being, largely as a result of your doing. There are numerous personal messages of thanks to others, which are richly deserved, and which I hope in due time to get off, but your efforts have been so special I wanted you to know that I deeply appreciate them. Parenthetically, I was virtually bowled over by Sherman Hazeltine's contacts among the Western bankers, not only from deep appreciation of his efforts but from extraordinary admiration for the effectiveness of their congressional contacts. Maybe that is why bankers have more influence than lawyers."[31]

Hazeltine was president of the First National Bank of Arizona. O'Connor had been elected to the bank's board of directors in January 1971, the first woman director in the bank's ninety-two-year history and one of only a few women bank directors nationwide.[32] O'Connor had sent Rehnquist copies of letters Hazeltine had written to selected U.S. senators, and she had added a personal note of encouragement to the nominee: "We certainly regret the unpleasant experiences you must have had during the hearings, but it will all be worthwhile when you are confirmed." The benign phrase "unpleasant experiences" belied the nature of the nomination battle underway in Washington, and the vociferous criticism of Rehnquist.[33]

Clarence Mitchell, director of the Washington bureau of the National Association for the Advancement of Colored People (NAACP), was among those who claimed that Rehnquist had harassed African-American voters in Phoenix. "During the long and dramatic struggle of black citizens for rights and equality of treatment there have been many frustrations and fears," Mitchell said during his testimony against Rehnquist. "However, if there has been any fixed star by which they could set a course that would take them to their goal, it has been and up until now is the United States Supreme Court. The Rehnquist nomination raises a grim warning. Through that nomination the foot of racism is placed in the door of the temple of Justice."[34]

During the hearings, Rehnquist denied harassing blacks at the polls. He said he had been there merely to check the credentials of voters and that he had actually intervened when another lawyer questioned African-Americans too aggressively. Rehnquist testified before the Senate Judiciary Committee that he had come to believe that the Phoenix law prohibiting race discrimination in restaurants and other public places benefited society. He refused to answer many questions about his involvement with harsh Justice Department policies on wiretapping and other government surveillance. He said he had been speaking in his official capacity and did not want to elaborate with his own views.[35]

After the hearings were over but before the Senate vote, *Newsweek* magazine reported on a newly uncovered memo written by Rehnquist in 1952, while he was a clerk to Jackson and the Court was considering the *Brown v. Board of Education* school-segregation disputes. In the memo, Rehnquist appeared to defend the "separate but equal" doctrine in government treatment of blacks and whites. "I realize that it is an unpopular and unhumanitarian position, for which I have been excoriated by 'liberal' colleagues, but I think *Plessy v. Ferguson* was right and should be re-affirmed...."[36] The memo's revelation exacerbated some senators' concerns about Rehnquist's views of civil rights. Rehnquist defended himself by saying that he had been stating Justice Jackson's views for his own use as he deliberated with fellow justices. Richard Kluger, who later examined the question in *Simple Justice,* his seminal work on *Brown v. Board of Education,* wrote: "A far more plausible explanation might be that the 'I' of the memo is Rehnquist himself, referring to the obloquy to which he may have been subjected by his fellow clerks, who discussed the segregation question over lunch quite regularly, who were almost unanimous in their belief that *Plessy* ought to be reversed, and who were, for the most part, 'liberal.' "[37]

But senators were satisfied enough with Rehnquist's explanation on this and other points of contention to confirm him by a vote of 68–26 on December 10, 1971. The activists who a year earlier effectively opposed Judges Haynsworth and Carswell "found it extremely difficult to crank up for a third major fight at the end of the legislative season," wrote Leon Friedman, a lawyer and Supreme Court analyst. "Moreover, some of their efforts had been dissipated early in the game when they mobilized against the rumored nominations of [other potential nominees] submitted to the American Bar Association before the President settled on Messrs. Powell and Rehnquist." Friedman also observed that law school professors did not as actively oppose the nominee as they had previous conservatives, which Rauh, of the Leadership Conference on Civil Rights, explained by saying, "They think that a reactionary A student is better than a reactionary C student and that it's O.K. for him to go on the bench. None of the important leaders of the bar came out against Mr. Rehnquist, largely because his professional competence was unquestioned." [38]

Goldwater was impressed by how Rehnquist held up. On December 11, the day after the Senate vote, he wrote to him, "Before going home for the holidays I want you to know how deeply proud I am of you and the manful way that you stood up to the false attacks by Bayh and company. We now have a Court that will be a delight to the Founding Fathers as they sit up in Heaven and begin to watch decisions made on their words and not on the whims and wishes of a sociologist. It will be a great honor for me to call you Mr. Justice." [39]

When Rehnquist was sworn in on January 7, 1972, amid the white marble and intricate bronze-work of the Supreme Court, O'Connor was there. It was her first time inside the Supreme Court. She found the brief ceremony inspiring and affecting. "It was an emotional moment for me as I contemplated the potential benefits which can accrue to our nation by virtue of that eight-minute ceremony," she wrote to one of Rehnquist's supporters. Then, in a gesture that was disarmingly dutiful and classically O'Connor, she added: "Unfortunately, there was no program or other memento of the occasion. I purchased the enclosed volume of 'Equal Justice Under Law' and requested Bill to sign and date it on page three as a memento for you in appreciation of all the help you gave Bill in connection with his confirmation. If you believe additional copies of this volume would be appreciated by others who likewise assisted, please let me know."[40] The deed also marked O'Connor's place in Rehnquist's confirmation. She wrote letters telling people about the few days after the ceremony spent with Rehnquist and his family. He had regaled her with anecdotes from his first days in chambers and the cases that awaited him.[41]

O'Connor's sense of optimism for Rehnquist's tenure stood in contrast to President Nixon's closing response to Rehnquist's appointment. "I will give you one last bit of advice, because you're going to be independent, naturally," Nixon told Rehnquist, "and that is don't let the fact that you're under heat change any of your views. . . . So just be as mean and rough as they said you were." The remarks apparently were made in the only private conversation recorded between Nixon and Rehnquist.[42]

In the end, O'Connor's work for Rehnquist was not decisive. There was no real groundswell of opposition in Phoenix for her to confront. Arizona Senator Campbell decided against flying to Washington to testify, believing the nominee had the votes and satisfied that his written remarks on Rehnquist would be put into the record by Senator Kennedy. Most U.S. senators were not troubled by the testimony against Rehnquist regarding civil rights.

But the young Arizona legislator had given her all. The episode might have instilled in her a sense of what was possible for herself. After Rehnquist was confirmed, she filed away her personal score-sheet of senators' votes, along with all the letters, notes, phone numbers, and news clippings she had collected. She stuffed in, too, a cartoon she had seen in the *Arizona Republic* that November. It featured a disheveled but happy man looking into a hospital nursery window at his newborn daughter. He says to the nurse by his side, "Just think, she might someday become a Supreme Court justice."[43]

4

"NEVER ONE OF THE BOYS"

If Sandra O'Connor's long-range ambitions remained loosely formed and divided between politics and law in the early 1970s, her commitment to community was as strong as ever. Returning from her 1972 trip to Washington for William Rehnquist's investiture, she expanded her political and social networks. American women were leaving the kitchen and moving away from their role as hostess, but for O'Connor, entertainment remained a priority. The contrast to the social isolation that Harry and Ada Mae Day experienced on the ranch could not have been starker. Or, perhaps, O'Connor had achieved with the social elite of Phoenix what they might have wanted but never could have found in the rough ranch world around the Lazy B. In any case, O'Connor genuinely enjoyed throwing big parties, and she understood that her social activities paid dividends in her professional life.

Some of the galas she and John hosted had whimsical themes. In June 1972, they held a "So long school, hello summer" square-dancing party. The women wore calico dresses, the men Levi jeans and cowboy shirts.[1] A few months earlier, a small bridge the O'Connors had constructed across the arroyo to a pool and guest quarters behind their house prompted friends to stage a campy bridge dedication. Men sported top hats and tails with white shorts and sneakers. Women wore gowns and pith helmets. Boiled beef, potatoes, and English muffins were served. Bagpipes wailed;

festive helium balloons abounded. As covered by the Society pages of the *Arizona Republic,* the gala brought out a Who's Who of Phoenix.[2]

O'Connor sought civic board appointments. By the mid-1970s, she was on the board of trustees of the Heard Museum, a world-renowned collection of Native American fine art. Her interest in Indian artifacts had begun on the Lazy B, where she sometimes found arrowheads as she wandered the ranch with her mother. O'Connor also became a member of the Stanford University board of trustees. Sharon Rockefeller, already a trustee when O'Connor was appointed, said O'Connor jumped into discussions, ignoring the kind of advice women often received about sitting back and figuring out how the men dealt with each other. Rooming with O'Connor at Stanford's Faculty Club when they were there for meetings, Rockefeller said she was struck by how O'Connor could close off the other worries of the day—whether they had to do with her sons or the job back in Arizona. "She didn't wallow in problems or reveal self-doubt," said Rockefeller.[3]

O'Connor's early focus as a state senator had been job opportunities for women and equal pay for equal work. It seemed fitting that one of the first initiatives of this task-oriented legislator was removing from the books a 1913 Arizona statute prohibiting women from working more than eight hours a day. It was not easy legislation to push through against the opposition of labor activists, some Democrats, and other women. "Let's give the women a chance for a better life and a bigger pocketbook," O'Connor said in a speech on the Senate floor. Many women were discriminated against in seeking and keeping jobs, she said, because of the eight-hour limit. One of O'Connor's most vocal opponents was another woman. Democratic senator E. B. Thode argued that repealing the law would hurt the working poor and asked if Arizona "really wants to go back to the sweatshop days?"[4] O'Connor's bill passed the Senate by a single vote, and became law later in 1970.

But as O'Connor showered her colleagues with facts about women's unfair wages, she did not directly challenge people to change their attitudes. It was an approach that kept her in good stead with the business community. When the Phoenix Advertising Club named her "Woman of the Year" in 1972, the brochure for the annual awards banquet began with this description of the honoree: "While other women are marching and shouting, Sandra O'Connor quietly carries the standard of successful

women. She is regarded by thousands of people all over Arizona as a woman who by her performance and comments, as distinguished from her complaints, has done much to advance the status of women in this state."[5] The not-so-subtle message was that female rabble-rousers would not be rewarded by the established institutions of Arizona. But, of course, O'Connor knew that.

At an early age, on the Lazy B, O'Connor learned to work hard and not to complain. A letter Harry Day wrote to his sister Eleanor during negotiations over the settlement of a family estate attested to that. "I have raised my children to work and they all like to work and expect to work during their lives," he told his sister. He asserted his belief that "a person leads a fuller and more satisfying life if they work, are occupied, doing something constructive or enterprising during their lives."[6]

IN 1968, RICHARD NIXON had staged one of history's greatest political comebacks by winning the presidency. Four years later, he was headed toward easy reelection over Democratic senator George McGovern. In Arizona, Nixon's reelection effort was being run by Sam Mardian, a former Phoenix mayor and the brother of Robert Mardian, a former assistant attorney general and now deputy to Nixon's campaign manager John Mitchell, the former attorney general. In spring 1972, Sam Mardian was under pressure from the regional office to add a woman to the ranks of the organization, and he decided to ask O'Connor to be his cochairman. "She could easily have had twenty-five significant 'firsts' as a woman," recalled Sam Mardian. "But you didn't get the feeling that you were talking with a woman. You got the feeling that you're dealing with a cohort and trying to achieve something of substance."[7] O'Connor accepted his offer.

Thomas C. Reed was Southwest regional director for Nixon's reelection effort and had urged Mardian to choose a woman cochair to broaden the appeal of the reelection effort. Upon meeting O'Connor, Reed thought she was exactly what the Arizona campaign needed: a fount of energy who refused to rest on the belief that Barry Goldwater's home state would automatically produce a Nixon majority and that would be that. "Now here's a lady who understands phone banks," Reed said years later. "She gets it, that you can use the high numbers [of people turning out for the presidential race] to win legislative elections."[8]

Reed shared O'Connor's belief in cultivating Mexican-American voters in the Southwest and was impressed after their first meeting when she wrote him a note that said, "I would appreciate receiving at the earliest possible date a list of prominent appointments to public office of Mexican-Americans made by President Nixon, with names, positions, and addresses."[9]

O'Connor also tried to generate support in the state's Native American community. She had begun talking with Peter MacDonald, a charismatic Navajo tribal chairman. Their conversations focused on the Nixon administration's proposal to move the Navajos off rangeland that had long been claimed by the rival Hopi tribe. About six weeks before the November election, O'Connor wrote to Senator Goldwater, urging a postponement of hearings on the Navajo-Hopi land bill and offering an optimistic prediction, "Recent estimates indicate that as many as 25,000 Navajos may have registered to vote. Discussions with Peter MacDonald, the Navajo Tribal Chief, indicate that there is a good chance that almost all the Navajo votes could go to President Nixon and other Republican candidates this time, provided there is not a major revolt due to the Senate hearings on the Navajo-Hopi land bill presently scheduled for September. I'm sure you realize the depth of feeling in the Indian community concerning this bill. . . . I feel strongly that it would be very advantageous politically to reschedule the hearings on the land bill after the November elections. If this could be done, it assures us an unprecedented opportunity to capture Republican votes in the northeastern corner of the state this fall."[10]

The tone of O'Connor's letter was cheerful and collected. But it ignored a deteriorating relationship between MacDonald and Goldwater. Three weeks earlier, MacDonald had upbraided Goldwater's party in a *Washington Post* story, declaring that unless Republicans supported the Navajos in the land dispute he might "have to support George McGovern."[11] The threatening rhetoric was typical of MacDonald, but Goldwater took it personally. Since Goldwater had not taken sides in the land dispute—and he had close friends among both the Navajo and Hopi— he felt betrayed by MacDonald's statement. Goldwater was in a position to strike back. MacDonald was scheduled to be one of the speakers at the Republican National Convention who would put Nixon's name before the convention. Shortly before the Miami event, which O'Connor at-

tended, Goldwater saw to it that MacDonald's name was dropped from the list of nominating speakers.[12]

Either O'Connor was oblivious to the open enmity between MacDonald and Goldwater or she chose to ignore it. The letter offered a window into O'Connor's political approach at this point. She was an organizer of people and a synthesizer of facts—always working to get out ahead of a situation. No volunteer in her purview would ever be short of campaign materials saying "President Nixon: Now More Than Ever." On the other hand, she lacked an intuitive grasp of the grudge matches that bred in politics. She took people at their most positive selves, often signing letters to campaign coworkers and volunteers at the strip-mall headquarters for the reelection of President Nixon with, "I love you."[13]

Goldwater wrote back to O'Connor about a week later, saying, "I think I am safe in saying that Peter MacDonald muddied up the water so badly back here that in spite of efforts of Paul Fannin and myself, hearings are going to be heard on the bill." Then Goldwater addressed her assumptions: "Sandra, the number of Navajos who are registered to vote would be closer to 2,500 rather than 25,000 and because of the fact that they tend to vote Republican, the three counties, all Democratically controlled that contain the reservation, will not provide enough polling places for that number of voters, so it is not a matter of great political urgency. . . . I have worked on the Navajo Reservation more than any other Republican and while I don't claim to have all the answers, I have gotten a few."[14]

When she responded, O'Connor acknowledged her error only this way: "I have personally checked the registration figures for Apache County, and I concur with your view that they will not be a major factor in this year's election. There is a tremendous potential there, however, for the future, and I hope we can continue to build good relations with the Indians of both the Navajo and Hopi tribes. I am certainly grateful for your tremendous knowledge of the Indian people and their area."[15] It was classic O'Connor: no reference to the put-down or her larger gaffe, no apologies, no return sarcasm.

Nixon won in a landslide. It was the first Republican sweep of the once-solid Democratic South since Reconstruction.[16] In Arizona, Nixon won 67 percent of the major-party vote.[17] The public seemed not to care about news stories connecting a June 1972 break-in at the Democratic national headquarters in the Watergate office building to the president's re-election campaign.

Through her connection to the campaign, O'Connor's reputation was enhanced. Shortly before the November election, regional director Reed wrote to Anne Armstrong at the Republican National Committee, urging her to suggest O'Connor for a job in the administration's second term. "She is an attorney, attractive, about my age, with more brains and energy than can be utilized in all of Arizona." [18]

In a later interview, Reed said: "After the election, I remember asking, 'Would you like to come to Washington?' She gave a 1950s answer. 'Well, my husband has a good law practice. My kids are in school.' Then she said, 'Maybe something else will turn up.' " [19]

O'Connor also told Reed that she was about to become Senate majority leader, a position that had come quickly to the 42-year-old senator. After she had won her own reelection in 1972 and state Republicans kept their 18–12 margin over Democrats in the Senate, O'Connor's fellow Republicans elected her over Senator Dave Kret of Scottsdale, who had been majority leader for two terms. O'Connor also managed to knock out another senator who had been majority whip and was attempting to move up the ranks to majority leader.[20] Apparently, just as O'Connor was earning a reputation for working with the GOP leadership, Kret was pursuing "his lone wolf policies regardless of what the GOP majority program called for." [21] As *Arizona Republic* political editor Bernie Wynn reported on the plan being devised by Republican leaders, he wrote, " 'Sandy,' as she is known around the Capitol, is a sharp gal. She is articulate, has a steel-trap mind, boundless energy, and a large measure of common sense." [22] After she had been elected, Wynn added, "Sandy O'Connor should be quite good at this if she can learn to smile while the minority is trying to shove a political knife in her ribs. She has a lovely smile and should use it often." [23]

The majority leader post, the number-two spot after the Senate president, was responsible for getting the leadership's legislative program passed. Superficially, the job appeared ideal for the detail-oriented O'Connor, who strove for good relations with all colleagues. But once she became majority leader, O'Connor found herself challenged almost immediately by lawmakers on both sides of the aisle. "Mrs. O'Connor continually is being tested in the Senate," reported the *Tucson Daily Citizen,* "partly because she is new on the job this year and partly because she's a woman—the only woman majority leader in any of the 50 state legislatures as far as she knows."[24]

O'Connor discovered that elective politics was not just a game of smarts, preparation, and skill—all of which she had. Hardball maneuvering—which did not come naturally to her—was also required. O'Connor did not look for unstated motives. O'Connor was by nature a centrist, as well, and in the mid-1970s, Arizona was moving decidedly to the right. Goldwater, who had famously said at the 1964 Republican National Convention, "extremism in the defense of liberty is no vice" and "moderation in the pursuit of justice is no virtue," would witness a conservative upheaval that made him look like a moderate in his own state. With the constant influx of new residents, the emerging political milieu made Phoenix the heart of the new conservative Sunbelt.[25]

O'Connor had been a protégé of Old Guard Republicans. Now, Goldwater and longtime GOP party chairman Harry Rosenzweig were losing their influence. A new brand of social conservatives was emerging. Their numbers would swell—and not in small measure due to a bombshell from the U.S. Supreme Court.

Three weeks after O'Connor was sworn in as Senate majority leader, the Supreme Court issued its decision in *Roe v. Wade,* making abortion legal nationwide and creating a new force in politics. On January 22, 1973 in the case of a Texas carnival worker who claimed she had been raped, the Supreme Court declared that women have a constitutional right to decide whether to end a pregnancy. The justices grounded the right in the Fourteenth Amendment's due-process guarantee of personal liberty. They set out a three-part approach to be used when assessing state laws regulating abortion: During the first trimester of pregnancy, the decision to have an abortion was left entirely to a woman and her physician. During the second trimester, the state could regulate the abortion procedure in ways reasonably related to maternal health. And during the third trimester, the state could, if it wished, forbid all abortions except those necessary to protect the mother's health.[26]

Coincidentally, former president Lyndon B. Johnson died the day of the ruling, so news of *Roe v. Wade* initially was overshadowed. But its magnitude soon became clear. For some women, the decision was a liberating force. But for many Americans, it challenged religious convictions

about when life begins and, for some, was nothing short of an endorsement of murder. As such, *Roe* immediately created the national "Right to
Life" movement focused on winning its reversal. The most socially consequential decision since the 1954 ruling in *Brown v. Board of Education*,
Roe presented a new and difficult dynamic in electoral politics and fueled
cultural wars that endured in America.

In Arizona, abortion opponents first turned to the state legislature to
try to win new regulation of the abortion procedure and to try to push
through a resolution that would urge Congress to protect the unborn.
They did not presume that O'Connor would be on their side.[27] In 1970, a
few months after she had been appointed to the Senate, O'Connor had
voted in a committee meeting for repeal of a state law that banned abortion except to save the mother's life. The committee approval of a
proposed repeal of criminal laws pertaining to abortions came by a 6–3
vote. According to news reports about the April 29, 1970, action,
O'Connor made an unsuccessful attempt to add a provision requiring
abortions to be performed only by licensed physicians.[28] Catholic groups
vehemently opposed the repeal, and three Catholic bishops issued a statement calling the bill a "moral evil."[29] Some Protestant ministers and rab-
bis, meanwhile, issued a letter that said in part, "We firmly believe in the
ethical and moral rights of a woman over her own body in making such
deeply personal choices as whether or not she will have a child. Arizona's
abortion law abridges this right." The legislation stalled in 1970 and
never made it to the floor of the Arizona Senate.[30]

After the Supreme Court's *Roe v. Wade* decision in 1973, O'Connor opposed state proposals for stricter antiabortion regulations and for a resolution asking Congress to prohibit abortion.[31] She also voted against an
antiabortion provision on an appropriations bill for expansion of the University of Arizona football stadium. O'Connor said she did not think the
amendment to ban abortions at the University of Arizona hospital was
relevant to the bill. The amendment passed over her protests.[32] The
amendment's sponsor, who declared that the university hospital had become "an abortion mill," said he deliberately chose the unrelated but popular stadium bill for his proposal, to ensure adoption of his measure.
O'Connor also backed legislation that restricted Arizona state funds for
abortions for poor women and a bill that gave hospital personnel the
right to refuse to participate in abortions. Her actions, taken as a whole

over half a decade of Senate tenure, make her appear more sympathetic to abortion-rights proponents than to opponents but far from a major player on the issue, in any event.

Newspaper reports of the day cast Senator O'Connor as more interested in matters of women's equal rights. In spring 1972, when the U.S. Senate was considering whether to send the Equal Rights Amendment to the states for ratification, O'Connor had written to Arizona senators Goldwater and Fannin, urging them to vote for it. The amendment, which had been approved by the U.S. House of Representatives in 1971, said, "Equality of rights under the law shall not be denied or abridged by the United States or by any state on account of sex" and that "the Congress shall have the power to enforce by appropriate legislation the provisions of this article." It was intended to nullify laws that discriminated against women.

The U.S. Senate voted for the amendment 84–8 on March 22, 1972. Both Goldwater and Fannin were among those opposed.[33] A few weeks later, Goldwater explained in a letter to O'Connor, "Your opinion, especially on a legal matter of this nature, means much to me and I am sorry that I just could not vote for the Equal Rights Amendment. . . . First, I do not think any law can change the design of the Lord by making men and women identical. Second, I dislike tampering with the Constitution. Third, I believe the problems which have been raised of discrimination in society can be treated under existing statutes or the Fourteenth Amendment."[34] Goldwater could make his views of women known in a more recklessly blunt way. Not long after that ERA vote, he teased that he would not oppose a woman for vice president "as long as she can cook and comes home on time."[35]

The day after the ERA passed the U.S. Senate, and before she had received Goldwater's letter, O'Connor rose from her desk in the Senate chamber and vigorously urged her colleagues to vote for what could become the twenty-seventh Amendment. She said the ERA was in the tradition of the women's liberation movement that began in the nineteenth century. News accounts said it was an unexpected show of enthusiasm by the senator from Paradise Valley.[36]

But as the years passed and the amendment gained little momentum in Arizona, and the national Republican Party cooled on the measure, so did O'Connor. She would be of two minds, mirroring some of the natural ambivalence of her state and the times. The pioneer woman was a symbol of the West, and when Arizona achieved statehood in 1912, it immediately gave women the right to vote in its elections. But the state also was distinctly conservative—increasingly so with the influx of Republicans. Even as state legislators were considering action on the ERA, the Maricopa County assessor in Phoenix refused to let his women employees wear pantsuits until the vice chief justice of the Arizona Supreme Court issued a directive permitting it. Unrelated to that dispute, O'Connor said in one mid-1970s interview, "I grew up in an age when they (pants) weren't popular and I never changed my style from dress to pants. I feel dresses are more feminine, make a better appearance."[37]

By early 1973, only twenty-two of the requisite thirty-eight states had ratified the Equal Rights Amendment. Arizona was not one of them. At O'Connor's urging, the Arizona Senate Judiciary Committee considered trying to put the ERA to a vote of the state electorate. "We've heard each side say they're representing a majority of the people," O'Connor said during a committee meeting. "Personally, I think amendments to the Constitution of the United States should be referred to a vote of the people of this state, like amendments to our Arizona Constitution."[38] But she was overruled by colleagues on the Judiciary Committee who wanted an opinion from the state attorney general about whether the legislature could seek a public referendum on an issue in the legislative domain.

As the months wore on, ERA proponents and opponents held rallies at the Capitol, in the shadow of its seventeen-foot high statue of winged Victory atop the building. First, ERA supporters came bearing carnations for legislators. Then opponents arrived with homemade bread. One leader of the second group, representing Homemakers United Effort, said, "The great majority of women are happy in the role of wife, mother, and homemaker. There is no more noble, satisfying, or creative career."[39]

O'Connor took the competing sentiments to heart. "I find myself in a difficult position concerning the Equal Rights Amendment," she wrote in her stock reply to constituents in early 1974. "I do not share the concern expressed by some that its ratification would threaten family life as we know it or that it would deprive women of their freedom. On the contrary, the Equal Rights Amendment recognizes the fundamental dignity and individuality of each human being and rests on the basic principle that sex should not be a factor in determining the legal rights of men or women. The Amendment affects only governmental action. It does not affect private actions or the private and personal relationships of families and husbands and wives. . . . On the other hand, many sincere and genuine questions have been raised about the interpretation of the broad general language of the Amendment, and these questions would, no doubt, require litigation, to resolve them."[40]

In March 1974, the attorney general's office announced its determination on whether the Equal Rights Amendment could be put to the state voters. It said that, contrary to O'Connor's interests, the legislature could not refer an advisory question on ratification of the ERA to the electorate. The opinion said the legislature had the option to ratify or to reject the amendment but that it could not be referred to the people.[41] The following month, the Senate Judiciary Committee voted 5–4 against sending the measure to the floor, effectively killing it. O'Connor was one of the four senators in the minority.[42]

"Women who expected Sen. Sandra O'Connor to use her power as majority leader to give the bill an assist have been disappointed," *Phoenix Gazette* columnist Janet Sanford wrote, taking stock of the situation in early 1974. "In fact, Sen. [Scott] Ulm [a Tucson Democrat who introduced the ratification measure] lays the death of the ERA bill in committee last session at her door. While O'Connor's disinterest may have surprised some since she gave lip service to women's rights prior to her elevation to the leadership post, it makes good sense to the politically astute. For the first female majority leader to immediately attach herself to a feminist cause might dilute her effectiveness as majority leader, a risk she cannot afford to take at this point in her career."[43]

Everything O'Connor had done as a public official suggested she thought about how to be most effective, where to spend her capital, and what fights were worth picking. Whatever her reasons for retrenchment on the ERA, it made O'Connor less of a threat to the male GOP movers and shakers who were in power in the mid-1970s and who would become her main supporters in 1981. (The Republican Party formally dropped its support of the ERA with its 1980 presidential convention platform.) O'Connor had a way of separating herself from unpopular causes. Shirley Odegaard, one-time chair of the Arizona Statewide Coalition on the Equal Rights Amendment, later told *Ms.* magazine: "Sandra . . . didn't want a floor vote because she feared polarization and felt it would be hard to bring opponents around. We urged her to use her leadership and power to make the ERA a trade item with other bills. . . . She favored issues we could win and she began to think the ERA was a lost cause."[44] Odegaard put her finger on a distinctive trait of O'Connor: she attached herself to issues on which she could prevail.

BY 1974, THERE WERE many frustrations for O'Connor as state Republicans clashed with Democrats and each other. Famous for her ability to control her temper, at one point at the end of the legislative session, O'Connor let her anger fly at a fellow Republican. A Senate committee chairman who was furious that his pet project had failed to reach the floor told O'Connor, "If you were a man, I'd punch you in the mouth." Her response: "If you were a man, you could."[45]

O'Connor's family life was also becoming more complicated. Her sons were growing up and required the attention teenagers need. She tried to impose discipline, but as O'Connor's longtime friend Diane Cooley said, "she had a crew that was eager for shore leave."[46] Brian, her middle son and the family's true nonconformist, was sometimes in trouble at school.[47] He worked out his restlessness with various adventures, such as backpacking alone in the mountains. Brian tried to keep some of his exploits from his parents. "I had begun hang-gliding secretly in high school," he recalled. "I stored my hang-glider at a friend's house. My mother found out about that. She was not happy. At that time, it was the early stages of hang-gliding. . . . She said, 'I would rather see you jump out of an airplane.' And I said, 'Is that a promise?' And she said, 'Yes.' Within a couple of weeks, I went to her with a parental permission slip [for parachuting]."[48]

O'Connor tried to keep her boys busy with chores. "We examine the job to be done and set compensation for work performed," she said in one interview. "We don't pay by the hour—they could drag it out."[49] She also forced them to take care of their own needs around the house. "My return to the job market necessitated that our three sons learn to be self-sufficient to a degree that would not have been true had I remained at home," she later wrote. "They learned to cook and, when necessary, wash their clothes, and even to iron a shirt now and then."[50]

At the other end of the family spectrum, John and Sandra O'Connor's parents were aging and requiring a different kind of attention. John's parents, "Gigi" and John O'Connor, had moved from California to Arizona and were in a residence community for seniors nearby. Down at the Lazy B, as Harry Day entered his 70s, Sandra's brother, Alan, assumed more responsibility on the ranch. But both father and son complained to Sandra about who was more ham-fisted at maintaining the Lazy B. Alan believed that their father was stubbornly refusing to look at modern ranching methods. Harry complained that Alan's return to the ranch after college was "against my wishes and . . . better judgment."[51] Alan, it would turn out, was responsible for extending the family's ownership of the ranch into the 1990s.

At several points in the 1970s, Harry Day felt that Alan, with Sandra's support, was trying to muscle him out of management of the ranch—at one point, by bringing in a legal advisor. O'Connor tried to calm her father down. Harry wrote back: "Thanks for your letter and thanks for the flattery. I guess that makes me feel better. Since I have spent my life devoted to Lazy B Ranch I guess I get emotional about it—anything that hurts Lazy B hurts me, in fact I am more concerned about Lazy B's financial welfare than I am about my own personal affairs. . . . It hit me like a blow when I realized that even though I am still head of Lazy B (president) I was being maneuvered out of the picture. I know, I am an old fogey and don't like any changes. However, I am still alive and I have feelings and wishes like I have always had. . . . This is not the first time there has been a movement to put us out and I still don't like it."[52] As the carbons of many letters saved in his personal files demonstrate, Harry had a way of being quarrelsome even while claiming to take the high ground.[53]

In spring 1974, O'Connor decided not to seek reelection to the state Senate. Just five years after she had hustled to get in, she issued a formal announcement that it was time for her to move on. She said she wanted to give someone else a chance.[54] She also wanted more control of her time. Maybe she simply had wearied, too, of the pushing and shoving of the political scene. One of her later comments about her time in the legislature attested to her frustrations: "I was never one of the boys."[55]

NATIONALLY, SUPPORT FOR Richard Nixon was eroding and the Republican Party was in retreat. Two months before O'Connor announced her retirement from the Senate, in February of 1974, the U.S. House of Representatives had voted to authorize the House Judiciary Committee to see if sufficient grounds existed to impeach the president. Goldwater was still backing Nixon, and Arizona Republicans, including O'Connor, played host to one of Nixon's last public appearances. On May 3, 1974, just three months before his resignation, President Nixon flew to Phoenix, accompanied on Air Force One by Goldwater and the rest of the Arizona delegation, for a speech at the city Coliseum. After the band played "Hail to the Chief," balloons and confetti descended from the rafters. In his only mention of Watergate, Nixon said, "The time has come to get Watergate behind us and to get on with the business of America."[56] In the cheering crowd were O'Connor and her boys.[57]

In later years, Goldwater said of Nixon, "He had lied to the people, had lied to his friends in Congress, including me. I was wrong in protecting him as long as I did."[58] Goldwater never shook off his disappointment. (In 1994, he refused to go to Nixon's funeral.)

O'Connor's friends and family said she was not disheartened by Nixon. "She would be the last one to be discouraged or disillusioned about politics because of that incident," former Phoenix mayor John Driggs said, referring to Watergate. Perhaps that was true. O'Connor was a pragmatist. Maybe she never idealized Nixon the way some other Republicans had.[59]

The tentacles of Watergate reached Arizona. O'Connor saw Sam Mardian's brother Robert, who worked directly with Mitchell, convicted for taking part in the cover-up of the Watergate burglary. (His conviction was later thrown out on appeal.)[60]

One month after O'Connor announced she was not going to seek reelection, she said she was going to run for a new superior court judgeship created by the Maricopa County Board of Supervisors. "As a lawyer, I am naturally interested in the judiciary and would find it a great opportunity to be of service," she said on May 23 as she announced her intention to run for the spot. She told a local newspaper reporter she had had no idea the judgeship was going to be created when she announced less than one month earlier that she would not seek Senate reelection.[61] If that was the case, it was a striking bit of good luck and fortuitous timing.

O'Connor soon found herself in a heated primary race. Because she was still in the state Senate when the seat was created, she could not ask Republican governor Jack Williams to appoint her as a temporary measure before the regularly scheduled election. He appointed another Republican, David Perry, who turned out to want the judgeship permanently. "As a rule, seats on the Maricopa County Superior Court bench are seldom contested in party primaries any more, and when they are, they attract little more than stifled yawns from most voters," the *Phoenix Gazette* wrote. "Sandra O'Connor and David Perry apparently never heard the rule." Perry told the reporter he had long wanted to be a judge. He also drew a line between himself and O'Connor by suggesting that he was a real lawyer and she was not. "No judge I know ever remembers seeing Mrs. O'Connor in the courthouse," he said.[62]

O'Connor countered by talking about the work she did with Tobin in the late 1950s. She also said the position involved much more than judging. "There are lots of lawyers who can go in and fill the functions of a judge," she said, "but they may not be able to make constructive changes. We need to ask which person has demonstrated some leadership and capacity to improve the system. I think I've done that." She was cautious about what she said about Perry personally. "It's really an advantage to the public, when one party has a choice of good candidates," she said in her constantly upbeat way.[63]

O'Connor made several appearances throughout the county. In her campaign literature, she asserted, "As a lawyer and as a legislator I am deeply concerned about the need to strengthen the enforcement of the laws that govern our conduct. As a citizen, a wife and a mother, I want to help replace fear in our streets with strength in our courtrooms."[64] Perry used more media advertising and billboards. In the end, O'Connor won with 70 percent of the votes in the Republican primary. She had no Democratic opponent, and took the seat in early 1975.[65]

Once established in the basement chambers of an old county courthouse, O'Connor thrived. "It has a certain atmosphere," she told a reporter. "The cockroaches are its only drawback. I keep bug spray around, but it would take a meat ax to kill some of them." The job offered her exactly what she wanted: control over her schedule and a chance to interpret the substance of the law. "The whole experience of presiding over a trial in court is a remarkable experience," she said. "You see every kind of human emotion and human value expressed and you see people in very tense situations and you listen in detail to some remarkable problems and situations of every kind. . . . You have an inside look at crime and the kind of criminal behavior that we've all wrung our hands in an effort to stop. . . . There are moments of great pathos in a courtroom and there are moments of levity and there are moments of boredom."[66]

The crimes were run-of-the-mill. One of O'Connor's most widely publicized sentences arose in the case of a Scottsdale businesswoman, the mother of two young children, charged with passing $3,500 worth of bad checks. She pleaded guilty and, in an emotional appeal, asked O'Connor not to give her a sentence that would separate her from her children.

Responding from the bench, O'Connor said, "You have intelligence, beauty, and two small children. You come from a fine and respected family. . . . Someone with all your advantages should have known better." When O'Connor read the sentence—five to ten years in prison—the defendant wept. "What about my babies?" she cried. O'Connor quickly left the courtroom. Alone in her chambers, the steely judge burst into tears herself.[67] O'Connor later called the decision to jail the woman—who rejoined her children after serving eighteen months in prison—the toughest she had ever made.[68]

Meanwhile, O'Connor kept up her political contacts even as a judge. In 1978, state Republican leaders began talking to her about possibly running for governor. Party leaders reportedly were dissatisfied with the potential GOP gubernatorial crop, which included auto dealer Evan Mecham and insurance executive Jackson Londen.[69] At first, O'Connor told them she did not want to run. But GOP movers and shakers who feared a fiasco at the top of the ticket persisted. *Arizona Republic* columnist Wynn wrote that O'Connor said she would agree to try for the gubernatorial nomination if the party stalwarts would meet three conditions: unqualified support from Senators Goldwater and Fannin and from the state's U.S. Representative John Rhodes, also a Republican; sufficient funding so that she would not incur any personal campaign debts; and a first-rate campaign manager. Among those making the overtures were former Arizona Senate president Jacquin and former state Republican chairman Rosenzweig.[70]

But the new state Republican chairman Jim Colter was backing Mecham, who had tried vainly for statewide office three previous times. Colter had taken over the party organization two and a half years earlier in 1975 and imposed "rigid ideological standards to separate the good guys from the bad guys," according to the *Arizona Republic*.[71] Political columnist John Kolbe of the *Phoenix Gazette* added: "Colter & Co. took over in 1975 after a hard-fought battle in which they promised to 'open up' the party after a decade of clubby (but effective) rule by Harry Rosenzweig's 'old guard' faction. And once in office, they proceeded to close the shop to all but the true believers in their own hard-right purity."[72]

As O'Connor was trying to make her decision in early 1978, Colter said it was too late for O'Connor or any other candidate to enter the gubernatorial race to be held that fall. House Majority Leader Burton Barr, a political ally and friend of O'Connor, criticized Colter for failing to be neutral and said Colter's efforts were an attempt to discourage O'Connor from entering the race. If that is what they were, they worked. O'Connor announced she would not seek the nomination. "I think it's a sad day for the party because she would have been an outstanding candidate," Barr said. "She has all the credentials you need for the office and she's never lost."[73]

Publicly, O'Connor said she wanted to spend more time with her family. But her sons were moving off on their own. Scott was finishing his junior year at Stanford, Brian was a freshman at Colorado College, and Jay was a junior in high school. O'Connor likely realized that with key party leaders equivocating, she would have a tough time of it. Congressman Rhodes had been among those recruiting O'Connor, but as *Gazette* columnist Kolbe wrote, Rhodes still had to be mindful of "a district full of right-wing crazies, who regard the touches of moderation required by his [U.S. House] minority leader's position as signs of incipient communism, and constantly threaten to challenge him. He would have had to wait at least until the primary deadline" to publicly endorse O'Connor.[74]

It appeared the tactfully ambitious politician who had long positioned herself for higher office suddenly was the victim of transformed state politics and rare bad timing. But it would be only a matter of months until O'Connor's connections paid off in a different way.

John Driggs, the Phoenix mayor who had enlisted O'Connor's help on the historical commission in the fall of 1971, had a brother-in-law, Mark Cannon, who was Chief Justice Warren Burger's administrative assistant. Driggs had been trying to get Cannon to visit Arizona when he discovered that Cannon was coming with Burger to Flagstaff for a judicial conference. Driggs asked Cannon if he and Burger would like to cap off that trip with a houseboat vacation on Lake Powell, situated just over the border in Utah and known for its spectacular sheer red rock formations. Cannon and Burger agreed. Driggs then called John O'Connor to see if he and Sandra wanted to join them for a three-day vacation in August 1979.

"Would we ever," John O'Connor said.[75]

Driggs's wife, Gail, later recalled that they thought, because both O'Connors were lawyers, they would help the conversation if it began to lag. "Sandra can discuss anything: from changing diapers to world events," she said. Once the guest list was arranged, Gail Driggs and Sandra O'Connor immediately began planning the menu and gathering the ingredients for homemade chocolate ice cream and the marinade for the fish to be caught.[76] At Lake Powell, they all swam and water-skied and enjoyed nightly conversations on the deck of the houseboat. Burger regaled them with stories about his Minnesota childhood and life in the law. Pictures show the chief justice of the United States and then-trial judge O'Connor engaged in animated conversation as they sit in beach clothes on the boat. Years later, Mark Cannon said Burger was impressed with O'Connor's personal warmth and legal experience and began thinking about ways to involve her in national legal conferences.[77]

O'Connor was moving up in Arizona, too. Democratic governor Bruce Babbitt, who had defeated Mecham in the 1978 election, appointed O'Connor to the Arizona Court of Appeals to succeed Mary Schroeder, whom President Carter had just named to the U.S. Court of Appeals for the Ninth Circuit. Babbitt said years later that his appointment of the Republican O'Connor reflected an effort to demonstrate bipartisanship in judicial selections and some deference to his lawyer wife, Hattie Babbitt, who had practiced before O'Connor. "Hattie made the case quite forcefully that this was a really important time to select the most qualified person who also happened to be a woman," Babbitt said. Asked about the speculation at the time that he could have been trying to remove a potential Republican opponent for future gubernatorial elections, Babbitt said, "That really wasn't in the calculus."[78]

O'Connor was formally sworn in to the appellate court on December 4, 1979. With her sons looking on, husband John helped her glide her arms into her black robe. Friends and colleagues came to the investiture.

As John Driggs approached to shake her hand, she whispered, "Guess what? The chief called me last week and invited me to go to England with him for a judicial conference."[79] Burger had invited her to be one of the U.S. judiciary's representatives at an Anglo-American legal conference in London.

Five days later, O'Connor sent a handwritten note to Mark Cannon, Burger's assistant. "I am thrilled about the Anglo-American Legal Exchange. It is a wonderful opportunity to learn more of the British system. They do many things well in their system." She added that she had been reading in the newspapers about a controversial new book illuminating the inside workings of the Supreme Court: *The Brethren,* by Bob Woodward and Scott Armstrong. "It disturbs me when one such as Justice Burger is discussed in such unflattering terms," O'Connor wrote to Cannon. "We found him to be a delightful, warm, and impressive person. We trust time will heal any wounds and that Justice Burger is not too disturbed by current press releases."[80]

5

REAGAN'S CHOICE

With less than eight weeks until Election Day 1980, Ronald Reagan's top strategists thought that the momentum of the campaign was slowing. The former California governor was still ahead in the polls, but incumbent president Jimmy Carter was running neck-and-neck in key northern states.[1] Trying for a second term, Carter was unpopular largely because of the nation's economic problems and his failure to negotiate release of the hostages held in Iran. But he was raising serious doubts about the 69-year-old former actor's ability to lead the United States. Reagan's key advisor on the campaign plane was Stuart Spencer, a disheveled but thoughtful Californian who in the 1960s had been one of Reagan's earliest political advisors. Spencer understood instinctively that the Reagan campaign had gone "flat."[2]

Women, especially, were reluctant to support Reagan. In fact, Spencer realized, women as a group had liked Reagan when he was an actor, but each year since he had left the screen, they had grown less fond of him. Spencer and pollster Richard Wirthlin worried about what would later be called the "gender gap." They attributed it to Reagan's opposition to the then-pending Equal Rights Amendment, which he had once supported, and to permissive abortion-rights laws, but, even more so, to the sense among undecided women voters that the military buildup advocated by Reagan might lead to war.[3]

Spencer had what in the context of an otherwise predictable campaign was a daring idea. He urged candidate Reagan to promise to appoint the first woman to the Supreme Court. Reagan already had said that he "probably" would consider putting a woman on the nation's highest court, but he had never committed to it. At first, Reagan resisted such a promise. He was not certain he would get the opportunity to appoint any Supreme Court justice. President Carter had no vacancy in four years. Still, Reagan liked the idea of making a big deal of his intention to appoint a woman. So, at the behest of Spencer, Reagan held a news conference in Los Angeles on October 14, 1980, to say: "As you know, a number of false and misleading accusations have been made in this campaign. During the next three weeks, I intend to set the record straight. One of the accusations has been that I am somehow opposed to full and equal opportunities for women in America. . . . I am announcing today that one of the first Supreme Court vacancies in my administration will be filled by the most qualified woman I can find."[4]

The announcement made the front page of the *New York Times,* which called it a bold move.[5] But the Carter camp dismissed it as a cynical gesture. "Equal rights for women involves more than just one job for one woman," President Carter asserted, adding that if Reagan truly believed in equality he would be supporting the ERA.[6] First Lady Rosalynn Carter told reporters that her husband planned to put a woman on the Court once a vacancy arose. The name of Shirley Hufstedler had been circulating for months as Carter's first choice, should an opening occur. Hufstedler, a 55-year-old Californian who was one of the first women on the federal bench, had given up a seat on the Ninth U.S. Circuit Court of Appeals based in San Francisco to head the new Department of Education in Carter's cabinet. When Hufstedler was named to the post in January 1980, White House officials told reporters that she had received a commitment that she would "not be precluded" from appointment to the Supreme Court. There was speculation at the time that Justice William Brennan, then age 73 and the eldest of the nine, would soon retire.[7]

Reacting to Reagan's press conference, women's rights leaders said the candidate was merely trying to divert attention from his ERA opposition. The vow of a woman justice injected some new energy into the Reagan campaign, although it was not the decisive event. That came two weeks later, in Cleveland, at the only debate of the campaign between the presidential nominees. In that forum, Reagan effectively blamed Carter for the faltering economy. When Carter rebuked Reagan for opposing Medicare, Reagan accused him of distorting his record and, in a memorable retort, declared, "There you go again." After the debate, Reagan surged ahead in most polls. Although his promise to put a woman on the Supreme Court was an almost forgotten issue, Reagan remembered that he had made it and, given a chance, meant to keep his word.[8]

By spring 1981, when Justice Potter Stewart told Attorney General William French Smith of his intention to retire, Sandra Day O'Connor had not, like Hufstedler, been appointed to a federal court. But she was a state appellate court judge and well connected, notably with Arizona U.S. Senator Barry Goldwater and Chief Justice Warren Burger. O'Connor's name also had surfaced earlier in 1981 as a possible choice to run the Justice Department's civil division, reportedly by way of the old-boys network of Stanford University Law School.[9]

O'Connor's blend of lawyerly seriousness and Western common sense had captivated Burger since he first met her on the Lake Powell houseboat vacation. Having stayed in touch with successive administrations since his appointment as chief justice in 1969, Burger understood how Washington worked. He made sure he kept lines of communication open to the new administration. Shortly after Reagan's election in November 1980, the chief justice had arranged for Reagan to call on the Supreme Court in an informal session with tea and cookies. Later, Burger began sending notes to Reagan's top people. "He wasn't talking about cases," recalled Fred Fielding, Reagan's White House counsel at the time. "He was more interested in how a swearing-in or other event would go, that it was done right, the imagery."[10] In one January 1981 episode, Burger contacted former U.S. ambassador to Great Britain Walter Annenberg to have him relay one of Burger's speeches about dealing with the news media to Michael Deaver, a top Reagan aide. "The Chief Justice was most anxious that the President be apprised of . . . the enclosed speech. . . . I am sure you will agree that Chief Justice Burger could have no other purpose than to be constructive," Annenberg wrote to Deaver.[11]

A decade earlier, when President Nixon was looking for nominees to succeed John Marshall Harlan and Hugo Black, Nixon told his aides that Burger was "totally against" the notion of a female justice.[12] Now, in

1981, Burger was quietly putting O'Connor's name before White House officials, including Fielding. Burger invited the 42-year-old counsel to his suburban Virginia house for lunch one Saturday. "He had a little garden and we walked around in it," recalled Fielding. "We talked about a prospective vacancy."[13]

Fielding had a feel for delicate situations and the people maneuvering in them. A farm boy from Bucks County, Pennsylvania, whose father died when he was 11, Fielding went to college and law school on scholarships. After a stint in the army and a few years in the Philadelphia office of a prominent New York law firm, Fielding was hired in 1970 as deputy to White House counsel John Dean, who became a leading player in the Nixon Watergate scandal. Fielding took over day-to-day operations in the counsel's office when Dean left the White House and eventually went to prison for his role in the cover-up. Full cheeks and a jovial temperament masked Fielding's cunning. Thinking back to his conversation with Burger in spring 1981, Fielding said, "There are a couple of things he wanted to plant in my mind that day and Sandra O'Connor's name was one of them."

Burger's former administrative assistant Mark Cannon recalled the chief justice talking up O'Connor. "He was a master at timing. He also specialized in knowing how to get from point A to point B," said Cannon, adding that Burger would have made sure that both Fielding and Attorney General William French Smith had her name.[14]

As even O'Connor herself would observe years later, her credentials were not obviously those of a Supreme Court candidate.[15] Most appointees in the recent past had been on a federal court or top state court. Newest justice John Paul Stevens, appointed by President Ford six years earlier, had been on the U.S. Court of Appeals for the Seventh Circuit based in Chicago for five years before being elevated. Burger had been a judge on the U.S. Court of Appeals for the District of Columbia Circuit for thirteen years before Nixon named him chief justice of the United States in 1969. Harry Blackmun was elevated in 1970 from the U.S. Court of Appeals for the Eighth Circuit, where he was a jurist for more than a decade. William Rehnquist and Lewis Powell, both appointed by Nixon in 1972, were, respectively, an assistant attorney general in charge of the Office of Legal Counsel, and a prominent Richmond lawyer who had been president of both the ABA and American College of Trial

Lawyers. Most of the other appointees of the twentieth century had served on a federal court or their state's highest bench.

If O'Connor's name was not recognized among the legal elite, her name was known among exactly the right people at a time when a new president from the West was looking for an attractive woman candidate. When Stewart publicly announced his retirement on June 18, U.S. senator Dennis DeConcini, an Arizona Democrat and member of the Senate Judiciary Committee, put out a press release recommending O'Connor based on his local interest.[16] He described O'Connor as a conservative with sound credentials. His comments made the news wires but were not seriously picked up by the national press. DeConcini, who had known O'Connor since the mid-1960s, when he worked for Democratic Arizona governor Sam Goddard and she was in the attorney general's office, said, "I knew she was smart. I knew she was politically astute."[17] They were often on opposite sides of legal matters, but O'Connor had never made an enemy of DeConcini.

As REAGAN'S AIDES KNEW, his choice had to take into account the issues of the day and the politics of the moment. In the 1980s, abortion was *the* issue to be confronted. This was the legacy of the Supreme Court's *Roe v. Wade* decision that said the Constitution gives a woman a right to end a pregnancy. The ruling was at the fulcrum of religion, culture, and women's rights. Nearly overnight, the 1973 decision created the "Right to Life" movement and gave political force to religious fundamentalists who eventually organized into the Moral Majority, led by Baptist minister and televangelist Jerry Falwell. Abortion presented a no-win situation for most politicians, because there seemed to be no middle ground.

Administration lawyers searched O'Connor's record for any position she had taken on abortion rights, and, more broadly, for anything in her background that would disqualify her. Justice Department lawyer F. Henry "Hank" Habicht flew to Phoenix and looked up legislation O'Connor had sponsored. He interviewed people whose names had been quietly passed on from key Arizonans, including Bob McConnell, an assistant attorney general for legislative affairs. McConnell had grown up in Arizona and had worked for the state's former U.S. Representative John Rhodes, a Republican.

Habicht got the impression that O'Connor was able to be "very feminine around men and did not make them feel threatened." He said it also appeared that "she was always looking for the next opportunity to assume a leadership role." Before he took the trip, Habicht had read through all of her rulings. He was impressed with her accomplishments but thought she seemed a bit cool personally. In Phoenix, however, colleagues spoke warmly about her and how she could come across in Senate hearings. "I felt like we had the whole package here."[18]

That was the informal word among Smith's top aides by the end of June. Attorney General Smith asked his assistant Ken Starr to make plans to visit O'Connor in Phoenix. He also asked Starr to arrange to fly to Detroit to interview U.S. Appeals Court Judge Cornelia Kennedy, who had not been entirely excluded. Former president Gerald Ford, Reagan's one-time rival, had forwarded Reagan a letter he received from five judges in Kent County, Michigan, endorsing Cornelia Kennedy for the vacancy. In his cover letter to the new president, Ford wrote in detached prose, "Over the years, I have closely observed the judicial performance of Judge Cornelia Kennedy as she has served both Michigan and the United States Court systems. She has carried out her judicial duties with great distinction and, in my judgment, would serve our nation exceedingly well as a member of the United States Supreme Court."[19]

The White House wanted to keep the process secret to make sure that any flaw in a potential nominee's background could be found first by the administration, rather than the press or a potentially hostile member of the Senate.[20] "One woman we'd been interested in for a judgeship turned out not to have paid her income taxes—in fact, she hadn't even filed for a number of years," Smith wrote in his memoir about judicial choices generally, without naming the woman in question. "The FBI check had revealed her to be a superb candidate, with this single astonishing exception." Referring specifically to the 1981 Supreme Court vacancy, Smith wrote, "A couple of our other candidates who also looked good initially turned out, on closer inspection, to have oversized skeletons in their closets." Again, he named no one.[21]

When Smith called O'Connor for the first time on June 25, even many administration insiders did not know that the Arizona judge was being considered. Wendy Borcherdt, associate director of presidential personnel, responsible for placing women in the executive branch of government, wrote to Fielding on the same day, suggesting five names: Kennedy, the federal appeals court judge; Mildred Lillie, a California appellate court judge who had been considered by Nixon in 1971; Carla Hills, secretary of Housing and Urban Development under President Ford; Sylvia Bacon, District of Columbia Superior Court judge and former Justice Department lawyer under Nixon; and New York Republican lawyer Rita Hauser, who had been a representative to the United Nations Commission on Human Rights between 1969 and 1972.[22]

Those names were raised in various media reports, too. But it was almost as if their legal prominence worked against them. "There was a sense that this new president wants to present someone who is like him," Starr recalled. "Judge Kennedy, for example, came across as a professional jurist. Judge O'Connor, in contrast, had an aura of a very intriguing, well-balanced individual, who was more accurately reflective of the personality of Ronald Reagan. I don't want to underestimate the connection of being from the West."[23]

Recalling O'Connor's engaging manner, Fielding said, "she had to be identified" through contacts with Burger, Goldwater, and others, "but she sold herself." Edwin Meese, a Californian who had once worked with the brother of O'Connor's first law partner, Tom Tobin, and in 1981 was counselor to the president, recalled that she offered an appealing combination: "She had been a judge. She had been a legislator. She was from the West."[24]

O'CONNOR MET REAGAN in the Oval Office at about ten-fifteen on July 1, 1981. Also in the room were Attorney General Smith, Chief of Staff James Baker, Deputy Chief of Staff Michael Deaver, and Smith's secretary, Myra Tankersley, who had picked up O'Connor at Dupont Circle and quietly brought her to the White House. O'Connor and Reagan talked about horses and ranch life. When the conversation turned to substantive issues and abortion, she told Reagan she was personally against abortion. She said she considered the procedure "abhorrent." Then they moved on to other topics. The two had more in common than superficial similarities of boom-state backgrounds and outdoorsy interests. Both had had somewhat isolated childhoods. They each had developed rarely revealed inner lives and, in their early public careers, had been underestimated. Reagan was sold on her, so sold that he consistently brushed off any criticism that surfaced about O'Connor.

Years later, in an interview on an Arizona television station, O'Connor recounted the forty-five-minute meeting with a minimum of detail and an unconvincing declaration that she did not want the job: "He was pretty interested in my ranch background and fixing fences, riding horses, and a few things like that, but he did ask questions of substance as well. . . . Then it was time to go, and I said good-bye to the president and the other people who were there and left. I went to the airport to fly back to Arizona that afternoon. When I got on the airplane, I said to myself, this has been the most interesting time to go to Washington . . . to meet with the president's close advisors and to meet with the president himself in the Oval Office. That was fantastic. But thank goodness I don't have to go do that job, because I really didn't think I would be asked to serve. It seemed so unlikely to me when there was already someone from Arizona on the Court—William Rehnquist. And we had been in the same law school class. Typically the Court doesn't end up with two members there from the same state, and certainly not one as small as Arizona. And so I breathed a sigh of relief and came home."[25]

It is hard to imagine the striver O'Connor breathing a sigh of relief that she might *not* be chosen. This was a woman who engineered her appointment to her first political office in 1969, who quickly rose to be state Senate majority leader, and who, when she sought a switch from politics to the bench in 1974, beat the incumbent for a local judgeship.

Reagan did not want to meet with any other prospective nominee, and he went off to the cabinet room for a session on economic policy. He knew the staff had more work to do on an O'Connor nomination, but as far as he was concerned, she was the one. Reagan and O'Connor were a good fit. Both were naturally optimistic, pragmatic, and had benefited from luck and good timing in their careers. Throughout his life, Reagan had seized opportunities, and this was a tremendous opportunity for him—and for O'Connor. Years later, Attorney General Smith would give credit to Reagan himself for putting her name on a short list.[26] Smith's one-time aide, Bob McConnell, remarked that many people claimed to have given O'Connor's name to Reagan. "That is all real interesting," Smith responded in his low-key way, "because before the [1980] election, the president handed me a piece of paper with several names, and her name was on it, in his own handwriting."[27]

After her Oval Office meeting with the president, it was safe for White House aides to leak O'Connor's name to reporters.[28] Then another ritual of judicial nominations began, as special interest groups weighed in. Abortion opponents were wary. They had helped Reagan win the Republican nomination and then the White House, but now they worried that they were being taken for granted. They had seen Reagan make the economy a priority rather than concentrate on their effort to get abortion banned.

O'Connor's name was not really known outside Arizona, but one of the leaders of the National Right to Life Committee happened to live in Phoenix. Even more coincidentally, that leader, Dr. Carolyn Gerster, had, like O'Connor, sped through her school years, broken down barriers in a male-dominated profession, and worked full-time while raising a family.[29] Gerster had lobbied state senator O'Connor in vain to pass antiabortion legislation. She felt certain O'Connor was on the side of abortion rights, and Gerster believed she should do everything possible to stop O'Connor's nomination.

Opposed to abortion since her early medical-school days, Gerster stepped up her public activism after the 1973 *Roe v. Wade* ruling. She became involved in the National Right to Life Committee, and in Arizona pushed for a legislative resolution against the decision and tougher regulation of abortion.[30] As a state senator, O'Connor had not taken an intense interest in abortion rights, but what she had done on the subject put her in opposition to Gerster as far as Gerster was concerned. In 1970, as a member of the state Senate Judiciary Committee, O'Connor voted for a bill to legalize abortion.

After O'Connor left the legislature and became a local judge, Gerster remained active in the state and national antiabortion movements. When Reagan was running for the GOP presidential nomination in early 1980, he won a crucial endorsement from the political action committee of the National Right to Life after meeting with Gerster, then the PAC chairman, in January. At the time, Gerster told reporters that "it was an extremely hard decision," because Senator Robert Dole of Kansas and U.S. Representative Phil Crane of Illinois, also seeking the GOP nomination, held solid antiabortion positions. Gerster said, however, that Reagan seemed to be the strongest candidate for the party's nomination, and she believed that if he got a chance to name a justice, he would seek out someone against abortion rights.[31] So, in June 1981, when Gerster saw O'Connor's name promoted as a Supreme Court nominee, she wanted to block any chance O'Connor had for the appointment.

Gerster alerted abortion foes around the nation, and the White House began to hear from them. "Over the past three or four days, I have received a number of calls from people in and around the right-to-life movement. Similar calls, I gather, have been made to others at the White House," Michael Uhlmann, a deputy to Meese, wrote to his boss on July 6. "The burden of the message was that the nomination of Judge O'Connor would trigger a nasty political protest against the President." Sensing that Reagan's top advisors were not worried about O'Connor's actions on abortion, Uhlmann added, "It is important to bear in mind the special significance that right-to-lifers attach to Supreme Court nominations. The federal judiciary in general, and the high court in particular, have in their view been engaged in a systematic effort to prevent the public from working its will on the subject of abortion. Whatever one may think of that argument, or of the merits of abortion itself, the intensity of right-to-lifers on the issue of judicial power should not be underestimated."[32]

He was right. Social conservatives had supported Reagan in part because they thought he would change the judiciary that had delivered *Roe v. Wade* and other decisions that they believed eroded American values. Their allies in the Senate began to make their interests known as O'Connor's name circulated. Oklahoma Republican Don Nickles privately warned White House aides he might not support her. North Carolina Republican Jesse Helms and Idaho Republican Steve Symms also complained about O'Connor. Gerster sent a telegram to Reagan on July 6, asking him not to make a decision on the nomination until she and her team could send him a package of information about O'Connor's votes.[33]

But the men who were responsible for getting O'Connor to this point were not fervently against abortion rights. That was certainly not a concern of Chief Justice Burger, who had voted with the majority in *Roe v. Wade*.[34] For Meese, Baker, and Deaver, abortion was not a priority. Still, the antiabortion groups could not be ignored. Attorney General Smith asked Starr to talk to O'Connor again about her legislative record on abortion. Was there any validity in the reports coming from the Arizona abortion opponents?

At the same time, some of Reagan's closest aides were urging him to seize the moment. Amid the flurry of correspondence over abortion on July 6, Fielding sent Baker a memo titled "Supreme Court Nomination—Game Plan." Fielding recommended the O'Connor announcement be made immediately. He assumed that any problems the nominee would face were already out: "initial leakage has probably surfaced all potential problems (pro-lifers, etc.)" Fielding also proposed that O'Connor not be at the White House with Reagan when he made the announcement—"too difficult to get to Washington unnoticed"—but he suggested a White House press aide be sent to join O'Connor in Phoenix for her appearance before the media.[35]

Reagan decided to proceed, apparently with no qualms about O'Connor's position on abortion and obviously not interested in waiting for Starr's report. At 5:20 p.m., July 6, Reagan called Goldwater and told him he was going to nominate the daughter of Arizona. Reagan and Goldwater talked for about five minutes. Administration aides began leaking the news, including to the chambers of Chief Justice Burger. Around six p.m., Burger called O'Connor in her Arizona office to tell her it appeared the nomination was hers. They had not gone far in the conversation when O'Connor got word that the president himself was calling. She hung up with Burger. When the president got her at 6:10, they talked for ten minutes.[36]

"Sandra, I'd like to announce your nomination to the Court tomorrow," she recalled him saying.

"I was thunderstruck, really, and very concerned, because it's a very hard job," O'Connor said years later, "and I didn't think that my experience on Arizona's courts, as nice as it had been, had prepared me for that." The president was not only offering her a chance to be on the nation's highest court. He was choosing her to break the tradition of 192 years and 101 male justices. "It's fine to be the first, but you don't want to be the last."[37]

The next day, on July 7, at 10:46 a.m., Reagan walked into the White House briefing room and made it official. Taking a line from Longfellow, he said, "Those who sit in the Supreme Court interpret the laws of our land and truly do leave their footprints on the sands of time.

Long after the policies of presidents and senators and congressmen of any given era may have passed from public memory, they'll be remembered."

He said he would send O'Connor's name to the Senate for confirmation as an associate justice of the United States Supreme Court. "She is truly a person for all seasons, possessing those unique qualities of temperament, fairness, intellectual capacity, and devotion to the public good which have characterized the 101 brethren who have preceded her."[38]

When reporters started shouting questions at him, President Reagan tried to refer them to Attorney General Smith, who stood nearby. But as reporters kept pressing Reagan on the abortion issue, he acquiesced.

"Can you give us your feelings about her position on that?"

"I am completely satisfied," Reagan answered.

"On her right-to-life position?"

"Yes," said Reagan.

"And did you interview her personally?"

"Yes," he said.

In Phoenix, O'Connor held a news conference with help from White House deputy press secretary Peter Roussel, who had flown into town. "If confirmed," she told reporters nervously, "I will do my best to serve the Court and this nation in a manner that will bring credit to the president, to my family, and to all the people of this great nation." She looked stiff. Her shoulders were uncharacteristically hunched, her arms glued to her sides. Here was a woman who operated best when she understood the context. This was all so new.[39]

Fortunately for O'Connor, even if she was not quite ready, the nation was.

"Judge Sandra Day O'Connor's place in history is already secure, based on today's announcement that she will be President Reagan's nominee as the first woman on the United States Supreme Court," a report on the front page of the *New York Times* said.[40] "The symbolism was stunning," *Time* magazine added. "By giving the brethren their first sister, Reagan provided not only a breakthrough on the bench but a powerful push forward in the shamefully long and needlessly tortuous march of women toward full equality in American society." The magazine quoted Barbara Jordan, a former Texas congresswoman: "I congratulate the President. The Supreme Court was the last bastion of the male: a stale dark room that needed to be cracked open. I don't know the lady, but if she's a good lawyer and believes in the Constitution, she'll be all right."[41]

O'Connor's sheer female presence was nearly enough. Goodwill flowed her way, and she did not squander it. She kept smiling and spoke of how grateful she was, how this was so unexpected for "a ranch girl." The White House coached her on the media, warning her not to say anything substantive.

"It was very intense," O'Connor recalled of those days. "I couldn't move without a battery of television cameras following my every step."[42] Her sons remembered this as an exciting time and were thrilled, rather than put off, by all the cameras outside their house. Son Jay, who had just finished his freshman year at Stanford University, took up duties as a press officer in Phoenix, organizing information about his mother and acting as the contact for family questions. Gail Driggs, O'Connor's longtime friend, set up a bank of typewriters in Driggs dining room and enlisted other women to help answer the letters pouring in to the first female nominee.

"The announcement produced an avalanche of telephone calls, letters, and even visits to my parents," O'Connor later wrote. "Everyone they had ever known wanted to contact them and say how pleased they were. The ranch, which had always been a quiet backwater, suddenly became the focus of national attention."[43]

An *Arizona Republic* reporter sought out the nominee's father and found him in his office at the Lazy B. "I'm Harry Day, and I'm busy," Harry said, at first barely looking up at the reporter and continuing to balance the ranch checkbook. The story captured the cantankerous but proud father.

"I used to call her for legal advice every once in a while. But since she became a judge, she couldn't give me advice anymore. . . . She'd just say, 'Well, this is what the law says.' And I'd say, 'Well, hell, I know what the law says; I want to know how to get around the law.' "

Harry also told the reporter that he thought his daughter would be a good judge because she would not be like former Chief Justice Earl Warren.

Ada Mae cut in, "Now, now, Harry, you don't want to be quoted saying that."

"Well, hell," Harry said, "why not? It's the truth, and I'd say it again."[44]

People across the country wrote to O'Connor. "I cannot begin to describe with what delight I viewed the surprising headlines in Chicago's newspapers the day of your nomination," one woman wrote in a letter that O'Connor later said was typical. "I actually stood there with my mouth hanging open and an idiotic grin on my face, feeling overwhelmingly euphoric and proud." But then there was this postcard that came in that showed another set of attitudes: "Back to your kitchen and home female! This is a job for a man and only he can make the rough decisions. Take care of your grandchildren and husband." It was signed "Senior Citizen."[45]

Another kind of criticism, related to O'Connor's credentials, was raised by a few publications. The liberal magazine *The Nation* asserted: "In the general satisfaction—which we share—over the selection of a woman, no one seems to have noticed that in choosing Judge O'Connor, President Reagan has overridden some fundamental conservative principles and basic policy of his administration: for the highest Court in the land he has picked a person barely qualified for the post, almost entirely because of her sex and not on the basis of individual merit. Despite the many kind words of her friends, Judge O'Connor's record is not even close to Supreme Court quality. She was not an exceptional lawyer or legal scholar, nor is she an outstanding judge."

But such observations—made more as political strikes against the Reagan administration than as reasons for rejecting O'Connor—had little traction. They were barely spoken elsewhere, and even *The Nation* agreed that "Judge O'Connor could become a fine Justice. Like so many other beneficiaries of affirmative action, she may make a great deal out of the unexpected opportunity."[46]

The American Bar Association, which had been screening prospective candidates for the Court since the nomination of William Brennan in 1956, gave O'Connor a "qualified" rating, meaning she met the ABA's standards of integrity, professional competence, and judicial temperament. The ABA reserved its highest rating, "well qualified," for those who merited its strongest endorsement. Members of the screening committee said that her legal background "has not been as extensive or challenging" as that of other potential nominees.[47] Mark Cannon, Burger's administrative assistant, said that the chief justice made sure the screening committee had the names of prominent lawyers with whom O'Con-

nor had traveled on the Anglo-American exchange trip.[48] At another
time and with another nominee, there might have been more public attention on the limits of her professional experience. But O'Connor ex-
uded competence and professionalism.

Any attention to her lack of credentials was eclipsed by critics' focus on
her abortion record. Starr had finished his additional research. But what
could he really say at this point? President Reagan already had put himself on the line with the nominee. Starr did not aggressively pursue outside complaints about O'Connor's abortion record. He talked mainly to
O'Connor and simply reported back what she had told him. "We felt our
mission was to identify her judicial philosophy," Starr said in a later interview, "and not to, in any way, probe into how she would vote and not
to extract [a] . . . commitment of how she would vote."[49]

Starr's three-page memo addressed to Attorney General Smith began,
"As a trial and appellate judge, she had not had occasion to rule on any
issue relating to abortion. Contrary to media reports, she has never attended or spoken at a women's rights conference on abortion." Starr said
he talked by phone to O'Connor twice on July 6 to get information about
her positions. Regarding the 1970 bill to decriminalize abortion, Starr
wrote, "There is no record of how Senator O'Connor voted, and she indicated that she has no recollection of how she voted." She was matter-of-
fact, hardly defensive, he would recall later. Starr said he had no reason to
check local newspapers to see if her vote had been recorded. If Starr had
taken such a step he would have discovered that the proposed legislation
was front-page news and the subject of considerable controversy in Arizona eleven years earlier—and that O'Connor had voted for the measure
to decriminalize abortion.

In his memo to Attorney General Smith, Starr added that "Judge
O'Connor further indicated, in response to my questions, that she had
never been a leader or outspoken advocate on behalf of either pro-life or
abortion-rights organizations. She knows well the Arizona leader of the
right-to-life movement, a prominent female physician in Phoenix, and
has never had any disputes or controversies with her."

That assertion, as well as playing down the 1970 vote, would cause
trouble for Starr and O'Connor, because the "prominent female physician," Gerster, plainly considered O'Connor an adversary. Starr had
taken O'Connor's word for everything and never contacted Gerster. If he

had, he would have heard otherwise. "I had an adversary position with Sandra O'Connor," Gerster told columnists Rowland Evans and Robert Novak soon after, calling O'Connor "one of the most powerful pro-abortionists in the [Arizona] Senate." She told reporters the president had been misled.[50]

Administration aides worked to diminish the Starr memo's importance in the selection process, adopting the party line that it "was not intended to be a decisional memo, but rather was for informational purposes." McConnell, the assistant attorney general for legislative affairs, called old contacts in Arizona to verify O'Connor's version of events. "After vetting it to our satisfaction," he recalled, "the job was to get her confirmed."[51]

The inimitable Goldwater, who had not lost his edge at age 72 and whose conservative credentials could not be questioned, lent his heft. When Moral Majority's Jerry Falwell declared that O'Connor would support "abortion on demand," Goldwater interceded. He said he had known O'Connor for twenty years and that she "epitomized the American ideal of a mother and wife and community-spirited person. . . . I was present at the wedding of my nephew last year when she made a beautiful speech about 'marriage being the foundation of the family, the basic unit of society, the hope of the world, and the strength of the country.' Now, what quarrel can Moral Majority take with this creed?" At another point, after Falwell was quoted as saying "All good Christians should oppose O'Connor," Goldwater declared, "All good Christians should kick him in the ass."[52]

Using a cane because of a hip ailment caused by arthritis, Goldwater went to see his Senate colleagues, particularly conservatives, such as North Carolina Republican Jesse Helms. On the day after Reagan's announcement of O'Connor's nomination, a White House liaison to Capitol Hill, Max Friedersdorf, prepared a memorandum for the president: "Helms said he expects to receive 'flak from the other Senators,' if he supports the nomination, but gave the impression that he is now leaning that way. Apparently Senator Goldwater has worked on Helms, because he mentioned that Barry had requested Helms help with the nomination. As you know, Senator Helms can be changeable at times, but he sounds positive today."[53]

Strom Thurmond, the then-78-year-old Republican chairman of the

Senate Judiciary Committee, backed the nomination, too. But he wrote privately to Reagan to notify him about the possible obstacles to O'Connor's confirmation. Thurmond expressed concerns about O'Connor's record on abortion and questioned her association with what he suggested were distasteful feminist causes. In response, the president's team cast O'Connor as a conscientious woman concerned about job discrimination, not a feminist firebrand. White House officials told Thurmond and other senators that she had not campaigned for the Equal Rights Amendment. They acknowledged that she considered the measure to be an important one. After all, they said, who would not have? It had passed Congress by a two-thirds vote and was submitted to the states for consideration. "Her activities as a state senator were directed at *securing the full consideration of the ERA,*" not necessarily seeing it passed, they wrote in talking points for senators.[54] White House aides reminded her to mention in meetings with senators that she never voted one way or the other on the merits of ERA. But she once had spoken out for its ratification and written letters to members of Congress to secure its passage—activities that her White House handlers ignored.

Attention to the ERA was approaching a crescendo at the time. The amendment, which had been pending since 1972, needed to be ratified within the year, or it would die. Ratification required the approval of three-fourths of the states—thirty-eight—and it was becoming clear that this approval was unlikely. On June 30, the day before O'Connor and Myra Tankersley had driven over to the White House to meet with Reagan, at least three thousand supporters of the ERA had rallied in nearby Lafayette Park to launch their final push to win ratification before the deadline of June 30, 1982. Actor Alan Alda spoke at the press conference, one of more than one hundred events that were staged by the National Organization for Women (NOW) to commemorate the beginning of the last year for the ERA. Betty Friedan and other feminists were hoping that Reagan's opposition to the ERA would backfire and generate more support for the amendment. Although the ERA had been ratified in thirty-five states, three more were needed before it could become part of the Constitution. No additional state had ratified the amendment since 1977, four years earlier.

Democrats who might have been ready to resist Reagan's nominee could not help but extol his choice of a first woman. "Democrats and other detractors are, again, writing on the blackboards of their minds, 'Do not underestimate Ronald Reagan,' " opined *Washington Star* columnist Mary McGrory. "These are the people who were sure that the conservative Republican President would not nominate the first woman in history for the Supreme Court. Or, in the unlikely event he did, just to fulfill a fairly porous campaign promise, that he would pick some right-wing harridan, given to shutting up shoplifters and putting down minorities. Much more likely, they predicted, he would choose some howlingly conventional white male. But the President confounded them by hitting on Sandra D. O'Connor, a 51-year-old Sun Belt overachiever who has had an incomparable contemporary reality training, being the mother of three sons, with experience in three branches of state government and a long history in Republican politics."[55]

Rival politicians did not shrink from expressing their admiration for Reagan's move. House Speaker Thomas P. ("Tip") O'Neill, a Democrat from Massachusetts, called it "the best thing he's done since he was inaugurated." A *New York Times* report observed that the bipartisan enthusiasm arose partly because Washington "still recalls that a little over a decade ago President Richard M. Nixon had to face political humiliation when the Senate rejected two of his Court nominees, Clement F. Haynsworth Jr. and G. Harrold Carswell."

The fate of Haynsworth and Carswell was a reminder that Supreme Court confirmations never occur in a vacuum. They reflect the partisan divisions, the issues, and the grievances of the time. In May 1969, Abe Fortas was forced from the bench partly because of fallout from President Lyndon B. Johnson's bid to elevate him to chief justice the previous year. The departure of Fortas, an LBJ confidant, was the climax of a furor brought on by the disclosure in May 1969 of Fortas's dubious financial activities.[56] After that episode embarrassed their party's president, Senate Democrats were predisposed to reject two of newly elected President Nixon's nominees, Haynsworth and Carswell, who had problems of their own. Harry Blackmun subsequently won Senate confirmation in May 1970 to succeed Fortas.

After nearly two hundred years of male justices, the public at large embraced O'Connor. A Gallup Poll in mid-July 1981 found that 86 percent of those questioned approved of a woman serving on the Supreme Court, and 69 percent believed O'Connor was qualified to serve on the

Supreme Court. (Four percent said she was not qualified, and 27 percent said they had no opinion.)

The one sticking point was the far Right of the Republican Party. "The sound you hear, beneath the loud reveling at the president's precedent-shattering nomination of a woman to the Supreme Court, is the cracking apart of Ronald Reagan's Great Coalition," asserted Patrick Buchanan, a former Nixon aide, denouncing the president for the way he executed his "frivolous campaign promise." Buchanan, who at the time was a columnist but would eventually join the Reagan White House, said the president owed the Right for helping him win the GOP nomination.

Buchanan presumed Reagan wanted to nurture the Right wing. But, as *Washington Post* reporter Bill Peterson wrote, the president seemed eager to use the O'Connor nomination to separate himself from the far-right organizations that had helped elect him. Columnists Evans and Novak observed that while Carolyn Gerster believed the president had been misled by his advisors, "the more plausible explanation is that Reagan shares the view of Jim Baker and his aides that the Moral Majority is not vital to his political coalition."[57]

How O'Connor felt about the controversy over her abortion record is not easy to discern. At the time, she declined to answer any questions about it, saying she was waiting for the Senate hearings. She told family members that abortion was one of those issues on which no matter how you acted, you would displease half of your constituents.[58] Her style was to look for public consensus. But agreement on abortion was not easy to find in the early 1970s when she was a legislator—still less so in 1981, when she had to face the Senate.

O'Connor did not fret over the single issue of abortion. Rather, she devoted herself to homework on every topic for the Senate hearings. She had learned from helping Rehnquist a decade earlier that adversaries could be neutralized. She studied senators' records, so that when they brought up a topic she could refer to their work. As she recalled about her years in the state Senate, "My approach as a legislator was to try to develop as much background knowledge and expertise as possible in the subject areas of the legislation, and to develop community contacts that would provide the necessary public support for my positions."[59]

Whenever she obtained advice from a White House official, she wrote a thank-you note. She also was in contact with some of the men who would be her colleagues. After hearing from Justice Lewis Powell through a mutual friend, she wrote to him and his wife, Josephine: "I know that it will be a special pleasure to know you and to work with you." She enlisted them in her effort to find a place to live, asking: "If either of you know of a two bedroom furnished apartment which might be available temporarily as of September 1, you might let me know. I do not want to decide on a permanent dwelling until I am better acquainted with the area." When Powell asked his secretary to file away O'Connor's letter, he attached a note directing her to put it in "My file on communications with other Justices. She will be one soon."[60] O'Connor and her husband eventually rented an apartment in the Watergate as a temporary home—through a friend of the Powells.

In mid-July, O'Connor returned to Washington to be introduced to senators who would decide the fate of her nomination. Photographs of that visit show O'Connor smiling broadly as she greeted each senator, leaning in close as she clasped their hands. The epitome of good manners, she appeared to be the host rather than the guest. White House aides instructed her to use the meetings to ease relations for the forthcoming hearings before the Senate Judiciary Committee. "A principal purpose of courtesy calls is to show the senators exactly who the candidate is and why she is qualified to assume this high position," the administration team wrote in one of the hundreds of documents prepared for O'Connor. "Thus, the exercise should not be viewed simply as replying to specific questions with responsive answers; rather, the courtesy calls permit the designee to take the initiative and convince senators of the merits of the President's selection."

Justice Department lawyers prepared several large briefing books containing materials on Supreme Court decisions, excerpts from prior confirmation hearings, and questions likely to be asked—along with suggested answers. What they encouraged her to say came from what she had told them about herself, processed through their political machinery. For example, Ken Starr and his colleagues wanted her to stress her legislative experience that she herself touted. They offered her this language: "I have had to face the people directly and answer to them on very hard issues, and then to hear from them at the ballot box. That is the essence of a republican form of government—having to answer at election time to the people who sent you to the capital. It is because I have been through the process that I fully understand the difference between a legislator and a judge." On abortion, they reminded her that her personal view was that abortion is morally repugnant. And, of course, they said, she could not comment on *Roe v. Wade*.

She was most nervous about her meeting with Helms, who had the power to single-handedly block her if he wanted to lead the antiabortion opposition.[61] O'Connor talked about her regard for family. "When she was finished, he got up and embraced her and said good luck," recalled McConnell, the assistant attorney general who accompanied O'Connor to Helms's office. "We walked down the hallway and got in an elevator and I said, 'There will be no organized Senate opposition.' I absolutely knew after he embraced her."[62]

By the end of the week, O'Connor had visited thirty-nine senators, the House Republican and Democratic leaders, and several representatives of the American Bar Association. Documenting her visits, the White House's senate liaison reported to Baker, Meese, Deaver, and Fielding: "Thurmond advised Judge O'Connor repeatedly not to let herself be 'pinned down' on how she would rule as a Justice. Thurmond seemed to be satisfied on the ERA issue and indicated he himself had supported the measure in the early 70s. . . . O'Connor described herself to Senator Thurmond as 'a conservative judge from a conservative state.' Thurmond raised the question of O'Connor being 'alright as long as Reagan is in,' implying she would vote liberal afterwards. Thurmond said this was a question he had received. O'Connor responded that her record as both a legislator and judge will reflect her strong convictions and commitment on the issues." The implication: O'Connor was handling the senators.[63]

On the Democratic side, Senate Minority Leader Robert Byrd of West Virginia told O'Connor he intended to vote for her confirmation. The ranking Democrat on the Senate Judiciary Committee, Joseph Biden of Delaware, said he knew of no Democrats who would oppose her.

Senator Kennedy, the embodiment of Senate liberalism, similarly welcomed her. When she and McConnell entered Kennedy's office in the stately Russell Building, they immediately were struck by all the Kennedy family memorabilia, including a picture of a young John F. Kennedy, bare-chested in dog tags aboard his World War II PT boat. "Then there was this awkward moment of not knowing how we start," recalled

McConnell, "and Sandra leaned over and said, 'Well, Senator Kennedy, how is your mother?' "

That drew an amusing anecdote from Kennedy, who a year earlier had run for the Democratic nomination for president. "I was with her last weekend and her mind is as sharp as it can be about things in the past," Kennedy said of a visit to his mother, Rose. "But as you get closer it gets fuzzier. You can have wonderful conversations with her about who won what flag football game and who won what sailing race we had among us, and all of those details about growing up. But, as I was getting up to leave, she said, 'Ted, you didn't get the nomination, did you?' "[64]

Everywhere O'Connor went, crowds of people gathered around. She was even greeted warmly by U.S. Representative Henry Hyde, the white-haired, six-foot-three hulking Illinois Republican whose name was synonymous with a law denying federal funds for abortions unless the life of the woman was threatened by her pregnancy. However, Hyde was one of the few members of Congress who did not want his picture taken with her.[65]

The courtesy calls turned up eight Republican senators who were resisting O'Connor's appointment, but as Friedersdorf said in his account to the White House, the meeting with Hyde "was positive" and he agreed to help with those senators: "Hyde indicated he believes the anti-O'Connor activities by the Right-to-Life groups are damaging to those groups; agreed to call on the eight 'problem' senators with the following line: Mrs. O'Connor is going to be on the Court, she cannot be defeated, so why make an enemy. Hyde also indicated he would make a supportive statement at the appropriate time."

At the end of the week, President Reagan hosted a party for O'Connor in the Rose Garden. "We're delighted to have her here and look forward to when she'll be here, you might say, permanently," he told reporters before he was to meet with his nominee. A White House photographer recorded a moment in the Oval Office before the festivities were to begin: Reagan and O'Connor became locked in a conversation. He wore a tan suit, striped tie, handkerchief tucked neatly into his breast pocket. Legs crossed at the knee, he was laughing with O'Connor, who sat to his left, in a pink suit with pink blouse, leaning forward, hands wrapped around her knees. Her brown hair was coiffed in a short bob. If one did not know

O'Connor, one would have thought her playing the ingenue laughing with an older man at a party.

When O'Connor came back to Washington for the final run of study sessions, briefings, and mock hearings before the main event, she had a sense of purpose in her stride. She was seen going in and out of the Justice Department with large, legal-size folders of materials balanced on her hip, smiling, in good spirits. By day, she underwent mock question-and-answer sessions in the attorney general's conference room, a high-ceilinged expanse that Attorney General Bobby Kennedy had used as his office in the early 1960s. She continued to ask Smith's assistants for more materials, on homosexuality, abortion, and busing. In the evenings, she went to dinner, socialized with new friends, and attended a Kennedy Center performance of the musical *Annie*.

The night before the hearings began, she lay in bed and worried about "how [she] would be treated and how well [she] would be able to respond to the questions."[66] But once inside the Dirksen Senate Office Building, she had one of the most receptive audiences a Court nominee ever faced. In the cavernous but packed hearing room, Chairman Thurmond escorted O'Connor to the witness table. He then walked to the dais and took his place in the center seat. "This is truly an historic occasion," the chairman said in his South Carolina drawl, "as it is the first time in the history of our nation that a president has nominated a woman to serve on this august body."[67]

Wearing her favorite lavender suit, O'Connor presented herself to a national television audience. She began by echoing some of the themes from her preparation: "I want to make only one substantive statement to you at this time. My experience as a state court judge and as a state legislator has given me a greater appreciation of the important role the states play in our federal system. . . . Those experiences have strengthened my view that the proper role of the judiciary is one of interpreting and applying the law, not making it." She also warned them at the outset that she would not be able to answer questions about cases that might come before her.

Then she introduced her family. "By way of preamble," O'Connor said, "I would note that some of the media have reported correctly that I have performed some marriage ceremonies in my capacity as judge. I would like to read to you an extract from a part of the form of marriage ceremony which I prepared: 'Marriage is far more than an exchange of vows. It is the foundation of the family, mankind's basic unit of society, the hope of the world and the strength of our country. It is the relationship between ourselves and the generations which follow.' "

Defining herself as a traditionalist, a woman of family values, she told the senators that her nomination had brought her family closer together. She then introduced her three sons: "Scott graduated from Stanford two years ago. He was our state swimming champion. He is now a young businessman, a pilot, and a budding gourmet cook. Now my second son, Brian, is a senior at Colorado College. He is our adventurer. He is a sky-diver with over four hundred jumps, including a dive off El Capitan at Yosemite last summer. I look forward to his retirement from that activity, so he can spend more time in his other status as a pilot. Now my youngest son, Jay, is a sophomore at Stanford. He is our writer, and he acted as my assistant press secretary after the news of the nomination surfaced, and did a very good job keeping all of us quiet. If I could promise you that I could decide cases as well as Jay can ski or swing a golf club, I think that we would have no further problem in the hearing. Finally, I would like to introduce my dear husband, John. We met on a law review assignment at Stanford University Law School and will celebrate our twenty-ninth wedding anniversary in December."

Later, in response to questions from DeConcini, she linked her regard for family to her position on abortion. "I have indicated to you . . . my own abhorrence of abortion as a remedy. It is a practice in which I would not have engaged, and I am not trying to criticize others in that process. There are many who have very different feelings on this issue. I recognize that, and I am sensitive to it. But my view is the product, I suppose, merely of my own upbringing and my religious training, my background, my sense of family values, and my sense of how I should lead my own life."

The answer satisfied DeConcini but not Senator Jeremiah Denton, an Alabama Republican, who tried hard to pin down the nominee on her views. Denton, 57, a former carrier pilot and Vietnam POW, had spent four years in brutal captivity. At one point, when the North Vietnamese paraded him before a television crew, he blinked the word "torture" in Morse code. After emerging from imprisonment in 1973 and returning home, he became involved in politics and was elected Alabama's first

GOP senator since Reconstruction. He was a conservative on social issues. He told O'Connor that when he came home in 1973, he was appalled to find out that the Supreme Court had legalized abortion
nationwide.

As he questioned her, she tried to strike a balance. "Senator Denton,
for myself, it is simply offensive to me. It is something that is repugnant to
me and something in which I would not engage. Obviously, there are
others who do not share these beliefs, and I recognize that. . . . I am 'over
the hill.' I am not going to be pregnant anymore, so it is perhaps easy for
me to speak. . . . For those in the legislative halls, it poses very difficult
problems for them in drawing those lines legislatively."

For Denton, who regarded abortion as "even more fundamental than
the issue of slavery" in the nineteenth century, such answers were inadequate.

"Well, with all due respect, we are dealing with such nitty-gritty distinctions as rape, incest, and so forth, save the life of the mother," he said.
"I am asking your personal reflection on the offensiveness with respect to
those kinds of conditions. Where do you think it occurs? Where does it
become offensive?"

"I find that it is a problem at any level," she said. "Where you draw the
line as a matter of public policy is really the task of the legislator to determine." She was saying, in effect, it is up to elected lawmakers to decide
when abortion should be allowed.

Her first session in the witness chair was over. Afterwards, McConnell
dropped her off at her Watergate apartment. He planned to return to the
Watergate around eight p.m. to go over materials for the second day of
hearings, but he wondered whether that would be productive. O'Connor
had seemed exhausted. As McConnell apprehensively approached her
apartment later that evening, O'Connor threw open the door, wearing a
Groucho Marx nose, mustache, and glasses. "Bob, we need to lighten up,"
she said. McConnell recalled that he did not know whether the Groucho
stunt was a way to help herself, her Justice Department handlers, or both.
But the gesture seemed just right.

The next day, Denton asked more questions, this time focusing on the
Starr memo and questioning why O'Connor would ever say she was not
an "adversary" of Gerster. O'Connor began by saying, "We have children
who have attended the same school, and I have seen her on any number

of occasions." Then, with Denton interrupting at several junctures, O'Connor insisted that when she disagreed with some request from a lobbyist or constituent, she did not believe that made them adversaries. "As a legislator, I had many instances in which people would come before the legislature and espouse a particular position with regard to a particular bill. I, as a legislator, was obligated to listen to those views along with the views of others, and then ultimately cast a vote. . . . I think that it is important to recognize that what I am trying to reflect is that because I may have voted differently than Dr. Gerster would have, had she been a legislator, does not mean that we are adversaries." For those who had known O'Connor, the remark was believable. She looked for common ground. She did not nurse grudges.

Denton said he could not believe that she would have forgotten her position on the 1970 legislation to legalize abortion in Arizona: "Somebody in Arizona has said that was the equivalent of not remembering how one would have voted on the Panama Canal issue."

"We voted on literally thousands of measures and that bill never went to the floor for a vote," O'Connor responded. She said that at the time she believed that the abortion law needed to be repealed because it would have prevented a rape victim from undergoing a prompt procedure to prevent pregnancy. But, O'Connor added, her awareness of a need for abortion regulation had risen. She said that she would not now vote for a repeal of the Arizona law.

"Senator Denton, again I would ask you to reflect on the fact that we are talking about the year 1970. That was a time when, at least my perception as a state legislator in Arizona, indicated that this subject was not the subject of the public attention and concern that it is today."

Activists on both sides read into her words what they wanted to hear—with the exception of Gerster, who was standing by, ready to testify against her. Falwell, leader of the Moral Majority, took O'Connor's testimony as a promise to oppose abortion. "I think the judge will work overtime now not to be an embarrassment to the president." Abortion rights groups took away the exact opposite message, heartened by what they knew of her record as an Arizona legislator.[68]

In the end, O'Connor's three days of testimony revealed little. But confirmation hearings were rituals designed to appease rather than to expose. Nominees were coached to disclose just enough to make senators believe their questions have been answered but not enough to rouse them to ask more penetrating questions. She told the Senate Judiciary Committee she favored the death penalty and believed judges had been too lenient on some criminals. When asked about busing to desegregate schools, she said she was opposed to the policy and invoked her own childhood of having one year made a seventy-five-mile roundtrip bus ride to school. Busing "can be a very disruptive part of any child's education," she said. But she also testified that federal judges sometimes are justified in ordering drastic measures such as busing to remedy violations of individuals' constitutional rights. In the end, O'Connor warned senators about reading too much into her personal views, saying they did not control her judicial votes.

In ways that mattered most in Washington and to people watching the proceedings on television, she presented herself as a loving mother, loyal wife, and competent lawyer. Like the president who had nominated her, O'Connor spoke of family values and moral imperatives. She appeared to represent a tidy world of working mothers who could have it all—and would always do the right thing by their husband and children. She favored more opportunities for women without being on the cutting edge of the feminist movement.

After she overcame a few nervous moments, her testimony was first-rate. She demonstrated that she had researched all potential queries and the men who might ask them. Fred Barbash of the *Washington Post* reported, "She knew each senator's pet project on the committee and could congratulate them on network television for their 'fine work' in seeking solutions to the crime problem or the problem of caseload backlogs in the federal Courts. And through it all, she was the very essence of composure and self-confidence: even-voiced and even-tempered, no nervous quaver to her voice, no fidgeting, a smile when appropriate, a serious and intent gaze for serious and intent questions."

Senators could not keep their enthusiasm in check. "May I compliment you on your tour de force [in testifying]" Senator Arlen Specter, a Republican from Pennsylvania, said. "According to the television last night, you did very well," Senator Charles Grassley, an Iowa Republican, added. Thurmond told her she "will make an outstanding associate justice of the Supreme Court." There were other witnesses still to testify, but these key senators made it clear that they did not expect anything damaging to surface. When Democratic Senator Biden said, "I just don't want you to wall yourself off. You have an obligation to be an advocate for women," the audience burst into applause. O'Connor smiled and said nothing.[69]

Years later, she recalled, "After sitting in the witness chair on national television answering endless questions about the Constitution, various cases, and my personal feelings on some of life's great issues, I began to think that the hearings would never end." But at the time, she kept her impatience to herself.[70]

Next, the Senate Judiciary Committee heard from other witnesses: Gerster and John Wilke, president of the National Right to Life Committee, testified that O'Connor should be rejected because she had not promised to vote to overrule *Roe v. Wade.* Gerster spoke of the difficulty of opposing a home-state judge. "I have known Sandra Day O'Connor since 1972," Gerster told senators. "Our children were members of the same Indian Guide group. We attend the same church; we have the same friends. She is a very gracious and a very gifted lady. Quite apart from our social contact, however, we were in an absolute adversary positions during 1973 and 1974 due to Senator O'Connor's position on abortion-related legislation when she served as Senate majority leader."

Republican Senator Robert Dole of Kansas asked Gerster whether O'Connor's testimony might have led Gerster to support the nominee. "Senator, I wanted that with all my heart, I really did. You have no idea of the burden that this has placed on me as an Arizonan and as an acquaintance of Judge O'Connor. I listened to every minute of testimony on public television and took extensive notes, looking for some word. . . . I can say that I came here prepared to tear up my testimony and to enthusiastically support Judge O'Connor's nomination." But, sighed Gerster before a dwindled audience, nothing O'Connor said reassured her.

The White House was nearing unanimous support and attending to the few Republican holdouts. On September 15, Reagan wrote to Senator Alfonse D'Amato, a New York Republican, to assure him that a vote for O'Connor's nomination "will not in any way be inconsistent with the commitments that both of us made during our successful campaigns in 1980. . . . We conducted a thorough screening of all potential candidates for the Supreme Court beginning last March. Based on my review of Justice O'Connor's record, I am confident that she is going to make an outstanding Justice of the Supreme Court. I am satisfied with her views on judicial philosophy and with her position with respect to the right-to-life issue."[71]

Reagan also called Denton to make a personal pitch for O'Connor. Friedersdorf and Powell Moore, an aide to Reagan for legislative affairs, had described Denton in a note to the president as "probably the one senator standing in the way of a unanimous Senate confirmation of Judge O'Connor."[72] The call paid off. On September 21, O'Connor was confirmed by the Senate, 99–0. The only person who did not vote was Max Baucus, a Montana Democrat who favored O'Connor but was in his home state when the roll was called. Senator Helms waited until the last minute to announce that he would vote for confirmation. "Uncertainty yet exists to some degree," he said about her stand on abortion. "But I will vote for Mrs. O'Connor because I have faith in the president of the United States and faith that she would not allow the president to be misled" on the abortion question. If she voted for abortion rights, Helms suggested, she would be doing more than upsetting conservatives; she would be revealing that she had deceived the president.[73]

O'Connor listened to the vote in Senator Thurmond's Capitol hideaway office. Earlier that day, the Senate Judiciary Committee chairman had told reporters, "The people of this country want a woman on the Supreme Court and this nomination is highly satisfactory to the public." After the 99–0 tally was announced, O'Connor strode outside to the Capitol steps accompanied by Thurmond, Goldwater, DeConcini, and Vice President George H. W. Bush. "I am absolutely overjoyed at the expression of support from the Senate," she told the reporters and tourists looking up at her. Gazing across the Capitol lawn to the marble-columned Supreme Court, she said, "My hope is that ten years from now, after I've been across the street at work for a while, they will all be glad that they gave me that wonderful vote."

Her face was open, her smile wide, her eyes lit. O'Connor threw open her arms, the embodiment of intelligence, determination, and good luck. The contrast to July 7, 1981, when she stood before reporters in Phoenix with her hands rigidly at her side, was striking. Now, she reached out to the crowd below. Like Reagan, she was one of them.

6

THE MARBLE PALACE

With Chief Justice Warren Burger clutching her arm, Sandra Day O'Connor descended the wide marble steps of the Supreme Court. It was noon on Friday, September 25, 1981, the day of her investiture as a justice on the nation's highest court. Gathered on the plaza below were scores of photographers, reporters, Court employees, and tourists. Out on the streets, people were waving and cheering for the first woman to sit with the brethren. As O'Connor, wearing a black robe, navigated the sun-blazed marble steps, Burger smiled broadly, his chin up, his chest out. Thriving on such pageantry and attention at the columned building, he had taken it upon himself to preside over the gala surrounding O'Connor's investiture. With his white mane and chiseled face, he was the Chief Justice from Central Casting. Burger had been among the first to recommend O'Connor to the Reagan administration, and he had laid the groundwork before Justice Potter Stewart revealed his retirement plans. Burger's support for O'Connor was not lost on his colleagues, some of whom said privately that they expected Burger to quickly wrap O'Connor in conservative robes and be assured of her vote.

O'Connor had been quietly taking it all in, sizing up relations among her new colleagues. Since President Ronald Reagan had announced on July 7 that he had chosen her to fulfill his campaign vow to appoint the first woman justice, her life had been a whirlwind of legal tutorials and social events. Throughout the confirmation process, even when confronted by bombastic senators, antiabortion picketers, and pushy reporters, she had been the picture of decorum—a lady in pastels, white handbag dangling at her elbow. Her appeal was nonthreatening, and the nation was captivated. There were still questions, of course. Would she be a Burger conservative, a middle-of-the-roader, a liberal even? Was she the well-mannered matron she had shown Washington and the nation, or as hard-nosed and calculating as some of the men who had come before her? For now, simply being the first of her gender was enough.

On the wide steps beneath the frieze declaring "Equal Justice Under Law," O'Connor's descent of the Court's steps was her last public appearance before the investiture. Burger had choreographed this moment as a photo opportunity and a sighting for those who did not have seats for the two p.m. swearing-in. Several thousand requests for places had been made to the Court, but the room would hold only four hundred—and that was with extra chairs squeezed into aisles and alcoves. No television cameras or tape recorders were permitted.

Under her black robe, O'Connor wore a V-neck dusty-rose dress, belted at the waist, and a gold necklace. As the cameras clicked, Burger clutched her arm as if she were a wife or daughter. After a dozen years in male-dominated politics, O'Connor indulged such gestures. When they reached the plaza, flanked by giant stone figures signifying the Contemplation of Justice and the Guardian of Law, Burger shouted to reporters: "You've never seen me with a better-looking justice." O'Connor did not wince. She shouted to a friend to take pictures of the photographers for her scrapbook.[1]

The rest of the justices watched her warily. They were old and they were old-fashioned. A majority of them were born in the first decade of the century and were now in their 70s. Would her views as a woman set her apart? They were curious about what a celebrity she had become. "The town is agog about the first lady Justice," Justice Lewis Powell wrote to his family. But mostly they wondered whether she was really qualified. Privately, they had expressed their doubts and compared notes. Bill Rehnquist, who knew her from Stanford and Phoenix, vouched for her qualifications. "In view of what Bill Rehnquist said about her, she may be a good appointment," Powell allowed in a letter to the newly retired Potter Stewart, adding, "If she meets your qualifications, it will be good to have a woman on the Court."[2]

To outsiders, the brethren looked ready for the first sister. They had dropped the traditional "Mr. Justice" designation from written opinions, in favor of simply "Justice" a year earlier. But some of the justices had misgivings about the change—not necessarily out of sexism but for reasons of protocol. "If you are maintaining a permanent record on the vote to eliminate the use of 'Mr.,' " Justice Harry Blackmun wrote to Burger on November 17, 1980, "please record me as in opposition. It seems to me that of late we tend to panic and to get terribly excited about some rather inconsequential things. I regard this as one of them. . . . As Hugo Black once despairingly said (and how well I remember), 'All these changes around here!' " Powell agreed with Blackmun: "[T]he choice of a woman may well be overdue, given the glacial changes in our society over the past two decades. But it does seem more dignified, and perhaps less anticipatory of a political judgment, to defer making a change at this time. It certainly will be appropriate when a 'Sister' joins us."[3]

"With Harry and Lewis," Burger wrote to all eight associate justices, "I thought we moved much too fast on the 'Mr. Justice' business. . . . But the [majority] voted to make the change." It had been released to the press, so, Burger said, the Court could not retreat. The chief justice then offered a bit of solidarity to the dissenters: "You may recall that I do not address the Ms. Counsel as 'Mizz' [during oral arguments]."[4] He was referring to the contemporary "Ms." designation that some women preferred over either "Miss" or "Mrs.," which were tied to marital status.

Now, in the courtroom at the heart of the building, they were ready for the woman who would yank them into the contemporary world. The nine black leather chairs of the justices were perfectly spaced along a curved raised bench made of Honduran mahogany. Boxing the courtroom were twenty-four white Italian marble columns; red velvet drapes hung in the intervals. At one minute before two p.m., Marshal Alfred Wong escorted President Reagan into the courtroom. Simultaneously, Supreme Court chief clerk Alexander Stevas escorted O'Connor to the front of the room, to an armchair used by Chief Justice John Marshall in the nineteenth century. She now wore only her rose-colored dress, without the black robe; her official robing was part of the investiture. With the sharp rap of Wong's gavel, the main event began. Attorney General William French Smith officially presented O'Connor to the eight justices and submitted President Reagan's official commissioning of her as an associate justice. Her new colleagues watched solemnly as O'Connor placed her left hand on a Bible, raised her right hand, and swore to "well and faithfully discharge the duties of the office on which I am about to enter. So help me God." Burger then said simply: "Justice O'Connor, welcome." She was helped into her black robe and took the chair that was assigned to her by virtue of seniority, next to Rehnquist, at Burger's extreme left. It all took no more than fifteen minutes.

As O'Connor looked down from the bench at her husband and three grown sons, her mother and father, sister and brother, and the President and Mrs. Reagan, her eyes welled up. It was "a moment suspended in time," she wrote later, "bridging the life in the harsh desert terrain of the Lazy B and the fast-paced sophisticated life in Washington, D.C."[5] Her father, 83, and mother, 77, could hardly walk without help. Years of cigarette smoking had taken its toll on both of them, and her mother was in the early stages of Alzheimer's disease. At one point, her mother remarked of Reagan, "I think I've seen him somewhere before." But she still had extended periods of lucidity and told reporters, "It is a very proud day for me. And for the country, really."[6]

The justice's brother and sister would recall the whole event in a blur of activity: the frantic pace of the week, the constant sound of camera shutters and sight of television lights, and the adulation of a sister who was the apple of their parents' eyes. They watched their sister in the receiving line after the investiture, observing that she looked each guest in the eye and tried to find something personal to say.[7] The time since her Senate confirmation on Monday, September 21, had, in fact, seemed one great and continuous receiving line. The investiture followed a week of so many parties, toasts, and photo opportunities that a White House aide called the prelude to her swearing-in a "mini-inaugural."[8]

The Tuesday before the investiture had been an exception. That day O'Connor had gone back to Arizona for funeral services for her mother-in-law, Sally "Gigi" O'Connor, who had died on the previous Friday. Oddly, the woman who had been trailed at every turn for two months was able to return to Arizona almost unnoticed. O'Connor's presence at the funeral was recorded only with a picture in a local paper.[9] But the personal sadness amid a week of professional success would be a harbinger of the dual challenges to come. As the first woman justice, she would more personally face the test of the intertwined cycles of work and family.

President Reagan and First Lady Nancy Reagan stayed for a brief courtyard photo session and then returned by motorcade to the White House. Reagan's work was done. He had electrified the nation with his selection. "My appointment has probably done more to give women confidence in true equal opportunity than a thousand speeches," O'Connor wrote to the president after the investiture.[10] She seemed to have it all, and in 1981, many women believed that possible. Women were beginning to deluge law schools with applications, and O'Connor's appointment to the high court reminded many women of their own potential. "Yes, I will bring the understanding of a woman to the Court, but I doubt that that alone will affect my decisions," she told the *Ladies' Home Journal* shortly after she was sworn in. "I think the important fact about my appointment is not that I will decide cases as a woman, but that I am a woman who will get to decide cases."[11]

But first she had to navigate the rituals of the building dubbed "The Marble Palace" by Court scholar John Frank. Even moving around the place—with its four internal courtyards—was difficult at first. She lost her way getting from the parking garage to her office. Finding sunlight was even harder. There were times when the daughter of the West would seek out a corner of the courtyard and hold her face up to the sun to feel its heat.[12]

Allowed two secretaries and up to four law clerks, as given all justices, O'Connor hired the three clerks selected by Potter Stewart before he retired. For the fourth, she brought in Ruth McGregor, a 38-year-old partner from her husband's firm of Fennemore, Craig. McGregor sought out the clerkship with O'Connor after working on a team that helped O'Connor prepare for the Senate confirmation hearings. When McGregor requested the position, O'Connor asked, "What does Bob think about this?" She wondered whether McGregor's physician husband would mind his wife being away in Washington for a year. At a time when the nation was holding O'Connor up as a symbol of women's liberation, the question revealed her traditional side. McGregor told O'Connor that she and her husband had worked it out. The justice-to-be was satisfied. Once at the Court, McGregor—ten years older than most other clerks, and dressed in expensive professional suits—confused some Court police officers. They mistook her for the justice herself. "It took me a while to realize they didn't stand up for every woman who came by," said McGregor, who would eventually become an Arizona Supreme Court Justice.

The reception for O'Connor might have been rousing, but some of the business of being a justice had been neglected. McGregor recalled, "We went into her chambers. No one at the Court had set them up. [Documents] were just in stacks, all along the periphery of the office, where the secretaries sit. It wasn't just that we lacked a filing system . . . we literally didn't have file cabinets." Yet, O'Connor had immediate business to handle. In three more days, on September 28, the justices' first meeting—or "conference," as it is called—for the upcoming term was scheduled to occur. O'Connor was faced with a mind-boggling pile of hundreds of appeals that had come in over the summer. "I can remember John O'Connor and the Justice and I getting ready for [the first] conference. We went through the hundreds of [cases] and put them all in numerical order, which seemed reasonable. But that's not always the way they do it. So that whole first conference, she had to be flipping back and forth through her notes."[13] The numbered cases often were not in pure chronological order. The list depended on when all the filings were in hand and on whether an individual justice, seeking to do more research, had asked to have a case postponed for discussion.

At these conference meetings, the justices decided which of the filings, known as "petitions for certiorari," they would grant and schedule for further briefing and oral arguments. It was also where, as the term unfolded, they voted on cases that already had been argued. The conference was held in an oak-paneled room off the chief justice's chambers. The decor was relatively spare: dominating the room was a rectangular-shaped table where the justices sat. On the north wall was a large black-marble fireplace. Above it was an oil portrait of John Marshall, considered the nation's greatest chief justice, who served 1801–1835. A glass chandelier hung in the center of the room, and the conference table was additionally lit by nearby lamps. The chief justice sat at the head of the table, with the eight others around him, in order of seniority. It was indicative of the justices' elaborate rules of protocol and decorum that in

August 1981, as Justice Stewart was leaving, Blackmun wrote to Powell, "This is just to let you know that I've decided to retain my middle seat at the conference table. I had promised to inform you when I had reached a decision on this 'very important' matter. I suppose this enables you to move over to the corner place previously occupied by Potter." Powell then wrote to Chief Justice Burger, "In view of Harry's decision, I will move up to Potter's place at the conference table." Burger sent back a note: "OK, indeed excellent!"[14]

As the newest justice, O'Connor sat in the place nearest to the door, because it was the junior justice's job to act as doorkeeper and to hand messages or requests for material to the messengers stationed outside the room. By tradition, the junior justice also took notes of the proceedings for the benefit of the Supreme Court's clerk. Some of her colleagues, worried about the appearance of her undertaking this secretarial role, raised the possibility of exempting O'Connor from the necessary but menial tasks. But Justice John Paul Stevens, who had been the junior justice until O'Connor's arrival, recalled in an interview that he objected to the suggestion that O'Connor not take up the duties, believing that she would be insulted by the special exemption. He also thought "everyone should have a turn." In the end, tradition reigned and O'Connor assumed doorkeeper duties.[15]

Because it was the only time when the nine were alone, without the benefit of law clerks or secretaries, the conference was a unique and important part of the Court's routine. Here was where the justices first put themselves on the line, sometimes firmly declaring a stand, sometimes tentatively casting a vote. Most of the time, the views and votes stuck. But in a handful of cases each term—sometimes the most consequential disputes—the conference offered only the first round of a case's resolution. O'Connor appreciated the power of these justices-only meetings. "It was just an electric moment for me," she said.[16]

Crossing the threshold as the only woman, she was the odd one, the outsider. But the eight men carried their own mixed history together. The justices were still feeling the aftershocks of the publication of the book *The Brethren,* Bob Woodward's and Scott Armstrong's account of the Court's inner workings and personal tensions. Based on interviews with unnamed justices and many of their former law clerks, the book depicted a bickering group of old men maneuvering around one another on

the law. Warren Burger was portrayed as especially small-minded and
unpopular. It stung and made Burger more distrustful of some of his colleagues. Other justices tried to disparage the book, but, of course, some
had cooperated with the authors.[17]

The truth was that Burger's personal style inspired rivalries. Some of
the other justices thought he used a bait-and-switch technique to control
the opinion-writing assignment. Burger sometimes would waive his turn
to speak first in the justices' conference. Then he would vote with the side
that had a majority, which would give him, as senior member for that
side, the power to assign the writing of the opinion in the case. Some justices believed this was intended at times to rob senior liberal William
Brennan of the right to compose the opinion or to assign it to another justice. Potter Stewart had compared Burger to a "show captain" on an
ocean liner who takes women to dinner while the real captain pilots the
ship.[18] Even Burger's ideological soulmate Rehnquist once said of Burger
that he "sometimes . . . gives the impression of a southern senator conducting a filibuster."[19] But while his personal relationships could be
strained, Burger made the Court, as an institution, work better. His
touch ran throughout the building, from the glassware in the cafeteria to
the flower plantings outside. He had the long mahogany bench, at which
the justices heard cases, cut into three sections, for a winged, half-
hexagon effect. That enabled the justices on the two far sides to better see
and hear each other during oral arguments.

On the substance of the law, Burger was a strong adherent of judicial
conservatism, and did not believe the Constitution was a mandate to
solve social problems. As O'Connor had learned from the tales of his
childhood during their fortuitous houseboat vacation in 1979, Burger
was born in St. Paul, Minnesota, of Swiss-German Protestant stock. He
spent his early life on a farm, worked his way through local colleges, and
attended night classes for a law degree from St. Paul College of Law.[20]
After he had served three years as an assistant attorney general in the
Eisenhower Justice Department and thirteen years as a judge on a federal
appeals court, President Nixon named him chief justice in 1969.

Next in seniority, and the eldest and longest-serving justice at the time
of O'Connor's arrival, was William Brennan, 75. He looked beyond the
outcome of individual cases to the long horizons of the Court's role in
America. He had a liberal vision of the Constitution as an evolving docu-

ment that could be used to correct perceived social wrongs. A slight figure with a broad forehead, narrow chin, and big grin, Brennan also was a master of the fine art of compromise and getting five—the number of justices needed for a majority on a case. A 1956 appointee of President Dwight Eisenhower, Brennan had been the chief strategist of the liberal Warren Court and still held great sway twelve years into the Burger Court. Born to Irish immigrants in Newark, his father active in the labor movement, Brennan was relentless in putting together a majority for his side. He had a twinkle in his eye and was known to charm even those who rejected his view of the law. If he lost a colleague, he would not hesitate to go after him the next time around.[21] Unlike some of his brethren, Brennan was willing to compromise, accept "half a loaf rather than a full loaf,"[22] if that was necessary to obtain a majority and take steps toward a broader interpretation of constitutional individual rights. Former justice Felix Frankfurter, whom Brennan studied under while at Harvard Law School, was on the Court when Brennan took his seat at conference. In a 1962 *Look* magazine piece, the year he retired, the conservative Frankfurter was quoted as saying, "I taught my students to think for themselves, but sometimes I think that Bill Brennan carries it too far." But as bold as Brennan was on the law, he had a quiet manner and rarely asked questions during oral arguments. His health was declining. He already had had one stroke, which slightly disabled his right arm and hand.[23] For the conference, Brennan would often write out his remarks beforehand and deliver them verbatim from the written page.

Next in seniority was the firm-jawed, bespectacled Byron White, 64, who had been a scholar-athlete and decorated navy officer. In England, as a Rhodes scholar at Oxford University, he met John F. Kennedy, whose father, Joseph, was ambassador to the Court of St. James. The young Kennedy and White established a bond. When Kennedy became president, he made White deputy attorney general, and then, in 1962, appointed him to the high court. Born in Colorado, where his father was in the lumber business and a mayor of the small town of Wellington, White ranked first in his high school class and dominated on the football field. He first became a national figure as an All-American halfback at the University of Colorado in the 1930s. He went on to play professionally for the Pittsburgh Pirates (who became the Steelers in 1940) and the Detroit Lions, and was one of the first big-money players in the National Football League. In the off season, he went to Yale for law school and in 1946–1947 was a law clerk to then–Chief Justice Fred Vinson. His early press attention caused him to dislike the media, and he especially hated the college nickname of "Whizzer" that stuck through the years. So it was now White's habit to stand in the background. He had become a man of few words with a gruff demeanor. When he announced the majority opinion in a case, he would rarely read more than one or two sentences of it from the bench, in contrast to his colleagues who would go on for several minutes so that spectators would actually know what had been decided. Feared for his viselike handshake, White was a regular on the building's top-floor basketball court. He decided each case on its facts and resisted broad judicial philosophies.[24] By the time O'Connor joined the Court, he was voting more and more with the conservative wing. He and O'Connor were neither natural allies nor adversaries. Their Western origins gave them a common bond, and they had the distinction of being the first two justices publicly spotted dancing together. "The fleet-footed pair," as a *Washington Post* Style writer described them in a December 1981 item, waltzed at the Sulgrave Club ballroom in Washington, D.C.[25]

More distant from his colleagues was Thurgood Marshall, 73, the first African-American justice and a consistent defender of individual rights. Appointed by President Lyndon B. Johnson in 1967, Marshall was a physically imposing man with a distinctive gravelly voice. Born and raised in Baltimore, he wore his hair slicked back and sported a bushy mustache and big, square glasses. His father was a yacht-club steward, his mother an elementary-school teacher. The great-grandson of a slave brought to the United States from Africa, Marshall drew his name from a paternal grandfather, who had chosen "Thorough Good" for himself when enlisting in the Union Army during the Civil War. Marshall later changed it to Thurgood. He graduated from the all-black Lincoln University in Chester, Pennsylvania, and then obtained his law degree from Howard University. As a lawyer for the National Association for the Advancement of Colored People (NAACP), Marshall played a crucial role in developing the strategy to challenge the "separate but equal" doctrine and win the series of cases culminating in *Brown v. Board of Education* (1954). On the Court, Marshall continued to side with minorities and the underprivileged. He opposed the death penalty in every case. By 1981, he was increasingly impatient with the continuing struggle of blacks in

America, and easily dispirited. At Court social occasions, he sometimes looked like a man who had made it into a club he would rather not have joined. But he was a raconteur, a teller of the hundreds of stories he had lived—and that endeared him to O'Connor. Sharing the distinction of "firsts" in the ranks of this legal fraternity, Marshall and O'Connor felt a special bond.[26]

Harry Blackmun, 72, a 1970 Nixon appointee, was a hard worker who seemed plagued by self-doubt. Born in Nashville, Illinois, he grew up in St. Paul, Minnesota, where his father owned a grocery and hardware store. A small, wiry man with piercing eyes and graying hair, he had received a scholarship to Harvard College, where he majored in mathematics, then stayed for a law degree. Drawn to both medicine and the law, he became resident counsel at the Mayo Clinic in Rochester, Minnesota. Blackmun and Burger, old friends from St. Paul, were allied at first and dubbed the "Minnesota Twins" by the press. But over the years, Blackmun had moved to the left. He was best known for writing the 1973 *Roe v. Wade* decision that made abortion legal nationwide and transformed American society and politics. Blackmun's most suspicious and testiest side typically emerged in quarrels with Chief Justice Burger, the friend who now seemed to have little regard for him.[27]

When aides to Burger notified the justices that Burger would be reviewing their requests for guest seating at O'Connor's investiture, Blackmun fired off a memo to Marshal Wong. "I have already indicated to your office that I would like my seats in the box reserved for Mrs. Blackmun, our daughter Sally, and Sally's husband. I would like assurance that both my secretaries, the husband of [one of the secretaries], my law clerks and my messenger will be able to attend. I assume the law clerks will have available the usual seats in the front of the west side. If seats are not available for the secretaries there, I would like them to be placed in the seats allowed to me in the body of the courtroom. I emphasize front seats because my clerks have so much to do that they are not able to get in an hour in advance to acquire the better seats." When Wong wrote back saying he could not confirm seats and that Burger's chambers would have the final say, Blackmun immediately sent a second memo saying, "I expect my usual seats to be available to me at the ceremony . . . and I insist that your office reserve them for me."[28] Blackmun's prickliness was well known. Passing through the receiving line at O'Connor's investiture, retired justice Arthur Goldberg told Blackmun that he had better be nice to the new justice.[29] That turned out to be a challenge. Blackmun was the only justice who made regular use of the justices' small private library, down a corridor from a larger ornate library available to all Court staff. When O'Connor broke the pattern and showed up in what he considered his quarters, he harrumphed and let her (and the rest of his colleagues) know he thought she was intruding.

In marked contrast, Lewis Powell, 74, a 1972 Nixon appointee, was the gentlemanly peacemaker in the group. After publication of *The Brethren,* he took the unusual step, as the New Year of 1980 was dawning, of toasting in a memo to all of the justices "our Chief who has borne the recent highly commercialized libel with urbanity, dignity, and wonderous good humor."[30] Powell was a descendant of one of the original Jamestown colonists and a native of Virginia's Tidewater region. His father was a successful businessman in Richmond, his mother a homemaker. Powell had a law degree from Washington and Lee and a master's degree in law from Harvard. He was slender, with spectacles and gray hair, a toothy smile, and impeccable courtesy. As an Army Air Corps intelligence officer during World War II, he helped decipher German military communications. On the Court, Powell was the voice of moderation and the classic "man in the middle" on the substance of the law.

As his history in Phoenix and then the Nixon Justice Department championing government surveillance techniques had suggested, William Rehnquist was the sure conservative on the Court by the time O'Connor joined. He had a minimalist view of constitutional protection for individual rights, which often left him in lone dissent. But socially, his wry sense of humor and ready grin put him in good stead with his colleagues. One April 1, he hired a man to stand with a life-size photo of Chief Justice Warren Burger outside the Court and offer tourists a chance to pose for pictures with it.[31] Now slightly stooped from a bad back, Rehnquist knew O'Connor as well as anyone in Washington, D.C. did, and, at 57, was closest to O'Connor in age on the Court.

Soon after she arrived, Rehnquist and his wife, Nan, hosted a dinner for her. Nan Rehnquist prepared all the food herself in a Court kitchen, using hired help only to tend the bar and serve the dinner. It was a feat that impressed the other justices. This social occasion aside, Rehnquist was not able to offer much help as his old classmate learned the ropes in the early months of her tenure. He had his own troubles. The painkillers he was taking for longtime back problems were causing him to slur and stutter, on and off the bench. Moreover, a few weeks before the term began, he caught viral pneumonia. His run of bad luck included losing his wallet when he went to the Bethesda Naval Hospital Emergency Room to be treated.[32]

John Paul Stevens, 61, a 1975 appointee of Gerald Ford, was silver-haired, with an easy manner and lack of pretense. The son of a wealthy Chicago developer and an English teacher, he graduated first in his class at the University of Chicago and at Northwestern University law school. Between undergraduate and law school, he was a naval officer in World War II, earning a Bronze Star. Like White and Rehnquist, Stevens had been at the Court before, as a law clerk to Justice Wiley B. Rutledge in the 1947–1948 term. Stevens was not a crusader for either ideological side. But, unlike Powell, he had a distinct, sometimes idiosyncratic, approach to the law that often found him in lone dissent rather than in the middle. Stevens was slowly amassing a record on the left. With his bow ties and familiar stance of crossed arms, a hand holding his chin, Stevens some-times resembled comedian Jack Benny. But he was a serious competitor who had won national bridge and tennis championships. He piloted his own small airplane.

Before each conference meeting, the nine justices shook hands all around. O'Connor liked that. Touching hands made people feel closer, less antagonistic, she believed. The nine were alone in conference, but they came with materials prepared by their law clerks. It was those recent law school graduates, typically the cream of their Ivy League schools, who first winnowed down the seven thousand or so annual petitions to the Court. Four votes were needed to accept a case (to actually decide the case required five votes). In the early 1980s, the justices were taking about 150 cases for review each term as they sat, clerks' memos in hand, voting aloud by seniority, starting with the chief justice.

The procedures were new to O'Connor, so she worked hard to avoid missteps. She regularly asked her law clerks to come into the office on Saturdays. She brought lunch, usually a crockpot full of chili or other meal influenced by her Southwestern background. For each case the Court accepted for briefing and argument, she read as much background material as possible, including the parties' briefs, memos prepared by her law clerks, and law review articles. "I think that most everything you do in life requires preparation," she said at the time, "and if you are prepared and have thought about it, then things won't be a problem. If you feel you are not prepared . . . that's grounds for concern."[33]

She asked many questions in the private conference and from the bench, sometimes writing these questions out beforehand. The *New York Times* called her an "impeccably prepared questioner" who at times "has left lawyers squirming in discomfort."[34] But it was she who was being more closely watched, by people both inside and outside the Court. Many of the justices were still taking her measure, although by late October, Powell wrote to his children: "Justice O'Connor is off to an impressive start. It is quite evident that she is intellectually up to the work of the Court. Perhaps I have said before that she is the Number One celebrity in this town."[35]

The Reagan administration had brought new social glitter to the nation's capital, and O'Connor was an immediate A-list attendee. At one point in her first term, *Newsweek* reported, "If O'Connor's jurisprudential position is still undefined, her social standing couldn't be clearer. She and her husband, John, who is practicing law in Washington, have their pick of parties. She plays tennis weekly with a foursome that often includes the wife of her predecessor, Potter Stewart. And she has kept in touch with old friends, relying on visiting Arizonans to bring fresh tortillas that she turns into crab-meat enchiladas." The magazine also said people would ask for her autograph when she went grocery shopping.[36]

The *Washington Post* later wrote that O'Connor "hit the Washington party circuit hard even before she received the Senate's blessing to sit on the high bench. . . . Since then she has been as visible on the social scene as the ubiquitous purple Ridgewell's [high-end catering] truck."[37] As her clerks in the early years attested, if there was a state dinner, an exclusive theater opening, even a new panda at the National Zoo, O'Connor was there. She was game for anything, and insisted on exposing her law clerks, too, to the sights of Washington. She took them to museums, the National Archives, and on jaunts to see the annual spring blooming of the cherry blossoms at the Tidal Basin along the Potomac River.

John O'Connor, who accepted a job with the law firm of Miller and Chevalier in Washington, D.C., told the *Ladies' Home Journal* it was not hard to be the spouse of the first woman justice, in part because of all the opportunities in the nation's capital: "My life has become vastly broadened and vastly enriched by her appointment. I am not only happy for Sandra because she is so competent and so deserving, but I am happy for myself and my family because all our lives have become more interesting. Sandra's accomplishments don't make me a lesser man; they make me a fuller man."[38]

In addition to the public oral arguments—the hourly sessions held Monday, Tuesday, and Wednesday, in which lawyers for each side of a case argued before the justices—there was a steady pattern to the Court's work that involved the screening of requests for review, the study of the papers in cases accepted for argument, and the crafting of decisions in cases already heard. Each case was put to a vote within a few days of oral arguments. The most senior justice in the majority decided who would write the opinion for the Court. The most senior member of the losing side assigned the main opinion for the dissenting viewpoint. The other justices were free to write their own statements, but it was the majority opinion that spoke for the Court and guided lower-court judges.

A Supreme Court majority opinion, while specifically addressed to the facts of the case at hand, established precedent for all similar disputes. So, for example, if the justices struck down a particular city contracting policy as racially discriminatory, all similar policies nationwide were, by implication, invalidated. If the Court majority declared one state's abortion regulations unconstitutional, similar regulations would be implicitly voided.[39]

The justices sometimes found it difficult to write an opinion that garnered a ready majority, because of variations in their legal approaches. Sometimes justices discovered through crafting an opinion and trying to justify it with prior Court rulings that the case was not what it seemed. That happened early to O'Connor, when, in her first month, she surprisingly switched her vote in a case brought by taxpayers in St. Louis County who claimed their property was being unconstitutionally overassessed. "When we discussed this case at conference, we had been told at oral argument that the [taxpayers] had exhausted their remedies [at the state level] as to some of their claims. A closer inspection of [their] complaint, however, reveals that state administrative remedies" remain open. "Wow," Powell later wrote in a note to his clerks. But the taxpayer dispute was not a close case, so her switch did not affect its outcome.[40]

They all worked simultaneously on several cases. There was no apparent horse-trading, as there was in the legislative and executive branches. A justice would not be inclined to swap a vote for a colleague in one case in exchange for his vote in another dispute. In the same vein, a justice might have been angered by a colleague's position in one case but turn around and join him (or her) in another the same day. These negotiations played out on paper, amid a constant flow of memos and draft opinions, all constituting a conversation leading to a decision announced to the public. Generally, the nine justices kept all colleagues in the written conversation but sometimes—and this was when it got interesting—conversations played out in factions, rivalries developed, pairs of justices broke off.

And so it was in O'Connor's first term. Conservative and liberal factions split off to work privately on some opinions. And the seeds of her relationships with other justices were sown, as she collaborated with Powell, fell into an adversary role with Brennan, and was a regular target for Blackmun's cutting remarks. At one point, Blackmun wrote of O'Connor's arguments in a first-term case: "While these rhetorical devices make for absorbing reading, they unfortunately are substituted for useful constitutional analysis." She tried to stay cool in the face of provocation. She responded to Blackmun's criticism by calling it "disingenuous" and "absurd."[41]

O'Connor's substantive approach emerged, too. She was tough on criminal defendants and became a leading proponent of limiting state prisoners' appeals to federal courts. She also articulated a line of reasoning on the federal-state relationship that would become, over time, her signature. For decades, the Court she joined had been allowing an expansive regulatory role for the federal government, at a cost to the states' own agendas and autonomy. In a dissenting opinion during her first term, the former Arizona legislator offered a blueprint for reversing that trend and protecting states from federal intervention. "State legislative and administrative bodies are not field offices of the national bureaucracy," she wrote. A quarter century later, her view was generally that of the majority.

IMMEDIATELY IN THE FALL of 1981, disputes over prisoners' appeals roused O'Connor's states' rights interest. They also landed her in the middle of an ideologically split bench—a position that would become all too familiar. The case of *Rose v. Lundy,* involving a Tennessee prisoner, came to her and the other justices as all cases did: distilled into a bloodless, dispassionate set of briefs with page limits, margin standards, and requisite colors for the covers (blue, red, green, or gray, depending on who was filing). Federal law permitted state prisoners, after they had lost state court appeals, to challenge their convictions through petitions to federal courts for writs of habeas corpus. Loosely translated from the Latin, "habeas corpus" stood for "you have the body," and a writ ordered the government holding the prisoner to release him so he could make his case in court. Inmates sought the writ, for example, to claim violations of the right to counsel, the privilege against self-incrimination, or other constitutional guarantees.

Sometimes referred to as the "Great Writ," habeas corpus had long been viewed as central to personal liberty in the face of government oppression. By the early 1980s, however, Reagan administration officials and other conservatives argued that the writ was overused, that prisoners were bringing frivolous petitions, and that federal courts were interfering with state judgments. It irked conservatives that a single Federal judge could overturn a conviction that had been imposed and upheld by state trial and appellate courts.

O'Connor had spent four years on an Arizona trial court and one and a half years on an appellate bench, and she had strong opinions in this area. "[S]tate appellate court judges occasionally become so frustrated with the extent of federal court intervention that they simply abdicate in favor of the federal jurisdiction," she had written in an article in the *William and Mary Law Review* the year before her appointment. She began the piece by saying, "We appear to be the only major country with two parallel court systems," and asserted that "the labyrinth of judicial reviews of the various stages of a state criminal felony case would appear strange, indeed, to a rational person charged with devising an ideal criminal justice system."[42]

What might have been a lofty and arcane debate over judicial review often made newspaper headlines, because prisoners' access to federal courts through habeas corpus regularly determined the fate of the condemned on state death rows. The Supreme Court had broadly struck down states' capital punishment systems in 1972, saying they were arbitrary in operation, but then made clear four years later that states could cure the problem by adding safeguards to their sentencing processes. Still, the ultimate punishment remained an uneasy topic for the justices. A vivid reminder came during a session of oral arguments soon after O'Connor joined the Court. As the justices were hearing a death row appeal from a 16-year-old Oklahoma boy guilty of the unprovoked shotgun murder of a policeman, Rehnquist asked a lawyer for the state of Oklahoma whether it would be cheaper "from the taxpayers' point of view" to execute the defendant than to confine him for years of psychiatric treatment for his turbulent childhood. The normally quiet Justice Marshall jumped in: "Well, it would be cheaper just to shoot him when you arrested him, wouldn't it?"[43] Public opinion polls showed Americans favoring capital punishment, but as Powell had put it in a note to Rehnquist a few months earlier, "In theory there is a substantial majority sentiment for capital punishment. In practice there simply is no stomach for it."[44] With O'Connor's new vote, a Burger Court majority began losing patience with the long delays in executions and sought to ensure that death sentences were carried out.

The fall 1981 habeas corpus case involved a Tennessee man who had been sentenced to 120 years in prison for rape and sodomy. Noah Lundy made several claims to a federal court in challenging his conviction.[45] Some of Lundy's claims, however, had not been fully aired in state court, as was required before a state prisoner turned to federal court. Nonetheless, a federal judge decided to go ahead and consider all of Lundy's allegations and ended up overturning Lundy's conviction. Tennessee officials appealed, saying the judge should have dismissed the so-called "mixed" petition and insisted that all claims be exhausted in state court before any of them could be considered in federal court. But the U.S. Court of Appeals for the Sixth Circuit affirmed.

Now state officials were before the justices, urging them to reverse the decision favoring Lundy. Defendants' right advocates were closely watching the case because prisoners, who often filed habeas petitions without the benefit of legal help, generally did not understand that they could present claims for federal habeas only if they first had presented the claims in state court. As a result, a large percentage of the petitions to federal courts presented a complicated mix of both exhausted and unexhausted claims.

In their conference, a majority of the justices sided with Tennessee against Lundy. Burger assigned the opinion for the Court to O'Connor. On November 23, she circulated to the other justices a draft opinion holding that U.S. district court judges must dismiss such "mixed petitions" without considering any of the claims, leaving the prisoner to return to state court to present the "unexhausted" claims or to amend the habeas petition to present only exhausted claims to the U.S. district court. She also wrote that a prisoner risked forfeiting review of his unexhausted claims in federal court if "he decides to proceed only with his exhausted claims and deliberately sets aside his unexhausted claims" in the face of a U.S. judge's refusal to consider his mixed petition.

Burger and Rehnquist immediately endorsed her opinion. In opposition, Stevens told her that he was "persuaded that the position taken . . . will increase rather than lessen the burdens on both state and federal judges." Blackmun also said he would dissent, believing that O'Connor's standards were "a trap for the uneducated and indigent" prisoners. He also thought it would delay the resolution of claims that were not frivolous, and increase, rather than lessen, the caseload burdens on both state and federal courts.[46]

The longest, most detailed response came from Brennan, who said he believed she was misinterpreting a major 1963 Court precedent on habeas corpus petitions. That case, *Fay v. Noia,* was written by Brennan and had allowed state prisoners in some circumstances to challenge imprisonment through habeas corpus even if they had not already appealed through state courts.[47] "My analysis is so at odds with yours that I cannot join your opinion as it now stands," Brennan wrote at the end of three single-spaced pages. That memo and those from the others prompted Rehnquist to write O'Connor one of the more prescient notes of their early years together: "I am sure you realize by the conference discussion and the letter which Bill Brennan has sent you today that you are 'in the middle' where you will probably find yourself on more than one occasion." But Rehnquist had a more substantive message: "I was somewhat disappointed that your opinion did not place any more stringent requirements on the availability of habeas corpus to state prisoners than it did, but am willing to go along with it as it now stands. If it were to be changed to meet Bill Brennan's criticism, I could not join it. . . ."[48]

The middle position might have been new to O'Connor on the Court, but it was not new in the span of her career. In her legislative days, O'Connor took naturally to the role of consensus builder across ideological and political lines. Coincidentally, the day Rehnquist wrote his note, November 25, O'Connor was back in Arizona for a "welcome home" gala organized by Democratic governor Bruce Babbitt. More than two hundred people gathered on the state Capitol grounds under cloudy skies to honor O'Connor, who, in turn, declared, "It's not Sandra Day O'Connor who brought honor to Arizona, but Arizona that brought honor to Sandra Day O'Connor."[49]

Back at the Supreme Court, she amended some of her references to prior case law as Brennan requested, and separated out passages to which he objected, so he could specifically dissent from that portion of her opinion and join other parts. But the concessions were small. She stuck with the stance that would make it harder for state prisoners to get into federal court—and insulate some state courts decisions from federal review.

"The most telling part of Justice O'Connor's opinion," Richard Cordray and James Vradelis later wrote for the *University of Chicago Law Review*, "was her suggestion . . . that a prisoner should be required to present all claims together, in the same petition for the federal writ, and to do so only when they have all been exhausted [in state court]. . . . In other words, Justice O'Connor seems to regard the shift from seeking state remedies to seeking federal relief as more akin to crossing the Rubicon than it is to crossing the street to another courtroom."[50]

A few weeks later, another case involving prisoners' access to federal courts arose—and it cast in stark relief both the legal and stylistic differences between O'Connor and Brennan. Three inmates were seeking federal court review of alleged flaws in their trials in the state courts of Ohio. They had appealed their convictions for various violent crimes and had lost. They then began filing habeas corpus petitions challenging the jury instructions used by the judges at their respective trials. None had made these objections earlier, and the legal question was whether they could raise a constitutional claim in federal court after forfeiting it under state procedures. Lower federal courts sided with the prisoners, reasoning that because relevant Ohio law had not become clear until after the convictions, the prisoners' lawyers reasonably believed that objections would be futile.

Siding with the state, O'Connor's opinion for the Court said the prisoners had lost their right to make the claims. The writ of habeas corpus "extends the ordeal of trial for both society and the accused," she wrote, explaining that rigid rules are necessary for "finality" of punishments. With a nod to her own experience, she added, "Over the long term . . . federal intrusions may seriously undermine the morale of our state judges."[51]

O'Connor's opinion was signed in full by Burger, Rehnquist, White, and Powell. Dissenting, Stevens criticized the opinion for its "preoccupation with procedural hurdles." Blackmun agreed that the lower-court ruling should be reversed, but applied wholly different legal reasoning. The most stinging response to O'Connor's opinion came from Brennan: "Today's decision is a conspicuous exercise in judicial activism," Brennan began. When Powell saw that line in Brennan's draft, he wrote to one of his clerks: "No one is kinder or more generous than WJB until he takes up his pen in dissent." To the charge of judicial activism, Powell penned, "Who's calling who what!?"[52]

Brennan accused O'Connor of distorting facts in the case to reach her result. He referred to O'Connor's decision as "incomprehensible," containing "several pages of tortuous reasoning." Then, with a clerk-inspired rhetorical flourish that has survived the decades and become part of Court lore, Brennan accused her of disregarding her own ruling in *Rose v. Lundy,* released a few weeks earlier. "Sic transit Gloria Lundy," Brennan punned, with the loose translation being "Thus passes the glory of Lundy." He continued the pun: "In scarcely a month, the bloom is off the Rose."[53]

O'Connor responded in footnotes that Brennan's views "carry more rhetorical force than substance." News reporters called it one of the sharpest exchanges of the term, and the *Wall Street Journal* used it as Exhibit A to refer to "a pattern of unusual sarcasm from Justice Brennan" and to comment on the fact that tensions seemed higher this first year of a woman justice.[54]

However, one notable clash between O'Connor and Brennan occurred under reporters' radar at the time, just as the Court was about to take its Christmas recess. As the justices turned away from the immediacy of regular oral arguments, they began to address issues of their burgeoning caseload. It was a problem that had been building for years, but it suddenly became obvious that the justices had added so many cases to their argument calendar that it was already booked through April, when oral arguments end. Normally, cases would continue to be added through the end of January.

Within the privacy of their cloister, O'Connor made a proposal. Influenced by Burger and Rehnquist, who were most persistent in seeking a more efficient judicial machine, she suggested they have the formal option to dispense with oral arguments in cases that have been accepted for review and to resolve the disputes after simply ordering written briefs from the parties. "Would it help to amend our rules to provide for the option of ordering briefs without oral argument? If so, a simple revision in the form attached might suffice," she wrote to her eight colleagues.[55]

Burger readily endorsed the idea in a memo to all the justices. So did Rehnquist. "As one who earlier proposed something in the nature of what Sandra has suggested in her letter to you of December 14th," Rehnquist wrote to all of his colleagues, "I am in substantial accord with the proposed change in rules which she suggests in that letter." Some of the others were more tentative. Powell said he "could agree with Sandra's proposed change" but said, "My only concern is that we might abuse this privilege. I believe in the utility of oral argument, and also in the symbolism it portrays for the public. Accordingly, if the rule is changed as suggested, I would hope that we would use this option sparingly."

Stevens wanted to study the proposal further. "I would hope that we could postpone a decision on Sandra's proposed amendment . . . until a time when we can consider it in the context of other changes in our procedures that we might want to adopt."[56]

Most of them seemed willing to at least discuss O'Connor's suggestion and explore other ways to address what was truly getting to be a problematic workload. But not Brennan. He fired off a mortar that made his position clear: "Dear Chief: I could *not* agree to Sandra's proposed change. . . . I expect my reaction is influenced by my New Jersey experience [and] the [past] practice of the [state's] highest court in deciding almost all cases on briefs without oral argument. The low quality of final judgments was traced directly to that practice . . . Thus the New Jersey Supreme Court rule [now] requires oral argument of every case granted review. Lewis rightly says that one of the values of oral argument is the 'symbolism it portrays for the public.' For me, that is a very cherished value because it enhances the public image of our complete impartiality." Sending copies to all the justices, Brennan closed with a warning that ratcheted things up and ultimately ended the discussion: "I feel so strongly about this that I must publicly dissent if the rule is changed."[57]

Brennan felt no need to indulge the new justice or acknowledge that it might be a start to discussion of other options. The substantive legal views of Brennan and O'Connor differed sharply. But they were even more at odds personally. She did not go for his natural cajoling. And to Brennan's mind, his usual "Hiya, pal" greeting and linking of arms with a justice on the walk to conference did not seem right with the first woman. Perhaps it was inevitable that these two personally different but politically savvy jurists would clash.

Still, Brennan and O'Connor were smart enough to know they needed to find common ground. She would not let on that she felt slighted. It was not Brennan's style to hold a grudge, either. Hers was a vote he needed, and as he always said, "With five votes you can do anything." Sometimes, as he made that remark, he would hold out his hand, with his five fingers splayed, suggesting, "Five, count 'em, five."

In the court of public opinion, O'Connor was more than fitting in. Gallup Poll's annual survey of the "most admired women" listed her third, behind First Lady Nancy Reagan and British prime minister Margaret Thatcher. Meanwhile, a survey of 107 women executives in some of America's largest corporations reported that a majority admired Justice O'Connor more than any other public person, man or woman. She and her husband, John, spent New Year's Eve in Palm Springs. Their hosts were Walter Annenberg, billionaire publisher and former U.S. ambassador to Great Britain, and his wife, Lee, serving as U.S. chief of protocol. President Reagan and top administration officials also attended, and O'Connor began 1982 playing a round of golf with Reagan, Attorney General William French Smith, and Secretary of State Alexander Haig.[58]

Back in Washington, as the calendar page turned over, Rehnquist's health took another dive. He was hospitalized for severe back pain and treated for a withdrawal reaction to the painkiller drug he was taking to help him sleep. The drug had caused his noticeable slurring during oral arguments. When he returned to the bench two weeks later, his speech was clearer, and no longer did lawyers have to ask him to repeat his questions.[59]

The new year also brought record low temperatures. Snow and high winds whipped Washington, D.C. By January 13, blizzard conditions made roads throughout the area impassable, and the city's Metro rail system was partially shut down. Chief Justice Burger encouraged his colleagues and the staff to leave early. O'Connor drove herself home through the snow. It took the justices several hours to go just a few miles, but they had not yet seen the worst of the day. Shortly after four p.m., as the snowstorm continued, an Air Florida Boeing 737 tried to take off from National Airport, clipped a bridge, and plunged into the icy Potomac River. Seventy-six people, including two motorists, were killed and dozens were injured. It was a brutal way for Washington to start the year.

At the Court, Brennan was beginning a series of behind-the-scenes maneuvers that would lead to a ruling prohibiting states from denying a free public education to children of illegal immigrants. Brennan's moves in the case from Texas offered a window into the careful attention required to build a majority and the power that comes to a swing-vote justice.[60]

Plyler v. Doe began as a class-action lawsuit on behalf of schoolchildren of Mexican origin in Smith County, Texas, who had come to the United States with their illegal-alien parents. Since 1977, the Tyler Independent School District had required "undocumented" children to pay tuition rather than enroll free-of-charge as other children did. Lower federal courts held that the exclusion of the children from free public education violated the Constitution's equal-protection guarantee.

Brennan realized that if he was going to secure a majority, he had to make some quiet moves in advance. At conference a few weeks earlier, four of his colleagues had been inclined to agree with him and forbid schools from shutting their doors to children of immigrants. But their reasons were not unanimous, and Powell, who would be the critical vote, was especially ambivalent. "It's hard," he said. "On equal protection, I would recognize that the classification is children and that they have no responsibility for being there. It is hard to think of a category more helpless than the children of illegal aliens. I don't think that education is a fundamental right, but if some children get it I can't see how they can deny it to others." The morning of the conference meeting, according to Richard Fallon, one of Powell's clerks, the justice had arrived at the Court looking as if he had not slept.[61]

Proper education of the nation's children was deeply important to the man who had been president of the Richmond School Board and then head of the Virginia State Board of Education. But for Powell, a legal rationale was problematic. Eight years earlier, Powell had authored an opinion saying the Constitution held no fundamental right to public education. In fact, as Stanford University law professor Gerald Gunther wrote, that 1973 case of *San Antonio Independent School District v. Rodriguez* embodied the post–Warren Court's reluctance to expand the constitutional guarantee of equal protection of the law to new areas.[62]

Aware of the difficult task ahead, on January 25, Brennan wrote to Powell, "I am taking what is for me the unusual step of circulating only to you, Thurgood, Harry and John, an un-proofread draft of a proposed opinion for the Court in the alien children cases." Brennan knew that he, Powell, Marshall, Blackmun, and Stevens would have to cooperate if he was going to keep the majority. He also knew that if he kept his draft quiet, his conservative adversaries would not have a chance to criticize it or make their own pitch to Powell at the same time.[63]

Powell told Brennan he would join a bottom-line judgment favoring the children, but he was not sure he could accept Brennan's legal rationale. Brennan worked for weeks to come up with a more measured approach to the issue of constitutional equality in education to satisfy Powell. In the end, even after Burger began pressuring Powell to switch his vote, Powell signed Brennan's opinion, as did Marshall, Blackmun, and Stevens.[64]

On June 15, 1982, Brennan announced that the Supreme Court would not tolerate the creation of an "underclass" in American society, one permanently oppressed by the denial of a free public education. His opinion said, "Public education is not a 'right' granted to individuals by the Constitution. But neither is it merely some government 'benefit' indistinguishable from other forms of social welfare legislation. Both the importance of education in maintaining our basic institutions, and the lasting impact of its deprivation on the life of the child, mark the distinction." Writing for the four dissenting justices, Burger responded that,

"The Constitution does not provide a cure for every social ill, nor does it vest judges with a mandate to try to remedy every social problem. When this Court rushes in to remedy what it perceives to be the failings of the political process, it deprives those processes of an opportunity to function." O'Connor, who was the Court's only native of a border state, joined Burger's opinion and apparently felt no compunction to write any separate statement. (It would become clear in cases through the years that this Arizonan was not especially sympathetic to the plight of foreigners who had illegally crossed U.S. borders.)[65]

A week after *Plyler v. Doe,* Powell, again navigating the middle, gained a majority in a divisive case testing presidential immunity from civil lawsuits for damages. A. Ernest Fitzgerald, a widely publicized whistleblower of the late 1960s, lost his position with the Department of the Air Force in 1970. He was fired, he claimed, because of his testimony before a congressional subcommittee about cost overruns in the design and construction of the C5-A transport plane. Fitzgerald's lawsuit asserted a violation of his First Amendment and statutory rights, and the named defendants included former president Nixon as well as other officials. The issue for the Supreme Court was whether the president could be sued for his acts in office. As Powell labored to keep a majority together for an opinion giving the president immunity from such civil suits, Burger warned him not to make any concessions to Justice White, who was writing the main dissent. "Let Byron rant," Burger told Powell, and "don't fall into the trap of answering him and rendering the opinion unacceptable to me." The finished ruling emphasized that "Because of the singular importance of the President's duties, diversion of his energies by concern with private lawsuits would raise unique risks to the effective functioning of government." In a biting dissent, Justice White, joined by Brennan, Marshall, and Blackmun, called the majority position "tragic." Wrote White: "Attaching absolute immunity to the office of the President, rather than to particular activities that the President might perform, places the President above the law. It is a reversion to the old notion that the King can do no wrong . . ."[66]

O'Connor increasingly turned to Powell as she felt her way through the rigid customs of the Court and Washington protocol. She and her husband, John, dined often with him and his wife, Josephine. At one point, after the *Washington Post* published an article that she believed took her comments at a public hearing out of context, Powell penned a handwritten note telling her to disregard it. "Some reporters make a living trying to make public officials look irresponsible," he wrote. "Dear Lewis," she wrote back. "No wonder all who know you speak of you in the most glowing fashion. Thank you. I will chalk it up to experience."[67]

The other seven justices, with their varying temperaments, tried to keep up a collegial spirit, particularly as they faced June deadlines. It was the most difficult month, when all the opinions were to be completed and "holding five" votes for a Court-majority opinion became all the more urgent. By this month, most of the Court's easiest cases had been decided and the knottiest ones remained. There were constant negotiations over legal reasoning, down to individual paragraphs and footnotes. Justices regularly compromised on language to keep a colleague's needed fifth vote. And they found other ways to avoid needless friction. In O'Connor's first June, Rehnquist wrote to Justice Marshall in a child welfare case, with copies all around: "If this were November rather than June, I would prepare a masterfully crafted dissenting opinion exposing the fallacies of your . . . discussion. Since it is June, however, I join." That was an easy one for Rehnquist: Marshall already had all the other justices with him on the opinion.[68]

In a separate case, Marshall added some humor to the deadline crunch after he lost the majority in a dispute testing the constitutionality of the Illinois Business Take-Over Act in the case of *Edgar v. Mite.* On June 18, after Rehnquist and Burger suddenly had switched votes and Justice White had firmly claimed the majority, Marshall charted the twists and turns in the case for his colleagues:[69]

1. Justice Marshall circulates opinion for the Court.
2. Justice Brennan joins.
3. Justice Rehnquist joins.
4. Justice Powell joins.
5. Justice White circulates a dissent.
6. Justice Stevens circulates a dissent.
7. Justice Blackmun joins Justice White.
8. Justice O'Connor joins Justice Stevens.
9. The Chief Justice joins Justice Marshall.
10. Justice Rehnquist changes his vote.

11. The Chief Justice changes his vote.
12. Justice White circulates opinion for the Court.
13. Justice Marshall circulates a dissent.
14. Justice Brennan joins Justice Marshall.
15. Justice Stevens circulates concurring opinion.
16. Justice Rehnquist circulates a dissent.
17. The Chief Justice joins Justice White.
18. Justice O'Connor concurs.
19. Justice Powell concurs.
20. Justice Blackmun concurs.

Such efforts at good humor coexisted with some sniping. A majority opinion O'Connor wrote in June 1982 enhancing the ability of employers to limit the back pay they owed in job-discrimination cases provoked a caustic Blackmun dissent. He said she "simply and completely misstates the issue" and declared that her opinion "only confirms how far removed from the real world" she is. O'Connor responded to it in a footnote but said she did not want to engage in an "ad hominem," or personal argument, with Blackmun.[70]

Another spat erupted when she dissented from his opinion in a federal energy regulation case. Blackmun's opinion for the majority rejected arguments that the Tenth Amendment, which reserved to the states powers not expressly given to the federal government, protected Mississippi from restrictions under a federal energy conservation law. Blackmun's opinion for the Court upheld enforcement of a federal statute, requiring state utility regulators to consider adopting various pricing policies to spur conservation. Justice O'Connor filed a twenty-three-page dissenting opinion that laid out her view of the lines of authority between Washington and the states. It was a task that excited her as few others did that term.[71] She said that in finding the law constitutional, the majority "permits Congress to kidnap state utility commissions into the national regulatory family" and "undermines the most valuable aspects of our federalism." In one of her clearest and most passionate opinions, she said states were separate political units that must be able to operate without federal intervention. "I am not ready to surrender state legislative power to the Federal Energy Regulatory Commission," she concluded.

O'Connor's dissent, joined by Rehnquist and Burger, prompted

Blackmun to lash out in his majority opinion. He called her observations "apocalyptic . . . overstated and patently inaccurate."[72]

That did not bother O'Connor much. But a few weeks later, it was wholly different when she felt robbed of the majority. Blackmun withdrew his previous support for her opinion in a capital punishment case that same June. The question was whether the Eighth Amendment's prohibition on cruel and unusual punishment stopped a state from executing a defendant who had been convicted of a felony murder but who did not kill, or specifically intend to kill, the victim. The dispute in *Enmund v. Florida* dated to April 1, 1975, when Sampson and Jeanette Armstrong approached the backdoor of Thomas and Eunice Kersey's Florida farmhouse, pretending to need water for their overheated car. When Thomas Kersey retrieved a water jug, Sampson Armstrong grabbed him, held a gun to him, and told Jeanette Armstrong to take his wallet. Hearing her husband's cries for help, Eunice Kersey came around the side of the house with a gun and shot Jeanette Armstrong. The Armstrongs returned the fire, killing both of the Kerseys. Meanwhile, Earl Enmund had been in a parked car by the farmhouse, waiting to help the Armstrongs escape. He was convicted of murder and sentenced to die.

Enmund was challenging his death sentence, and O'Connor thought she had a majority of the Court to uphold it. When she ran a draft by Powell, he praised it and, realizing that Blackmun's vote was crucial, noted that "As you have largely followed Harry's reasoning in [a 1978 case involving crimes that warrant capital punishment], I would expect him to join." She then sent her draft opinion to all the other justices.

Blackmun was not persuaded, he wrote to White: "Sandra's opinion now has been joined by the Chief, Lewis and Bill Rehnquist, so she is close to having a Court [majority]. I find, however, that I cannot join [all] of her opinion." Blackmun proposed signing on to White's position that Enmund's death sentence be reversed, but also writing the following separate statement: "Although I continue to believe that the Eighth Amendment does not require in every case a finding of actual intent to kill before a capital sentence may be imposed . . . I agree with Justice White that the death penalty may not be inflicted where the defendant did not take life, did not attempt to take life, and did not intend to take life." Once Blackmun had cast his lot in with White, Brennan and Marshall joined White's rationale, too. Powell wrote to O'Connor, "It now appears that your fine opinion will not command a Court. The ironic result is that two Justices [Brennan and Marshall] who join Byron will never vote for capital punishment. Thus, you have a majority of the only seven Justices who really judge these cases."[73]

Blackmun's switch in *Enmund v. Florida* added to the exceptions the Court had begun to impose after reinstating the death penalty in 1976. Now it was clear that the death penalty could not be used as a punishment for rape (as the justices had said in a 1977 case) or for a defendant who participated in a murder but who did not commit the crime or intend to do so.

"I am somewhat frustrated and quite concerned that my draft failed to attract a majority," O'Connor wrote to Powell when the dust settled. "As you correctly observe, it is particularly ironic since it does represent a majority of those actually deciding these matters." But she added, "In this business one must learn to 'grin and bear it.' "[74]

O'Connor did not like to lose. But this was only the beginning. In time, she would figure out how to recoup her early defeats, including *Enmund v. Florida*.[75] Even for this first term, there was one more big case awaiting resolution. Or, as Professor Kenneth Karst would put it, "the Court faced a case that would become 'major' because of Justice O'Connor's opinion."[76]

7

THE GENDER TRAP

In her early months on the Supreme Court, Sandra Day O'Connor showed herself to be a conservative justice who wanted more deference to the states. But before her first term was out, that desire ran into a thorny case involving a state policy that discriminated on the basis of sex. Joe Hogan had been denied admission to an exclusively female, state-run nursing school in Mississippi. At the forefront of the case was a challenge to traditional notions of women's work and sexual stereotyping of men and women. Inside and outside the Court, there was great anticipation about how O'Connor would vote. Would she allow Mississippi to preserve its women-only school for nurses? Or would the new justice accept Hogan's argument that the school practiced unconstitutional sex discrimination with outdated notions of women and men? As she began to understand the rituals and customs among her long-tenured colleagues, the case of *Mississippi University for Women v. Hogan* offered O'Connor an early chance to make a mark on the law.

First at the lectern below the bench was Hunter M. Gholson, representing the Mississippi University for Women. "Mr. Chief Justice, and may it please the Court," Gholson said, opening with the requisite salutation this March 22, 1982. The room was quiet, rapt spectators sitting on the red, upholstered benches. Mississippi senator John Stennis, an old friend of Gholson, had just slipped into a seat near Gholson. Gholson understood that the venerable Stennis, who at the time had been in the Senate thirty-five years, was giving him a vote of confidence and showing the flag of Mississippi against those contesting its tradition of a women-only nursing school.[1]

"I would like to say at the outset that we are not here to perpetuate a nineteenth-century finishing school to teach young women needlecraft and kindergarten keeping," Gholson said. "Mississippi University for Women is a contemporary university which tries to prepare women to meet the challenges of today."[2] A year earlier, the U.S. Court of Appeals for the Fifth Circuit had struck down the ban on male students, saying that the state-run school had violated the Constitution's equality guarantee by excluding a man solely because of his sex. Gholson, a proud son of his native Mississippi, was hired by the school's alumnae association to take up the appeal. Instead of pouncing immediately, as was typical in more controversial cases, the justices let Gholson talk for a few minutes.

"I think it is interesting to look for a moment at the history," he said. This was the "first state-supported institution for the higher education of women in the country. It was founded in 1884, after the University of Mississippi had become co-educational, so it cannot be said that it was founded for the purpose of relegating women to some inferior school."

Arrayed along the bench from Gholson's left to right were: John Paul Stevens, Lewis Powell, Thurgood Marshall, William Brennan, Warren Burger, Byron White, Harry Blackmun, William Rehnquist, and Sandra Day O'Connor. Sitting erect in her high-back leather chair, O'Connor was well aware of the attention on her. Since her swearing-in six months earlier, the media glare had hardly dimmed, and she was viewed not as the new justice, but as the new *woman* justice. A few weeks earlier, she had passed on to Justice Powell a newspaper cartoon typical of the quips of the day. It was a sketch of Justice O'Connor sitting on the bench next to a curmudgeonly-looking man and saying, "Excuse me Mr. Powell, could you get us all some coffee?" Attaching a quick note, she told the man who was becoming her closest colleague: "I am forwarding it for a chuckle with your morning coffee."[3]

The case before them presented a nontraditional victim of stereotype and discrimination. Hogan, a 26-year-old surgical nurse at the Golden Triangle Regional Medical Center in Columbus, wanted to improve his job prospects. He had applied to the nearby Mississippi University for

Women for a bachelor's degree in nursing. As he told a reporter at the time, he was seeking the degree because "the trend is to eliminate the two-year nurse and make the four-year degree the only professional nurse."[4] Hogan said he had once hoped to attend medical school but could not afford it. Hogan was going with his best alternative—nursing school—yet he and his wife did not want to have to move away from Columbus to obtain the four-year degree. When Hogan was turned down by "The W," as the Mississippi University for Women was known locally, the rejection notice came with a printed sheet stating that the school accepted only women and that this exclusion had been approved by the courts.[5]

Hogan sued anyway, alleging unconstitutional sex discrimination. He lost before a U.S. district court judge, who said the state was justified in providing a specific program for women only. But on appeal, Hogan won at the Fifth Circuit. That panel declared that the policy excluding men violated the equal protection guarantee of the Constitution's Fourteenth Amendment. That court noted that men were able to audit nursing classes but were barred from joining the degree program. So, while women in the Columbus area who wanted a four-year nursing degree were provided a special school, there was no corresponding single-sex education for similarly situated men. The appellate court also pointed out that the state legislation that created the MUW was "based on role concepts for women that are no longer acceptable." At the core of its legal rationale, the Fifth Circuit agreed that Mississippi had "a significant and traditional purpose of providing for the education of all of its citizens," but it said the state's policy of "providing a unique educational opportunity for females but not for males . . . does not bear a substantial relationship to this important objective."[6]

As a result, in August 1981, Hogan became the first man in the school's ninety-seven year history to be admitted into the degree program—but not without protests from the students, faculty, and alumnae. "To me, his coming here is diametrically opposed to what, for nearly a century, Mississippians have calmly and quietly done well, and that is educate women," declared Carolyn Vance Smith, president of the alumnae association.[7]

Beyond the saga of one male nurse, Hogan's case arrived on the steps of the Supreme Court at a time of flux for women's prospects on the job and legal standards covering sex bias. As the *Washington Post* reported shortly after Ronald Reagan nominated O'Connor for the Court, although women were "still heavily concentrated in so-called female job ghettos such as the typing pool, government figures show small but meaningful signs of change in a number of previously male preserves." Using O'Connor's nomination as an angle on trends among working women, the story went on to say, "In 1960, when Sandra Day O'Connor was still an obscure attorney in private practice in Arizona, only 3.3 percent of her fellow lawyers and judges were women. . . . [W]hen she became the first woman nominated to the Supreme Court, that percentage had almost tripled." The report noted large gains for women in other fields—for example, accounting, banking, and medicine.[8] Conversely, there had been slight gains in the percentage of men in traditionally women's jobs, such as nursing.

The Supreme Court already was playing a role in changing attitudes toward sex stereotyping and the integration of the workplace. In the 1970s, it had begun applying tougher judicial scrutiny to government policies classifying people by sex. The Court rejected differences in Social Security benefits, terms of employment, and liquor laws. Many of the disputes that had ended up before the justices had been brought by men, such as Hogan, rather than by women. This was partly because of a strategy of women's rights lawyers, who sought to paint a picture for an overwhelmingly male judiciary of what it was like to be excluded because of sex. They also wanted to show that some laws ostensibly benefitting women were based on gender stereotypes.

In an important case from 1976, the Court threw out an Oklahoma statute that prohibited the sale of "non-intoxicating" 3.2 percent beer to males under 21, while allowing purchases by females at age 18.[9] A leading women's rights advocate, ACLU lawyer Ruth Bader Ginsburg, had argued in a "friend of the Court" brief that while the beer statute might appear to discriminate against men, "upon deeper inspection, the gender line drawn by Oklahoma is . . . a manifestation of traditional attitudes about the expected behavior of males and females, part of the myriad signals and messages that daily underscore the notion of men as society's active members, women as men's quiescent companions."[10] Striking down the drinking age double standard, the Supreme Court majority had invoked a test that would allow sex distinctions only when they were "substantially related to an important governmental goal." The majority in the case of *Craig v. Boren* observed that the government's objective was to decrease incidents of drinking and driving—the theory being that men drink and drive more than women. But the Court found that only 2 percent of men aged 18–21 were arrested for drunk driving. So, linking the ability to buy alcohol to the purchaser's sex was not "substantially related," as required, to the stated goal of preventing drinking and driving.[11]

But in two cases in early 1981, just months before O'Connor joined the Court, the justices had applied a seemingly more lenient test for government policies that enforced separate rules for men and women. The Court refused to invalidate a statutory rape law that punished men but not women and, separately, permitted the exclusion of women from military draft registration. Writing for the Court in both cases, Justice Rehnquist had said it did not breach the Constitution to treat men and women differently if they were not "similarly situated." Because of longstanding differences in the treatment of men and women, the "similarly situated" rule could be less demanding on government than the "substantially related" test from *Craig v. Boren.*

While sounding esoteric, the levels of "scrutiny" established by the justices to determine whether a governmental policy violated the Constitution's guarantee of equality were much of the battle for any two litigants. A challenged policy was more likely to be struck down if it were subjected to the strictest scrutiny, more likely to stand if subjected to the most lenient. Generally, government policies that classified people based on their race required the strictest scrutiny and least judicial deference. The Court would allow the policy only if it served a "compelling" governmental interest and was the "least restrictive" way to achieve that interest. Policies that separated people on the basis of gender generally were subjected to "intermediate" or "heightened" scrutiny. These laws could stand if, as *Craig v. Boren* dictated, they were "substantially related" to the achievement of an "important" objective. Finally, for routine governmental policies not specifically affecting any constitutionally protected class of people, the Court said judges should look simply at whether the policy was a "reasonable" measure designed to serve a "legitimate" government purpose. This easiest standard was known in the law as the "rational basis" test.

As O'Connor arrived, these standards seemed in flux. She came with her own experience and views, too, of course. The first woman justice had spoken compellingly of her own rejection by law firms after finishing Stanford Law School. "I had graduated high in my law school class and had been on the board of editors of the *Stanford Law Review* and had done all the things that, today, would qualify one for a very good position in a law firm," O'Connor said in one interview. "It did in those days, too, if you were a man."[12] In Arizona, as a state senator and then a judge, she had followed developments in bias law. She complained in the early 1970s that women were forced to work mainly as secretaries, waitresses, and teachers—earning about half of every $1 earned by a man—and she sponsored legislation that repealed a law barring women from working more than eight hours a day. But O'Connor was not known—even in Arizona—for the fervor that defined the women's movement nationally and helped Ruth Bader Ginsburg make her name.

In the courtroom, Gholson's attention went to his right, as Justices Rehnquist and O'Connor, next to each other, asked the early questions. Rehnquist, whose record in the area plainly put him on Gholson's side, posed the first query. If the flagship University of Mississippi was already coeducational, he asked, why did the state need to set up a school only for women?

"The reason was that women perceived a special need for some of them for education especially tailored to the needs of women," Gholson responded, and quickly added, "and I would certainly say that not all women perceived this need." He contended that the women-only policy helped make up for past discrimination against women. Justice Marshall then asked about the fact that men were allowed to audit classes, and questioned why only women could obtain a degree if men were attending classes anyway. Gholson said the men attended mostly at night, so women did not have to see, or compete with, the men very much.

Justice O'Connor jumped in next. She homed in on the legal standard for sex discrimination cases and whether the Court was bound by its decision in *Craig v. Boren* that struck down the age variation for beer purchasers.

"Mr. Gholson, is a finding that the Board of Regents had a belief that single-sex education benefits women sufficient in and of itself for us to uphold the provisions for that institution? And what level of scrutiny do we have to apply?"

"I think, Your Honor, that *Craig v. Boren* certainly sets out that there must be a necessary state purpose, and this must serve as an essential element of fulfilling that purpose," Gholson said. "But I think that *Rostker v. Goldberg* [the case involving the male-only draft registration] indicates that the majority of the Court certainly stopped short of saying that all gender classifications are suspect in the highest sense of the word."

Gholson was hoping for a watered-down standard. More broadly, Gholson thought he could win O'Connor's vote and that of Justice Marshall with the argument that this was educational affirmative action for women. But neither appeared receptive, and Gholson fairly quickly—he recalled later—considered O'Connor "antagonistic" to his views.[13] Gholson emphasized the consequences if the Court did not side with Mississippi: "Will we next be facing challenges of whether we have coeducational versus single-sex dormitories?"

When the white light on the lectern popped on, indicating that Gholson had five minutes left of the thirty allotted minutes for his side, he began to speed up. He wanted to be able to respond to the case put forward by the other side, so he quickly said, "If I may, I will reserve the remainder of my time."

"Very well," said Chief Justice Burger.

Stepping next to the lectern was Wilbur Colom, a young, African-American lawyer from Mississippi, who, in his own words, was "living a lawyer's fantasy."[14] The Supreme Court bar was (and is) overwhelmingly white and filled with members of the legal elite. In the Court's first case of the morning, former justice Abe Fortas had been one of a pair at the lectern. After the Mississippi case, the justices would be hearing cases that brought U.S. Solicitor General Rex Lee and Harvard University law professor Laurence Tribe—both prominent oral advocates—to the lectern. One of a handful of mavericks who show up each term, Colom was building up his practice by taking on unpopular but high-profile cases such as Hogan's.

Born to civil rights activists in Ripley, Mississippi (the Deep South birthplace of William Faulkner), Colom had grown up challenging Jim Crow laws and the racism of the 1970s.[15] After attending Howard University, he went to law school at Antioch in Washington, D.C. Among his many odd jobs was a clerical internship at the Supreme Court. So, the marble-columned building was not foreign to him, but the position just six feet from the justices was. "The question presented for resolution to this Court today is whether one nurse, Joe Hogan, will be barred from receiving academic credit toward a BS degree in nursing simply because he is male," Colom told them. Quickly turning to Gholson's claim that the nursing school was compensating for past discrimination against women, Colom said, "We never heard anything regarding affirmative action for women as a purpose for the W, as they call it, at the trial level. We never heard it at the Fifth Circuit." Colom's point was that the university was not set up to compensate women or to eliminate disparities in men's and women's education and career opportunities. Rather, it was founded to prepare women for domestic duties and traditionally "female" vocations. Colom added that in the field of nursing, women do not need affirmative action.

Leading women's rights groups were backing Hogan. The National Women's Law Center, NOW Legal Defense and Education Fund, the Women's Equity Action League, and the Women's Legal Defense Fund had joined together in an amicus curiae brief that said: "Even when a gender line has the purported aim of helping women, if the classification in fact only helps some women but hurts others by perpetuating 'role typing,' it violates the Constitution's equal protection guarantees. In fact, the stereotyping of nursing as 'women's work' operates to harm both men and women. Men have been excluded or discouraged from entering the field. The resulting job segregation is often described as responsible for the low status and low wages of women in nursing, as well as in other 'women's jobs.' "[16]

With O'Connor quiet for a moment and taking in Colom's argument, other justices asked about the unique character of the nursing school and whether there was something important for women in the all-female environment. Colom acknowledged that school officials touted the nurturing environment for women students but added that the opportunity for leadership role models for the women was overstated. "Of the ten presidents of this college, this university, all have been male," Colom told the justices. "The vice president for academic affairs, the dean of many schools, the director of admissions, personnel, extended services, the library . . . [have] been . . . men. . . . How can they provide the role models [that school officials seek]?"

Two days later, on March 24, the justices met in their conference room off Chief Justice Burger's chambers to discuss the case. O'Connor was carefully watching how the justices maneuvered among one another. She had an eye for hierarchies. It was her natural instinct to observe how the other justices did things and then adapt their lessons to her style. She went into the male-dominated, tradition-bound world of the Supreme Court believing that she *could* fit in, that she would not be excluded, despite her sex, despite her inexperience, despite her open demeanor in the face of reserved and cool Washington. She had been this way since childhood: a girl who thrived among the cowboys, a transient student forced to make her way far from home, and then a Stanford coed younger than her peers. Aside from the law-firm rejections after graduation, she claimed she had never faced any discrimination.[17]

Seated around their rectangular conference table, ready to consider the Mississippi University for Women's appeal, Burger was first up. He wanted to reverse the lower-court ruling and side with the university. "I don't think that the all-woman college must go down the drain," he said. Next came Brennan, who wanted to affirm and preserve the standard he had used in the 1976 *Craig v. Boren* case. Reading from his notes and looking up occasionally through thick lenses in wire frames, Brennan told his colleagues they had before them a narrow question, one that involved only the school of nursing. "We can assume without deciding that a state could [meet the Court's test] for permissible single-sex schools," he said, stressing that there is no reason to get rid of systems that provide men and women with equal educational opportunities. This is not a case of separate-but-equal facilities, Brennan urged, because Mississippi offered no all-male nursing school, or even an all-male university. O'Connor, the most junior justice, listened as Brennan then took on the affirmative action argument: "The school's statutory statement of purpose and aim is the perpetuation of sexual stereotypes rather than any affirmative action. Moreover, it is difficult to believe that any affirmative action is needed in nursing programs—a traditionally female career."[18]

Next, Justice White, taciturn and to the point, agreed with Brennan that the lower court should be affirmed. But he also made clear that he did not want to look beyond the nursing school and set policy for the whole Mississippi University for Women.

Marshall, too, agreed to affirm: "I would decide this case narrowly." Next was Blackmun, who said he was troubled by the university's founding mission of preparing women for traditional work, but he feared that to strike down the policy would force every state-run school to be coeducational. So, he voted for the university.

Powell, speaking with more certainty, said he wanted the policy of the Mississippi University for Women to stand. A traditionalist, Powell liked the idea of single-sex schools. He believed they had long benefited both men and women. "There are perfectly justifiable educational reasons for one-sex schools," Powell said. "So this guy could go to one of the coed nursing schools." He did not think Hogan was in any way a victim of sex discrimination. Agreeing with Powell, Rehnquist also wanted to reverse the Fifth Circuit and let the MUW policy stand. Men have not been discriminated against, Rehnquist said flatly, and there is no need to be concerned with them being excluded here.

The eighth justice to speak, Stevens, wanted to affirm the Fifth Circuit based on Brennan's grounds. He agreed that the nursing school context was different because men traditionally did not seek to become nurses. Stevens's vote tied it. With him, Brennan, Marshall, and White, there were four justices on Hogan's side. Voting for the MUW were Burger, Blackmun, Powell, and Rehnquist.

It fell to O'Connor, the only justice who had been the victim of real sex discrimination, to decide the case. If her predecessor, Potter Stewart, had still been at the table, he likely would have gone with Burger and those who favored the MUW. In cases decided before he retired, Stewart had been of the mind of Rehnquist, urging a softer standard for government policies that drew a line between men and women for various rules and benefits. But O'Connor sided with Brennan. She wanted to let Hogan, and any other man, obtain a nursing degree at the MUW. She cautioned, however, that she was not ready to say that states must never create single-sex schools. But in this instance, she said, clearly the state was unfairly discriminating against men.

So, by a single vote, the Court was ready to strike down the no-men policy at the nation's oldest public college for women. The justices moved on to the week's other cases. In the next few days, as O'Connor well knew, it would fall to Justice Brennan, as the most senior justice in the majority, to decide who would write the opinion for the Court. He could keep it for himself, as he had in past sex-discrimination cases, or he could, perhaps, give it to the first woman. Brennan certainly was aware that he would not have had a majority without her. And he was cognizant of the public significance of the first woman justice taking up the pen in an important sex-discrimination case.

As the rituals within the conference were unfolding so were the social initiations of Court life. Two days later, on March 26, O'Connor celebrated her 52nd birthday, toasted with a glass of wine by her colleagues, as was the custom. The next night, she attended one of the more glamorous galas of political Washington: the annual white-tie Gridiron Dinner. President Reagan and his wife, Nancy, headlined the guest roster for the press corps' song-and-dance show. Rehearsed for months, the Gridiron featured veteran newspaper reporters and a few talented ringers playing the roles of Washington officials and spoofing their deeds. Seated at the head table with cabinet officials, several ambassadors, and other dignitaries, O'Connor was to witness one of the livelier Gridiron shows. To the surprise of just about everyone, Nancy Reagan took the stage and brought down the house with a rendition of "Secondhand Rose," spoofing her clotheshorse image and the controversial $200,000 White House china she had ordered. During the journalists' portion of the show, O'Connor's arrival on the Court was memorialized by a Burger impersonator who sang: "Gone are the days of the nine men good and true/Now there's a clear gender dif'rence in our crew." An O'Connor impersonator stepped onto the stage, singing to the tune "One of the Girls": "I'm one of the girls who's become one of the boys/Sharing one man, one vote, as a smart dame enjoys/Oh, I'm the first female, no tie and no shirt." [19]

When O'Connor returned to the Court the following week, Brennan asked her to write the majority opinion in the Hogan case. Brennan knew she was ready to reinforce his handiwork from *Craig v. Boren*. Brennan also recognized that if O'Connor did not have control of the Hogan decision, there was a chance that one of the more liberal justices in the majority might go farther than she wanted; Brennan could lose her crucial fifth vote.

There was some irony in Brennan's work to ensure a strong statement against sex discrimination. He was known for hiring only male clerks. Susan Estrich, who was at the top of her class at Harvard Law and editor of its law review, wrote in her book, *Sex and Power,* "The most liberal member of the Court, the most articulate opponent of sex discrimination, wouldn't hire me because I was a woman." It was 1975 when Brennan refused to hire Estrich, whose position on the *Harvard Law Review* would have assured her a Brennan clerkship if she were a man. She ended up landing a position with Justice Stevens. As Estrich noted, the word was that Brennan believed his chambers worked better when it was just him and the "boys."[20]

There was another point of inconsistency in the Hogan case: Blackmun's position. He had been with Brennan in the 1976 *Craig v. Boren,* endorsing a standard intended to limit government differentiation between men and women. But in 1982, Blackmun resisted signing on with O'Connor. He told his colleagues he was worried about the "inevitable spillover" effect and possibly losing "all values that some think are worthwhile." In his written dissent, he ended up saying, "I have come to suspect that it is easy to go too far with rigid rules in this area of claimed sex discrimination." Some news accounts at the time also showed him developing a personal rivalry with O'Connor, which might not have made him open to her approach. In an article focused on spring 1982 cases, Stephen Wermiel of the *Wall Street Journal* wrote: "The frequency with which Justice Blackmun has made comments, always off the record, about Justice O'Connor, surely suggests some hard feelings. Some Court watchers suggest that Mr. Blackmun may resent the favorable publicity and attention focused on Mrs. O'Connor's arrival last fall. . . . But the justices scoff at suggestions of feuds."[21]

In an interview with the fledgling Cable News Network a few months later, Blackmun acknowledged clashing with O'Connor and said she appeared to have joined the Court's conservative wing. But he added, "The Justice is able, articulate. She gives no quarter, she asks no quarter and she's a fine Justice."[22] Years later, Blackmun's once-private correspondence revealed that he was put off by all the media hoopla surrounding the new justice and her constant socializing. He did not appreciate her conservative votes and he also could not abide that this freshman justice was not showing the apprehension and angst that still enveloped him.

Whatever rivalries there were among the justices in O'Connor's first years, she appeared to look beyond them. Whatever slights she felt, she kept to herself. Whatever grudges she nurtured, she kept them secret. In fact, she would write to Blackmun as her first term wound down: "As the term concludes, I wanted to tell you what a privilege it has been for me to work with you this year. Your knowledge and the care you exhibit with all you do sets a wonderful example."[23] As she had in legislative politics, she always struck an outwardly positive note.

As O'Connor was drafting the opinion for the majority in the Hogan case in spring 1982, she worked in an office that was distinct from the black-leather furnishings of her brethren. She filled her chambers with Navajo rugs and other Western art from the Heard Museum in Phoenix. In time, she would put up sepia-toned photographs from the family ranch. She would display a pot by ceramicist Maria Martinez and bring from the Lazy B an Indian carving of an American eagle, an ancient Anasazi pot, a piece of Arizona petrified wood, and baskets made by Apache, Papago, and Pima artists.[24] "I miss the atmosphere of the desert," she told the *Ladies' Home Journal*. "I miss the open vistas, the clear sky and the availability of the outdoors."[25]

But the O'Connors were moving easily into the orbit of Washington. They bought an apartment in the exclusive Kalorama section of Washington, D.C. She began entertaining and socializing with her usual vigor. She invited law clerks to dinner, went to the theater with Justice Powell, and found tennis and bridge partners among the movers and shakers she met at parties. For O'Connor, it was more than a matter of making connections. She liked to be busy, and made it a point of bringing along those who worked with her. "When it seemed like we were all about to break from the workload," recalled former clerk Scott Bales, "she would come running in and say, 'I just arranged for an outing to this new exhibit at the National Gallery.' "[26] Glen Nager, another clerk in her early years, who toted up field trips to the FBI, the Natural History Museum, and cherry blossoms, said, "She was not raised to sit still."[27]

By mid-April, the Hogan case dominated the O'Connor chambers. As she worked on parts of the opinion in longhand on a legal pad, her clerks gathered information about the school. O'Connor incorporated into her opinion a statement by the MUW Alumnae Association, which she thought illustrated the bygone era the university was trying to perpetuate. "In the aspect of life known as courtship or mate-pairing, the American female remains in the role of the pursued sex, expected to adorn and groom herself to attract the male," the alumnae association told the Court. It said a women's college "can free its students of the burden of playing the mating game while attending classes, thus giving academic rather than sexual emphasis."[28]

Shortly before she was ready to circulate her first draft, O'Connor had her first major opportunity to speak as a justice of the Supreme Court outside of Washington. She was the keynote speaker at a conference of women judges at the Johnson Foundation's Wingspread Center in Racine, Wisconsin. Sponsored by the National Center for State Courts, the gathering was billed as the first nationwide forum to study the needs of women judges. O'Connor was upbeat, speaking mostly of service women can do for others, rather than complaining of any wrongs done to women. Many of the women in the audience were thrilled to have this embodiment of female success appear before them. But some wanted more recognition of the struggles and discrimination women faced in rising to the upper reaches of the profession. In an exchange after O'Connor's speech, a woman asked a familiar question: How did O'Connor balance work and family? Women should always put family first, O'Connor declared, according to Stanford University law professor Barbara Babcock, who was at the conference. Babcock, who had been a Justice Department lawyer in the Carter administration, said she recalled thinking of the "family first" answer, "How could that be? Most of the women in the room were there because they had sometimes put their careers first or even sacrificed family."[29]

The mixed response to O'Connor's appearance would become part of a pattern of divided reactions among women to the new justice. The split often would be ideological. Liberals were inclined to think she was letting them down by not being more of a feminist advocate. The bully pulpit was not O'Connor's preference in her early years, as would soon be clear by her words in *Hogan*. The opinion was shaping up to be straightforward and fact-laden. On May 27, she circulated her first draft, which said that "the challenged policy expressly discriminates against applicants on the basis of gender" and that Hogan had a right to be admitted into the school.

Her draft disturbed Powell, with whom she otherwise was growing close. "In my view, the long experience with education in women's colleges—viewed as educationally desirable—supports the existence of a legitimate state interest," Powell said as he dictated some random thoughts to try to figure out how to deal with O'Connor's opinion.[30] "Perhaps I should add as a footnote that I have experienced it personally with a wife and three daughters." Powell mused to his staff that he could not understand why a man would want to be a nurse. That was Powell—generous, gentlemanly, but behind the times.[31]

As she continued to work on her opinion for the majority, O'Connor also engaged in what would become a practice of regular travel throughout the United States and abroad. That May, she went to Columbia College in Columbia, South Carolina, to give a commencement address. Four days later, she traveled to Philadelphia for the Gimbel Awards. At the end of the month, she was at Colorado College, where her middle son, Brian, was graduating, and gave the commencement address, "One Step at a Time and Keep Walking." Still on the move as she worked on Hogan's case and opinions in at least a dozen others, she returned to Philadelphia on June 11 to give the commencement address at the Jefferson Medical College. Her husband, John, went along on these trips. That, too, became a pattern. In moving to Washington, John had given up his established law practice and a longstanding association with a prestigious firm. Even after he joined the Washington, D.C., law office of Miller and Chevalier, his practice was limited by his lack of contacts in the nation's capital and the potential legal conflict of a spouse on the Supreme Court. Still, John thrived on the opportunities to travel widely and mingle with power brokers in the nation's capital. Since July 1981, when Reagan called O'Connor, John had been keeping a diary of Sandra's doings and their activities together.

During the second week in June, they flew to California for what might have been O'Connor's most significant speech of the season, in light of the Hogan ruling she was writing. Speaking at her alma mater, Stanford University, and taking a passage from the Talmud, she began, "In every age, there comes a time when leadership suddenly comes forth to meet the needs of the hour. And so there is no man who does not find his time, and there is no hour that does not have its leader."

"At first blush," she continued, "this ancient saying suggests merely that there will always be a Moses when Moses is needed. Yet, on further examination of the words 'there is no man who does not find his time,' we realize that the message conveyed is that each of us, in our own individual lives and the crises we face, will have a time to lead. Whether we will lead only a family, or a handful of friends, and where and how we will lead, is up to us, our views, and our talents. But the hour will come for each of us."[32]

O'Connor delivered the Hogan opinion on a hot, cloudless July 1. She said the Constitution does not permit a state-run school to provide a special education for one sex to the exclusion of the other. Befitting the woman who had repeatedly fought sexual stereotypes, she looked at the practice not only from the point of view of Hogan but also from that of the female students. Excluding males from nursing training, she wrote, tends "to perpetuate the stereotyped view of nursing as an exclusively women's job." She rejected Mississippi's claim that the single-sex admissions policy "compensates for discrimination against women and, therefore, constitutes educational affirmative action." She observed that the state had not shown that women lacked opportunities in the nursing field.

She adopted Brennan's standard from *Craig v. Boren* for sex discrimination—a legal test that asked whether the challenged policy bore a direct or substantial relationship to the state's proposed objective—and found that Mississippi's policy failed. She said the state lacked the requisite "exceedingly persuasive justification" for the ban on men. In a footnote, O'Connor made clear she was not intending to assert that all state-supported single-sex education was inherently unequal and a violation of the Equal Protection Clause: "Mississippi maintains no other single-sex public university or college. Thus, we are not faced with the question of whether states can provide 'separate but equal' undergraduate institutions for males or females."[33]

As she closed her opinion, she cited the Supreme Court's 1873 decision denying an Illinois woman, Myra Bradwell, a license to practice law. O'Connor used it as an example of government efforts to keep women out of jobs because they were believed the weaker sex. With implicit irony, O'Connor then invoked Justice Joseph P. Bradley's concurring statement in *Bradwell v. Illinois* that it was right to stop a woman from practicing law, "in view of the peculiar characteristics, destiny, and mission of women."

Most distressed and impassioned among the four dissenters was Powell. He praised single-sex colleges and noted that many women across the country chose to attend all-female schools. "Left without honor—indeed, held unconstitutional—is an element of diversity that has characterized much of American education and enriched much of American life," Powell wrote. He concluded, "The Court, in this case, may have departed farther from the intent and purpose of the Equal Protection Clause than in any other prior case." That was a surprising assertion from a justice who was typically more moderate in his rhetoric. Could Powell have believed that the ruling was more troubling than, say, *Plessy v. Ferguson,* which in 1896 upheld a state law requiring trains to provide separate but equal facilities for black and white passengers?

The time limit for the Equal Rights Amendment's ratification elapsed the day before the *Hogan* ruling was announced July 1, 1982—a fact picked up by many commentators. "How fitting that the same week the ERA went out of business—at least for now—the Supreme Court decided, in a case that gives hope to the women's movement, that sex-based discrimination can be attacked in a variety of other ways," the *Washington Post* said in an editorial. "This is true notwithstanding the fact that the immediate beneficiary of the court's action was a man. . . . The Court was right."[34]

The night of the decision, Ruth Bader Ginsburg, who in 1982 was a judge on the U.S. Court of Appeals for the District of Columbia Circuit, brought a copy of the ruling home to her apartment in the Watergate Building to show her husband, Martin. Realizing as he read it that the opinion reflected much of his wife's thinking, he remarked lightheartedly, "Did you write this?"[35]

Eleanor Smeal, president of the National Organization for Women, said the ruling was particularly welcome "on the day after the ERA deadline," but expressed concern about the one-vote margin of the decision. This was a worry for naught. *Mississippi University for Women v. Hogan* endured. The majority's rule that government show an "exceedingly persuasive justification" for any sex classification was invoked when the Court found in 1994 that women cannot be eliminated from juries without explanation (in an opinion by Blackmun) and, in 1996, when the justices (in an opinion by then-Justice Ruth Bader Ginsburg) said women could not be excluded from a state-run military school.

The Mississippi case helped define O'Connor. Equal rights between the sexes was a subject that had long engaged her, and she crafted an opinion that she believed made a difference in American life. As the curtain came down on her first term, the case also offered O'Connor a way to show that she could not be cast plainly on the ideological right or on the left.

Hogan would receive his four-year nursing degree, and lawyer Colom later wrote, "Feminist leaders across the nation heralded the decision. We brought out bottles of champagne. A man had won his sex discrimination case, yet we toasted the women of the feminist movement."[36]

O'CONNOR WOULD NOT be the toast of feminists for long. In the early 1980s, gender divisions also were playing out on abortion rights, and in the next term, a series of abortion cases came before the justices. The most significant of the three cases centered on an Akron, Ohio, ordinance passed in 1978 and intended to discourage abortions. The ordinance required all abortions after the first trimester of pregnancy to be performed in a hospital. It also imposed a highly detailed "informed consent" provision that forced a doctor to provide considerable information about the fetus's development and to tell the woman that the fetus "is a human life from the moment of conception." The law prohibited the physician from performing an abortion until twenty-four hours after the woman had signed the consent form.[37]

In their first, preliminary consideration of the case, O'Connor was one of four votes cast (with Burger, White, and Rehnquist) to hear Akron officials' appeal of a ruling invalidating the ordinance. O'Connor's vote at that private conference was the first sign to her colleagues of where she stood on abortion rights. Ever since Reagan nominated her, O'Connor's position on abortion had been the source of much speculation. The president had fought off immediate criticism from Moral Majority's Jerry Falwell and others in the religious right who believed O'Connor was not a true abortion opponent. In Arizona, she had supported abortion rights as a state senator. But during her Senate Judiciary Committee hearings, she said she regretted voting in 1970 for a bill to repeal Arizona's criminal abortion statute. She also said legislators, not judges, should draw the line between permissible and impermissible abortion laws.

The drama over abortion rights went back to 1973, when the Supreme

Court first declared that women have a constitutional right to end a pregnancy. That decision in *Roe v. Wade* transformed national politics and created new and powerful movements: the antiabortion, or "right to life" groups, and the "pro-choice" organizations. As O'Connor could see by looking out her window each January 22, the anniversary of *Roe v. Wade,* the decision remained white-hot. The occasion brought tens of thousands of protesters to the nation's capital. Across the street from the Court, Congress was under constant pressure from advocates and opponents of abortion rights. The Hyde Amendment, named for U.S. Representative Henry Hyde, which limited federal funding of abortions under Medicaid programs to pregnancies that threatened the woman's life, had cleared Congress. But federal lawmakers continually rejected proposals to amend the U.S. Constitution to end the abortion rights established by the Court in *Roe.*

O'Connor was the first member of the high court ever to have felt a fetus within her, and now, in only her second term, she found herself directly in the middle of the abortion controversy. The religious right was watching her, as were women's groups.

The Akron case provided another forum for conflict between O'Connor and the liberal-leaning justices, particularly Blackmun, who was the author of *Roe v. Wade.* Blackmun was proud of the admiration he had won from women's groups and even took it as a badge of honor that he constantly received hate mail from those on the other side. In the 1973 decision, he had written, "The Constitution does not explicitly mention any right of privacy [but] the Court has recognized that a right of personal privacy, or a guarantee of certain areas or zones of privacy, does exist under the Constitution. . . . This right of privacy . . . is broad enough to encompass a woman's decision whether or not to terminate her pregnancy." But, said Blackmun, who was once general counsel to the Mayo Clinic, it is a qualified right. A "state may properly assert important interests in safeguarding health, in maintaining medical standards, and in protecting potential life."[38]

During oral arguments in the Akron case on November 22, 1982, Blackmun was ready to defend his handiwork. His questioning of a Reagan administration lawyer provided a theatrical high point of the session. Waving the Reagan administration's legal brief, which asked the Court to approve the stringent Akron restrictions on abortion, Blackmun leaned forward, looked down at Rex E. Lee, the solicitor general of the United States, and asked: "Mr. Solicitor General, are you asking that *Roe v. Wade* be overruled?"[39]

"I am not, Justice Blackmun," Lee answered in a deep, confident voice.

"Why not?"

"That is not one of the issues presented in this case, and as amicus appearing before the Court, that would not be a proper function for us," Lee said, referring to the Reagan administration's joining the side of Akron as a "friend of the Court" and not being a main party to the case.

"It seems to me that your brief in essence asks either that or the overruling of *Marbury v. Madison,*" Blackmun said sarcastically. The 1803 *Marbury v. Madison* case was a landmark that established the Court's right to review legislation and declare it unconstitutional. Blackmun's assertion drew gasps from spectators.

Finally, just as Lee was finishing his argument favoring the Akron regulation, Blackmun said in a tone of disgust, "Mr. Lee, did you write this brief personally?"

"Very substantial parts of it, Justice Blackmun," Lee said, just as his time ran out.

The exchange was classic Blackmun, emotional, proprietary, and personal.

O'Connor, sitting erect, her silver tumbler of water to her right, a small rack of pencils on her left, focused on the city's asserted interest in imposing the regulation. Alan Segedy, lawyer for the city of Akron, had told the justices in remarks before Lee's: "This Court has recognized interests in maternal health, potential life, and maintaining medical standards."

"Counsel," O'Connor asked, "is the city relying on all . . . of the alleged state interests that you described in this instance?"

"That's correct, Your Honor."

"Okay. Thank you."

When Stephen Landsman, representing the Akron Center for Reproductive Health, took the lectern to urge the Court to invalidate the regulation, he recalled O'Connor's question to Segedy and observed that when the city appealed the case, it referred only to one legal ground: "Justice O'Connor asked Mr. Segedy what interest does the state rely on in this case [to defend the regulations]. I would cite to the Court the 'questions presented for review' [by Akron] in this case. Akron relies on one and only one interest in its questions, whether the state's interest in maternal health and well-being is such that it may regulate abortion." In other words, Landsman maintained, the Court needed to focus on whether the regulations interfering with a woman's right to abortion could be justified by the city's original asserted interest in a mother's health and well-being.

Soon after the arguments, when the justices took up the case, O'Connor was ready to vote to reinstate the regulations that the lower court had struck down. That put O'Connor in the dissent. Voting the opposite, against most of the restrictions, were Burger, Brennan, Marshall, Blackmun, Powell, and Stevens—a majority. They believed the regulations were intended to interfere with abortions rather than to protect the mother's health. Burger assigned the opinion to Powell. "As you already know," O'Connor told Powell on March 7, 1983, when he sent around his first draft of an opinion for the majority, "I have a different view in this matter. In due course, I will circulate something."[40]

Although O'Connor knew how she wanted to come down, she took longer than even she expected to put her opinion together. On May 4, O'Connor sent Powell a handwritten note. "Dear Lewis, don't despair. I think I can give you all of the separate writing in the three abortion cases tomorrow. I regret it has taken so long but there was a great deal for me to review and consider before putting it on paper."[41] The next day, she passed around her first draft with the strong, forceful sentiment: "[T]he trimester approach is a completely unprincipled and unworkable method of accommodating the conflicting personal rights and compelling state interests that are involved in the abortion context." O'Connor reconsidered a few weeks later and took out the word "unprincipled." But she attacked the legal underpinnings of *Roe* in phrasing that would stay largely in her opinion.[42]

She concentrated on Blackmun's trimester analysis. As he had explained in *Roe,* the state's interest changed as the pregnancy progressed. In the first trimester, the state had no interest sufficiently compelling to warrant interfering with the abortion decision. In the second trimester, when the abortion was more likely to affect the health of the mother adversely, the state had a compelling interest in protecting her and could therefore regulate the abortion procedure, by requiring, for example, that it be performed in a hospital. In the third trimester, when the fetus presumably could survive on its own, the state's compelling interest lay in protecting that life. To that end, Blackmun wrote for the Court, a state could forbid abortions in the third trimester except when necessary to protect the life or health of the mother.

In O'Connor's mind, modern medicine had pushed fetal viability back to an earlier point in pregnancy while technology also had permitted women to have safe abortions in later months. So, she wrote: "The *Roe* framework . . . is clearly on a collision course with itself. As the medical risks of various abortion procedures decrease, the point at which the state may regulate for reasons of maternal health is moved further forward to actual childbirth. As medical science becomes better able to provide for the separate existence of the fetus, the point of viability is moved further back toward conception."[43]

She said states have "a compelling interest in . . . protecting potential human life" from the moment of conception—not simply from the time of viability, as set forth in *Roe v. Wade.* In a reflection of her regard for state prerogatives, she quoted Justice Oliver Wendell Holmes: "legislatures are ultimate guardians of the liberties and welfare of the people in quite as great a degree as the courts." She noted that Akron officials had held several hearings before adopting the ordinance and said, "legislatures, with their superior fact-finding capabilities, are certainly better able to make the necessary judgments . . . than are courts." In the end, O'Connor was approaching the case not in terms of a woman's right to privacy but, rather, through the lenses of federalism and institutional roles—which organ of government should set such policy? Her answer was: the state legislature, not the federal judiciary.

Her dispassionate prose belied how emotional the case was, how pictures of dismembered fetuses were distributed in antiabortion mailings, how blockades of clinics were becoming a regular occurrence. Although the Court had not been directly asked to overturn *Roe v. Wade*—and O'Connor certainly did not want to address that core question—the legitimacy of that decision was constantly under attack. So, when Justice Powell read his decision from the bench in his soft, Southern inflection on June 15, he made clear that the Court was not ready to turn away from its 1973 landmark. "In *Roe v. Wade,* this Court recognized a woman's constitutional right to choose abortion—subject to state interests also recognized by the Court. *Roe* was decided a decade ago. None of our subsequent cases has questioned *Roe*'s authority as a constitutional precedent. Today we reaffirm *Roe*." Striking down the Ohio and other legislative restrictions on access to abortion, the Court appeared particularly distrustful of the highly detailed "informed consent" provision. "It is fair to say," Powell wrote, "that much of the information required is designed not to inform the woman's consent but rather to persuade her to withhold it altogether."[44]

By the time the decision was announced, O'Connor had softened her dissenting rhetoric against the framework of *Roe v. Wade*. As would happen often as the years unfolded, she was straddling two camps. She insisted that *Roe*'s trimester formula was "unworkable," but did not call for its reversal. Devising her own standard, she contended that a regulation should be allowed if it is not unduly burdensome on a woman's ability to seek an abortion. If a regulation were found to be an "undue burden," she wrote in her patented language, then it could be subject to strict judicial scrutiny. But she did not believe anything in Akron's ordinance, including a second-trimester hospital requirement and a mandatory twenty-four-hour delay, impermissibly interfered with a woman's choice to end a pregnancy. A regulation that increased the cost of the procedure (for example, by requiring a hospital stay) is not an undue burden, she said, so no constitutional right is invoked.

The White House was watching. The day of the ruling, a Reagan aide wrote a memo to top officials laying out how the votes broke down. O'Connor's position vindicated President Reagan, and a few days later, he singled out her dissenting statement for special praise.[45]

O'Connor's views drew bitter denunciations from women's rights advocates. Janet Benshoof, an American Civil Liberties Union lawyer on the team challenging the Akron restrictions, said O'Connor's position was "unprincipled." "I'm personally disappointed," said Jane Gruenebaum, spokesman for the National Abortion Federation. "It would have been nice to have a woman on the Supreme Court who was a stronger advocate of a woman's right to abortion."[46]

O'Connor was, to all appearances, oblivious and upbeat. She penned a note to Powell, saying she was heartened that he, rather than Blackmun or others in the majority, spoke for the Court: "I was very glad you wrote for the majority. It kept the rhetoric dispassionate throughout and I think will not stir up any more public outcry than is already extant anyway."[47]

For his part, Blackmun was curious about why O'Connor had watered down her criticism. One of his clerks pursued the matter, then wrote, "At breakfast, you asked whether I knew why SOC had made several wording changes in her dissent—particularly why she had taken out 'unprincipled' . . . The answer is rather interesting. When the dissent first circulated, SOC's clerk . . . came by to see what I thought and whether I was still talking to him. We discussed the dissent, and I mentioned that I thought the language was a bit strong; the word 'unprincipled' especially struck me as gratuitous. Apparently several other clerks made the same comment. [The O'Connor clerk] mentioned this to SOC, and she insisted on taking the word out immediately; . . . [s]he wanted to avoid anything that even indirectly appeared to be an ad hominem attack."[48]

Blackmun's one-time majority of seven justices for abortion rights had dwindled. There now apparently were six votes for *Roe* and three votes against it. In time, Burger would switch sides, and *Roe*'s fate would be even more precarious. Perhaps Blackmun sensed this, or perhaps he was anxious about the overall direction of the Court. But O'Connor's presence made for a more troubled Blackmun. As John Jenkins wrote in a *New York Times Magazine* piece in 1983, Blackmun openly expressed his fears about the increasingly conservative tenor of the high court. "Just as Justice Blackmun sees Justice O'Connor's appointment as adding a third solidly conservative vote to the Court, he sees it as his responsibility to correct the imbalance her presence creates." Jenkins's piece also highlighted Blackmun's desire to prevail on a Court with shifting majorities, quoting the justice as saying: "I think this job is very competitive among the nine of us. . . . If a vote goes 5–4 on a given case—a tentative vote—and one is assigned the opinion to write, he circulates it. And somebody on the down side, on the four, is preparing a dissent. You're locked in combat. It's competitive to that degree. You're struggling for the fifth vote."[49]

AS MUCH AS O'CONNOR was beginning to understand the power of five votes, she was attuned to the subtler relations among the justices, their manners and customs, down to the various office collections: for a silver tray when a justice's child married, for the "mess" fund supplying coffee and sweets. As her third term was starting in fall 1983, Burger let them all know they were running low on the "mess" fund. He inspired a clever round of responses from the justices and found O'Connor ready to one-up them all.[50]

"Our auditors advise me that we have a total of $4.00 in the 'mess fund,' " Burger wrote whimsically to the group.

Justice White responded first, "With gratitude for your administration of the mess fund, I enclose one likeness of Lincoln and five of Washington. Perhaps a Hamilton would have served as well, but he lost a duel." "In New Jersey, of course," White added in his own hand, at the end of his note.

Justice Stevens jumped in: "Not having won any duels lately, I enclose a likeness of Hamilton. Like Byron, I appreciate your excellent administration of the fund."

Rehnquist picked up next, also focusing on White's note and referring to the 1804 duel in which Aaron Burr mortally wounded Alexander Hamilton: "I enclose my check for $10.00 in order to keep the 'mess fund' healthy. Byron's similar letter of transmittal of his share refers to Hamilton losing a duel 'in New Jersey, of course.' Since he has brought up the subject of New Jersey, and since New Jersey is the ancestral home of one of our colleagues, I cannot help but recommend to you all a recent article in *Harper's* about New Jersey being the cancer center of the nation. It appears that the New Jersey Tourist Agency had adopted a slogan for a new campaign to get people to come to New Jersey, a slogan which consisted of the punchy phrase 'New Jersey's Got It!' It seems that they had to withdraw the slogan, because too many New Jersey wags were adding 'And I Hope I Don't Catch It!' "

Brennan, the New Jersey native, wrote back the same day: "I enthusiastically join Byron, Bill and John in thanking you for your magnificent administration of the 'mess fund.' I too am happy to enclose a likeness of Hamilton. I overlook Byron's and Bill's snide references to New Jersey. It's enough to say it's too bad for Hamilton that Burr was a better shot. I hope neither Byron nor Bill catches it."

In response, White, the one-time pro football star, responded to Brennan, "In view of the Giants and now the Jets, I withdraw my aspersive reference to the Garden State in my recent note to the Chief Justice."

"Enough of this historical stuff!" declared O'Connor in a note to Burger, with copies all around. "My contribution in the form of 4 million Mexico pesos was sent to you yesterday via Pony Express. It should approximate 10 gringo dollars. Hasta la vista, Sandra."

In the same spirit, about the same time, O'Connor chided the *New York Times* for referring to the Supreme Court as consisting of "nine men." The mention came in a September 29, 1983, editorial page piece that complained about the proliferation of acronyms in the government. The paragraph that prompted Justice O'Connor to write a letter to the editor said: "Is no Washington name exempt from shorthand? One, maybe. The chief magistrate responsible for executing the laws is sometimes called the POTUS (president of the United States). The nine men who interpret them are often the SCOTUS. The people who enact them are still, for better or worse, Congress." In her letter, O'Connor said, "According to the information available to me, and which I had assumed was generally available, for over two years now SCOTUS has not consisted of nine men. . . . If you have any contradictory information, I would be grateful if you would forward it as I am sure the POTUS, the SCOTUS, and the undersigned (the FWOTSC) would be most interested in seeing it." FWOTSC was her self-coined shorthand for "First woman on the Supreme Court."[51]

Women's groups, however, continued to be split in their assessments of whether she advanced their cause. In the spring of 1984, when the New York Women's Bar Association chose to honor O'Connor with its President's Special Award on Justice, a group of sixty lawyers and law professors wrote a letter calling the choice "incomprehensible and extremely disturbing." They said she was hostile to abortion rights and civil rights. "As women attorneys," the critics said in a letter to bar president Madeline Stoller, "we must not give legitimacy to token appointees who undermine our goals, but must insist upon and reward only demonstrated commitment to the cause of women's and human rights." Stoller defended the choice to honor the newest Supreme Court justice, which had been approved unanimously by the board of the New York Women's Bar: "The vast majority of our organization find Justice O'Connor a glowing example of what women attorneys can achieve in the law." Stoller said she was "a role model" for female lawyers.[52]

O'Connor had no public comment. She had seen it before: the expectations people had, simply because she was a woman. And she had more significant worries that spring. Her parents were in very ill health. Ada Mae Day's Alzheimer's was worsening, and Harry's emphysema required him to always have handy a tank of oxygen and inhaler.[53]

Harry Day, the hard-driver who so shaped the first woman justice's life, died on April 10, 1984, of heart trouble related to the emphysema. O'Connor heard the news from her brother. "It wasn't a huge traumatic thing," Alan said later. "We were expecting it, not today maybe, but soon. Then Sandra came out and just took charge. . . . We decided to have the memorial service at the ranch. We didn't want some preacher who had never even known him to give a talk, so we decided that all three of us would each get up and say something." At the Court, her law clerk Glen Nager remembered seeing tears spilling onto a legal pad as she sat at her desk drafting the eulogy.[54]

Nearly fifteen years earlier, Harry Day had written to his daughter, telling her what he wanted when he died: "I can't stand the thought of a conventional funeral service at the mortuary . . . with the Baptist or Methodist minister—the obituary and music by local talent. . . . I would like a brief service by an Episcopal rector, ashes to ashes and dust to dust, right here in my home, if possible, with just family and relatives and a few close friends present, possibly a few of my old cowboy friends but most of those are gone. I do not want an expensive casket and I do not want a lot of flowers. However, I doubt if any of it makes any difference after you have gone over the divide."[55]

At the ranch house, O'Connor placed baskets of poppies next to a photograph of her father. The family took his ashes to the top of a mountain, "a place," she wrote, "to see the sunrise and the sunset, and always to be reminded how small we are in the universe but, even so, how one small voice can make a difference."[56] Her sentiment echoed the speech she had made at Stanford University in the run-up to the Mississippi sex-discrimination ruling.

Unlike Harry, who had missed out on college and was resigned to life on the ranch, his daughter had found opportunity at every turn. He watched from afar as she reversed his defeats. Back at the Court, the justices took up a collection for a memorial offering. As was their way in matters large and small, they circulated memos about who already gave, who needed to contribute, and which charities to use. Their rituals continued like clockwork. Harry Day's time had ended. His daughter's hour was beginning.

8

ASCENDING THE BENCH

As Ronald Reagan's second inaugural approached, the Supreme Court kept to its appointed rounds. On January 18, 1985, the justices met in the private conference room off Chief Justice Warren Burger's chambers. Only eight justices were present; Lewis Powell was recuperating from prostate cancer surgery at the Mayo Clinic in Rochester, Minnesota. The justices voted on the week's cases, and because it was two days before the presidential inauguration, they discussed logistics for the swearing-in that would assemble the highest levels of the executive, legislative, and judicial branches. As tradition dictated, Burger would administer the oath to Reagan while the other justices watched from choice seats among the dignitaries. But Washington was experiencing a chilling cold front, single-digit temperatures that confounded White House planners and the justices who worried about staying warm on the wind-swept steps of the Capitol, where the inauguration was to be held.

Associate Justice William Rehnquist, a Wisconsin native, was following news of the temperature plunge. As the justices were leaving their conference, he remarked that a weather forecaster said it was about to turn cold.

"Turn cold?" responded Sandra Day O'Connor, accustomed to the mild winters of Arizona. "It's been cold here for the last ten days."

"I guess it all depends on your point of view," Rehnquist retorted.

In a note to the convalescing Powell, Rehnquist recounted this exchange and reported on what had transpired in the justices' conference.[1] At 77 and rail thin, Powell was slow to recover from his surgery. He had been expected back in chambers by now, and his physical condition was a concern to his colleagues. It also was a point of political interest to top Reagan aides and outside legal analysts. If Powell, a moderate and influential jurist who kept the Court centered, was forced to retire, the balance of power on the Court could shift. For an administration eager to put its stamp on the bench, a Powell retirement would mean an opportunity to appoint a more conservative justice.

"We have now finished our January argument calendar, of course, and I must say I can't ever remember a less interesting or stimulating group of cases," Rehnquist wrote, trying to cheer up Powell. "If you had to miss one oral argument session, I don't think you could have picked a better one to miss. Even the conference today got a little bit testy, as it does at times. Some of the Chief's discussion is quite good, when he feels very strongly about something and when he feels he has a majority with him; but some of it can be singularly uninspiring. Sometimes when he runs out of things to say, but he doesn't want to give up the floor, he gives the impression of a southern Senator conducting a filibuster.

"I sometimes wish that neither the Chief nor Bill Brennan would write out all their remarks beforehand and deliver them verbatim from the written page," Rehnquist continued. "Bill is usually thorough, but as often as not he sounds like someone reading aloud a rather long and uninteresting recipe. Then of course Harry Blackmun can usually find two or three sinister aspects of every case which 'disturb' him, although they have nothing to do with the merits of the question. And John Stevens, today, as always felt very strongly about every case, and *mirabile dictu* had found just the right solution to every one. As you might imagine, my conference discussion was, as always, perfectly suited to the occasion: well researched, cogently presented, and right on target!"

Rehnquist easily joshed with his friend Powell. They had joined the Court together in January 1972, the final two of Nixon's four appointees. Powell and Rehnquist shared Court gossip. Powell also turned over to Rehnquist cartons of Merit brand cigarettes. As a former board member of Philip Morris, Powell, a nonsmoker, received free tobacco products.

When Powell finally returned to a full schedule months later, Rehnquist penned a note that said, "Your return to the bench yesterday made our sitting a truly joyful one—something that is hard to say about most of them. Fondly, Bill."[2]

Justice O'Connor, who had sought out Powell as a mentor, also missed his warm presence within the cold marble. "Surely you know how concerned your colleagues are about you," she wrote. "You will be in our thoughts and our prayers each day until you are among us again. Surgery is never easy. Mayo's the best place to be for it and we shall stand by and be ready to help you in any way we can." O'Connor followed up a few days later with a telephone call to Powell's wife, Jo, and encouraged her law clerks to write to the justice.[3]

The relationships among the nine justices supported, in important ways, the substantive negotiations over cases. As with any group, individuals paired off in special friendships, or had their rivalries. Feelings of trust, or distrust, influenced how they dealt with each other when crafting legal decisions. O'Connor was becoming more skilled at maneuvering among her male colleagues, most of them a generation older and considerably more experienced.

On January 20, the temperature sank below zero. The inaugural parade and outdoor festivities were canceled, and Reagan took the constitutional oath for a second term inside the Capitol. This was a relief to O'Connor, who at a celebratory brunch the day before had been heard telling Republican National Committee cochairman Betty Heitman, "I'm not going to do much this weekend, but the first thing I'm going to do today is go out and buy a pair of warm shoes."[4]

The public enthusiasm for Reagan—he carried forty-nine of the fifty states—resonated across Capitol Hill. "We can read," Thomas P. "Tip" O'Neil, the Democratic speaker of the House of Representatives, told Reagan at an inaugural reception. "In my fifty years in public life, I've never seen a man more popular than you with the American people."[5] The economy had rebounded during Reagan's first term. Spending was up, unemployment was down. Reagan had proclaimed, as his reelection theme, that it was "Morning Again in America," and so it seemed at this heady moment in American history. Unseen beyond the horizon were the second-term controversies that—in the country and on the Court—would turn as bitter as the Washington winter.

Justice Powell, who continued to miss oral arguments into the spring of 1985, was the bridge between the ideological poles on the Court, so his absence exacerbated tensions that had been rising over the past couple of months. The liberal justices found themselves increasingly in the minority. In an unusually pointed speech the previous fall, Justice Blackmun told a group that the Court was "moving to the right," going "where it wants to go . . . by hook or by crook."[6] Around the same time, William Brennan criticized the Court's conservatism before law students in Georgia. The Court has, Brennan said, "condoned both isolated and systematic violations of civil liberties." Separately, Thurgood Marshall accused the majority of denying effective remedies to victims of constitutional violations and "eroding" faith in the nation's legal system. Stevens, too, had criticized his conservative colleagues as casting aside judicial restraint to move the law to the right.[7]

They blamed the trend partly on O'Connor. In her early voting, she had been in step with Burger and Rehnquist, so much so that *Time* magazine dubbed her Rehnquist's "Arizona twin."[8] That expression was a variation on the one once used to describe Blackmun and Burger— "Minnesota twins." Blackmun had shed the label in the mid-1970s as he moved away from Burger. Now, a decade later, he was in the liberal camp with Brennan, who still carried the mantle from the Earl Warren era.

Blackmun, especially, scrutinized O'Connor's positions and was perturbed by her tendency to vote with Burger and Rehnquist. At the end of her early terms, he wrote an assessment of her work for his files. He tried to figure out her motivations and her "soft spots," as he referred to them, and encouraged his clerks to gather "the scuttlebutt" on where an opinion of hers might be headed.[9]

But if he had been able to see more of her correspondence, he would have realized that the first woman on the Court was making a turn from being a reliable conservative vote to becoming a more centrist justice. It was during this period that O'Connor showed herself—at least to some insiders—to be a shrewd player. She ran ideas by Powell and worked with him to obtain a majority. She made a practice of showing drafts of her opinions to other select justices to solicit interest, protect a vote she did not want to lose, or prompt a justice to be ready to circulate a memo of approval when she gave her draft opinion to them all. She kept tabs on a vacillating justice who might be a fifth vote for a position she favored.

Although relations remained prickly with Blackmun, O'Connor took a deliberately positive attitude toward him. She accepted his invitations to prayer breakfasts sponsored by ministers he knew and kept him apprised of small concerts and other social doings she and John arranged. She became an eager accomplice in 1984 when Blackmun asked her to slightly delay the announcement of the Court's decision in a Hawaii property-rights case, because he was vacationing in Hawaii: "Dear Sandra, the votes are coming in rapidly in these cases. I wonder if I may raise a point of personal privilege. I shall be in Honolulu May 20–22. Do you think the decision in these cases could be withheld until after the 22nd? I run into enough flak as it is these days, and I think it would be better if I were out of the State by the time the decision comes down. Sincerely, Harry." The case involved a challenge to a state land condemnation law that redistributed land previously controlled by original Polynesian settlers. The ruling was unanimous in upholding the law, and Blackmun did not write separately, so there would be no apparent reason for Court watchers to single him out for criticism. But O'Connor quickly said yes: "Dear Harry, I will be more than happy to get you safely back on the Mainland before lowering the boom by announcement of this decision. Sincerely, Sandra."[10]

Separately, in a 1985 criminal case, when O'Connor realized she might win Blackmun's wavering vote, she gave him an early copy of her draft opinion and wrote deferentially, "It does not fit neatly into any of our prior holdings. It is probably too long. I am open to any suggested changes or approaches." Four days later, he responded that he would be inclined to sign her opinion, but added, "I hope you will not mind if, when your opinion is circulated [to all of the justices], I write to say that I shall hold my final vote until I see the dissent." He did not want to reveal yet to the others that he was with her. But she did not care. The important fact was Blackmun's willingness to join her opinion. "Thank you very much for reviewing my draft in this case and for your letter," O'Connor wrote back immediately. "I will follow your advice and circulate generally, keeping my fingers crossed that I can obtain four other votes." O'Connor knew she had the other requisite votes, because in their conference meeting on the case *Illinois v. Class* she, Burger, Rehnquist, and Powell all had voted together. It was Blackmun's position that was in doubt.[11]

Such correspondence revealed what would become her trademark mode of operation. She worked both incrementally and broadly. As she developed her position, she monitored the views of the other justices. Her tactics were not unique, but they were more constant and increasingly effective, compared to most of the other justices. All of the members of the Court bargained with each other to various degrees. It was part of the collective process that produced a majority opinion. O'Connor, the former legislator, was particularly suited to this give-and-take. Further, her efficient manner helped her keep her mind on multiple topics and her hand in many cases. And a competitive nature made her want to win.

In negotiations with other justices, she often accentuated her state legislative and state court experience. Her message was that she knew the practical effects of rulings. In a 1984 case, she invoked her trial-judge tenure to persuade Powell to change his position and vote to reinstate the murder conviction of a Pennsylvania high school math teacher who strangled a student to death in 1966.[12]

The teacher, Jon Yount, was driving 18-year-old Pamela Rimer home from school. As they were talking in the car, he made advances toward her. She rebuffed him. Yount, who later said he panicked, then drove her to a farmhouse and killed her. Rimer's body was found with numerous wounds about her head and cuts on her throat. She died of strangulation as blood from her wounds flooded her lungs. The sensational case, including reports of Yount's apparent confession, dominated news in the Clearfield County area for months. Yount was convicted after a trial, but an appeals court reversed, finding that his confession had been obtained in violation of his right to counsel. After a second trial and conviction, a Federal appeals court ruled that reports of Yount's confession and prior conviction had tainted the jury pool. Now the state had appealed to try to win reinstatement of the conviction.

"Forgive me for sending you another letter," O'Connor wrote to Powell as the justices considered the Yount case. "You have enough to read without this added burden. I write because you are always willing to listen and because it seems most unfortunate to resolve this case by an equally divided Court. You qualified your vote to affirm as being 'tentative' and I hope you might be persuaded to consider a reversal."[13] (Justice Marshall had not participated in the case and it initially appeared that the justices would split 4–4, with the result being affirmance of the lower court ruling favoring Yount.)

O'Connor believed the appeals court had wrongly interpreted the effects of the publicity on jurors. Comments from one of the jurors had been a key basis for the lower court's reversal of Yount's conviction. The juror said that he had read news stories and believed Yount had committed the crime. But he also said he could be convinced otherwise by the evidence. In other words, while this juror did not appear to be operating with the requisite presumption of Yount's innocence, he professed an open mind. O'Connor told Powell that she had reviewed the colloquy between the juror and Yount's lawyer. "In many ways, it was like colloquy I heard when I was a state court judge. Prospective jurors are not lawyers, and they take their temporary roles in the legal system with great seriousness and sincerity. Lawyers sometimes confuse them with hypotheticals . . . It is easy for us, fourteen years later, to [examine] that colloquy and detect awkward statements that indicate inflexible bias. But . . . we have no ability to judge his credibility and veracity. The trial judge, however, was there and could. That judge expressly denied the challenge for cause because he believed what [the juror] said" about being open to the evidence.[14]

After receiving O'Connor's memo, Powell wrote a note to his clerk, saying that he was rethinking the case.[15] What happened next demonstrated the effect O'Connor had on Powell. He not only switched his vote, he took over the opinion for the Court, reversing the judgment favoring Yount.

In a strong dissent, Justice Stevens said that the deluge of publicity leading up to Yount's second trial had compromised the integrity of the guilty verdict and that the lower court judgment throwing out his conviction should stand. Stevens accused the justices in the majority of intervening because it looked as if Yount had committed the crime and was about to get off. "It appears that the facts motivated the Court to select this case for . . . review. . . . The desire to 'follow through'—to do something about such an apparent miscarriage of Justice—is difficult for judges as well as laymen to resist," he wrote.[16]

Another example of O'Connor's backstage strategizing had begun the day after Reagan's inaugural festivities, as the Court considered the First Amendment protections for defamatory statements. The case itself was relatively insignificant—it received scant attention from newspapers— and O'Connor did not even write an opinion in it. But a reconstruction of her correspondence and other dealings in the case opened a revealing window on the way she worked.

The Vermont-based dispute began when Dun & Bradstreet issued an erroneous credit report to a bank regarding a construction company named Greenmoss. A 17-year-old high school student who was paid to review Vermont bankruptcy pleadings for Dun & Bradstreet inadvertently had attributed to Greenmoss a bankruptcy petition filed by one of its former employees.[17] A trial court ruled for Greenmoss, awarding it $50,000 in compensatory and $300,000 in punitive damages for defamation and loss of business. Dun & Bradstreet moved for a new trial, which the lower court granted, but the Vermont Supreme Court reversed, keeping the judgment in place.

Dun & Bradstreet's appeal required the justices to return to the 1964 case of *New York Times v. Sullivan,* a landmark in which the Court for the first time gave broad protection to the press against lawsuits for most defamatory comments about public officials. The Court ruled that public officials claiming libel could recover damages only if they showed "knowledge or reckless disregard" of the falsity of the information.[18] Written by Brennan, the ruling said, "debate on public issues should be uninhibited, robust and wide-open." Now Dun & Bradstreet was arguing that its credit-reporting operations were protected by the principles of *New York Times v. Sullivan* and later related cases.[19] Brennan agreed. O'Connor, conversely, believed that the *New York Times* standard should not apply to a commercial transfer of information by an entity that was not in the traditional media. The speech in this case, she said, was related to "the marketplace of money, not the marketplace of ideas." She thought Dun & Bradstreet should be liable for the consequences of the erroneous credit report.[20]

At the first conference on the dispute, back in the spring of 1984, five justices had voted to reverse the Vermont Supreme Court (Brennan, joined by White, Marshall, Blackmun, and Stevens) and four to affirm (Burger, Powell, Rehnquist, and O'Connor). Brennan, the senior among those voting to reverse, undertook the opinion for the Court. Powell was preparing the dissent. But soon after, White realized he did not like how far Brennan wanted to go with his opinion, and successfully persuaded his colleagues to schedule new oral arguments by the litigants. Powell held out hope of winning White over and writing not a dissent but the opinion for the majority.[21]

When O'Connor talked to White in January 1985 after the new round of arguments, she realized that he was working on an opinion that would put him more in league with Powell than with Brennan. O'Connor wanted to alert Powell to this, but she also did not want to interrupt his recovery from prostate surgery. She wrote a personal letter for Powell, then scrawled on an attached note for her clerks: "Tell Powell chambers to just set this aside for Justice Powell to read once he is back and working again. It can wait until then. SOC." The personal letter said, "Dear Lewis, please do not read this until you are truly ready to go back to work. It can wait. This case has been making its uncertain way through this Court for two terms now. I am not sure the Court will succeed in resolving it in any way which I regard as satisfactory. But during your illness something has occurred which offers the possibility that four, and perhaps five, of us can partially agree on one significant feature."[22]

"Byron has shown me a rough draft of his proposed opinion," O'Connor continued, putting herself in the center of the negotiations. "He is not planning to join Bill Brennan, so there are potentially five votes in opposition to the circulating 'majority' opinion. This is reason enough to make it worthwhile to pursue every avenue of agreement among those in dissent, who might thereby become a majority. With that prospect in mind, there appears to be possible agreement by you, Byron, the Chief, Bill Rehnquist and me. . . ." Powell's clerk on the case decided O'Connor's message was important enough to send to Powell right away. The clerk knew Powell was holding out for White's vote and this could be a sign of a welcome turn of events.[23]

As O'Connor simultaneously worked on other cases during this, her fourth, term, she was keeping up a pace of extracurricular activities that would, over the years, become part of her national persona. In early February, just after she wrote the note to the convalescing Powell, she presided at a Pepperdine University moot court performance in Malibu, then went to the University of Utah in Salt Lake City to speak at its alumni banquet. She detoured to Park City, Utah, for a ski vacation with her husband and sons. She brought back Mrs. Fields cookies for Justice Powell just as he was returning from the Mayo in Minnesota. She sent them to his house with a note mentioning that Mrs. Fields was headquartered in Park City and saying, "Her cookies are guaranteed to add pounds to your body. Please eat."[24]

For most trips, John was at her side. O'Connor's status as a working mother and wife was highlighted at many of the events. Before an audience of one-thousand people at the Century Plaza Hotel in Los Angeles, Pepperdine president-elect David Davenport introduced O'Connor this way: "Amid a reported six-day, fifty-hour-and-more week, she remains a loving wife to John, her husband of more than three decades, and devoted mother to their three sons, Scott, Brian, and Jay. None can deny she is indeed a precedent setter."[25]

In Washington, O'Connor remained an A-list guest. It was not unusual for her to put in a full day of work, touch up her hair with the electric rollers she brought to the office, and change to a fancy dress for an embassy or other social engagement. John would often call for her after work in a tuxedo. "Sandra, why don't you let them go home," he sometimes remarked as they waved good-bye to the law clerks.[26]

O'Connor's clerks found her demanding yet attentive to their personal lives. In one breath, she could sternly convey that an opinion should be finished immediately. In another breath, she would ask, "How is your husband?" The consensus among clerks was that the faster something was written, the better. "When you're working with her, she's managing you," said one clerk. "The real warmth comes out later, after the clerkship." From the scores of applications that flooded her office, O'Connor tended to pick people who had clerked for prominent lower-court judges and had first-rate credentials. She did not take chances. She also preferred lawyers with steadier temperaments, and did not abide the demeaning of other justices in casual conversation or writing, as was sometimes allowed in other chambers.

O'Connor's organized field trips struck the various clerks differently. Some loved the chance to get exclusive tours of the capital's museums or to undertake the whitewater-rafting adventures. Others felt that the work demands were so difficult that the last thing they wanted to hear was O'Connor declaring, "We're going to see a museum exhibit today!" It was also an unspoken rule that female law clerks joined the aerobics class O'Connor began sponsoring as soon as she came to the Court, although not all believed in O'Connor's motto of daily exercise. "I think physical fitness is enormously important to your capacity to do mental fitness work," O'Connor told the *Saturday Evening Post* as she allowed a reporter into the class taught by a local YWCA instructor and held in the Court gym on the top floor. (The resulting story depicted the first woman justice, clad in leotard, throwing "herself *totus corpus* into various stretches, extensions, twists, head rolls and leg lifts."[27])

O'Connor's excursions on the town were frequent. At the annual white-tie Gridiron dinner in spring 1985, O'Connor engaged in a long and animated conversation with John Zaccaro, husband of the 1984 Democratic vice-presidential candidate Geraldine Ferraro.[28] Some Washington men still had a hard time thinking of O'Connor beyond the "first woman" role, however. Columnist Art Buchwald quipped to *Mc-Call* magazine, "My biggest fear in Washington is that I'll sit down next to Sandra O'Connor at a dinner party and say, 'What does your husband do?' "[29]

One highly publicized incident from a black-tie gala early in 1985 took on a life of its own. It occurred at the Washington Press Club's Salute to Congress dinner and involved Redskins running back John Riggins, who apparently had had too much to drink. "Come on, Sandy baby, loosen up," the intoxicated Riggins told her as they were seated together at a table sponsored by *People* magazine. "You're too tight." Riggins then walked over to John O'Connor, knelt beside him, and put his arm on John's shoulder. Riggins then dropped to the floor and fell asleep. With his black tie askew and his top shirt-button open, Riggins lay there for several minutes. Waiters stepped over him as they served dessert, according to the *Washington Post*.[30]

The next day, in an effort to apologize, Riggins sent roses to O'Connor and all the other women who were at the table. But the justice was more amused than insulted, and a few weeks later, the women in her morning aerobics class showed up in T-shirts that said, "Loosen up at the Supreme Court."[31]

Years later, when Riggins, who left professional football and tried an acting career, debuted in a Washington area community theater, O'Connor showed up with a dozen roses for his curtain call. Riggins was shocked. "Here's this very attractive woman in this really beautiful red dress and she's got these roses. It was Sandra Day O'Connor."[32] O'Connor had a knack for bringing a personal—and winning—touch to a situation when people least expected it.

IN CHAMBERS, AMONG JUSTICES, O'Connor managed the resolution of cases in a way that increasingly caught Brennan off guard. In the dispute over the Dun & Bradstreet false credit report, Brennan knew White had been a tentative vote to reverse the Vermont Supreme Court. But Brennan still thought he had the majority. That changed as O'Connor intervened. "Dear Lewis," she wrote to Powell: "By now you have seen Byron's response to your recirculation. I have also talked to Bill Rehnquist and the Chief Justice and I feel reasonably confident that you will have four votes for your proposed new circulation. Byron would at least be a fifth vote to affirm the judgment which would effectively place the plurality opinion in your hands."[33]

O'Connor, like Brennan, knew how to persuade colleagues. They shared an understanding of the decision-making process as collective and believed that several justices could walk away happy from the culmination of drafts and compromise.

When Brennan began to feel things shifting in late March 1985, two months after O'Connor wrote the first confidential letter to the convalescing Powell, he proposed a new version of a majority opinion: "The attached draft in the above has been substantially revised in light of the circulations of Byron and Lewis." It included a lengthy defense of the 1964 New York Times ruling, which prompted Justice Stevens to write an immediate personal note to Brennan about how this draft could backfire with their conservative colleagues and to suggest ways to gain White's backing.[34]

Brennan was committed—understandably—to his opinion in New York Times v. Sullivan. It marked not only a shift in protection for free speech but also, amid the struggle for civil rights in the South, a limit on the free rein that all-white Southern juries had enjoyed in their efforts to punish criticism by mostly Northern newspapers about segregation. The subject of the libel case was a Times advertisement that called attention to the strong-arm tactics of Montgomery, Alabama, police during a civil right protest at the state capitol. It was placed by Southern civil rights activists, members of the clergy, and union organizers, among others. The high court reversed a jury's $500,000 damages award for statements the Court deemed neither reckless nor knowingly false.[35]

Any advice Brennan drew from Stevens to make the *Dun & Bradstreet* opinion more palatable to White was too late. White and Powell were together to uphold the jury verdict in favor of Greenmoss. Writing for the Court, Powell said only "matters of public concern" merited the First Amendment protection of *New York Times v. Sullivan*. Brennan, joined by Marshall, Blackmun, and Stevens, objected to the distinction, saying, "This Court has consistently rejected the argument that speech is entitled to diminished First Amendment protection simply because it concerns economic matters."[36]

In the whole scheme of First Amendment law, this case, enhancing the ability of some individuals to recover damages for libel, was not a momentous ruling. The facts were "idiosyncratic," as Brennan wrote. But for those who knew the role O'Connor had undertaken, it revealed how she could take a page from Brennan's own playbook to build a majority.

AT THE SAME TIME, in early 1985, O'Connor was far more invested in another case—one involving a subject rooted in her frontier past and experience as a state legislator. The case tested whether federal minimum wage and overtime standards could be imposed on state and local governments.[37] The U.S. Labor Department had sought in 1979 to enforce the minimum wage and overtime rules against a mass transit system in San Antonio, Texas. Transit officials claimed that the department lacked the authority to force the municipality to pay public employees the higher wages, and sued. San Antonio won a ruling in a U.S. appeals court that the transit system was immune from the federal wage law, under a 1976 Supreme Court decision that protected some state and local government actions against congressional regulation. The Labor Department, joined by public transportation workers, appealed.

When the case of *Garcia v. San Antonio Metropolitan Transit Authority* first arrived at the Court in October 1983, O'Connor was in the majority with all four Nixon appointees: Burger, Blackmun, Powell, and Rehnquist. They agreed that the federal government could not impose minimum-wage and overtime rules on municipalities, and voted to affirm the lower court.

They believed the Tenth Amendment could be used to protect states from potentially intrusive federal regulation. Their approach recalled the Supreme Court of the early 1900s, which struck down federal labor laws as applied to the states. In the 1976 case of *National League of Cities v. Usery,* the contemporary Court had first resurrected that view. Now the question was whether the Court was going to further reinforce a trend protecting states from the federal government, or adopt a view that had generally held since the New Deal era of great power for the federal government.

In conference, O'Connor called *Garcia* a "watershed case."[38] She believed, as she had written in a case in her first term, that "the true 'essence' of federalism is that the states as states have legitimate interests which the national government is bound to respect even though its laws are supreme."[39] With her background, it was easy for her to see states as political entities that should operate as autonomously as possible.

But as the justices began the months-long process of writing opinions in the San Antonio transit case, Justice Blackmun switched his vote. In a note to his colleagues, Justice Blackmun wrote, "I have spent a lot of time on these cases. I have finally decided to come down on the side of reversal. I have been able to find no principled way in which to affirm" the 1976 precedent that weakened federal power.[40]

"Wow!" wrote Justice Powell, when he received the June 11, 1984, memo from Blackmun revealing his change of heart.[41] O'Connor was equally surprised—and distressed. Suddenly, a majority of the five liberal-leaning justices was siding with the federal government and labor unions. They were prepared to write a decision giving Congress broad power in the business of state and local governments and, in a practical vein, allowing state workers to sue for overtime pay. "Needless to say, Harry's circulation today supporting a reversal of the judgment . . . is unexpected," O'Connor wrote to her colleagues. "Because our summer recess is right around the corner, I, for one, would prefer that the case be reargued rather than reassigned."[42] She did not want resolution of the case simply turned over to the liberals now in the majority. She wanted it subjected again to oral arguments and full briefing. Rehnquist and

Burger agreed. They wanted the case held over until the new term that would begin the next October.

But Blackmun and Brennan, the most senior of the justices on the prevailing side to apply the wage law to states and municipalities, saw no reason to prolong resolution. Marshall did not want to have the case submitted to new arguments, either.[43]

Stevens suggested in a note to Burger that politics was in the air. "I find it difficult to believe that the four Justices who have supported the motion to reargue do not have the capacity to prepare a dissent in the time which remains this month," he wrote. Then, mulling their motives, Stevens said, a "possibility, of course, is the thought that the membership in the Court might change over the summer and thereby produce a different outcome. In my view, this would not be a proper ground for reargument."[44]

All the justices were exasperated and tense, but Burger prevailed on the issue of new arguments, and the case was rescheduled for the next term. There was no change in personnel or sentiment at the Court by early 1985, however, so Blackmun continued with the majority opinion, imposing federal wage standards on the states. Burger assigned the main dissent to Rehnquist, "[s]ince it is 'your ox' that is being 'gored.' "[45] Burger was referring to the fact that Rehnquist had written the Court's opinion in the 1976 *National League of Cities v. Usery,* in which (contrary to what was now prevailing in the San Antonio case) the Court said Congress exceeded its power to regulate interstate commerce when it extended wage and overtime standards to state and local government employees. Rehnquist had written then that some local government roles are so "traditional" that they cannot be regulated by the federal government.[46]

Although O'Connor shared most of Rehnquist's views on the issue, she told him that she wanted to write a separate statement in the San Antonio case. She felt strongly that states should be able to control what they paid their workers. Powell was pleased she was going to write separately. "After all, you and I are the only members of the Court who have had extended experience in state and local government," he told her. "Your experience, of course, was of a more important character, as mine was limited to serving on boards."[47]

In her dissent, handed down with the February 1985 ruling, O'Connor said that the Framers envisioned a republic "whose vitality was assured by the diffusion of power not only among the branches of the federal government, but also between the federal government and the states." She was irked that the Court was retreating from its 1976 federalism stance. She said she "would not shirk the duty" to reverse that in the future. Rehnquist issued a separate one-page dissent, signed by O'Connor, presaging the changed Court of the 1990s. He said he did not "think it incumbent on those of us in dissent to spell out further the fine points of a principle that will, I am confident, in time again command the support of a majority of this Court."[48]

The *New York Times* carried an editorial denouncing the views of O'Connor and the other dissenters: "They like to be seen wearing the robes of judicial restraint. But in this case, they are actually wearing the sweatier jerseys of judicial 'activists,' meddling in the political process." But to O'Connor's mind, her stand was just the opposite. She believed that the majority was meddling in the states' political processes by letting the federal government set the wage rule.

The San Antonio case demonstrated how a single justice on a closely divided Court—here, Blackmun—could significantly change the law. That made O'Connor's moves at the center all the more crucial, and heightened the anxiety among Court observers for any changes among the nine.

By the summer of 1985, the White House had become increasingly watchful for any signs that one of the older justices, particularly Brennan, Marshall, or Blackmun, would step down. White House communications director Patrick Buchanan, who had been a political columnist at the time of O'Connor's nomination, wrote to the president's chief of staff Donald Regan in July 1985, "The battle for control of the Supreme Court appears imminent. . . . The stakes here are immense—whether or not this President can leave behind a Supreme Court that will carry forward the ideas of the Reagan Revolution—into the 21st century." He said the president's "best bet" would be a sitting jurist "who has already run the gantlet of the Judiciary Committee and the full Senate." Focusing on two judges Reagan appointed to the U.S. Court of Appeals for the District of Columbia Circuit, Buchanan said, "While [Robert] Bork is [an] ex-

Marine and a brilliant judge, I would lean to [Antonin] Scalia for the first seat. He is an Italian-American, a Roman Catholic, who would be the first Italian ever nominated—a tremendous achievement for what is America's largest ethnic minority, not yet fully assimilated into the melting pot—a minority which provides the GOP its crucial margins of victory in New Jersey, Connecticut and New York. . . . An ancillary benefit of such a nomination would be to contradict the vicious but popular libel that Italian-Americans are somehow a hoodlum-prone people."[49]

Buchanan concluded, "Given the cruciality of the Supreme Court to the Right-to-Life Movement, to the School Prayer Movement, the anti-pornography people etc.—all of whom provide the Republicans with the decisive Presidential margins—the significance of this first nominee is not easy to exaggerate."

Since its early days, the Reagan White House had put an emphasis on changing the federal bench to reflect its conservative priorities. For the lower courts, the administration developed a system for screening young conservatives that became the model for future Republican administrations. It sought out jurists who would work to get courts out of the business of solving society's problems. Reagan was making a lasting mark, but he would not get a new vacancy on the Supreme Court in 1985.

For the time being, there was enough shifting of influence among the current nine. O'Connor continued to present herself as the dutiful colleague rather than power broker, more Donna Reed than Wonder Woman. (The *Saturday Evening Post*'s story that featured her aerobics class also included the justice's recipe for crab enchiladas and tomatillo sauce.) But, with O'Connor, there was more than met the eye. Behind the scenes, she was becoming adept at affecting the law through her negotiations with the justices and her separate "concurring" opinions.

Typically, in each case, there was an opinion issued for the majority and another for the dissent. But when a justice in the majority wanted to offer a caveat regarding the legal reasoning of the main Court opinion, or lay the groundwork for new legal doctrine for future cases, that justice penned a concurring statement. A concurring opinion became particularly significant if written by the justice who was the critical fifth vote and joining the majority only with a caveat. (Court tradition held that when justices in the majority had differing rationales, national precedent was set only on the narrow points on which at least five agreed.) O'Connor's concurrences, more often than not, emphasized the discrete facts of a dispute and had the effect of narrowing the breadth of a Court ruling.

Sometimes O'Connor advanced a different rationale altogether, which while consistent with the majority, reoriented the law for future cases. An example was the 1984 dispute of *Lynch v. Donnelly,* which allowed a city-sponsored display of a Nativity scene. The key fifth vote to allow the crèche, O'Connor joined Chief Justice Burger's majority opinion, but then wrote a concurrence that laid the foundation for the "endorsement" inquiry that in time would be central to deciding whether a local government had violated the constitutional mandate against the establishment of religion.[50]

A NEW AFFIRMATIVE ACTION case in fall 1985 presented the perfect opportunity for O'Connor to use the power of her concurrence. In the early 1980s, white teachers in Jackson, Michigan, had been laid off to protect the jobs of African-American teachers with less seniority. The whites had been let go and the blacks shielded under the terms of a collective-bargaining agreement that required the school district, when conducting layoffs of faculty members, not to lower the overall percentage of minority faculty.[51]

Wendy Wygant and other laid-off teachers claimed they had been discriminated against because of their race, in violation of the Fourteenth Amendment's guarantee of equal protection under the law. But lower federal courts ruled that the collective-bargaining deal was a permissible way to remedy past societal discrimination and ensure role models for minority schoolchildren.

On Friday, November 8, the justices prepared to vote in their private conference on the closely watched appeal brought by the white teachers. Earlier in the week, heavy rains had roiled the Potomac River and flooded parts of the nation's capital. To keep tourists away from the swollen Potomac, officials had closed the Washington Monument and Lincoln and Jefferson Memorials. Finally, on Friday, Washington awoke to blue skies, and tourists milled around the Supreme Court for the first time in days.

O'Connor and the other justices gathered in the room adjoining Burger's chambers for their regular session. Although she was now in her fifth term, Burger still assigned O'Connor opinion-writing duties for second-tier cases. But her vote in this affirmative-action case could make the difference, and that might land her authorship of the opinion.

O'Connor believed remedial programs could be imposed—but only for limited time periods and only if the harm to whites was slight. As a young person, O'Connor had known few people who were African-American. "Like most of my counterparts who grew up in the Southwest in the 1930s and 1940s," she wrote at one point, "I had not been personally exposed to racial tensions before *Brown [v. Board of Education]* . . . I had no personal sense . . . of being a minority in a society that cared primarily for the majority."[52]

As they spoke by seniority around the large rectangular table, the justices' views and votes on *Wygant v. Jackson Board of Education* were predictable, based on their positions in earlier cases. Burger spoke against the school board's affirmative-action policy. White voted with Burger, as did Powell, who had seen integration battles as the president of the Richmond School Board. Rehnquist, invariably opposed to a special government boost for African-Americans at the expense of whites, joined them.[53]

Brennan voted to affirm the decision to lay off whites to retain less senior black teachers, as did Marshall, who said, "discrimination is worse today than before." Blackmun also voted to uphold the lower-court ruling that endorsed the board's decision to lay off whites for the sake of blacks. Stevens did the same.

So, the vote was tied 4–4 when the case came around to O'Connor. She wanted neither to affirm nor to reject the school policy. She thought the best alternative was to refer the case back to a lower court for a hearing. Justice O'Connor wanted the school board to be given a chance to justify its remedial action based on past discrimination in the district.

Some of her fellow justices were annoyed. Her vote did not really break the tie. Blackmun wrote "tentative" and three exclamation marks next to his note about her comments. When he returned from the weekly conferences, he often mimicked O'Connor to his law clerks, applying her distinctive cadence and saying: "I vote tentatively, very tentatively . . ."[54] Burger said he would assign the *Wygant* opinion in due course, and the nine moved on to other cases.

When Burger gave the opinion to Powell, Brennan was surprised. He dashed off a note to Marshall, Blackmun, and Stevens: "I thought the vote at conference was four to reverse (the Chief, Lewis, Byron and Bill), and we four to affirm, with Sandra voting to vacate (and return the case to lower Court). I must assume that since the conference Sandra has joined the Chief, et al., or they have come around to her vote to vacate."[55]

But the situation was not that clear-cut. She was not ready to reject entirely the school-board policy. If O'Connor was frustrated by the assignment of Powell to the Michigan case, she did not show it. Maybe she was used to it. Political Science Professor Beverly Cook observed, "Like Marshall, O'Connor was not assigned to write the Court opinion by the Chief Justice in a single significant case between 1981 and 1986."[56] For his part, Powell, wiser than Burger in his relations with people, knew he had to woo O'Connor to get her vote on this affirmative-action case.

"I am not really at rest on this but I am inclined to think there is a legitimate state interest in promoting racial diversity in public school facilities," she wrote to Powell a month after his initial note telling her he had the case. She also said a school board that believed it had engaged in past race discrimination should be able to take extraordinary steps to ensure blacks were hired and remained on the job.[57]

This worried Powell. He could not go as far as O'Connor wanted and still keep Burger, White, and Rehnquist on the opinion. Meanwhile, Brennan had asked Marshall to write a dissenting statement for the four justices who favored an affirmative-action remedy. Marshall thought he could sway O'Connor and capture a majority. His draft opinion opened by noting that the Court might need more information from the school board to decide whether its affirmative-action plan was constitutional. Brennan wrote Marshall a private note, saying, "It is really a great job and ought to change some votes."[58]

Powell, meanwhile, worked to secure O'Connor's fifth vote to strike down the layoffs. "It is obvious that I need your vote rather badly," he wrote to O'Connor in March 1986. "I therefore would welcome any suggestions you may care to make." Over the next few weeks, Powell and O'Connor inched toward a compromise. Eventually, Powell would recall the contentious 1982 dispute over the Mississippi University for Women nursing school that would not admit men. She had written the opinion for a five-justice majority. Now, four years later, Powell told O'Connor, he "probably should have joined" her opinion in that case of *Mississippi University for Women v. Hogan*.[59]

In the *Wygant* dispute from Michigan, O'Connor ended up signing enough of Powell's opinion to invalidate the layoff of the white teachers. But she wrote a separate opinion spelling out her rationale for when government could use affirmative action. Once legal analysts and news reporters read the opinions issued on the morning of May 19, 1986, attention shifted from Powell to O'Connor. She had articulated "certain core principles," as she termed them, namely that public employers could use affirmative action to remedy past discrimination as long as it does not "unnecessarily trammel rights" of "innocent individuals."[60]

"In what may have been the most noteworthy aspect of the ruling," the *New York Times* reported, referring then to O'Connor and the four liberals, "at least five Justices . . . rejected the . . . broad position that the Constitution bans governments from using any racial preferences in employment that, at the expense of innocent whites, benefit members of minority groups." The *Washington Post's* news story mentioned O'Connor's opinion before getting to Powell.[61]

Justice O'Connor had limited her opinion to the facts in the *Wygant* case and signaled that she would not oppose all race-based measures. Through her concurrence, she had prevailed. Her receptiveness to affirmative action was noticed, and in a section of the opinion that would become relevant years later in a major dispute over the legality of racial preferences in college admissions, she also wrote that compensation for past discrimination should not be taken to be the only justification for affirmative action. Five votes approved a government role in deliberately bringing together individuals of all races, and O'Connor had a critical voice in the forms such policies took.

"We all have a strong voice here," she said years later in an interview, when asked about her position in the *Wygant* dispute. "It is the strength of the reasoning that matters in each case."[62]

ONE MONTH AFTER that ruling, Warren Burger announced he was stepping down. Given early notice by the Chief Justice, President Reagan was ready that June 1986 to announce immediately his choice of Rehnquist to succeed Burger. To take the open associate-justice seat, Reagan chose appeals court judge Antonin Scalia, a favorite of conservatives such as Pat Buchanan.

Some news reports at the time said that White House officials briefly considered elevating O'Connor but that they thought her too inexperienced. *Time* magazine wrote, "Reagan aides may have also been disturbed because she seemed to show mild symptoms of the Earl Warren syndrome, lately developing a disconcerting streak of independence."[63] Later conversations with top aides suggest the junior justice was never really in the running. But her moves were being closely observed.

Scalia, whose quick wit played well before the Senate Judiciary Committee, skated through the process. He sidestepped questions about his substantive views and the hearings did not focus on the intense conservatism for which he would become known once on the high court. The 50-year-old appeals court judge showed off his family of nine children and demonstrated enough charm through the hearings to draw compliments across the political spectrum. Senator Kennedy, the Massachusetts Democrat, said that although Scalia, who at the time was on the District of Columbia Circuit, was a conservative, "he is clearly in the mainstream."[64] The political reality was that Senate Democrats were not going to turn down the first Italian-American justice. Italian-Americans were a significant constituency in a number of northeastern states, including Massachusetts. Scalia was approved by a vote of 98–0.

Democrats focused their opposition on Rehnquist's nomination to be the sixteenth chief justice of the United States. With his record as the most conservative member of the Court, Rehnquist was targeted by liberals who complained about his votes against affirmative action and abortion rights and in support of the death penalty and other harsh law-enforcement policies. In a reprise of questions that had been raised when he was nominated to be an associate justice in the fall of 1971, Rehnquist was asked about accusations that he had harassed African-American voters in Phoenix in the 1960s and, as a law clerk in 1952, had tried to persuade Justice Robert Jackson to uphold the "separate but equal" doctrine. Rehnquist denied both charges.

One of the witnesses who disputed Rehnquist's version of events at the Phoenix polls was James Brosnahan, a former assistant U.S. attorney who investigated complaints at one precinct in 1962. He said voters had singled out Rehnquist as the cause of their problems. Brosnahan's testimony, challenging Rehnquist's assertion that he was at the polls to arbitrate disputes, sparked a dramatic exchange with Utah Republican senator Orrin Hatch. The senator maintained that Rehnquist was the victim of mistaken identity and that the problem-maker was an aggressive GOP contender about the same height and weight as Rehnquist. Hatch pointedly asked Brosnahan, a lawyer in a San Francisco firm, whether he truly remembered Rehnquist at the scene.

"Do you think I really would be here to testify about the qualifications of the Chief Justice after 27 years of trying lawsuits if I wasn't absolutely sure? If it was even close, I would be at Jack's Restaurant in San Francisco for my Friday afternoon lunch," Brosnahan said.[65]

In the end, Rehnquist won confirmation on a Senate vote of 65–33, which at the time was more opposition than any other successful Supreme Court nominee in the twentieth century had faced. Rehnquist became the fifth associate justice in the history of the Court to be elevated to chief justice.

For O'Connor, Rehnquist's elevation was a boon. She would now get choice assignments. All of the justices would get a fairer shake. Rehnquist believed that each justice should have a chance to speak once in the private meetings before anyone spoke twice. "Nowhere was the change in leadership more apparent than at conference," wrote John Jeffries, Powell's biographer. But at the same time that the justices lost the blustery Burger they gained a voluble junior justice who would upset things in other ways. Scalia immediately alienated Powell. "Politically, Powell and Scalia were not so far apart," Jeffries wrote, "but personally they were like oil and water. Scalia's cheerful lack of deference rubbed his senior colleague the wrong way. His volubility struck Powell as bad manners. In Scalia's first oral argument he asked so many questions that Powell finally leaned over to Marshall and whispered, 'Do you think he knows that the rest of us are here?' "[66]

Burger had often taken Powell for granted, as he pressed him to broker compromises that worked to the chief's advantage. But Powell still felt a kinship with Burger. They were born within two days of each other in September 1907. "Burger's departure marked the beginning of the end for Powell's generation," Jeffries wrote. "The promotion of a younger colleague to Chief Justice and the appointment of a man nearly three decades Powell's junior told Powell what he desperately did not want to hear: Soon he, too, would have to go."[67]

Powell did not act immediately, and intervening events transformed the nomination politics that awaited his would-be successor. Democrats gained eight Senate seats—winning the close elections as they had lost them six years earlier—and regained the majority in the Senate. Now, any new Reagan judicial nominee would go before a Senate Judiciary Committee controlled by the opposing party.[68]

The justices themselves had kept their eye on the 1986 Senate elections—primarily for sport. Some of them placed wagers—a practice encouraged by the poker-playing Rehnquist and naturally competitive O'Connor. Joined by Powell and Stevens, the foursome placed bets on all the Senate races. When the Republicans lost their majority in the Senate, Rehnquist and O'Connor were the biggest losers in the pool. They had bet mostly on Republicans. For that miscalculation, O'Connor revealingly referred to herself and the chief as misguided "optimists." In a further political twist, O'Connor had bet on her old confirmation-hearing nemesis, Jeremiah Denton, to win reelection in Alabama. The single-term Republican Denton lost to Richard Shelby.[69]

"I enclose my calculations on the election prediction pool," O'Connor, who handled the paperwork on the bets, wrote to Rehnquist, Powell, and Stevens after the election results were in. "You may audit if you wish. By my calculations the two optimists (WHR and SOC) owe some money. Each of us agreed to put $16 in the pool.... The net win/loss result is WHR, down $7.33; LFP, up $14, JPS, up $2.67 and SOC [down] $9.34. I am transmitting my total loss to Lewis. The Chief should send $2.67 to John and the balance to Lewis. Cheers, SOC.... P.S. I have now retired as a political pundit. At least until 1988."[70]

A few weeks after the November 1986 election, O'Connor and her husband, John, went to the University of Pennsylvania in Philadelphia, where she had been asked to judge a moot court competition. While she was inside the law school, more than forty demonstrators protested outside. They particularly complained about her record against abortion rights and chanted, "Look at her, she's Sandra Day—doing it the Rehnquist way."[71]

Yet, increasingly, O'Connor's record was not "the Rehnquist way." She was moving to the center, as seen with the *Wygant* affirmative-action case and others, as the 1980s wore on. Even Justice Brennan observed in an interview for the *New York Times Magazine* that O'Connor was voting less along conservative lines. "It is just so important that all federal judges are independent, not the voice of any administration," Brennan said, as he answered a question about O'Connor. "As a Justice feels more comfortable here, the judicial independence tends to put some distance between the political people who were so excited, initially, about the appointment."[72]

Brennan and O'Connor's respective positions of influence were tested in several cases in the late 1980s. In one match-up over government affirmative action, Santa Clara County in California had instituted a plan to move more female public employees into higher-ranking positions. The plan allowed Diane Joyce to be elevated to road dispatcher over Paul Johnson, who scored marginally higher on a qualifying interview. The vote among the justices to uphold the preference policy was 6–3, with O'Connor in the majority. As the most senior of the six, Brennan had the power to assign the opinion. He kept it for himself.[73]

As the justices began sending around their draft opinions, O'Connor could not abide Brennan's sweeping endorsement of preference policies for women and minorities in government jobs. She wanted to make sure that any remedy for past bias was devised cautiously. Brennan never outright refused her requests for alterations in his opinion. Instead, he tried to placate her with a string of modest changes in the wording of his draft. She suggested he was stonewalling and told him pointedly in a memo that his tactics "compel me to change" the opinion that would have endorsed much of his majority statement. Brennan already had the requisite five votes for his rationale. He simply sat back as she wrote a concurring opinion criticizing his "expansive and ill-defined approach to voluntary affirmative action by public employers," which she suggested could lead to unfair discrimination against white men.[74]

The fact that Brennan could not win the endorsement of the one woman justice was not lost on legal analysts. "It was another sign of her independence," *Newsweek* observed.[75] Coincidentally, it was the same case from Santa Clara County that set off Scalia on a rant against affirmative action. During the justices' early conference on the dispute, Scalia had harangued O'Connor and the rest of his brethren on the evils of hiring preferences based on sex or race. To which, O'Connor rejoined: "Why, Nino, how do you think I got my job?"[76]

Two months after the Santa Clara decision was handed down, Justice Powell announced his retirement. Powell had set the equilibrium: he had cast the key vote and written the opinion in the seminal *Bakke* case that allowed affirmative action in higher education. He was the decisive vote for the death penalty but with safeguards. By the time he retired, he seemed to be the fifth justice keeping abortion rights in place.

As influential as he turned out to be, Powell had resisted becoming a member of the Court. In 1970, when the Nixon administration first asked him to become a justice, he turned down the offer. In 1971, after saying yes, he reconsidered. On the morning of October 21, 1971, after a sleepless night, Powell called Attorney General John Mitchell and asked if it would embarrass the president if he withdrew his acceptance. "His answer was an emphatic 'yes,'" Powell wrote in notes to himself recorded at the time. "I reluctantly concluded I should adhere to my prior acceptance."[77]

On June 26, 1987, when Powell told O'Connor he was leaving, she was overwhelmed. "Your announcement leaves me devastated," she wrote. "No one on the Court has been kinder than you. There is no one with whom I have felt as free to discuss our cases and how to resolve them than you. There is no one for whom I have greater respect and affection than you. In short, you are irreplaceable."[78] Yes, irreplaceable as a human being who was unfailingly decent to them all. But not irreplaceable as the justice in the middle who would make the difference on the law. That would now be O'Connor's role.

9

"THE TRANSITORY
NATURE OF LIFE"

Vice President George H. W. Bush was slightly ahead of Massachusetts Governor Michael Dukakis in the polls on the first Monday of
October 1988, when the Supreme Court opened its term. A Bush victory
would cement the legacy of President Ronald Reagan, whose imprint
was already evident at the Court. Three of the associate justices who took
their seats in the magisterial courtroom were Reagan appointees: Sandra
Day O'Connor in 1981, Antonin Scalia in 1986, and Anthony Kennedy
just eight months earlier, in February 1988. In addition, in 1986, Reagan
had elevated William Rehnquist to chief justice. As Rehnquist took the
center chair on the bench, Kennedy was the justice in the media spotlight.
The bespectacled, earnest-looking former federal appeals court judge
from California had succeeded Justice Powell after the Senate's rejection
of Robert Bork. Kennedy had a reputation for conservatism, but his
views on many constitutional questions were unknown, which led reporters to speculate that he might become the Court's key vote.[1]

Powell had said the justices work as "nine little law firms,"[2] and the
relationships among them were still shifting after his departure in summer 1987. Beyond the columned building, the political fallout from the
Senate confirmation fight over Bork remained in the air. Democratic sen-

ators and liberal interest groups had mobilized quickly when President Reagan nominated Bork to succeed the retiring Powell. In effective but obvious overstatement, Senator Edward Kennedy had declared on the Senate floor, "Robert Bork's America is a land in which women would be forced into back-alley abortions, blacks would sit at segregated lunch counters, rogue police could break down citizens' doors in midnight raids, children could not be taught about evolution, writers and artists could be censored at the whim of government."[3] The momentum only had continued to build against the brilliant but ideologically polarizing appeals court judge. That Bork was named to succeed Powell, whose moderate vote had kept the Court centered, raised the stakes and brought the nominee more criticism than might have occurred if he had been named to replace a different justice. The Senate rejected Bork by a vote of 58–42.

Reagan aides and Senate Republican leaders had tried to enlist the help of some justices in the fight for Bork.[4] The recently retired Powell felt the most pressure. Senator Strom Thurmond, of South Carolina, ranking Republican on the Judiciary Committee, pleaded with Powell to testify on behalf of Bork. After Powell said no, then–vice president Bush called him. The retiring justice again refused to go public with any support for Bork. Then President Reagan called to ask Powell to support Bork. Reagan told Powell that he "might make a difference" in getting Bork approved. While ratcheting up the pressure on Powell directly, White House aides were also urging Rehnquist to intercede with the retiring justice. Rehnquist declined. In a note for his permanent files, detailing the White House pressure, Powell wrote, "In my view, the White House, and perhaps the nominee himself, have taken an unprecedently active part in attempting to win public support. . . . In major part I suppose this was a reaction to the type of campaign against Bork waged by special interest groups." Indeed, even newspaper editorial pages that had opposed Bork's nomination criticized how his liberal opponents had demonized the judge.[5]

President Reagan's second choice to succeed Powell was U.S. Appeals Court Judge Douglas Ginsburg, who, like Bork, sat on the District of Columbia Circuit. But his name had to be withdrawn within days of Reagan's announcement because of reports that Ginsburg had smoked marijuana while a professor at Harvard Law School.[6] Reagan's third choice was Anthony Kennedy, a judge on the U.S. Court of Appeals for the Ninth Circuit, who had grown up in a politically connected Sacramento family and, in his early years as a lawyer, been a consultant to then–California governor Reagan. Kennedy won Senate approval by a unanimous vote. When he was sworn in on February 18, 1988, Justice Kennedy filled the seat next to Justice O'Connor, which had been empty for the first four of the seven argument sessions in the 1987–1988 term.[7]

Justice O'Connor was happy to have the media spotlight now on the 52-year-old Kennedy. In fall 1988, she was just back from a trip West. In Oregon, she told a group of lawyers that in her early years on the Court she had longed for obscurity.[8] She compared the press scrutiny she underwent to being "engulfed by a tidal wave, the strength of which you didn't anticipate." She said it took a while to believe she was up to the task of sitting on the nation's highest bench. "It was several years before I felt confident in granting or denying" the hundreds of petitions that came to the Court annually, she said. But now, her apprenticeship years were over, and the trip to Oregon, and another to Idaho for a conference, had lifted the justice's spirits.[9] Once back in Washington, O'Connor and her husband of thirty-six years settled into an expansive Victorian-style home that they had recently bought in the Maryland suburb of Chevy Chase. Their three sons were on their own. The oldest, Scott, was married now, and Justice O'Connor was hoping for her first grandchild. John was finalizing negotiations for a new position with a law firm, Bryan Cave, that would set him up in a Phoenix office for part of each month and allow him to take advantage of the contacts he had made before he moved with his wife in 1981. John had been limited in his work at Miller and Chevalier. He could not handle anything that would end up before the high court. Even when another of the firm's lawyers argued at the Court, Justice O'Connor disqualified herself to avoid any conflict of interest.

The new 1988–1989 session could not have been better designed as a test of a new justice—or, for that matter, of a veteran who was becoming adept at maneuvering among her brethren. On the calendar that fall were disputes over the validity of racial preferences in government contracting and rules for sex-discrimination lawsuits. There were cases testing the constitutionality of the death penalty for the mentally retarded and for defendants who committed crimes when they were under 18. A significant abortion case from Missouri was headed toward the Supreme Court, too.

As the substantive business of the term commenced, the justices began their familiar routines and conversations-by-memo—unseen beyond the Court walls but so much a part of their day-to-day operations. "The Court is just kicking off its annual United Fund campaign, which has a goal of $13,000 for a little more than 300 employees," Rehnquist wrote to the others, with the rebuke that "Last year participation by the Justices' chambers declined in three respects: Total number of chambers donors decreased . . . ; total amount of chambers' gifts decreased . . . ; average chambers giver's gift declined. . . ."[10] Rehnquist had a way of lighting a fire under the justices who were slow—slow to turn out opinions and sluggish simply in doing their part in the business of the Third Branch. Another sign of how mundane details preoccupied the chief justice was Rehnquist's worry in the fall of 1988 over individual justices' circulating too many photographs (to be given to friends and acquaintances) for "hand-signing." Rehnquist said that a "signing machine" had been purchased to cut down on such requests for signatures. After he raised the topic, they agreed to limit requests for "hand-signing" of photos to ten each term. "I suggest that each chambers devise a system for assuring that any such item placed in the Conference room or otherwise circulated for hand signing show on its face the chambers in which the request has originated," Rehnquist added.[11] Such matters, as they cycled with the daily legal business each term, were patterns and routines on which O'Connor thrived.

But just as the first two-week session of oral arguments was winding down in mid-October, O'Connor received startling news. A spot had showed up on a routine mammogram. Something did not look right on the test, the physician told her. She felt fine, she said, but her doctor insisted she have more tests to determine whether she had breast cancer.

"The Big C," O'Connor would say later, as she recalled how subsequent tests showed that she had cancer.[12] The mere word overwhelmed her. Seven months earlier, appendicitis had required emergency surgery. But that was a threat of a different magnitude. Then she had recovered quickly. Now, the 58-year-old justice who was the most physically active of the nine had to stop everything. She was unprepared for the emotional jolt of the diagnosis.[13] "I couldn't believe I was hearing this," she re-counted to the National Coalition for Cancer Survivorship. Her face and her hands—her whole body—tingled, she said. "It couldn't be true. I'm too busy. I feel fine. You can't be serious."

Referring to the shock of the diagnosis and immediate concerns about treatment, she said, "I mean this was a world that was new to us. We didn't know the medical terms, we didn't have any experience with this and I wasn't sure I was even equipped to absorb the information I was hearing." She said that she and John tried to take notes as they talked to the various physicians but that the torrent of information was over-whelming.[14]

Justice O'Connor's youngest son, 26-year-old Jay, was working in Washington at the time and living in an apartment fifteen minutes from his parents' home. He went with his mother and father to some of the di-agnostic sessions. "She was very scared," Jay said in a later interview. "I had never seen her like this. My mom is so thoughtful and on top of things, and it really struck me to see her in a moment so helpless. She was crying."[15]

O'Connor wanted to wait to have the breast-cancer surgery, to under-stand her options, to get another round of oral arguments out of the way, to just catch her breath. Her physicians told her the surgery had to be done immediately. "There was definitely the possibility presented that she could die," Jay said. "I remember walking out of some of those ses-sions and thinking that if part of the goal was to reassure us, they didn't do it."[16]

O'Connor's cancer had progressed so far that she had to undergo a mastectomy, removal of the diseased breast. The woman who had felt so in control of her daily life was boxed in by medical imperatives. She vowed to take as little time off as possible and to be back in time for the next round of arguments. That would be ten days after the surgery.

The day before the October 21 operation, she kept a previously scheduled speaking engagement at Washington and Lee University in Lexington, Virginia, a three-hour drive southwest of Washington, DC. This was a gesture toward normalcy as well as a favor to Justice Powell. The university, named for George Washington and Robert E. Lee, was Powell's law school alma mater, and she did not want to break a commitment. In an expansive moot courtroom at the law school, before a standing-room-only crowd that had no idea what O'Connor would face the next day, the justice talked about a lawyer's mission. "The greatest joy you can have in life is to develop a skill and go out into the world and use it to help people who need it; and for the satisfaction of helping them, not for the money." An account in the law-school newspaper noted that she looked "poised and in control," and that she drew laughter with her "unexpected wit."[17]

The next day, O'Connor checked into Georgetown University Hospital, carrying legal papers in one of her bags. She had arranged for briefs to be delivered as she recuperated.[18] She had also taken time to prepare an explanation for her fellow justices. As she was getting ready for surgery on the morning of October 21, they found her memo in their chambers: "This is to let you know before you read about it in the newspaper that I am undergoing surgery today for breast cancer. Please do not be unduly concerned about it. The prognosis for my full recovery is in the range of 100 percent, and I do not anticipate having to miss any of the Court's oral arguments as a consequence of it. I will be back very soon among you. No flowers—just good thoughts. Sincerely, Sandra."[19]

As usual, her tone was controlled. But the nation's first female justice had won no dispensation from the terror befalling 1 in 50 American women. In 1988, breast cancer struck about 135,000 women in the United States every year. Survival rates depended on the size of the tumor and how much the cancer had spread before removal. The National Cancer Institute said the five-year survival rate for patients whose cancer was confined to the breast was greater than 85 percent; if it had spread to the lymph nodes, the survival rate dropped to 70 percent or less.[20]

For O'Connor, the possibly fatal disease came at an especially difficult time. The Court was beginning one of its most challenging terms in years. John's new job required him to spend about two weeks a month in Phoenix.[21] And her mother, Ada Mae, was in worsening health with Alzheimer's.

When the Court's Public Information Office released news of O'Connor's surgery, it made immediate headlines. Before she went to the hospital, O'Connor had prepared a brief statement to be issued, saying the cancer "was found to exist in a very early form and stage. The prognosis is for total recovery. I do not anticipate missing any oral arguments."

Court public information officer Toni House said she had no other details to release about the extent of O'Connor's operation or O'Connor's continuing treatment. But *Los Angeles Times* reporter David Savage sought out a breast cancer specialist at Georgetown University Medical School, who revealed what O'Connor had hoped to keep quiet: she had had a mastectomy. "Her tumor was more extensive than could be handled by a lumpectomy alone," the physician told the *Los Angeles Times*.[22] A lumpectomy involves removing only the tumor rather than the whole breast. Other news organizations repeated the *Los Angeles Times* report in their continuing accounts.

O'Connor's days in the hospital were wrenching. She reached out to Nancy Ignatius, a friend who had survived breast cancer. "It was so intense that I called that friend of mine at home and I said, could you come down to the hospital by any chance, do you have time, could you come down and see me? And she did. She dropped everything and came down and we shed a tear or two together, and we talked everything over and somehow that helped."[23]

Ignatius, who had known O'Connor since the justice's arrival in Washington, recalled getting the message on her answering machine and responding immediately. "We had a wonderful, open and frank discussion, but also a little bit teary," she said later. "There is a kind of sisterhood that happens. People are drawn together in ways that they never expected to be drawn together."[24]

Cancer was startlingly different from everything else O'Connor had faced in her fifty-eight years. With no clear recommendations for treatment, her natural decisiveness was foiled. As magazine writer Marjorie Williams wrote in a profile of O'Connor around this time, "The language of doctors, with all those possible outcomes and vague prognoses and admissions that they have no answers, only odds, is so different from the language of lawyers."[25]

O'Connor left the hospital on October 26, with five days to recover before she would return to the bench for another two-week round of oral arguments. She was exhausted. Hundreds of well-wishers wrote to her, and she could not begin to respond. She managed to write to a few friends. "It is wonderful to be out of the hospital and hopefully on the mend," she said in a note to Lewis and Jo Powell, two days after she returned home. "It has been a severe shock to be diagnosed and treated for cancer. It has become epidemic in our society and carries with it such a traumatic burden both to the body and the psyche. Depressing."[26]

"Depressing." This was a word O'Connor rarely used. Cancer was transforming. "This just wasn't me," she said when she first went public with her experience in 1994. "I'm not used to being tired. I've had a lot of energy in my life and I couldn't believe that I needed all that sleep."[27]

In the O'Connor family, where she had played the role of hardy problem-solver, she had never felt so defenseless. "My condition was causing distress to my family," she said. "My husband was affected by it. . . . My children were anxious." But the needs of others helped turn around her attitude, as she told herself, "You better shape up and make a go of this because you're causing a lot of distress for other people."[28]

Her doctors pushed her to "visualize" her treatment and recovery. "This was tough for me," she said. "I'm not a visual person. I'm a practical person, and I've never been someone who has sat around and gone to these encounter groups and thought these things through. . . . It would have been good in retrospect if I had understood some of these approaches to treatment." She adopted a characteristically hard-nosed alternative: she got a calendar, marked the chemotherapy treatment dates, and wrote down when expected side effects, such as hair loss, were to occur. As she passed through these phases, she checked them off. And although she naturally was guarded about her personal feelings, she turned to friends for advice on wigs and reconstructive surgery.

She was grateful to have her obligations and "a job that was hard and important." Decisions on cases had to be made. Opinions had to be written. The cycle kept going and she had to go with it. "So I just went down to my office and kept working," she said, wondering aloud how people without the mission of work would get through a similar ordeal.[29]

Her colleagues remember her keeping up through obvious discomfort. "She did what she had to do," Justice Stevens said later. "Everybody was aware of her problems. She didn't ask for any special treatment. She did her share of the work. She handled that in character."[30] O'Connor scheduled her chemotherapy treatments for Friday afternoons so she could use the weekends to recuperate from the nausea and other side effects of a regimen intended to destroy any cancer cells that might have spread to other parts of her body.

Within a few weeks, O'Connor resumed a full schedule of extracurricular engagements. She attended receptions and parties, even as she looked pale and uncomfortable. "That is vintage. This is who she is," explained her son Jay. "She has a real sense of service and commitment." [31] It was also natural to O'Connor's identity not to abide failure and to keep up appearances.

After O'Connor had reconstructive surgery, she could not drive, and John was regularly out of town with his work, so a longtime Phoenix friend, Gail Driggs, came to Washington and ferried her around to various social engagements. Driggs said O'Connor was undaunted in attending embassy affairs and other parties. Nancy Ignatius, who, with her husband, Paul, socialized often with the O'Connors, similarly recalled the justice continuing to go to parties throughout the chemotherapy. "I can remember her showing up at one of the waltz events [and] seeing her on the dance floor, looking absolutely ashen. But she was there." Ignatius added that in the Washington social scene, hostesses often were left wondering whether an invited senator, cabinet member, or other VIP would attend as promised, but that O'Connor had a different reputation. "If she says she is coming," Ignatius said, "she comes." [32]

O'Connor seemed more resolute in the way she dealt with her work and the other justices. "You can't go through that without coming face to face with your own mortality," Ruth McGregor, O'Connor's former law clerk and friend from Arizona, said. "It was the first time that she had to deal with a serious health threat. She faced it down. I just think it made her all the stronger. Not more aggressive, maybe. Just stronger." [33] Other law clerks around this time agreed that O'Connor seemed more forceful after the surgery. But one law clerk who joined her chambers soon after said that Justice O'Connor often seemed frustrated, irritable even, by how slow she was to regain her old stamina. "She was not at the top of her game, but there wasn't a ball she didn't swing at," the clerk said. [34]

In 1994, when Justice O'Connor went public with her feelings about surviving cancer, she said that not a day had passed without her thinking about the experience. "Having this disease made me more aware than ever before of the transitory nature of life here on Earth, of my own life. And it made me value each and every day of life more than ever before." As the ordeal gave her new strength and personal spirit, it may have awakened her to the greater possibilities of her place on the Court.

• • •

THE DAY O'CONNOR RETURNED to the bench, October 31, the justices heard a sex discrimination case that immediately placed her center stage. Her stamina was tested, as were her negotiating skills with a familiar rival, Justice Brennan. The case involving a female manager who had been denied partnership at a major accounting firm invoked sexual stereotypes and notions of how men and women were *supposed to* act.

Ann Hopkins, a senior manager at Pricewaterhouse's Washington, DC, office, had been turned down for a partnership in 1982. According to Court filings, she had been an able manager who specialized in securing contracts with federal agencies, including a $25 million contract with the State Department. She was smart and aggressive, but she also had an abrasive interpersonal style that became the focus of litigation related to her partnership rejection.[35] Colleagues described her as "aggressive" and "macho," and claimed that she denigrated underlings and used profanity. One critic said she needed to attend "charm school." The men who reviewed her partnership application said she had "lots of talent" but lacked "social grace." In comments that would be highlighted throughout the litigation, one Pricewaterhouse partner who supported Hopkins's bid for promotion told her after she was rejected that it might help to "walk more femininely, talk more femininely, wear makeup, have her hair styled, and wear jewelry."[36] Hopkins took the comments as evidence that she was denied partnership based on her sex and on illegitimate stereotypes. She sued Pricewaterhouse under Title VII of the 1964 Civil Rights Act, which prohibited job discrimination based on sex, race, religion, or national origin. Pricewaterhouse countered that a partnership advisory committee had rejected Hopkins for legitimate reasons related to how she dealt with people.[37]

Hopkins' lawsuit was known as a "mixed motive" case, that is, one in which an employer might have had valid reasons for denial of a promotion as well as illegitimate ones. Hopkins alleged that the partners did not think she was "feminine" enough, and essentially rejected her based on sex. A federal trial court judge ruled that Pricewaterhouse had unlawfully discriminated against Hopkins by giving credence to partners' comments based on sex stereotyping. A U.S. court of appeals affirmed, ruling that an employer allowing a discriminatory motive to play a part in a promotion or other job decision must prove by "clear and convincing" evidence that it would have made the same decision in the absence of discrimination. That was a far tougher standard for employers than many other lower-court judges were using in similar bias cases. The Supreme Court agreed to take up an appeal by Pricewaterhouse and to resolve conflicts among the lower courts—most of which had been putting the burden of proof more heavily on the workers who claimed job bias.[38]

The issue was playing out in offices, shops, and factories across the country. Women had been nearing numerical equality with men in various professions but still were likely "to be penalized . . . when they act[ed] in ways violating sex-related expectations," according to the American Psychological Association.[39] That is, female professionals had to walk a fine line between being aggressive enough for the job and feminine enough not to threaten traditional expectations. It was a line that O'Connor knew well.

Labor, management, and women's rights groups filed briefs with the Court, trying to influence the justices. The Equal Employment Advisory Council, a nationwide association of employers and trade groups, argued that the proof required by the federal appeals court for Pricewaterhouse was out of step with past Court cases and beyond the scope of Title VII protections. The group feared new difficulties in defending arguably valid workplace decisions. Coming at the issue from the opposite direction, a collection of women's groups led by the NOW Legal Defense and Education Fund urged the justices to put the "clear and convincing" evidentiary requirement on employers. Lawyers for the women's groups opened their amicus curiae brief by citing comments from Jeane Kirkpatrick, U.S. ambassador to the United Nations under President Reagan. Reflecting on her own experience as a woman in high government office, Kirkpatrick had said: "I've come to see here a double-bind: if a woman seems strong, she is called 'tough,' and if she doesn't seem strong, she's found not strong enough to occupy a high level job in a crunch."[40]

O'Connor understood those perceptions. Further, for all her ambition and drive, she reinforced the notion that women do best when their clothes are traditionally feminine, their hair is done, and their lipstick is on straight.

"We'll hear argument next in No. 87–1167, *Pricewaterhouse v. Ann B. Hopkins,*" Chief Justice William Rehnquist said, as lawyer Kathryn

Oberly, representing the accounting firm, stepped to the lectern. "Ms. Oberly, you may begin whenever you're ready."

"Mr. Chief Justice and may it please the Court," began Oberly, a former assistant to the U.S. solicitor general and, in 1988, a highly competitive appellate lawyer in private practice. "The district court in this case, after a five-day trial, found that Pricewaterhouse had legitimate nondiscriminatory reasons for that decision [not to make Hopkins a partner]. The district court also found that [Hopkins] failed to prove that those reasons were a pretext for discrimination. . . . But then something inexplicable happened in the district court's reasoning." Oberly said that the district court judge concluded that Pricewaterhouse violated Title VII because it failed to take steps to rid its decision-making process of any sex stereotyping. Oberly likened the result to "an O. Henry" story.[41]

In their questions, the justices focused on how to separate proper and improper grounds for a workplace decision and what burdens of proof employers and employees should bear in such "mixed motive" cases. On the latter point, Justice O'Connor jumped in early. "What is the liability situation in a case when there are two independently sufficient causes for a particular employer's action . . . ? "

"Then the situation we have, Justice O'Connor, is basically who wins in the case of a tie? Who wins if the district court, as was the case here, is unable to decide which motive actually caused the decision?" Oberly said. "And our position on that issue is that the answer has to be for [the employer]."

When it was time for James Heller, representing Hopkins, to speak, he pointed out that the lower-court judge had found that "although stereotyping by individual partners may have been unconscious on their part, the maintenance of a system that gave weight to such biased criticisms was a conscious act of the partnership as a whole."

The justices had few questions for Heller. O'Connor was not the only one who might have been tired that afternoon. The Hopkins case was the fourth of the day. After about fifteen minutes—with another fifteen minutes to go—Heller said, "If there are no other questions, I will then sit down." There were none.

Two days later, during the justices' conference on the case, all nine said they thought that the lower court had gone too far with a burden of proof for employers. But a six-justice majority, including O'Connor, determined nonetheless that Hopkins had met the appropriate requirement for showing discrimination. They believed she should prevail if the sex stereotyping was a "substantial" factor in the decision against her. In agreement with O'Connor were Brennan, Marshall, Blackmun, Stevens, and White. The six differed over how the burden of proof should shift between employer and employee, and the legalistic details would be worked out in the writing of opinions.

Meanwhile, three other justices—Rehnquist, Scalia, and Kennedy—wanted to side completely with Pricewaterhouse.

Brennan, who was the most senior justice of the majority, decided to keep the main opinion of the Court for himself. The thirty-two-year-veteran of the Court knew he had Marshall, Blackmun, and Stevens with him fully for a ruling that would enhance the ability of workers to bring cases such as Hopkins's, but do away with the lopsided standard used by the lower court in this particular case. Brennan wanted O'Connor (if not White) to sign his opinion, too, although Brennan was aware that she more narrowly interpreted the breadth of antibias law and was worried about subjecting businesses to increased litigation.

Brennan had long been known for his magnetic personality. But by 1988, the number of Reagan appointees was making it difficult for him to win a majority. In addition, he was now 82, fighting various physical ailments, and relying more on his clerks. Still, no one inside or outside the Court underestimated Brennan's continuing ability to pull five votes out of a hat.

Differences between O'Connor and Brennan in the Pricewaterhouse case played out through a series of memos that lasted nearly two months, during a period when both felt physically drained. In mid-December, Brennan was admitted to Bethesda Naval Hospital after experiencing high fever and chills. Tests revealed gallbladder disease that required surgery.[42]

Brennan had sent around his first draft in the Pricewaterhouse case before going into the hospital. O'Connor wrote back while he was out, saying she was "in general agreement" with his approach but worried that his decision could cause "stray remarks at the workplace, even by those responsible for employment decisions," to shift the burden of proof in a case to the employer.[43] She was concerned about frivolous lawsuits and unnecessary liability for employers. She laid out her worries over five pages. Working through his clerks, Brennan responded the next day: "Dear Sandra, thank you for your extensive and helpful memo. . . . I happily agree to make most of your requested changes, but for reasons that shall appear, I am unable to go along with all of them. Where I do not adopt your suggestions, however, I will add clarifying language that I hope will alleviate your concerns. . . . Again, many thanks for your comments; they have greatly improved the opinion."[44]

"Dear Bill," O'Connor wrote back, "I realize that it is much easier to cast suggestions over the chef's shoulder than it is to have one's head in the oven. Let me briefly lay out my remaining concerns with the proposed opinion." Their exchanges came down to differences over what would be required of employers trying to defend themselves against sex bias complaints. Brennan wrote at one point, "I had hoped that my most recent memo would persuade you that my proposed opinion in this case does not depart from the principles" of past cases. He wanted to reassure O'Connor that he was not breaking any new ground. "However, since— as we often say—five votes are better than four, I am willing to adopt your suggestion that we use the language from those cases in the opinion. . . . Will not these changes take care of your concerns?"[45]

In the end, Justice O'Connor "concluded that our differences in this case went beyond mere linguistics" and refused to sign his opinion.[46] She sided with Hopkins and employees generally, but with a more limited idea of the breadth of Title VII.

That is how it was between Brennan and O'Connor. Even when they were on the same side, they were not on the same page. And in this crucial term, O'Connor seemed less interested in indulging his attempts at persuasion.

When the ruling was handed down on May 1, 1989, six justices rejected Pricewaterhouse's view that Hopkins should have to prove she would have been promoted to partnership in the accounting firm but for sex discrimination. "An employer who objects to aggressiveness in women but whose positions require this trait places women in an intolerable and impermissible Catch-22: out of a job if they behave aggressively and out of a job if they don't," Brennan wrote in an opinion assigning to employers the burden of proving that bias had not been the reason for an adverse job decision. In his opinion, joined by Marshall, Blackmun, and Stevens, Brennan said once an employee shows that gender played a motivating part in an employment decision, an employer may avoid being found liable only if it proves by a "preponderance of the evidence" that it would have made the same decision even if it had not taken the employee's gender into account. The lower courts in Hopkins's case erred, he said, by requiring the firm to make its proof by clear and convincing evidence—a more difficult standard. Still, the standard invoked by the justices in the new ruling generally enhanced the ability of employees nationwide to prevail.

Justices O'Connor and White, each writing separately, concurred in that judgment but offered employers slightly more coverage when faced with "mixed motive" lawsuits. O'Connor wrote that it was important to avoid "unwarranted preferential treatment" of women. In her concurring opinion signed by no other justice, she said it was "strong medicine" to require the employer to bear completely the burden of proof, and that judges should make that demand only when the employer had knowingly given substantial weight to a sex stereotype or other impermissible factor. O'Connor added that if the majority had adopted Pricewaterhouse's position, as Rehnquist, Kennedy, and Scalia sought, it would seriously undercut Title VII's purpose of deterring intentional discrimination and compensating victims for their injuries.

In making this point, Justice O'Connor observed that Hopkins already had proved that sex stereotyping had been a substantial factor in the decision to pass her over. "It is as if Ann Hopkins were sitting in the hall outside the room where partnership decisions were being made. As the partners filed in to consider her candidacy, she heard several of them make sexist remarks in discussing her suitability for partnership. As the decision makers exited the room, she was *told* by one of those privy to the decision making process that her gender was a major reason for the rejection of her partnership bid. . . . One would be hard pressed to think of a situation where it would be more appropriate to require the [employer] to show that its decision would have been justified by wholly legitimate concerns." Justice O'Connor did not think it unfair to shift the burden to the employer "to convince [a judge] that, despite the smoke, there is no fire.' "[47]

As was her way, O'Connor also stressed that employers should not be in a position to seek the same number of men and women on the job to avoid litigation: "rather, all it need do is avoid substantial reliance on forbidden criteria in making employment decisions." When the Hopkins case returned to a lower court under the new standard, a trial judge ruled that Pricewaterhouse failed to show by a preponderance of the evidence that Hopkins's partnership was rejected for valid reasons. In that May 1990 decision, Pricewaterhouse was ordered to make her a partner and to provide back-pay dating to 1984 when Hopkins effectively was forced out.[48]

Paradoxically, the 1988–1989 term was noteworthy for the number of major job-discrimination disputes the Reagan-influenced Court resolved in favor of business. The Hopkins gender-discrimination case was the only one in which Brennan managed to pull out a victory—although tempered by O'Connor's concurring opinion. In the other cases, mostly involving race discrimination, the Supreme Court majority, which included O'Connor, significantly restricted the reach and remedies of federal civil rights laws.[49] With Brennan and the other liberals in bitter dissent, the decisions taken as whole made it harder to prove job bias and easier to challenge affirmative action programs. Revealing the tensions among justices, Blackmun's dissenting statement in one of the cases declared: "One wonders whether the majority still believes that discrimination . . . is a problem in our society, or even remembers that it ever was."[50] The Democratic-controlled Congress reacted by drafting legislation to counter the effects of the rulings.[51] Legal analysts interpreted the series as a sign that the Reagan appointees had coalesced, and the Court had taken a hard turn to the right.[52] The question, however, given the shifting relations among justices, was whether it would last.

———◆·✦·◆———

10

STILL IN THE GAME

In the early months of her illness, O'Connor worked hard to stay in the game, figuratively and literally. She began playing a little golf and tennis a few weeks after the October 1988 mastectomy. "It helped me, to resume physical exercise as soon as I could," she said. "I'm someone who just loves to have an exercise class . . . or . . . to play tennis or golf or ski . . . And it was hard because I lost the strength in my arm and it hurt."[1]

When she first returned to the Court, O'Connor had joined other justices betting on the November 1988 presidential election where the choice was between George H. W. Bush and Michael Dukakis. The Democratic challenger had been lagging in the polls for weeks, but as Election Day neared, some surveys showed that there might be a swing in Dukakis's favor. "I smell victory in the air, don't you," he asked the crowd at one rally. At another event, he declared that he was "rocking and rolling" as Vice President Bush was "slipping and sliding." The Massachusetts governor was betting on a big swing at the end.[2]

At the Court, pool participants were Rehnquist, Stevens, O'Connor, Kennedy, and retired Justice Powell. After the results were in, and Bush had beaten Dukakis with 53 percent of the popular vote, Rehnquist tallied up the results among the justices with an elaborate set of calculations. Rehnquist and O'Connor did the best. Reported Rehnquist: "John [Stevens] owes the pool $10.61, Tony [Kennedy] owes $0.22, Lewis

[Powell] owes $9.77. Sandra won $5.19 and I won $15.19. Those who owe should send their money to me and I will in turn send it to the winners."[3] Rehnquist typically did well in the election pools. Justice Scalia said in an interview, "I almost never participated, mainly because the Chief almost always wins."[4]

These habitual wagerers led by Rehnquist did not confine themselves to politics. Several months earlier, they had placed bets on exactly how many inches of snow would fall during a storm. Rehnquist, whose preoccupation with the cold began during his Wisconsin childhood and who worked at a weather station in Africa during World War II, conducted the snow measurements. But O'Connor had her own gauge. "It only took me five hours to get here today in order to verify your snow measurements. I know when to accept defeat. Enclosed is my dollar," she wrote to Rehnquist. Powell ended up besting them all with his prediction.[5]

AFTER THE CANCER SURGERY, O'Connor walked with noticeable stiffness. "There was constant media coverage," she recalled. Then, mocking the press, she said: " 'How does she look?' 'When is she going to step down and give the president another vacancy on the Court?' 'She looks pale to me. I don't give her six months.' It was really difficult."[6]

As a justice on the nation's highest court, O'Connor was under legitimate scrutiny. The fight over Robert Bork's nomination in 1987 demonstrated that any retirement could create a major political fight and have significant implications for the law. O'Connor had not made public the fact that she was undergoing chemotherapy, so reporters were on the lookout for a change in her appearance. The United Press International moved a story on its wires on November 28, a month after her surgery, that said, "Justice Sandra Day O'Connor appeared to be wearing a wig Monday as she heard arguments before the Supreme Court, suggesting she may be suffering hair loss from treatment related to her recent breast cancer surgery. O'Connor's hair is naturally thin, light colored and graying, but Monday it had more fullness and body and was a slightly darker shade."[7]

While the press speculated and the new year dawned, O'Connor remained active. In January 1989, she attended some of the inaugural festivities for President George H. W. Bush, including a cocktail party hosted by former deputy White House press secretary Peter Roussel, who in 1981 had flown to Phoenix to help O'Connor with her first news conference after being nominated by Reagan. The *Washington Post* reported that O'Connor, who played tennis with Barbara Bush, chatted with Wimbledon tennis champion John Newcombe of Australia, a friend of the Bushes, about the White House tennis court.[8] A week later, O'Connor and her husband went to Palm Springs, California, for a judicial conference. O'Connor's work and her social engagements became a rope to hold on to, to pull herself out of her illness.

At the same time, hardly a day passed without some high-profile case on her desk. The 1988–1989 term was to be an unusual one, because of O'Connor's health, the divisiveness among justices, and the substance of the cases before the Court.[9] About a week before the presidential inauguration, it became clear that she was the deciding vote to allow the execution of criminal defendants convicted of murder who were found to be mentally retarded. "Accordingly, I will plan to keep the assignment in this case," she told Rehnquist. She believed the constitutional ban on cruel and unusual punishment did not categorically prevent states from executing mentally retarded defendants, but she wanted the door open to change if a consensus among the states against it emerged.[10]

At the same time, serial killer Theodore Bundy, 42, pressed an emergency appeal asking the Supreme Court to block his scheduled execution in Florida. The case of the disarming psychopath had captured the nation's attention. A 1986 television movie starring Mark Harmon, called *The Deliberate Stranger*, had chronicled the terror Bundy wrought after gaining the confidence of unsuspecting women. Bundy, who had been called a "diabolical genius" by one lower-court judge, claimed he was mentally incompetent when he stood trial in 1980 for the killing of a 12-year-old girl in Lake City, Florida. Bundy reportedly was connected to at least thirty-six sex murders or disappearances of young women nationwide.[11]

For O'Connor and four other justices, action in the case was easy: deny Bundy's request for a stay of execution. Brennan and Marshall dissented, noting that they were against the death penalty in all circumstances but also saying they believed a judge's instructions to Bundy's Florida jury were flawed. Two other justices, Blackmun and Stevens, also voted to block the execution. Without the requisite five votes from the Supreme

Court to stay his execution and with no intervention from Florida officials, Bundy was executed on January 24, 1989, after a decade of court appeals.[12]

O'Connor was concerned with protracted inmate appeals, particularly in capital punishment cases. Regard for state-court decisions had been a priority of hers since she joined the Court in 1981 and was yet another point of contention between her and Brennan. In the 1988–1989 term, she ended up adopting one of the toughest stances ever—for her and ultimately for the Court—concerning the ability of state prisoners to be heard by federal judges. The occasion was the case of Frank Teague, an Illinois man convicted in 1980 of armed robbery and attempted murder of police officers. He claimed that he had not received a fair trial. Teague, who was African-American, had been tried by an all-white jury after the local prosecutor had used all ten of his "peremptory" challenges to excuse prospective African-American jurors. (Historically, each side in a case received a set number of peremptory challenges for screening potential jurors. Unlike challenges "for cause," based on grounds that a juror cannot fairly decide the case, peremptory challenges could be made for any reason and did not require an explanation. Still, the Court had ruled earlier that they could not be used to strike a person from the jury pool because of race.)[13]

In this case, Teague claimed the exclusion of blacks violated his Sixth Amendment right to be tried by a jury whose composition was representative of the community. The high court had decided to hear his appeal, apparently to determine the scope of the constitutional right to a fair jury. The Sixth Amendment required that a jury be drawn from a fair cross-section of the community, but earlier Court cases had focused on the overall pool from which particular juries were drawn. Teague's claim was aimed at the actual jury chosen.

Justice O'Connor did not think Teague should even be in federal court, for reasons that had nothing to do with the racial question at the core of the case. It had long irked this former state-court judge that state-convicted prisoners tried to defy state-court rulings by repeatedly petitioning federal judges on various grounds through petitions for habeas corpus. In the justices' private conference, a majority was with O'Connor for the bottom-line judgment that Teague was barred from a federal hearing on his claim that his right to a fair jury had been violated.

But things got sticky as she began circulating a draft of her reasoning to seriously curtail federal judges from hearing prisoners' petitions. Brennan and the other liberal justices were troubled. In her draft opinion distributed November 23, she first observed that the Court had previously held that the Sixth Amendment requires a jury pool to be drawn from a fair cross-section of the community but that it had never said that the jury chosen must mirror the community. Then, in the more far-reaching portion of her opinion, O'Connor wrote that the Court need not address the jury question, because any new Sixth Amendment rule could not apply retroactively to cases such as Teague's. With more assertiveness than she had demonstrated in past cases on the subject, she adopted a standard under which prisoners could rely only on the law already in effect when their convictions became final (after their direct appeals were complete) and, with few exceptions, could not benefit from any new rule of law that later emerged from a Supreme Court decision.[14]

Because of the evolving nature of constitutional law, the potential ramifications of O'Connor's opinion were great. Federal judges in habeas cases were often in the position to rule on questions for which there was not yet a directly controlling Supreme Court precedent. When Justice Stevens saw what O'Connor proposed, he sent around a note to the others reminding them that the issue before the justices involved jury composition and that the lawyers had not focused on when new rules could be applied to a prisoner's case. Stevens questioned "the wisdom of making an important ruling of this kind without the benefit of argument."[15] But in the end O'Connor effectively won a majority for her approach, with Chief Justice Rehnquist and Justices Scalia and Kennedy. Justice White, with whom O'Connor sometimes putted golf balls in chambers, did not join her opinion, but wrote a concurring statement that said O'Connor's approach offered "an acceptable application" in appeal proceedings.[16]

Stevens, joined by Blackmun, voted to reject Teague's appeal but objected to O'Connor's new standard for petitions from prisoners. Brennan's dissent, joined only by Marshall, was impassioned. He declared that O'Connor's opinion was undertaken "without regard for—indeed, without even mentioning—our contrary decisions over the past 35 years delineating the broad scope of habeas relief" for prisoners. Noting that even Illinois officials, protesting Teague's appeal, had not suggested that the Court go so far in restricting habeas petitions, Brennan declared her opinion an "unprecedented curtailment of the reach of the Great Writ."

O'Connor had taken the case beyond what anyone would have predicted when the Court agreed to hear Teague's case on the jury question. Yet, the ruling on February 22, 1989, barely made a ripple in the daily news. It came on the same day as a sensational decision in a Wisconsin child abuse case. The Court ruled that 4-year-old Joshua DeShaney's constitutional rights were not violated when county social workers monitoring his welfare failed to protect him from beatings by his father, which left the boy brain-damaged. Writing for a majority that included O'Connor, Rehnquist said that the Fourteenth Amendment's due process guarantee did not require states to protect individuals from harm by third parties when they were not in the custody of the state—for example, in a state institution. The Court said that the relationship between the welfare agency and the child did not rise to a level dictating a duty to protect him. The case prompted one of the most memorable Blackmun dissents: "Poor Joshua! Victim of repeated attacks by an irresponsible, bullying, cowardly, and intemperate father, and abandoned by [county welfare officials] who placed him in a dangerous predicament." [17]

Although the media focused on the *DeShaney* case, criminal law professors and defendants' rights advocates latched on to *Teague,* criticizing the ruling for making it more difficult for prisoners to get into federal court. [18] New York University law professor Barry Friedman wrote that the decision, although not itself involving a capital conviction, "plainly was the work of a Court anxious to speed the pace of executions." He said lower federal judges would be merely "traffic cops for the Supreme Court, doing little more than denying petitions and chastening the occasional errant state court that strays from the constitutional fold." [19]

O'Connor had long been looking for an opportunity to narrow habeas actions, and she seized on the Teague jury case to do it. More broadly, her level of confidence had been building with the years. And just as certainly, her role as pivotal justice was helped by the addition of another conservative, Kennedy, and by the weakened influence of liberal Brennan. But it is hard not to consider also the life-threatening experience with cancer among the factors that made O'Connor a force in these cases and others during the 1988–1989 term. The vestiges of the ever-dutiful, deferential former Arizona state legislator had disappeared. Her confrontations with fellow justices were overt and had a new clarity.

The battle with cancer had shaken her to her foundations. But the sustaining nature of her work was helping her overcome her illness, even as her illness altered the way she worked. The character it took to stand up to the disease strengthened her resolve. She was moving further away from her legislative days and early years on the Court when she had maneuvered in ways that relegated her to a supporting role. She was light-years from the woman who wrote letters on behalf of nominee Rehnquist or tried to influence an extra vote for Justice Powell. Abetted by the changes in Court membership that tilted in her direction, O'Connor was in a position to maximize her influence on the law.

In this term, O'Connor also undertook the opinion for the majority in an affirmative action dispute that ultimately would make her the voice of the high Court on the constitutionality of race-based policies. The dispute revolved around a Richmond, Virginia, ordinance requiring businesses contracting with the city to set aside 30 percent of their subcontracting work for companies owned by "black, Spanish-speaking, Oriental, Indian, Eskimo, or Aleut" people.[20]

Throughout America, such government policies designed to generate opportunities for racial minorities were common, but they ran the gamut from casual goals for diversity to firm hiring quotas based on color. In the late 1980s, whites increasingly challenged quota-driven and other hard-and-fast affirmative action programs. The phrase "reverse discrimination" became common. Politicians sometimes played on white resentment. (Three years after the Richmond case, North Carolina Republican Senator Jesse Helms would air a famous television commercial during his reelection campaign against Charlotte mayor Harvey Gantt, a Democrat and an African-American. In the television ad, a white hand crumpled up a job application after the job apparently went to a black man. Helms narrowly won.)

The Richmond ordinance specifically favored black and Spanish-speaking subcontractors, because very few Oriental, Indian, Eskimo, or Aleut people lived in the region. The J. A. Croson company, which lost a contract for installing plumbing fixtures at the city jail because it lacked the requisite minority subcontractors, sued the city over the policy, saying it violated the constitutional guarantee of equality. A lower federal appeals court agreed.

When the city of Richmond appealed, lawyer John Payton told the justices during oral argument, "By enacting this ordinance, Richmond was attempting to address one of the most difficult problems confronting our nation and its cities and states. Identified racial discrimination is a scourge of our society. Richmond focused on discrimination in the construction industry and proceeded to try to remedy that discrimination."

O'Connor asked Payton, a long-time civil rights lawyer working for a large Washington, DC, firm, what specific evidence of discrimination the city had to justify favoring the minority subcontractors. "Was there evidence before the city that [minorities] had been subject to discrimination in the Richmond construction industry?"

"There is no evidence in the record with regard to that," Payton answered. He then added that evidence of race discrimination in contracting had been well documented by the federal government.[21]

O'Connor had long struggled with the breadth of the Fourteenth Amendment's guarantee of equal treatment and the permissibility of race-based measures to atone for discrimination. In this case, she was troubled that Richmond had showed no direct evidence of race discrimination in public contracting, and she believed its set-aside program arose, in fact, from political favoritism. Blacks constituted about half of the population of Richmond, and five of the nine seats on the city council were held by blacks.[22]

In the opinion she wrote for the Court, she said, "While there is no doubt that the sorry history of both private and public discrimination in this country has contributed to a lack of opportunities for black entrepreneurs, this observation standing alone cannot justify a rigid racial quota in the awarding of public contracts in Richmond, Virginia ... [A]n amorphous claim that there has been past discrimination in a particular industry cannot justify the use of an unyielding racial quota."

Led by O'Connor, five justices said for the first time that all race-conscious policies, even when they benefit minorities, should be assessed by the standard known as "strict scrutiny." That meant that the same tough scrutiny that had been invoked for Jim Crow laws and other policies that discriminated against blacks would be applied to programs intended to give them a leg up.

But O'Connor insisted that "Nothing we say today precludes a state or local entity from taking action to rectify the effects of identified discrimination within its jurisdiction. If the city of Richmond had evidence before it that nonminority contractors were systematically excluding minority businesses from subcontracting opportunities, it could take action to end the discriminatory exclusion." The Court was not shutting the door on affirmative action in all cases but was making government accountable under stricter terms and requiring particular evidence of relevant past discrimination.

This time, O'Connor's words fell hardest on Justice Marshall, a man who had been denied seats in restaurants and the use of public restrooms because of the color of his skin. Marshall had spent much of his adult life working for equal legal rights for African-Americans. He found the decision written by O'Connor "a giant step backward." He pointed out the irony that the old Southern city of Richmond was being stopped from remedying a history of racial discrimination. "It is a welcome symbol of racial progress when the former capital of the Confederacy acts forthrightly to confront the effects of racial discrimination in its midst," Marshall wrote. He was joined by Justices Brennan and Blackmun. They attacked the majority for ruling that programs benefiting blacks should be judged by the same exacting standards as those that hurt minorities. They said O'Connor's position "sounds a full-scale retreat" from affirmative action for past discrimination, and warned, "The battle against pernicious racial discrimination or its effects is nowhere near won."

Marshall invoked Richmond's long history of racial discrimination, in voting rights, in housing, and—what mattered personally to the advocate who won the series of cases known as *Brown v. Board of Education*—in school integration. "As much as any municipality in the United States," Marshall declared, "Richmond knows what racial discrimination is; a century of decisions by this and other federal courts has richly documented the city's disgraceful history of public and private racial discrimination."

Editorial writers split in their assessment of the decision. In an editorial endorsing the ruling, the *Richmond Times-Dispatch* wrote, "[F]or all the high-sounding rhetoric about correcting 'stark and dramatic' evidence of racial bias, the ordinance turned out to be just another special-interest handout." But *New York Times* opinion-page columnist Tom

Wicker wrote of O'Connor, "[S]he and the majority know little about the South and little about racial discrimination."[23]

O'Connor believed she was bringing together such extremes to avoid, as she put it, "a politics of racial hostility." She tried to give both sides something. Her opinion rejected numerical set-asides but said some racial preferences might be permissible in other unspecified contexts.

ON A BASIC PERSONAL LEVEL, O'Connor simply was trying to stay busy and move beyond her illness. She had an especially productive spring in 1989, amid the miseries of chemotherapy and the constant rumors that she might have to step down. Looking pale and drained, she performed two highly public investitures of Bush administration appointees. She first swore in a former Republican congressman from New York, Jack Kemp, as head of the Department of Housing and Urban Development.[24] Three days later, O'Connor conducted the swearing-in of Clayton Yeutter as secretary of agriculture. President Bush spoke at the ceremony. Noting that Yeutter was named an "outstanding animal husbandry graduate" at the University of Nebraska, President Bush said, "Many kids want to grow up to be president—not Clayton. When he was a boy, he wanted to be secretary of agriculture. And here he is, and that's a lucky break for America."

"Are you ready to realize that ambition?" O'Connor quipped as she stood up to give Yeutter the oath.[25]

After O'Connor had sworn him in, Yeutter addressed her and recalled their work on the 1972 reelection campaign of Richard Nixon. He said he remembered meeting Arizona state campaign chairman Sam Mardian and O'Connor, who was cochair, when he visited Phoenix as director of Nixon's agriculture campaign issues. "At one particular point during the day, I said to the gentleman who was the campaign chairman, 'Where in the world did you get Sandra O'Connor? She is just fantastic!' And he said, 'You're absolutely right. She is fantastic.' "

Yeutter then told the investiture audience that Mardian had predicted to Yeutter in 1972 that O'Connor would be the first woman on the U.S. Supreme Court. O'Connor was not even a state trial judge in 1972. When asked later, Mardian recalled that he indeed had predicted that she would rise to the Supreme Court. "She was active politically and she had knowledge of the law," he said by way of explanation.[26]

Two weeks after the Yeutter investiture, on March 3, 1989, O'Connor endured another personal trauma. Her mother died. Ada Mae Day was 85. She was a turn-of-the-century woman who had graduated from college, then left the excitement of the city for the Lazy B and the love of her life. Harry Day often looked back to what might have been, but Ada Mae faced forward. "That's just the way it is," she often said of the vicissitudes of life. It was a phrase adopted by the first woman justice.

While O'Connor was in Arizona for funeral services, she learned that the *Washington Post* was about to publish a story alleging an ethical lapse on her part. A year earlier, O'Connor had sent a letter to an Arizona Republican activist Annetta Conant, which was then used by the state Republican Party to generate support for a party resolution declaring the United States to be "a Christian nation . . . based on the absolute law of the Bible." O'Connor's letter had cited statements in three Supreme Court cases "to the effect that this is a Christian nation." Two of the citations turned out to be in error, but the real furor was over the "Christian nation" sentiment.[27] The Arizona Republican Party's action in January 1989 prompted protests from Jewish community leaders and civil libertarians, who argued that the "Christian nation" movement arose from religious intolerance. (Arizona Republican Party officials quickly responded by adopting a resolution that said the party was open to all races and religions.)

Once the story was reported in the *Washington Post* in March 1989, lawyers across the ideological spectrum criticized O'Connor. She issued a statement saying: "I regret that a letter I sent to an acquaintance in response to her request for information was used in a political debate. It was not my intention to express a personal view about the subject of the inquiry, but merely to respond appropriately to one of the many requests for information which come across my desk."[28]

But the justice was not fully disclosing the facts of the matter. As Harvard University law professor Alan Dershowitz noted in a *New York Times* opinion piece, "the original request [to O'Connor] made it unmistakably clear that she was being asked to write her letter specifically for the Christian Nation Resolution being pressed by elements in the Republican Party."[29] The letter to O'Connor from Conant reportedly stated,

"Some of us are proposing a resolution which acknowledges that the Supreme Court ruled in 1872 that this is a Christian Nation. It would be beneficial and interesting to have a letter from you."[30] Dershowitz also reminded readers of a slip by O'Connor in 1987, in which she initially had agreed to give a "private briefing" to Republicans who had contributed $10,000 to a GOP political action committee. When news of the event became public, and legal ethics analysts criticized her participation, O'Connor pulled out. She said she did not know she was being used in connection with a fund-raiser.[31]

In 1989, even sympathetic nonpartisans disparaged O'Connor for the "Christian nation" letter. Newspaper columnist Edwin M. Yoder Jr. penned an opinion piece in the *Washington Post* that said he would assume, "as gallantry requires, that O'Connor's unfortunate letter was the product of some clerical slip-up or haste or was uttered on a day when she had far more important matters on her mind—or all three." Nevertheless, Yoder wrote, "The political embarrassment is acute, but considerably more embarrassing is the distorted idea of [the nation's religious identity] to which the Justice has lent unwitting support."[32]

Supreme Court staff suggested to reporters that O'Connor simply had adopted language from a 1975 letter by a Court librarian, written on behalf of Warren Burger in response to a request for similar information.[33] One way or another, O'Connor had blundered. If she was chastened, she was not going to explain herself. She did not address the narrow religious sentiment or inaccurate citations of her letter. All she said was that she was sorry that a personal letter was used for political purposes. She moved on.

Media attention increasingly focused on her even more consequential role on the Court. She was often the single vote controlling a resolution. In June, the *American Lawyer* magazine published a story observing that while "rumors have circulated persistently that she may leave the Court this summer . . . for now, at least, she is the one who determines which side wins the biggest 5-to-4 decisions and how broadly they are written. . . . She is the most moderate member of the new conservative majority, the closest thing we have, for better or for worse, to a living oracle of the evolving Constitution. To divine the direction of the law, watch what she does."[34]

Those words had particular resonance as the justices struggled to fin-

ish their momentous 1988–1989 term. In a closely watched pair of disputes from the Pittsburgh area over government-sponsored religious
holiday displays, O'Connor switched her vote at the last minute. She then
became part of narrow majorities striking down a Nativity scene on the
grand staircase of the Allegheny County Courthouse but finding permissible a display of an eighteen-foot Hanukkah menorah with a forty-five-
foot Christmas tree outside Pittsburgh's city-county building. Only she
and Blackmun were in the majority on both cases.

Earlier that spring, O'Connor had sided with Justice Brennan in voting against the menorah display. She had agreed in March to write the
dissenting opinion for Brennan, Marshall, Stevens, and herself. But on
June 6, with just a few weeks left in the term, she told Brennan that she
believed the Hanukkah menorah did not violate the requisite separation
of church and state. "This is a change from my conference vote and will
undoubtedly require a reassignment of the proposed dissent. This has
been a close case for me all along, but I am now firm in my approach," she
told Brennan. No regret. No mention of the sudden pinch Brennan was
in to write the dissent.

"Dear Chief," Brennan soon wrote to Rehnquist, "I'm very sorry but
the latest circulations of Harry and Sandra may require me to respond.
May the announcement of the case please go over until Monday?" That
would be July 3. Rehnquist agreed. The Court session was already extending into July—a rare occurrence under the ever-efficient Rehnquist—because of the last-minute wrangling, also involving O'Connor,
in an important abortion case from Missouri.[35]

In the menorah case, O'Connor wrote that Pittsburgh's erection of the
Jewish holiday symbol alongside the Christmas tree offered "a message
of pluralism and freedom of belief," rather than an endorsement of a particular religion. Her stance in that case was an extension of her position
taken in a 1984 dispute *Lynch v. Donnelly,* allowing the city of Pawtucket,
Rhode Island, to display a crèche scene surrounded by Santa's reindeer
and other secular holiday symbols. Her test was whether an objective reasonable observer would think the municipality erecting the display was
endorsing Christianity. In the current matters, Brennan believed O'Connor's position in *Allegheny v. American Civil Liberties Union* ignored past
cases requiring government neutrality not just among religions but between the religious and the nonreligious. He did not think the menorah

could be transformed into an innocuous, nonreligious symbol by virtue of what accompanied it at the site.[36]

Also in late June, O'Connor penned the controlling opinions in two important death penalty cases. In *Penry v. Lynaugh,* which she had begun writing around the presidential inaugural, she declared that the constitutional ban on cruel and unusual punishment did not prohibit a state from executing a mentally retarded convict who had been found competent to stand trial. In the *Penry* case, Scalia, the most conservative justice, was nearly as unhappy with O'Connor's rationale as was Brennan, the most liberal. "I do not plan to make changes to *Penry* in response to Bill's and Nino's writings," O'Connor told Rehnquist, sticking with her opinion that, as usual, navigated between two poles and largely (but not definitively) left the matter to the states. "As far as I am concerned [the decision] can be announced any day," she told the chief justice. O'Connor's rationale in the *Penry* case, which would become critical in later death penalty disputes, referred to the lack of societal consensus against executing mentally retarded defendants. She believed that "the clearest and most reliable objective evidence of contemporary values is the legislation enacted by the country's legislatures" and noted that at the time only one of the states imposing the death penalty banned the execution of retarded persons found guilty of a capital offense.[37] At the same time, O'Connor cast the fifth vote finding that the Constitution does not bar execution of a defendant who committed his crime when he was only 16 years old, in *Stanford v. Kentucky,* also based on the fact that no national consensus existed for the exception.[38]

IN THE GREAT MAJORITY of one-vote decisions during the 1988–1989 term, the five conservative members (Rehnquist, White, O'Connor, Scalia, and Kennedy) prevailed over the four liberals (Brennan, Marshall, Blackmun, and Stevens). That same lineup initially emerged in an Indian water-rights case the Court resolved just days before they recessed for the summer. Once again, O'Connor and Brennan were pitted against each other; she writing for the majority, he for the dissent. The case was yet another example of their competing approaches to the law and, for this particular term, the challenges O'Connor faced.

The dispute revolved around reserved water rights for Indians on the

Wind River Reservation, home of the Shoshone and Northern Arapaho tribes, in Wyoming. As trustee for the tribes, the United States had successfully contested a Wyoming state policy voiding the water rights. Wyoming claimed the rights had lapsed when the Indians failed to invoke them for irrigation or other projects. O'Connor was preparing an opinion for the Court that sided with Wyoming in its appeal and that would deny the Indians the water rights. It was her usual fact-laden ruling analyzing the various treaties and laws involved. As Brennan began the first draft of his dissenting opinion in the case, he criticized the majority and asserted that the tribes had not used the water rights in any irrigation projects because they had lacked the funds to undertake such projects. "The Court might well have taken as its motto for this case the words of Matthew 25:29: 'but from him that has not shall be taken away even that which he has.' . . . I cannot join in such a redistribution of rights at the expense of one of the most disadvantaged groups in American society—on the pretext that the Indians do not 'need' the water rights we strip from them." It was classic Brennan: focused on the human beings who would be affected by the ruling.[39]

Suddenly everything changed. O'Connor sent a memo to her eight colleagues on June 22, 1989, that said: "I am a minority stockholder in my family's ranching corporation. My brother, who manages the ranch, telephoned me this week to let me know the corporation has been named in a river water suit brought by an Indian tribe affecting the Gila River, which adjoins a portion of the ranch. For reasons I will not detail here, I believe the ranch will succeed in being dismissed from the suit as having no affected interest, but as of now I believe I must disqualify myself in this case."[40]

Taking herself out of the case meant that the Court was now split. A tie vote automatically affirmed the lower-court ruling, which had favored the federal government as trustee for the tribes. So, O'Connor's recusal, as it was formally known, meant that the justices who were once in the majority effectively lost. Four days later, the Court issued a two-sentence unsigned opinion stating that the lower-court decision favoring the Indians was affirmed by a divided Court. The statement said Justice O'Connor did not participate in the case. It gave no reason, as it never does. People outside the Court did not know how close the Indians had come to losing in *Wyoming v. United States.* (The dispute continued between Wyoming and the Native American community for years, and in 1992 a state-court ruling extinguished the tribe's water rights.)

In O'Connor's note to her colleagues saying that she would have to sit out the case of *Wyoming v. United States,* she aptly wrote, "The unexpected has become the order of the day this term."

HER AWARENESS OF "the transitory nature of life," and her increased determination, were accompanied by a new understanding of the dignity one clings to in the face of a potentially fatal disease. That was revealed in two later cases, one just a year after her surgery, one in the mid-1990s. In both, she adopted the perspective of the dying patient.

In the first dispute, which marked the justices' first foray into the ethics of an individual's "right to die," the parents of Nancy Cruzan, who had been unconscious since a 1983 automobile accident, wanted to remove her from life support. Cruzan was in what physicians called a "persistent vegetative state" and being fed through a tube in her stomach that provided food and water. The state of Missouri objected to her parents' desire to end the feedings, because Cruzan had provided no clear advance directive of what she would have wanted in such a dire situation. The high court ruled that a patient has a right to refuse life support, but by a 5–4 vote it sided with Missouri in declaring that a state may block parents' intervention when a patient's wishes were not clearly known. As she joined the Court majority's opinion by Chief Justice Rehnquist, O'Connor wrote separately to observe, first, the strong interest an individual has in refusing life support:

"Whether or not the techniques used to pass food and water into the patient's alimentary tract are termed 'medical treatment,' it is clear they all involved some degree of intrusion and restraint. . . . A gastrostomy tube [as was used to provide food and water to Nancy Cruzan] . . . must be surgically implanted into the stomach or small intestine. Requiring a competent adult to endure such procedures against her will burdens the patient's liberty, dignity, and freedom to determine the course of her own treatment."

Then, returning to her pragmatic self and with an eye to the states, O'Connor raised the possibility that parents or other relatives some day could be allowed to make the ultimate decision for an irreversibly comatose person: "Today's decision, holding only that the Constitution permits a state to require clear and convincing evidence of Nancy Cruzan's desire to have artificial hydration and nutrition withdrawn, does not preclude a future determination that the Constitution requires the states to implement the decisions of a patient's duly appointed surrogate. Nor does it prevent states from developing other approaches for protecting an incompetent individual's liberty interest in refusing medical treatment. As is evident from the Court's survey of state court decisions, no national consensus has yet emerged on the best solution for this difficult and sensitive problem."[41]

In the second related case, seven years later, the Court ruled unanimously that the Constitution does not guarantee Americans a right to commit suicide with the help of a physician. In a case that produced six separate opinions, attesting to the complexity of the subject, the Court upheld New York and Washington state laws that criminalized physician-assisted suicide. In her concurring statement, O'Connor said that the possibility existed that someday—after state legislatures had confronted the issue—the high court might find that certain individuals who are particularly suffering could have an individual right to assisted suicide.

"Death will be different for each of us," she wrote. "For many, the last days will be spent in physical pain and perhaps the despair that accompanies physical deterioration and a loss of control of basic bodily and mental functions. Some will seek medication to alleviate that pain and other symptoms."

In words that were by turns movingly warm and coolly theoretical, O'Connor concluded, "Every one of us at some point may be affected by our own or a family member's terminal illness. There is no reason to think the democratic process will not strike the proper balance between the interests of terminally ill, mentally competent individuals who would seek to end their suffering and the State's interests in protecting those who might seek to end life mistakenly or under pressure."[42]

Both her parents were gone. She had survived her own struggle with death. The O'Connor household would find more illness and heartache in the years ahead, and these events would be determinative forces in the justice she became.

SHIFTING GROUND
ON ABORTION

One final case of the arduous 1988–1989 term, *Webster v. Reproduc-tive Health Services,* brought to the forefront the enduring contro-versy over *Roe v. Wade.* Where did Justice O'Connor really stand on abortion? That great unknown was about to be answered as it became necessary for the first woman justice to cast the deciding vote on the most divisive of women's issues.

Three years earlier, in another abortion case, *Thornburgh v. American College of Obstetricians and Gynecologists,* Justice Harry Blackmun had said bluntly of O'Connor, "She just is against abortion." He had jotted those words in his characteristically neat, small cursive handwriting on O'Connor's draft opinion circulated in the case. That dispute involved a Pennsylvania statute designed to discourage abortions by imposing a waiting period and an "informed consent" requirement on women seek-ing the procedure.[1] O'Connor's dissenting opinion in the case was hand-delivered as customary by messenger. Blackmun was surprised by the forcefulness of her draft. O'Connor, who was not the swing vote at that time, had written, "Suffice it to say that I dispute not only the wisdom but the legitimacy of the Court's attempt to discredit and preempt state abor-tion regulation regardless of the interests it serves and the impact it has."

Blackmun put an exclamation point next to that sentence and then wrote his personal observation on what he believed was a hard-and-fast position against abortion.[2]

The vote in that case was 5–4. While Blackmun won the majority he needed at that time, he worried over the fact that the number of justices committed to abortion rights had dwindled since 1973, when *Roe v. Wade* became law.[3] It rankled Blackmun, the author of the *Roe* opinion making abortion legal nationwide, that O'Connor would vote to uphold restrictions Blackmun believed impinged on a woman's right to end a pregnancy. "Few decisions are more personal and intimate, more properly private, or more basic to individual dignity and autonomy, than a woman's decision—with the guidance of her physician and within the limits specified in *Roe*—whether to end her pregnancy," he had written for the majority.[4]

Now, sixteen years after *Roe* and three years after *Thornburgh,* much had changed at the Court. Antonin Scalia had become an associate justice, filling the seat of William Rehnquist, who became chief justice after Warren Burger retired. Anthony Kennedy had succeeded Lewis Powell, a consistent supporter of abortion rights who had been in the majority on *Roe*.

Politically, the nation was different, too. Newly elected president George H. W. Bush, and Ronald Reagan before him, had won the White House with support from the well-organized "Right to Life" movement. Now, with a new case testing a Missouri abortion law at the Court, the Bush administration was advocating reversal of *Roe*. Missouri's statute asserted that life began at conception and that the unborn have "protectable interests in life, health and well-being." It imposed several regulations on women seeking to end a pregnancy and the physicians who would conduct the procedure.

"Will *Roe v. Wade* go down the drain?" Blackmun had asked rhetorically of a University of Arkansas audience in the summer of 1988, a few weeks before the term began. "I think there's a very distinct possibility it will—this term."[5]

Decided on January 22, 1973, a date seared in the minds of activists on both sides of the abortion dilemma, *Roe* had extended for the first time the constitutional right of privacy to a woman's decision to end a pregnancy. By the late 1980s, the protests and picketing begun in 1973 were

escalating into more radical, even unlawful, tactics that included bomb-
ings at clinics that performed abortions. And the impact of the abortion
debate on politics, the law, and public understanding of the Supreme
Court could not be overstated. The fight over Reagan's nomination of
Robert Bork in 1987 traced largely to abortion politics.[6]

For Blackmun, the 1973 decision was a defining work. Written in his
third term on the Court, *Roe v. Wade* established the short, wiry Minnesota justice in the American mind—for better or worse. As O'Connor
knew firsthand, Blackmun had a habit of challenging new justices to be
with him or against him on abortion rights. He saw no middle ground.
After O'Connor criticized *Roe,* first in a 1983 case from Akron, Ohio, and
then in the 1986 *Thornburgh* case, Blackmun worried that she soon
would vote to reverse it outright. Only three of the justices who made up
the original seven-justice majority signing *Roe v. Wade* were still on the
Court: Blackmun, William Brennan, and Thurgood Marshall. All were
80 or older.

It was a coincidence of history that the Court faced pressure to reexamine *Roe* at a time when the crucial swing vote belonged to the first justice ever to have given birth and just as she faced a life-and-death
challenge in her personal life. She was still undergoing chemotherapy
treatments for breast cancer as the case first came to the justices. Advocates on both sides looked for signs of how O'Connor might rule. Her
public record over the years was ambiguous. In the 1970s, as an Arizona
state senator, O'Connor had voted to repeal state criminal laws against
abortion. She also had voted against a resolution in the state senate that
criticized *Roe v. Wade* and called upon Congress to try to reverse its effects. But when Reagan nominated her in 1981 and she testified before
the Senate Judiciary Committee, her expressed views seemed more ambivalent. "It is something that is repugnant to me and something in
which I would not engage. Obviously, there are others who do not share
these beliefs, and I recognize that. I think we are obligated to recognize
that others have different views and some would draw the line in one
place rather than another."[7]

Two years later, in 1983, O'Connor vindicated Reagan and abortion
opponents. Participating in her first abortion case, *Akron v. Akron Center
for Reproductive Health,* she cast a vote—in dissent—to uphold Ohio restrictions on abortion. She was critical of *Roe,* writing that because of

medical advances that allowed fetuses to live outside the mother at earlier stages, its trimester approach tied to viability was "clearly on a collision course with itself." In language that particularly concerned activists who feared interference with a woman's choice of abortion, O'Connor also wrote, "Potential life is no less potential in the first weeks of pregnancy than it is at viability or afterward."[8] She seemed to be valuing the fetus in a way that could compromise a woman's right to chose abortion in the first and second trimesters.

Yet, even as O'Connor criticized *Roe* and voted for abortion restrictions that a Court majority believed were contrary to *Roe,* she never said that the 1973 landmark should be reversed. The closest she came may have been when she included this phrase in her 1983 *Akron* dissent: "Even assuming there is a fundamental right to terminate a pregnancy. . . ."[9]

So, in early 1989, neither side could predict where her next step on abortion rights would go. Even O'Connor herself might not have been able to say how she would rule before the case was argued, all the facts and legal reasoning put forward, and the justices started laying out their positions on paper.

THE PREAMBLE TO the 1986 Missouri law at issue declared "the life of each human being begins at conception." It went on to bar the use of public funds for counseling about abortion and prohibited public hospitals and public employees from performing abortions not necessary to save the mother's life. If a woman seeking an abortion appeared to be at least twenty weeks pregnant, physicians were required to perform tests to see if the fetus was viable (based on age, weight, and lung maturity). This provision appeared to conflict with the core of *Roe,* which said states could regulate abortions during the second trimester (roughly, thirteen to twenty-four weeks) only to protect the mother's health.

A group of physicians and nurses at a state-run hospital challenged the provisions as a violation of *Roe.* Siding with them, the U.S. Court of Appeals for the Eighth Circuit struck down the ban on public employees performing abortions. The appeals court also said the preamble's reference to the interests of the unborn reflected "an impermissible theory of when life begins" that contradicted *Roe*'s assertion of a mother's right to end a pregnancy. The lower court rejected the viability-testing requirement, saying that such tests were unreliable and could add $250 to the cost of an abortion.

Two weeks after the Supreme Court's January 9, 1989, announcement that it would hear Missouri's appeal, sixty-seven thousand antiabortion demonstrators turned out on the National Mall as part of the annual anniversary protest against *Roe v. Wade.* As they gathered at the Ellipse, President Bush spoke to them from the Oval Office over an amplified telephone hookup. "After years of sober and serious reflection on the issue, this is what I think," Bush began. "I think the Supreme Court's decision in *Roe v. Wade* was wrong and should be overturned. I think America needs a human life amendment.... I promise the president hears you now and stands with you in a cause that must be won."[10]

In the administration's "friend of the court" brief to the Supreme Court on behalf of Missouri, Justice Department lawyers wrote: "Even assuming that the various 'privacy' cases relied upon by *Roe* established a generalized right to privacy, it does not follow that the abortion decision is encompassed within such a right. Abortion involves the destruction of the fetus, and is therefore different in kind from the decision not to conceive in the first place." The brief then quoted a previous writing by O'Connor, that "potential life is no less potential in the first weeks of pregnancy than it is at viability or afterward."[11]

As the drama escalated, seventy-eight "friend of the court" briefs were filed—more than ever had come before the Court in a single case.[12] The filings came from physicians, historians, elected officials, women's groups, and religious organizations on both sides. Thousands of letters also were being delivered, most addressed to Justice O'Connor. Some of the mail was graphic, including photographs of aborted fetuses and of coat hangers, the latter a symbol of illegal abortions.[13]

In early April 1989, two weeks before the scheduled oral arguments in the Missouri case, *Webster v. Reproductive Health Services,* three hundred thousand abortion-rights supporters marched from the Washington Monument to the Capitol, their first major demonstration since 1986.[14] The high turnout was evidence of concern from abortion-rights groups that this Court might be ready to jettison *Roe.* Some of the speakers attributed what they viewed as a dire situation to Reagan, O'Connor's benefactor: "You know what happened in the eighties," declared U.S. Representative Patricia Schroeder, a Democrat from Colorado. "Ronald

Reagan got elected and said, 'Put down your picket signs and put on your little dress-for-success suits.' Well, a lot of people put down their picket signs and lost their rights."[15] Whatever ground had been lost, abortion rights advocates believed this was their moment to catch up.

At ten a.m. on April 26, a short electronic beep sounded, followed by the marshal's traditional chant of "Oyez! Oyez! Oyez! All persons having business before the Honorable, the Supreme Court of the United States, are admonished to draw near and give their attention, for the Court is now sitting. God save the United States and this Honorable Court!" The justices took their places along the bench. From spectators' left to right were: Scalia, Stevens, Marshall, Brennan, Rehnquist, White, Blackmun, O'Connor, and Kennedy. Against the black robe, O'Connor's face looked pale, gaunt. Nearing the end of her chemotherapy treatments, she still wore a wig.

Oral arguments can have a distinct tenor, at once more passionate and less formal than legal briefs. Sometimes the give-and-take is combative, sometimes subdued; sometimes all is earnest, while on occasion a little levity creeps in. Stepping to the lectern first was William Webster, Missouri's attorney general, appealing the lower-court decision against the state. "We contend the government is certainly not obligated in and of itself to become an advocate for abortion," he told the justices. Their first queries were practical, directed at the timing of viability tests and the possible penalties imposed on physicians who did not follow the Missouri regulations. Webster tried to minimize the obligation for doctors. "We are not telling the physician what kind of test to require, we are not even requiring him to use these tests and have them to be determinate of viability. We are merely requiring that a physician, usually a proabortion physician, make findings and record them."

The arguments soon took a confrontational turn as Charles Fried, who was acting as special assistant to Attorney General Richard Thornburgh, took over. Five months earlier, as Reagan solicitor general, Fried had submitted the initial brief on behalf of the U.S. government. Fried argued that the right of privacy in the touchstone case of *Griswold v. Connecticut,* a 1965 ruling that said states could not stop adult couples from obtaining contraceptives, did not extend to abortion. He said abortion was different from traditional private family matters.

"The right involved in *Griswold* . . . was the right not to have the state intrude into . . . the details . . . of marital intimacy," Fried said. "There was a great deal of talk about inquiry into the marital bedroom, and I think that is a very different story from what we have here."

Leaning forward, O'Connor asked Fried, "Do you say there is no fundamental right to decide whether to have a child or not . . . a right to procreate? Do you deny that the Constitution protects that right?"

"I would hesitate to formulate the right in such abstract terms," Fried responded, "and I think the Court prior to *Roe v. Wade* quite prudently also avoided such sweeping generalities. That was the wisdom of *Griswold.*"

O'Connor pressed on with a startling hypothetical question: "Do you think that the state has the right to, if in a future century we had a serious overpopulation problem, has a right to require women to have abortions after so many children?"

"I surely do not. That would be quite a different matter."

"What do you rest that on?" O'Connor asked.

"Because unlike abortion," said Fried, "which involves the purposeful termination of future life, that would involve not preventing an operation but violently taking hands-on, laying hands on a woman and submitting her to an operation . . . ."[16]

When Frank Susman, a St. Louis lawyer arguing against the Missouri regulations, stepped next to the lectern, O'Connor's earlier questions were foremost in his mind. Susman began by picking up on Fried's argument that reversing *Roe* would not harm the broader right to decide whether to have children. "I think the solicitor general's submission is somewhat disingenuous when he suggests to this Court that he does not seek to unravel the whole cloth of procreational rights, but merely to pull a thread. It has always been my personal experience that when I pull a thread, my sleeve falls off. There is no stopping. It is not a thread he is after. It is the full range of procreational rights and choices that constitute the fundamental right that has been recognized by this Court."

Susman argued that advances in medicine and science had blurred distinct stages of fetal development after conception. But he also acknowledged that the state indeed did have a compelling interest in a fetus after it was viable. "Historically, both at common law and in early statute, this was always the line chosen. Whether it was called quickening or viability, there is little difference time-wise."

"Well there is a difference, is there not, in those two?" asked O'Connor, the only justice who would have experienced quickening.

"Technically," responded Susman, "between those two definitions, Justice O'Connor, yes. Quickening had less of a medical significance. It was [when] the woman could first detect movement."

"When the fetus was first felt by the mother," said O'Connor.

"A kick, yes," said Susman, "absolutely, approximately two or three weeks before what we would consider viability today. . . ."

Justice Scalia asked Susman how a right to abortion can be a fundamental right "unless you make the determination that the organism that is destroyed is not a human life."

"Can you, as a matter of logic or principle, make that determination otherwise?" Scalia asked.

"It is a question verifiable only by reliance upon faith," Susman said, turning to the far left of the bench where Scalia was seated. "It is a question of labels. Neither side in this issue and debate would ever disagree on the physiological facts. Both sides would agree as to when a heartbeat can first be detected. Both sides would agree as to when brain waves can be first detected. But when you come to try to place the emotional labels on what you call that collection of physiological facts, that is where people part company."

"I agree with you entirely," said Scalia, "but what conclusion does that lead you to? That, therefore, there must be a fundamental right on the part of the woman to destroy this thing that we don't know what it is or, rather, that whether there is or isn't is a matter that you vote upon; since we don't know the answer, people have to make up their minds the best they can."

"The conclusion to which it leads me," said Susman, "is that when you have an issue that is so divisive and so emotional and so personal and so intimate, that it must be left as a fundamental right to the individual to make that choice under her then-attendant circumstances, her religious beliefs, her moral beliefs and in consultation with her physician."

The question before the nine justices was that large. Religious and moral implications loomed.

The give-and-take in *Webster v. Reproductive Health Services* was fast-paced and tense. O'Connor and Kennedy were among the most vigorous questioners, seemingly on a search for answers, their minds not yet made up. When the session was over, lawyers, reporters, and spectators spilled out onto the white marble plaza blindingly illuminated by the sun. There was nothing more for the advocates on either side to do. The case was now a matter solely for the justices.

Two days later, on April 28, 1989, in their private conference room, the justices cast their votes and explained their reasoning. O'Connor was the only one who had given birth, but everyone there knew parenthood. The other justices were fathers from an era when they were not even allowed in the delivery room, but they nonetheless had experienced the wonder of new life and the demands of raising children. Some of them brought other distinctive experiences to the table: Blackmun had been counsel to the Mayo Clinic and had infused his *Roe* opinion with his medical expertise. Justices Brennan, Scalia, and Kennedy were Roman Catholics, members of a community that strongly opposed abortion, but the three plainly were not influenced in the same way by Church teaching. Chief Justice Rehnquist and Justice White, the two dissenters in *Roe,* were hoping that this term finally would produce a reversal of the 1973 case.

According to custom, Rehnquist, as the senior justice, began the discussion. Now 64, Rehnquist was known for his orderliness and fairness. He did not like rambling discussions. But at this point, Rehnquist was still dealing with several older, more tenured, loquacious colleagues, so the twice-weekly morning conferences often lasted past noon.

Rehnquist said he would vote to uphold all of the Missouri regulations. He wanted to reverse *Roe* and leave the matter to the states, but—perhaps knowing he should not push O'Connor too hard—he suggested modifying the standard of *Roe* rather than completely overruling the decision.[17] Next around the table was Brennan, who had turned 83 earlier in the week and was, as expected, taking the opposite tack from Rehnquist. *Roe* had been correctly decided and relied upon for sixteen years, Brennan said. Next, Justice White, 71, wanted to uphold the Missouri regulations. He reiterated his view that there should be no constitutional right to abortion. Marshall, 80, said he would affirm the lower-court invalidation of the Missouri policies, as did Blackmun, 80, next in seniority. Justice Stevens, 69, mostly wanted to affirm the lower-court decision. Separating himself from Brennan, Marshall, and Blackmun, Stevens said he did not think the preamble to the Missouri statute about life beginning at conception actually affected a woman's decision to have an abortion.

Speaking next was O'Connor, 59 years old, who thought the lower appeals court had misinterpreted the Missouri provisions to conflict with *Roe v. Wade.* She said she believed the viability tests were permissible, as were the restrictions on state medical personnel. But would she vote to change *Roe,* as the chief justice wanted? Her answer was not clear. She said she did not want to go further than she had in the 1983 and 1986 cases, when she voted for state regulations and was critical of *Roe* without saying it should be overturned. Still, she gave Rehnquist hope that she might sign an opinion significantly curtailing *Roe.*

Next, Scalia, 53, said he wanted to use the case to confront the 1973 ruling directly and overturn it. After him came the newest justice, Kennedy, 52, who told his colleagues that he used to teach *Roe* when he was a part-time law professor in California. He said he thought the issue should be returned to the democratic process and become a matter for individual states. California, Kennedy's home state, had pioneered passage of permissive abortion-rights legislation that was signed into law in 1967 by then-governor Ronald Reagan. Kennedy seemed to agree with Rehnquist about scaling back *Roe.*

When the conference was over, Rehnquist had the votes (White, O'Connor, Scalia, and Kennedy) to at least reinstate the Missouri regulations, and perhaps a majority to do more, depending on whether he could persuade O'Connor to address the larger constitutional question. The justices returned to their respective chambers. Rehnquist decided later to keep the Court's opinion in *Webster* for himself. The others began drafting concurrences—or, in the case of Brennan, Marshall, Blackmun, and Stevens—dissenting opinions.

The justices wondered what might influence O'Connor and whether she would join Rehnquist in what was expected to be an opinion extensively diluting *Roe.* One of Blackmun's law clerks, Edward Lazarus, wrote to him on May 1, two days after the conference vote in the *Webster* case, "My sources inform me that Justice O'Connor does indeed have a pregnant daughter-in-law. Apparently, this relative has been trying to have a child for years."[18]

O'Connor's eldest son, Scott, and his wife were expecting their first child in about five months. O'Connor, who guarded her privacy, likely would have been angered to know that personal lives within her family were being examined. But Scott had been candid about his situation with at least one reporter. As part of a magazine profile of O'Connor published in the *Washington Post Magazine* on June 11, 1989, Scott was quoted as saying that he and his wife "struggled for three years to get pregnant" and that his mother was aware of the difficulty. He added, "It's ironic that the issue is all the people wanting to terminate pregnancy, and we couldn't do it without trying for three years and lots of medical help. We spent three years trying to do something that half of America is trying to prevent." [19]

Lazarus, who later wrote a book about his experiences as a Blackmun clerk, said in that published account that some of the justices' female law clerks were so concerned about how O'Connor would vote in the *Webster* case that one of them considered pretending to be pregnant to show the justice the dilemma of a woman who might need an abortion. "[M]any of us thought O'Connor's decision would depend at least in part on her reflections about womanhood," Lazarus wrote. "And in the crazed vortex of *Webster,* that hunch even led a few pro-choice female clerks to consider fanciful schemes for reminding O'Connor of *Roe*'s value to their shared sex. One I recall was to take place after the all-female aerobics class that O'Connor hosted three mornings a week upstairs on the basketball court. The idea was to have one of the clerks fake an unwanted pregnancy and break down in the locker room when the justice was sure to overhear. The notion quickly passed, but the warping emotion and the desperate attention to O'Connor's vote—those lasted until the end." [20]

Even without such dramatics, O'Connor constantly was reminded of the fragility of one's existence in the world. She longed for that first grandchild. And her breast cancer made her aware of the fleeting nature of life. On the other hand, stories of unwanted pregnancies echoed in the Missouri case, as more than seven hundred letters were filed with the Court from women who had had abortions. One woman wrote, "I have heard it said that abortion is just a convenience, especially for middle-class women. I assure you, pregnancy is no mere inconvenience. A pregnancy consumes a woman's body, energies and resources for nine months, many times with complications, sometimes at risk to the woman's life. . . . Every woman must have the right to enter into this life-absorbing responsibility when she decides that she can." [21]

O'Connor knew she carried the burden of her womanhood in this case. Still, she never was motivated primarily by her sex. "Concerns for the integrity of the Court, the operation of the collective decision-making process and, most important, the law itself . . . exert an influence on my actions far greater than any uniquely feminine perspective I might bring," O'Connor wrote later.[22]

When she had addressed abortion rights for the first time on a national stage, during her 1981 confirmation hearings, she had said that her views were the product "of my own upbringing and my religious training, my background, my sense of family values, and my sense of how I should lead my own life."[23] O'Connor, an Episcopalian, regularly attended Sunday services at the National Cathedral's Bethlehem Chapel. But she had been raised outside of organized religion. As a girl, when she asked her father whether he believed in God and why they did not attend church, Harry Day had said he believed in God. "[W]hen you watch the world around us and see how the earth orbits the sun," he explained, "and how the moon orbits the earth, and see the laws of nature work, you have to believe that some power beyond us has created the universe and has established the way nature works. . . . And we don't have to go to church to appreciate it. It is all around us. This is our church."[24]

Justice O'Connor was a great synthesizer of many rationales, interests, and information. Her approach was wide-ranging; but her decisions, in the end, narrow. During her eight years on the Court, O'Connor had demonstrated no overarching ideology but rather a searching approach that tracked the center of the nation and rarely moved the law much.

As she undertook her decisive role in *Webster v. Reproductive Health Services,* her health turned a corner. "All the tests have been negative and the prognosis for total recovery is excellent," O'Connor said in a statement released through the Court's public information office on May 8, 1989. "I do not plan to leave the Court." A few days earlier, she acknowledged publicly for the first time that she had been undergoing chemotherapy treatments. In response to a request from a newspaper reporter, the public information office said that she had completed chemotherapy, a treatment that reporters had surmised from her hair loss.[25]

The Missouri case moved toward a climax in late May, as Chief Justice Rehnquist sent around a draft of his opinion upholding the regulations. Rehnquist invoked a new legal standard that would allow abortion restrictions if they "reasonably further the state's interest in protecting potential human life." If adopted, that standard would be a far more lenient test of abortion regulations and a significant departure from *Roe*. On the substance of the law, Rehnquist wrote that the ban on the use of public employees and facilities for abortions only restricted a woman's ability to obtain an abortion to the extent that she chose a physician affiliated with a public hospital. White and Scalia told Rehnquist they were with him. Kennedy, who was voting in his first abortion case, signed on, too.[26]

O'Connor did not. Usually, O'Connor was the picture of efficiency. She liked to get her opinions out quickly and let her views be known so that she could affect the process. She and Justice White often raced to be the first to have an opinion to announce. "Beat Byron," a law clerk recalled hearing another justice say jokingly to O'Connor one term. But abortion was a difficult issue for O'Connor, as well as a possible opportunity, especially now it was clear she was in the middle and would control the outcome.

Justice Stevens responded without hesitation to Rehnquist's draft in pointed terms. He challenged Rehnquist's view that a state regulation should be allowed if it "reasonably furthers the state interest in protecting potential human life." In his memo, Stevens wrote, "The woman's interest in making the abortion decision apparently is given no weight at all. A tax on abortions, a requirement that the pregnant woman must be able to stand on her head for fifteen minutes before she can have an abortion, or a criminal prohibition would each satisfy your test. . . .

"Because the test really rejects *Roe v. Wade* in its entirety, I would think that it would be much better for the Court, as an institution, to do so forthrightly rather than indirectly with a bombshell first introduced at the end of its opinion," Stevens asserted.

These were sharp words from Stevens, but Rehnquist's draft had provoked him. "As you know, I am not in favor of overruling *Roe v. Wade*," Stevens concluded, "but if the deed is to be done I would rather see the Court give the case a decent burial instead of tossing it out the window of a fast-moving caboose."

Justice Blackmun, meanwhile, began penning a dissent premised on the idea that Rehnquist was going to get O'Connor as a fifth vote to gut *Roe*. He focused on the social consequences, writing in an early draft, "[A]lmost an entire generation of women have grown up shielded by the protective umbrella of *Roe*. That protection is now lost. . . . [W]omen will continue to seek and obtain abortions, but only the affluent will be able early to obtain medically safe procedures. The poor and the deprived, and certainly an undue percentage of our minorities, will not be able to do this." Blackmun's early draft was all despair: "The simple truth is that *Roe* no longer survives and that the majority provides no substitute for its protective umbrella."[27]

Some researchers reviewing justices' once-private papers believe O'Connor initially agreed with Rehnquist in seeking to overturn abortion rights.[28] With the benefit of hindsight and private papers of the justices made available over the years, however, it appears that O'Connor never was ready to sign an opinion undermining the core of *Roe,* particularly as the fifth vote against it. It also was clear in retrospect that the Missouri case was a turning point in her acceptance of the right to abortion.

By many accounts, this term already stood out for its bitter divisiveness. Maybe it was the difficult run of cases covering anti-discrimination law, separation of church and state, and the death penalty. Maybe it was the chemistry among the nine at this particular time in their lives, their age, their health problems. Maybe it was the clerks, whom Lazarus portrayed as ideologically motivated and cliquish.[29]

Then, on June 21, just as O'Connor finally was finishing the first draft of an opinion that would chart a new middle course in the Missouri abortion case, the Court issued its most criticized decision of the term, holding that flag-burning was a form of political expression protected by the First Amendment. By a 5–4 vote, the justices said that a protester who had burned a U.S. flag at the 1984 Republican National Convention in Dallas should not have been convicted of a crime.[30] The decision in *Texas v. Johnson* set off a new furor in Congress. Senate Majority Leader Bob Dole, a Republican from Kansas who was seriously injured in World War II, called the decision "dead wrong." Within a day, the Senate passed a resolution expressing its "profound disappointment" with the Court decision by a 97–3 vote.[31]

There were now constant denunciations within and beyond their chambers, and the justices still had a long way to go on the abortion dispute. "The expected circulation from SOC has been delayed until sometime later this afternoon," Lazarus wrote to Blackmun on June 22,

adding, in a reflection of the rampant animosities, "Apparently, her tennis game with [First Lady] Barbara Bush this morning, and her luncheon
appointment, have precluded her final pre-circulation review."[32]

When O'Connor's draft arrived later that day, her fellow justices saw
that she had, as expected, voted to uphold the Missouri regulations. But
she was not going to join with Rehnquist and reject any of *Roe*. In fact,
with her vote now the decisive one, she was backing away from the critical statements about *Roe* she had made in earlier cases. Gone were the
references to the 1973 decision's "problematic" framework or its
trimester rationale being "on a collision course with itself." Gone, too,
were strong statements about the life of the unborn that could diminish
the mother's right to choose to end a pregnancy. Her approach would
allow states more latitude to regulate abortion than the approach taken
by Blackmun and the other liberals. But unlike Rehnquist and the other
conservatives, she wanted the heart of *Roe v. Wade* to stand.

Looking specifically at the Missouri regulations, she believed the viability testing requirements to be modest. She ended up writing, somewhat convolutedly, "It is clear to me that requiring the performance of
examinations and tests useful to determining whether a fetus is viable,
when viability is possible, and when it would not be medically imprudent
to do so, does not impose an undue burden on a woman's abortion decision." She minimized the effects of all the regulations on a woman seeking an abortion. To reconcile the *Webster* Missouri ruling with the Court's
1983 rejection of medical tests in the case from Akron, Ohio, she wrote,
"The second-trimester hospitalization requirement struck down in
Akron imposed, in the majority's view, 'a heavy, and unnecessary, burden,' more than doubling the cost of 'women's access to a relatively inex-
pensive, otherwise accessible and safe abortion procedure.' By contrast,
the cost of examinations and tests that could usefully and prudently be
performed when a woman is 20–24 weeks pregnant to determine
whether the fetus is viable would only marginally, if at all, increase the
cost of an abortion."

Then came the most important qualification of her decision, the reason she insisted on withholding her signature from Rehnquist's opinion:
"When the constitutional invalidity of a State's abortion statute actually
turns on the constitutional validity of *Roe v. Wade,* there will be time
enough to reexamine *Roe*. And to do so carefully."[33]

At bottom, her opinion reflected her brand of judging. In the face of strong anti-*Roe* rhetoric from the chief justice and a near majority, she had retreated from a position that could have reversed the 1973 landmark. This would happen in other areas of the law, too: she would step to the brink, and then back away. Her opinion in *Webster v. Reproductive Health Services* was a pivot that would set her in another direction. But that would be clear only when she took her next step.

In the past, O'Connor had not concentrated on privacy issues as she had on other subjects such as the power between the federal government and the states, sex discrimination, or the requisite division of church and state. But, as a justice attuned to where America was on social issues and one who knew how to take advantage of divisions among her colleagues, the abortion dilemma became hers to decide.

"For today, at least," Blackmun wrote in a dissent joined by Brennan, Marshall, and Stevens, "the law of abortion stands . . . For today, the women of this nation still retain the liberty to control their destinies. But the signs are evident and very ominous, and a chill wind blows." Once O'Connor's position was known, however, Blackmun had dropped the direst language of his draft opinions: "*Roe* no longer survives."

While the justices who supported abortion rights felt a reprieve, the conservatives were disheartened, angered, and—in the case of Scalia—infuriated. There was nothing veiled about Scalia's indignation. He wrote in a concurring statement to Rehnquist's opinion, "Justice O'Connor's assertion that a 'fundamental rule of judicial restraint' requires us to avoid reconsidering *Roe,* cannot be taken seriously. By finessing *Roe* we do not, as she suggests, adhere to the strict and venerable rule that we should avoid deciding questions of a constitutional nature."

In prose dripping with contempt, Scalia declared, "We can now look forward to at least another term with carts full of mail from the public, and streets full of demonstrators, urging us—their unelected and life-tenured judges who have been awarded those extraordinary, undemocratic characteristics precisely in order that we might follow the law despite the popular will—to follow the popular will. Indeed, I expect we can look forward to even more of that than before, given our indecisive decision today."

Such vitriol was so strong in the final days of the 1988–1989 term that retired Justice Powell was moved to write to O'Connor with concern, "I cannot recall a previous term in which there were as many concurring and dissenting opinions. Some of the intemperate language in dissents reached the level of personal criticism. This, if this trend continues, could lessen public respect for the Court as an institution."[34]

O'Connor likely agreed, but for her part, she did not look back. In fact, when all the opinions were released and Scalia's condemnation became public, she already had left for Britain. With her cancer behind her, O'Connor and her husband were attending the Cambridge Lectures at Queens College and then an Anglo-American Legal Exchange in London.[35]

Years later, Justice Stevens said of O'Connor's move in the Missouri abortion case, "She very wisely thought, let's not do anything faster than we need to. She is not prone to take giant steps when we can take a small one."[36]

Ruth Bader Ginsburg, who in 1989 was still an appeals court judge, recalled that she interpreted O'Connor's opinion in the Missouri case as a signal that she would not vote to reverse *Roe*.[37] In retrospect, it was clearly that. But at the time, O'Connor still was regarded by many abortion rights advocates as part of the threat to *Roe,* and the *Webster* decision produced a new activism among advocates. Their nationwide mobilization helped elect abortion-rights supporters L. Douglas Wilder of Virginia and James J. Florio of New Jersey, both Democrats, to governorships in 1989.[38]

Leading women's rights lawyers did not want to leave O'Connor's vote to chance. In a pointed law review article after the Missouri case was handed down, law professors Susan Estrich and Kathleen Sullivan wrote, "[I]t certainly did make one thing clear: eight men may read our briefs, but the real audience is one woman. Sandra Day O'Connor, the only woman in American history to sit on the United States Supreme Court, is in the position single-handedly to decide the future of abortion rights." They described their article in the *Pennsylvania Law Review* as "nothing more or less than our best try, using whatever legal and persuasive talents we have, to convince an audience of one to stand up to those who are turning their backs on women." Estrich and Sullivan emphasized the practical consequences of overturning abortion rights: "[A] world without *Roe* will not be a world without abortion but a world in which abortion is accessible according to one's constitutional caste. While affluent women will travel to jurisdictions where safe and legal abortions are available, paying whatever is necessary, restrictive abortion laws and with them, the life-threatening prospect of back-alley abortion, will disproportionately descend upon those without adequate resources to avoid them."[39]

If O'Connor was reading the commentary of the day, she certainly realized that other writers believed she had disappointed a major constituency. Columnists Roland Evans and Robert Novak recalled that when Ronald Reagan nominated her to the Court, antiabortion forces said the administration was ignoring "pro-choice" evidence in her record as majority leader of the Arizona Senate. "Ronald Reagan could have had the pro-lifer of his choice as the first female justice," Evans and Novak wrote in July 1989. "He chose not to."[40]

Retired Justice Powell must have believed she needed some bucking up. "You must know that I am fond of you personally and have a high opinion of you as a thoughtful and conscientious Justice," he added in his note at the end of the contentious term. "I have said publicly that the President could not have found a better qualified woman to be the first to serve on this Court. I also admire John. He has made a place for himself in this critical city, and is widely liked. My affectionate best to both of you."[41] Powell, of all people, understood the power—and the isolation—that came with being in the middle.

END OF AN ERA

W hen Justice Sandra Day O'Connor turned 60 on March 26, 1990, she saw her face on campaign-style buttons wherever she ventured in the Court building. A surprise prepared by her law clerks, the buttons were emblazoned with O'Connor's likeness and the words HAPPY BIRTHDAY, SOC. In the anteroom to the courtroom, as she and her colleagues prepared to enter at the bang of the marshal's gavel, the other justices in unison peeled back their black robes to flash their SOC buttons.[1]

It had been nearly a year since she completed chemotherapy treatment for breast cancer. She had returned to her routine of arising each day at five a.m., peering out the window of her Chevy Chase, Maryland, home, and impatiently awaiting delivery of the morning papers. After breakfast, she drove to the Court for her aerobics or yoga class. Then she began reading the briefs in the thousands of cases that came to the Court each year.

The justice, who treated her clerks as surrogate children, even to the point of encouraging them to marry and have "grand-clerks," had recently taken the current group of four to the Tidal Basin to see the blossoming cherry trees that signify the beginning of spring in Washington. The exquisite pale pink flowers, floating on thousands of trees, a gift to the United States from Japan, bloom for only two weeks each year.

This spring was especially busy and public for O'Connor. In May, she attended a reception at the Library of Congress for Raisa Gorbachev, wife of Soviet president Mikhail Gorbachev. There she mixed with a crowd that included Marilyn Quayle, wife of the vice president, Katharine Graham, chief executive officer of the *Washington Post,* and other prominent women.[2] Despite her many public appearances, rumors continued that O'Connor remained ill with cancer and was about to retire. Guarding her privacy and disdainful of the media's attention to her health, she disliked even acknowledging the reports. But as June approached, the chatter was getting louder. Exasperated, O'Connor sent a statement down to the Court's public information office for release: "I am not sick. I am not bored. I am not resigning."[3]

ANOTHER ROUND OF deliberations on abortion came in spring 1990. Under review was a Minnesota statute that required a physician to notify both biological parents of an underage teen forty-eight hours before an abortion was to be performed. The statute included an alternative provision if the Supreme Court found that the two-parent requirement was unconstitutional. That alternative provision allowed a girl under 18 to bypass her parents and present reasons for the abortion to a judge. Reproductive rights advocate and physician Jane Hodgson challenged the Minnesota law, saying it interfered with a teenager's right to abortion, particularly in divorced or dysfunctional families. She also argued that the possible judicial bypass provision would not help because of the fear and shame a pregnant girl would feel appearing before the judge, a stranger.

For O'Connor, it had been easier in the early 1980s, when there was a solid majority to uphold *Roe* and when her vote did not matter. She could dissent from decisions striking down abortion regulations without affecting the result and changing the law of the land. But now, as in the 1989 *Webster* case, she was in the middle. Voting to uphold the Minnesota requirement now before them were Chief Justice Rehnquist and Justices White, Scalia, and Kennedy. Against it were Justices Brennan, Marshall, Blackmun, and Stevens. Justices on both sides of the divide were vying for O'Connor's vote.

O'Connor had yet to see an abortion regulation she could oppose. But from the start in the *Hodgson* case, she was concerned about the predicament of pregnant teenage girls in abusive families having to tell both parents about a planned abortion. Justice Stevens, who was becoming an ambassador from the liberal justices to O'Connor, started quietly working with her on a decision that could lead to a ruling against the Minnesota provision. During oral arguments the previous November, American Civil Liberties Union litigator Janet Benshoof had argued compellingly about the danger to young girls if they had to tell an abusive parent or navigate between a divorced mother and father. O'Connor was moved by the argument.

By late March 1990, it looked as if Stevens could hold together a five-justice majority, with O'Connor as the key swing vote, to strike down the Minnesota law. Brennan asked Stevens to make a few changes in the opinion he was crafting for the four liberals and O'Connor, but added, "I realize that you are walking a tightrope in this one."[4]

In the end, O'Connor agreed that requiring both biological parents to be notified of the scheduled abortion was unconstitutional. She wrote, "the primary constitutional deficiency lies in [the statute's] imposition of an absolute limitation on the minor's right to obtain an abortion."[5] It was the first time she had voted to strike down any abortion regulation. She did not want to block a pregnant woman, even one who was underage, from all avenues to end a pregnancy. Years later, Stevens said about the *Hodgson* ruling, "She made the decisions herself. She had never taken an irrevocable step in either direction. I assumed that she was seriously thinking about the whole thing" involving a woman's right to end a pregnancy.[6] She was. In this first postcancer term, O'Connor reevaluated her thinking about abortion rights and began to refine her idea of what was an "undue burden" for a pregnant woman.

A MONTH AFTER O'CONNOR turned 60, Brennan celebrated his 84th birthday. Age was taking its toll. Sitting through four hours of oral arguments each day, reading the heap of legal briefs, fighting the conservative tide—all wore him down. Much of the winter, he had been sick with the flu and other ailments. A year and a half earlier, he had undergone gallbladder surgery. But the liberal standard-bearer on the Court would not resign. The possibility that President George H. W. Bush would appoint a conservative jurist as his successor troubled Brennan. In his thirty-fourth Court term, he held on to his well-worn motto: Five votes is what it takes.

Brennan was closely watching O'Connor's moves in a criminal case dealing with a suspect's right to remain silent. As he confided to Justice Thurgood Marshall, Brennan realized that he faced a "troubling strategic choice." He could stand firm on principle and refuse to recognize an exception to the *Miranda* ruling that required police to tell suspects in custody of their right to remain silent. Or, he could concede an exception for routine booking questions at police headquarters, as a majority of the justices wanted. If he chose the latter course, Brennan could use his position as the senior justice in the majority to assign the opinion to himself and bargain with the others to minimize the effect on *Miranda.* That way, as Brennan wrote privately to Marshall, he would "concede only what is absolutely necessary to prevent Sandra and the others from taking over."[7]

The case would be one of the last flare-ups between Brennan and O'Connor. The dispute, *Pennsylvania v. Muniz,* drew little public attention. But the process by which the justices decided it was a testament to the declining influence of Brennan and the ascension of O'Connor.

Inocencio Muniz had been found sitting in a parked car on the shoulder of a Pennsylvania highway by a police officer in the early morning hours of November 30, 1986. Muniz's face was flushed, his eyes were glazed, and his breath smelled of alcohol. Believing that Muniz was in no condition to drive, the officer told him to stay put. But as the officer returned to his car, Muniz sped off. After the officer caught up to him, he took Muniz to the local police station, where Muniz, without being advised of his rights under *Miranda,* was asked routine biographical questions, then put through a series of sobriety tests. He faltered seriously as police asked him the date of his sixth birthday.[8]

The tape of Muniz's shaky responses was admitted at trial as evidence of his condition, and he was convicted of driving while under the influence of alcohol. Muniz appealed, saying that the tape should not have been allowed because it was taken before he had been read his rights. The legendary 1966 *Miranda v. Arizona* decision required police to tell suspects in custody that they have the right to remain silent and that anything they say can be used against them.[9]

This was not the first Supreme Court case to test whether evidence could be used when police failed to read a suspect his *Miranda* rights. Physical evidence, like blood samples, had never required *Miranda* warnings, and since 1966, the Court had adopted some exceptions to *Miranda*'s rule for statements given by suspects. Still, *Miranda* was a Warren Court landmark shielding a person from self-incrimination, and Brennan was protective of it.

The Pennsylvania Supreme Court had ruled that Muniz's answer to the question about his sixth birthday and other statements made while performing physical dexterity tests should not have been admitted, because they were "testimonial" in a way that was incriminating. Pennsylvania officials appealed to the high court.

Brennan generally agreed that no exception to *Miranda* should exist for the kind of questions put to Muniz, and he wanted to affirm the Pennsylvania Supreme Court. But after a conference vote on the case, he realized that the only way to keep control of the opinion for the Court was to compromise. As he explained in a memo to Marshall, who opposed any retrenching on *Miranda,* "I have great difficulty acknowledging that any exceptions to *Miranda* exist. . . . I understand, however, that everyone except you and me would recognize the existence of an exception to *Miranda* for 'routine booking questions,' and at least five of our colleagues want that exception to be defined broadly . . . I made the strategic judgment, therefore, to concede the existence of an exception but to use my control over the opinion to define the exception as narrowly as possible."

Then Brennan summed up the situation in words that resonated well beyond the case of *Pennsylvania v. Muniz:* "Sandra forced my hand by threatening to lead the revolution."[10] He was worried that O'Connor would orchestrate the weakening of *Miranda.*

Brennan's eventual opinion for the Court drew a distinction between Muniz's answers to routine informational questions (such as his name and date of birth) and his responses to questions intended to test his ability to reason. Exchanges of the first type were akin to physical evidence (such as a blood or urine sample) sought for record-keeping purposes, Brennan said, and fell within a "routine booking question" exception. But, he said, the slurred answer to the sixth-birthday question constituted a "testimonial" response, because a jury could have believed it showed that Muniz's mental state was confused due to his prior drinking.

That statement should have been excluded under the Fifth Amendment's protection against self-incrimination.

Along the way, Brennan had kept an eye on Marshall's dissenting opinion. In his final note to Marshall on the case, Brennan wrote, "Thanks, pal, for permitting me to glance at your dissent in this case. I think it is quite fine, and I fully understand your wanting to take me to task for recognizing an exception to *Miranda,* though I still firmly believe that this was the strategically proper move here. If Sandra had gotten her hands on this issue, who knows what would have been left of *Miranda.*"[11]

O'Connor had sent mixed signals on previous *Miranda*-related cases—voting for some exceptions and not others—but she never had indicated she would gut it.[12] So, Brennan may have been unduly worried. Still, her ability to draw a majority to reduce the legal protections for defendants established in the Warren era was a valid concern. Whatever the *Muniz* case revealed of the chasm between Brennan and O'Connor on *Miranda,* it demonstrated that Brennan recognized the need to outmaneuver her.

By 1990, O'Connor typically began with more votes than Brennan. The addition of Ronald Reagan's final appointee, Justice Kennedy, in early 1988 had solidified the conservative bloc and extended O'Connor's tie-breaking power. Now she was exercising more than the swing vote. Nearly twenty-five years younger than Brennan and an emboldened survivor of breast cancer, O'Connor had figured out how to line up votes as effectively as Brennan could. His words—"Sandra threatened to lead the revolution"—testified to that. She had bested the men at their own game. The old hand recognized that, too. In fact, Brennan seemed the first among the men to understand the influence of this first woman justice.

Beyond the Court, O'Connor was not regarded as Brennan's equal. Perhaps it was because she had not articulated an overall vision of the law—as Brennan had, based on the Constitution's adaptation to modern ideals of human dignity, or as Scalia had, based on his views of the Constitution's eighteenth-century origins. Perhaps it was because the rhetoric of her opinions was spare and workmanlike, not eloquent or memorable. Or perhaps it was because she was still perceived as the "woman justice."

O'Connor was caricatured in the press as uptight, schoolmarm-like. The "Loosen up, Sandy baby" line of Washington Redskins running back John Riggins endured. Columnists continued to refer to it well into the 1990s. She had been typecast early on, partly because of her demeanor and the contrast between her style and that of the veterans on the Court. A 1981 cartoon by Bill Schorr of the *Los Angeles Herald Examiner,* titled "Snow White and the Burger Court," bore it out. There she sits, "Snow White" Sandra O'Connor, erect, prim, and eager in her seat at the bench, next to the slouching Sleepy, Happy, Dopey, Grumpy, Bashful, and the rest. In real life, O'Connor was still the proper lady, handbag at her elbow, amid the crusty old men.

In her appearances off the bench, O'Connor never said anything to suggest she was an in-the-trenches operator. But she was, and Brennan knew it. "You had your day," Mary Brennan was quoted as saying to her husband in 1990, as she sensed his discouragement at the hands of the conservatives. "Now let them have theirs."

"Yes, but I'm right!" he retorted.[13]

THAT THE COURT was slipping from Brennan's grasp into O'Connor's was overwhelmingly evident in criminal law disputes, such as those involving Inocencio Muniz and, in 1989, Frank Teague. In that case, O'Connor had ensured that Teague, who was black, could not use a later constitutional ruling in a separate case to challenge his conviction for robbery and attempted murder by an all-white jury after his conviction became final.

The case of *Teague v. Lane* reflected O'Connor's pattern of throwing up hurdles for state prisoners who wanted to contest the constitutionality of their convictions or sentences in federal court. That pattern would continue in four other cases during Brennan's last months on the bench.[14] These cases, involving procedures for federal court review in writs of habeas corpus, were complicated and rarely made front-page news. In time, they would seem more consequential as states' mishandling of capital cases became widely apparent, partly through the use of DNA testing.

Still, even in 1990, prisoner appeals constituted an important battleground for O'Connor and Brennan. It was an area of the law in which O'Connor's vote and legal reasoning did not simply endorse the status quo. In this area, she had confidence from the outset, and she set out to change things. While defendants' rights advocates complained about incompetent lawyers in capital cases and the likelihood of innocent people ending up on death row, O'Connor complained that the condemned were dragging out their appeals and frustrating state prosecutors who had worked to win the convictions in the first place.

A 1989 study by a judicial committee led by retired Justice Lewis Powell found that the average time between a capital defendant's conviction and execution was more than eight years. The delay stemmed partly from the many chances inmates had to contest their death sentences at the state and federal levels. Beyond the Court, politicians were making an issue of how long it took for states to carry out death sentences and, more broadly, of crime itself. In the 1988 presidential campaign, for example, then–vice president George H. W. Bush had effectively branded Michael Dukakis as soft on crime, with commercials that suggested the Massachusetts governor was responsible for the release and subsequent rampage of murderer-rapist Willie Horton.[15]

In 1990, the Court majority's focus—embodied in the opinions of O'Connor and over dissents from Brennan—favored state officials and echoed some of the concerns of Republican politicians. Justice O'Connor emphasized the "very real costs" of letting state prisoners appeal to federal courts. As she declared in a speech at a "crime summit" organized by the Bush Justice Department around this time, "[S]tate prisoners may raise federal challenges to their state convictions again and again and again. . . . [I]f the state does lose in federal court and the petitioner is released from custody, it is the state that must retry him. Retrial becomes very difficult, and sometimes impossible, when many years have passed since the original trial. Witnesses and evidence become difficult to relocate; memories fade. I don't advocate that any court may ignore the defendant's constitutional rights even though he has been found guilty. Quite the opposite. . . . I only point out that one of the prices we pay for independent federal review of state court decisions is that we increase the likelihood that the guilty will go free."[16]

To Brennan, these prisoner appeals were all about individual liberty. But his views did not prevail, and in the four cases the justices decided in the spring of 1990, the conservative five-justice majority, including O'Connor, restricted state prisoners from getting federal judges to look at their cases. In one of the disputes, Brennan wrote a weary dissent, concluding that the Court had stripped "state prisoners of virtually any meaningful federal review of the constitutionality of their incarceration."[17]

In another of the disputes, O'Connor took up the pen for the majority to reinstate a death sentence for Jimmie Wayne Jeffers. Jeffers had been convicted of killing Penelope Cheney in a Tucson motel, allegedly because Jeffers believed Cheney had tipped police to his heroin trafficking. Jeffers was sentenced to death after a jury found that the murder was committed in an especially heinous manner. A U.S. appeals court had ruled that Jeffers was entitled to a new sentencing trial because of vague jury instructions about when a murder that did not involve torture could be considered especially heinous. Overturning that decision favoring Jeffers, O'Connor's opinion recounted in vivid detail the hotel scene where Jeffers killed Cheney, first by an injection of an overdose of heroin and then by beating her. "[W]hile Jeffers was beating [Cheney] he called her 'a bitch and a dirty snitch' and, with each striking blow, said, 'This one is for so and so.' "[18]

A draft of the dissent that Justice Blackmun crafted for the liberals in the Jeffers case reveals the acrimony that these disputes fostered. Writing that Arizona's standard for the "heinous" elements warranting the death penalty was flawed in its vagueness, Blackmun said O'Connor's opinion "borders on the outrageous." Blackmun declared with brazen irony, "[I]t is unlikely that an opinion so cynical in its approach to the adjudicative process, and so patently devoid of reasoning . . . could garner the votes of five members of this Court were it not for the fact that a person's life is at stake."[19]

This struck Justice Stevens as excessive. He asked Blackmun to change "borders on the outrageous" to "is deeply disturbing" and to drop the last sentence about Jeffers's risk of the death sentence. "Even if you make these two changes," Stevens told Blackmun, "no one will underestimate the force of your opinion or its disagreement with the majority's handling of this and similar cases."[20] Blackmun acquiesced.

More furor erupted at the Court the following year, 1991, when O'Connor wrote for the majority in a ruling that barred Roger Keith Coleman, a Virginia coal miner convicted of the rape and murder of his sister-in-law, from challenging the fairness of his murder trial. Coleman protested he was innocent and pointed to the fact that although his clothes were covered with coal dust on the day of the victim's killing, no coal dust apparently was found in her home. He claimed that he had been denied the constitutionally required effective assistance of counsel partly because his court-appointed lawyers never had handled such a serious case.

The Supreme Court majority said Coleman could not present his claim in federal court. Because Coleman's lawyer had missed a Virginia deadline by three days when filing his state habeas appeal, the claim had not been presented to the state court as was required before Coleman could plead his case to a federal judge.

"This case is about federalism," O'Connor asserted, taking a no-excuses approach that valued procedural consistency above the importance of reviewing the merits of Coleman's plight and the life-and-death stakes. "It concerns the respect that federal courts owe the states and the states' procedural rules when reviewing the claims of state prisoners in federal habeas corpus."[21] O'Connor said it was fair for Virginia courts to penalize Coleman for his lawyer's missed state-appeal deadline, because the state was not constitutionally required to provide him with a lawyer at that stage of his case. She said he had gotten a fair hearing in state court on his claim that he did not have effective assistance at trial. Dissenting justices accused the majority of erecting "petty procedural barriers" in the path of prisoners with constitutional claims. The decision overturned a 1963 ruling—written by Brennan—that had allowed prisoners to get to federal court even when they had not properly filed their appeals in state court, as long as they did not "deliberately bypass" the state process.

"In the name of states' rights, the Court has produced a terrible injustice," the *New York Times* editorial page intoned. "Is it fair to penalize the prisoner for his lawyer's mistake? Certainly, says Justice Sandra Day O'Connor for the majority. . . ."[22] The opening of her opinion referring to federalism, rather than any of the individual persons involved, invited criticism. She was preoccupied with process and lines of authority between state and federal judges.

Coleman maintained his innocence to the end. On the evening of his execution in 1992, his last words were, "An innocent man is going to be murdered tonight."[23] As in many other areas of the law, O'Connor found it easy to trust the states. To her, the involvement of federal judges meant the undermining of state-court authority. She did not think federal judges should be excluded from reviewing state verdicts—she simply approached their involvement with skepticism. Growing up in Harry Day's anti–New Deal home, she had learned to be wary of the intrusive hand of the federal government. O'Connor's view was forged as a state assistant attorney general, state legislator, then state-court judge. She knew how long it took to develop evidence for a criminal prosecution. She could far more easily put herself in the shoes of the state attorney general than the likes of a Jimmie Wayne Jeffers or Roger Keith Coleman.

And O'Connor rarely second-guessed herself: "I do not look back and say, 'Oh, what if I had done the other thing,' or 'Oh, I should have done something else.' "[24] She turned her attention to her son Brian's upcoming wedding. After that, as scheduled, she packed for a judicial conference in Hawaii, and then was headed to Scotland.

To the vexation of O'Connor, Brennan managed to win one last significant affirmative-action case before his retirement. The dispute involved a Federal Communications Commission policy that favored blacks, Hispanics, and other minorities applying for television and radio broadcast licenses. Under the policy, the FCC awarded Rainbow Broadcasting, whose ownership was 90 percent Hispanic, a license for a UHF facility in Orlando. Metro Broadcasting, which would have gotten the license but for the policy, sued the FCC. It said the preference program violated the constitutional equality guarantee.

How far the government could go in compensating for past race discrimination or in bringing diversity to a particular activity was not easily determined. The principle of affirmative action, woven into the fabric of American life since the early 1960s, was beginning to fray. The Reagan administration had tried to dismantle the Federal Communications Commission's race-preference policies. But, beginning in 1987, Congress had blocked the effort by barring the FCC from spending any of its appropriated money to examine or change policies.[25]

O'Connor believed the new FCC case should be covered by her 1989 decision, *Richmond v. Croson,* which struck down a Richmond public-contracts program favoring racial minorities and demanded the strictest judicial test for policies based on race. But Brennan thought Congress had more latitude than local governments to engage in affirmative action. He persuaded Byron White, who had been with O'Connor in *Rich-*

mond v. Croson, that the federal government, unlike a local one, had sufficient interest in ensuring diversity on the airwaves to justify the set-aside program. White's experience in the executive branch—as deputy U.S. attorney general in the John F. Kennedy administration—made him especially open to Brennan's argument that the federal government had a special role to play in ending discrimination. White's overriding question was whether the FCC first had tried race-neutral alternatives, and Brennan played up evidence that it had so tried.

Announcing the *Metro Broadcasting v. FCC* decision on the last day of the 1989–1990 term—a day he did not know would be his final one on the bench—Brennan referred to "the history of federal efforts to promote minority participation in the broadcasting industry" and emphasized that "it is of overriding significance . . . that the FCC's minority ownership programs have been specifically approved—indeed mandated—by Congress."[26]

O'Connor believed that the FCC's broad-scale program was not justified by the government's asserted interest in broadcast diversity. "Social scientists may debate how people's thoughts and behavior reflect their background," she wrote in dissent, "but the Constitution provides that the government may not allocate benefits and burdens among individuals based on the assumption that race or ethnicity determines how they act or think."

She did not go so far as to say government should be completely colorblind and that all race-based remedies should end. But she seriously questioned the continuing appropriateness at the end of the twentieth century of programs that favored racial minorities. Who really was helped in the end? O'Connor believed such programs were stigmatizing, and thought they ended up limiting people's horizons. Perhaps some of her feelings about benevolence to women—that it was a false benefit—shaped her ideas about government policies that favored African-Americans and other minorities.

Less than a month after the *Metro Broadcasting* decision, Brennan suffered a small stroke. On his way to take a Scandinavian cruise with his wife, he fainted while waiting to board a plane at Newark Airport. He continued with the trip, but when he returned, he sent a resignation letter to the White House. "The strenuous demands of Court work and its related duties required or expected of a Justice appear at this time to be incompatible with my advancing age and medical condition," Brennan wrote on July 20, 1990. He said he was stepping down immediately. Brennan gave a copy of the letter to all of his colleagues the same day, to notify them of his decision. "I think each of you fully appreciates how very much it has meant to me to know each of you as a colleague and a friend during our years of service together."[27]

Brennan's departure after thirty-four years closed a chapter at the Court. Supporters and critics agreed that he had had more of an effect on the law than anyone else in the last half century. It was his legal strategizing that made a reality of *Brown v. Board of Education*'s desegregation mandate. Arriving at the Court two years after the 1954 decision that struck down the "separate but equal" doctrine, Brennan formulated the subsequent ruling in *Cooper v. Aaron* that denounced efforts by Little Rock, Arkansas, school officials to delay desegregation. He played a leading role in the Warren Court's development of political equality through the principle of "one person, one vote." His opinion in *New York Times v. Sullivan* gave the press more latitude to publish reports on public officials by protecting reporters from defamation liability. It was his *Fay v. Noia* opinion that laid out the modern-era rights of inmates to challenge their imprisonment through a federal writ of habeas corpus.[28]

Even after Nixon appointee Warren Burger became chief justice in 1969, Brennan was able to push the Court to take the lead on society's problems. In 1971, as the justices were considering a North Carolina school district's policy of forced busing to desegregate its schools, Brennan advised Burger to think about the "tone" of a decision upholding busing and how people would react to it. "The matter of approach has assumed major significance in light of signs that opposition to *Brown* [*v. Board of Education*] may at long last be crumbling in the South." Brennan pressed Burger to "avoid saying anything that might be seized upon as an excuse to arrest this trend." In that case, *Swann v. Charlotte-Mecklenburg County Board of Education,* the Court ruled unanimously that busing was an appropriate method of eliminating the vestiges of school segregation. There and elsewhere, Brennan kept an eye on what governors were up to and where they might be backsliding on racial equality. Brennan believed that the states would follow the Court.[29]

His views contrasted with the philosophy held by O'Connor, who took her cues from the states, then pushed them ever so slightly where she believed they should go. Unlike O'Connor, who focused on the discrete contours of a legal dispute between two parties, Brennan wrote opinions that were a call to action on behalf of the poor, the unpopular, and the disenfranchised.

In some ways, the start of Brennan's declining influence could be traced to O'Connor's appointment. As U.S. Appeals Court Judge Richard Posner, a former Brennan law clerk, observed, "For a quarter of a century, from the time of his appointment until the replacement of [Justice Potter] Stewart by O'Connor [in 1981], Brennan was part of a liberal bloc of either four or five Justices that could usually pick up a vote or two from other Justices as well; in the briefer period between the replacement of [Felix] Frankfurter by [Arthur] Goldberg [in 1962] and Warren by Burger [in 1969], he was part of a commanding liberal majority."[30]

Was O'Connor relieved that Brennan was gone? Did she believe there would be less friction in her daily work? O'Connor did not think in those terms. She was not the type to wish her lot were different. She accepted what she had and worked with it. Her mantra: "That's the way it is." Her ethic: "Deal with it."

If their paths had never crossed, it is unlikely O'Connor would have been fully the justice she became. She knew how to work the backrooms of politics when she arrived, to be sure. But her negotiations with fellow justices led her additionally to take a page from Brennan's playbook on gathering votes. Her work in the Dun & Bradstreet libel case from 1985, in which she worked with Lewis Powell to win Justice White's vote, recalled the Brennan mode of persistent persuasion. There was also a time when O'Connor seemed affected by Brennan on the substance of the law. His attempts to influence her, to pull her more to the left on race-based policies or protections for the rights of defendants, for example, caused her to dig in with a more conservative approach.

As was the custom, the rest of the justices took up a collection to give Brennan the high-back black leather chair he had used in the courtroom. Along with retired justices Burger and Powell, they each chipped in $5.60 to meet the secondhand value—as determined by the marshal of the Court—for the chair Brennan sat in for thirty-four years.[31]

13

──◆◆◆◆◆──

FINDING NEW BEARINGS

In the late 1980s, Justice O'Connor had faced her own mortality in the form of breast cancer and the painful rigor of chemotherapy. About the same time, her mother, Ada Mae, died after enduring Alzheimer's for a decade. Almost as profoundly unsettling as O'Connor entered the 1990s, was the final sale of the Lazy B, the childhood home that had so shaped her identity. "It was a heart-wrenching time for all the family," she wrote.[1] With none of O'Connor's sons nor their cousins willing to take on management of the ranch, and its long-term money-making prospects dim, in 1986 the family had decided to sell. Of Harry and Ada Mae's three children, O'Connor was the most reluctant to give up the ranch that had been in the family for more than a century.

Shortly after the sale was completed, Justice Blackmun unwittingly asked O'Connor about the Lazy B. Her response can be inferred from the note Blackmun then wrote to her, "Dear Sandra, I am afraid I opened old wounds (of which I had not known) when I made inquiry about the ranch the other night. Perhaps the two photographs enclosed will give you a chuckle. They go back to 1924 and Wyoming and a favorite horse."[2]

"These old photos of you on horseback are treasures," O'Connor wrote back. "Life on a ranch seemed so normal to me growing up. Now it is so distant, but the memories are special." Then she added, "Could you toss a lariat?"[3]

Negotiating a course through these life events, O'Connor's working relationships also changed as she adjusted to the retirement of William Brennan and, in time, other long-serving colleagues. The inner dynamic of the Court was changing as individual justices removed the black robes and others donned them.

Justice Brennan's successor, David Souter, was a dry-witted Harvard law graduate who had spent seven years on the New Hampshire Supreme Court and three months on the U.S. Court of Appeals for the First Circuit. When President George H. W. Bush selected him in July 1990, Souter had published just one law review article and had yet to write a single opinion as a federal appeals court judge. Remarking on Souter's lack of a "paper trail," Senate Judiciary Committee Chairman Joseph Biden, a Democrat from Delaware, said less was known about Souter than any other Supreme Court candidate in the past quarter century. When a reporter asked Souter how it felt to be snatched from obscurity, Souter responded with an unflappable Yankee style that remained evident throughout his Senate hearings, "I must say, I never thought of myself as that obscure."[4] Souter was approved by a vote of 90–9 (with Biden's support), and he took the judicial oath on October 9, 1990.

Souter owed his nomination to his close friend Senator Warren Rudman, a New Hampshire Republican, and to John Sununu, Bush's chief of staff and a former New Hampshire governor, who had selected Souter for the state supreme court. Sununu predicted Souter would be a "home run" for conservatives. That assertion turned out in short order to be a colossal misstatement, and Souter's move to the left intensified the reordering of alliances on the Rehnquist Court in the early 1990s.

O'Connor took the lifelong bachelor under her wing, inviting him over for Thanksgiving dinner and trying to set him up on dates. (O'Connor had once boasted about her matchmaking skills, saying that she was known as "the Yente of Paradise Valley."[5]) She asked him to the many parties she and John held at their 1918 stucco house in Chevy Chase, Maryland, including, early in Souter's tenure, an evening of "Fajitas and frivolity . . . Dress: Country Western or Effete Eastern."[6]

On the substance of the law, Souter took some time to get his bearings and initially did vote with the conservative wing. During his first term, for example, he was the fifth vote in *Barnes v. Glen Theatre,* an Indiana case upholding a prohibition on nude dancing, against a First Amendment free-expression challenge.[7] Years later when a similar case returned to the Court from Pennsylvania, he wrote that he had made a mistake and would apply a stricter First Amendment test to cities seeking to shut down adult clubs. "[M]y mistake calls to mind Justice Jackson's foolproof explanation for a lapse of his own, when he quoted Samuel Johnson, 'Ignorance, sir, ignorance.' I may not be less ignorant of nude dancing than I was nine years ago, but after many subsequent occasions to think further about the needs of the First Amendment, I have come to believe that a government must toe the mark more carefully than I first insisted. I hope it is enlightenment on my part, and acceptable even if a little late."[8] (In the later case, *Erie v. Pap's A. M. Kandyland,* Souter was in the minority. The opinion for the Court was written by Justice O'Connor and gave Erie greater latitude to prohibit nude dancing in the face of arguments that the suppression of its "erotic message" violated the First Amendment.)

The absence of Brennan, the initial unpredictability of Souter, and the likelihood of other retirements contributed to a sense of flux at the Court. Law professor and legal commentator Alexander Wohl wrote in the *American Bar Association Journal,* "Although it is far too early to draw conclusions about how this 'new' Supreme Court will evolve, one thing is clear: The old calculus is gone and a new one waits to be implemented. And with no Brennan-like dominating presence guaranteeing guidance, continuity or collegiality, the question of who can step into the judicial vacuum remains an open one."[9]

O'Connor was taking control, but not in a way that could be easily compared to Brennan's leadership. She lacked his sheer persuasive presence and overaching vision of the law. Her coalition-building style was not easily detected from the outside, and the reality was that her legal approach was always a work in progress. But in time, the "new" calculus would be hers.

Curiously, it was during the term after Brennan's departure that O'Connor took a rare public step to set herself apart from the other justices. In a punitive damages case arising from an insurance fraud dispute, she dissented in the most public way and also demonstrated that her usual states' rights views were not without exception.

Supreme Court tradition dictated that when a dissenting justice was particularly angry about the position adopted by the majority, he took the exceptional step of reading portions of that dissent from the winged mahogany bench. Justice Stevens said it was a way to ensure that the dissent did not get lost in the shuffle of the day's news.[10] In 1989, when the Court majority ruled in a Missouri abortion case that states could impose new restrictions on a woman's right to end a pregnancy, Justice Blackmun read his dissent to a hushed courtroom. A year earlier, when the Court upheld a federal law allowing independent prosecutors to investigate suspected crimes by high-ranking officials, Justice Scalia dissented in a nine-minute statement that began, "Frequently an issue of this sort will come before the Court clad, so to speak, in sheep's clothing. . . . This wolf comes as a wolf."[11]

But in her first ten years on the Court, Justice O'Connor never once felt compelled to read a dissent aloud. When she was on the losing side, she tried not to reveal hard feelings. So it was a telling moment on March 4, 1991, when O'Connor for the first time in her tenure offered a dissent from the bench.[12] The situation that outraged O'Connor stemmed from a dispute between an Alabama woman cheated by her insurance agent and the company that employed him. O'Connor—alone among the justices—sided with the company when it was socked with a million-dollar damages verdict.

In 1982, Cleopatra Haslip was admitted to a hospital emergency room with a kidney infection. As a government employee of Roosevelt City, Alabama, Haslip presumed that the insurance policy she held through the city would cover her medical expenses. But she discovered that the city's insurance agent, Lemmie Ruffin, apparently had pocketed the payments and her policy had been canceled. Haslip was stuck with $3,800 in uncovered medical bills and pursued by a collection agency. She sued Pacific Mutual Life Insurance, Ruffin's employer. A jury awarded Haslip $1.04 million, of which $840,000 was punitive damages. The Alabama Supreme Court upheld the award.[13]

Large jury awards had long been a point of contention in courts and legislatures. For more than a decade, Congress had been trying to write legislation setting limits. Business groups argued that juries often granted excessive awards based on emotion or other questionable motives. But trial lawyers and consumer advocates said punitive damages and other money awards were an essential check on the unbridled power of America's corporations.

In the *Haslip* case, business groups asserted that the Constitution's due process guarantee limited a jury's latitude to deter wrongdoing through punitive damages. But the Supreme Court majority ruled for Haslip, saying the judge's instructions to the jury and postverdict review in state court helped ensure that the award was not arbitrary. Writing for the Court, Justice Blackmun said, "One must concede that unlimited jury discretion . . . in the fixing of punitive damages may invite extreme results that jar one's constitutional sensibilities. We need not, and indeed we cannot, draw a mathematical bright line between the constitutionally acceptable and the constitutionally unacceptable that would fit every case."

O'Connor was the sole dissent—a rare spot for her. Beneath the cut marble figures of Moses, Hammurabi, Solomon, and other ancient lawgivers, O'Connor said, "The existing system is not rational." In the published dissent that would be distributed that morning, she wrote, "Punitive damages are a powerful weapon. Imposed wisely and with restraint, they have the potential to advance legitimate state interests. Imposed indiscriminately, however, they have a devastating potential for harm. . . . Rarely is a jury told anything more specific than 'do what you think best.' "[14]

O'Connor then quoted one of Justice Brennan's opinions on due process of law to argue that the instructions to the Alabama jury lacked sufficient safeguards for Pacific Mutual. It was a curious reference by O'Connor to Brennan's expansive view of due process. Equally puzzling was O'Connor's position in the punitive damages dispute. She, of all the justices, tended to believe in state control and resisted federal interference with local matters. Perhaps she came to the case predisposed as a businesswoman. O'Connor had been the first woman member of a bank board in Arizona. At another time, under other circumstances, she might have become a leader in the corporate world. O'Connor looked at the *Haslip* case from the viewpoint of Pacific Mutual, seeking greater predictability for business. (In time, her position would be partly adopted by the majority to impose substantial limits on punitive damages in *BMW v. Gore* and *State Farm Mutual Automobile Insurance v. Campbell*.[15])

ONE YEAR AFTER BRENNAN was forced into retirement by ill health, Thurgood Marshall decided to step down. Before his public announcement, he revealed his decision to the justices at their private conference, O'Connor began crying, and Rehnquist got up and uncharacteristically hugged Marshall.[16] Long in declining health and often aloof as a colleague, Marshall nonetheless remained an epic figure in their lives. He had overcome a discrimination none of them could know. The next day, on June 28, 1991, Marshall sat in the Court's ceremonial East Conference Room before dozens of reporters and photographers and talked about his reasons for leaving. His legs were crossed at the ankles, trademark white socks on display. In his right hand, he held the cane he used for walking. In his left hand, he dangled his glasses. "What's wrong with me?" Marshall said with obvious impatience. "I'm old. I'm getting old and coming apart."[17] He was five days shy of age 83.

Marshall sat wearily in his chair. The soft jowls of his face sagged. But the intensity in his eyes was undiminished. Underneath it all, this great-grandson of a slave and son of a Pullman car steward was still a fighter. He scoffed at suggestions that he was leaving because of anger at the conservative justices' dominance. He called that "a double-barreled lie."

The day before, the last of the 1990–1991 term, Marshall had denounced a ruling by the majority that said evidence of a victim's character and the impact of the crime on the victim's family could be used against a murder defendant at sentencing.

Pervis Tyrone Payne had been convicted by a Tennessee jury of the murders of a woman and her 2-year-old daughter and of assault with intent to kill her 3-year-old son. During Payne's sentencing hearing, the boy's grandmother testified that the boy missed his mother and baby sister. Payne was sentenced to death. The Tennessee Supreme Court affirmed the conviction and sentence, rejecting Payne's contention that the grandmother's testimony and prosecutor's comments about the effects of the crime on the victim's family prejudiced Payne's rights.

Chief Justice Rehnquist wrote for the majority, which included

O'Connor, that such evidence was merely another way of informing the jury about the specific harm caused by a crime. He also said it would be unfair to allow testimony about the defendant's character but not about the victim's. O'Connor wrote a concurring statement that emphasized state power to determine capital sentencing proceedings. She also detailed the brutality of the killings and questioned how the testimony from the grandmother could have inflamed the jury more than the information that the victims died after repeated thrusts from a butcher knife.[18]

Marshall and fellow dissenters Blackmun and Stevens believed that the value of the victim-impact evidence was outweighed by its prejudicial effect and potential to distract the jury from the defendant's character. They also thought it wrong to reverse Court precedent. The departure from recent precedent prohibiting such evidence from being introduced at the sentencing hearing because of possible jury prejudice prompted Marshall to write, "Power, not reason, is the new currency of this Court's decision making. . . . Neither the law nor the facts supporting [Supreme Court cases from 1987 and 1989 that barred such victim evidence] underwent any change in the last four years. Only the personnel of this Court did."[19]

Marshall's departure closed another chapter in Court history. He had broken color barriers as a civil rights lawyer, U.S. solicitor general, and Supreme Court Justice. As O'Connor often told her law clerks, "He's the only one of us who made history before coming here."[20] She said she first heard his voice on the radio as news of the 1954 ruling in *Brown v. Board of Education* was announced: "I had not yet been exposed personally to racial tensions [but as] I listened that day on the radio to Thurgood Marshall talking eloquently to the media about the social stigmas and lost opportunities suffered by African-American children in state-imposed segregated schools, my awareness of race-based disparities deepened."[21]

Despite their personal bond, O'Connor was not sufficiently moved to adopt Marshall's views in cases involving those victimized because of skin color. As a young legislator in Arizona, O'Connor sometimes minimized the economic disadvantages blacks faced, saying women made less doing similar jobs. Now, as a justice, she voted against government programs designed to compensate for broad societal discrimination. She generally thought it was time to move on. When she wrote the opinion in 1989 declaring that the city of Richmond had violated the equality rights of white contractors by setting aside 30 percent of its public contracts for black-owned companies, Marshall had responded, "I . . . do not believe this nation is anywhere close to eradicating racial discrimination or its vestiges." He characterized the view of O'Connor and others in the majority who believed such affirmative action was no longer needed as "wishful thinking."[22]

To SUCCEED MARSHALL, President George H. W. Bush nominated Clarence Thomas, a judge on the U.S. Court of Appeals for the District of Columbia Circuit. At 43, Thomas was ready to become the youngest justice of the nine, and only the second African-American in history to reach the nation's highest bench.

Thomas's childhood had been wracked by poverty and despair in Pin Point, Georgia. Thomas's father left the family when Thomas was two; his mother worked as a maid and shucked oysters for a commercial fishery. She coped alone with her three young children for five years, living in a house with no electricity or plumbing. When the house burned down, Thomas, then 7, and his younger brother were taken in by his maternal grandparents in Savannah. With a creed of hard work and self-reliance, grandfather Myers Anderson put Thomas to work before dawn, forced him to study hard, and imposed a strict moral code. "One of my grandfather's favorite admonitions," Thomas said later, "always spoken in a deep baritone voice with the seriousness of the Last Judgment, was: 'If you lie, you'll steal. If you steal, you'll cheat. If you cheat, you'll kill.'"[23]

But the story of hard times in Pin Point did not quell opposition from civil rights groups intensely focused on the loss of a reliable liberal Supreme Court justice and his replacement by a conservative. They denounced Thomas for positions he had taken as head of the Equal Employment Opportunity Commission in 1982–1990 that curtailed protections for victims of race, sex, and age discrimination. Benjamin Hooks, executive director of the National Association for the Advancement of Colored People, testified: "He talks about his experiences, that his grandfather was called 'boy,' but those experiences did not leave him with the lesson" of a need for extensive government remedies for bias.[24]

Opposition escalated when a former employee of Thomas suddenly emerged with allegations that he had sexually harassed her when she worked for him at the EEOC and Department of Education.[25] The charges from Anita Hill, who had become a University of Oklahoma law professor, galvanized women on Capitol Hill and across America. Thomas categorically denied the accusations. He ended up being approved in the Senate by a 52–48 vote, the closest vote for a Supreme Court nominee in more than a century.

As O'Connor and the other justices kept an eye on the confirmation hearings, they were transfixed by a more private worry. Natalie Rehnquist, or Nan, as she was known to them, was dying of cancer. She and O'Connor had been friends for nearly forty years. On October 17, 1991, two days after Thomas was confirmed by the Senate, Nan Rehnquist died at the age of 62. It was the day before a gala celebration for Thomas was to be held at the White House. In deference to Chief Justice Rehnquist, the White House considered postponing the party. But Thomas and his supporters already had arranged to have more than a hundred guests there, and the festivities went on.[26]

RAPPORT BETWEEN THOMAS and O'Connor was tested almost immediately in a case that played right into an area of the law that she had made her own—prisoner appeals. The dispute arose from a December 1978 break-in at a home in Westmoreland County, Virginia. Police discovered the stolen television sets, record player, and other items at the house of Frank Robert West, and West was convicted of grand larceny. His eventual appeal to the Supreme Court tested the procedures for state prisoners seeking a federal hearing.

The majority agreed that West's petition should be rejected, and Rehnquist assigned Thomas the opinion. But then Thomas, without the backing of the majority, wrote a draft opinion that proposed blanket deference to state-court rulings by federal judges, which would effectively overturn a 1953 precedent. It was a hard-line position that most angered the justice who arguably had gotten the Court to this point—O'Connor.[27]

She declined to sign Thomas's opinion and wrote a separate concurring statement accusing him of misinterpreting her ruling in the *Teague* case, of taking precedent written by Justice Powell out of context, and of giving short shrift to numerous other past cases. Her opinion was an unusually strident, item-by-item response to Thomas's opinion. Her bottom-line was: federal courts must independently evaluate the Supreme Court precedent that existed at the time a defendant's state conviction became final and whether that precedent would have changed the outcome of the case. Her fierceness startled some of the other justices. But Thomas was pushing the Court further than it had gone in restricting prisoner filings, and O'Connor was thrust into the role of a moderate. Justice Stevens signed on as soon as he saw her draft in the West case, as did Blackmun, who wrote, "You are so right." [28]

Nothing made O'Connor push back more than someone trying to pressure her. It was not that she merely resisted. She had an internal mechanism her two siblings had witnessed from childhood, which caused her to rise up fiercely when pressured.

Years later, Thomas recalled the differences between him and O'Connor in *Wright v. West*. "At first I thought, 'Whoa, she's a tough cookie.' . . . But they had been working on these [habeas corpus] problems for years and I come marching in like this." Thomas pumped his arms aggressively for effect. "I was the new kid on the block. I was brash. . . . I just took it like the rookie football player who gets clobbered by the linebacker: 'Welcome to the NFL.' " [29]

DESPITE SOME DIFFERENCES, the addition of Justice Thomas gave O'Connor a new advantage. His vote allowed her to turn some of her most vigorous dissents into majority opinions, particularly to curtail the policies of racial preferences that opinions by Brennan and Marshall had secured.

After the 1990 census and a new round of redistricting, the North Carolina general assembly had drawn an unusually shaped congressional district that meandered through black neighborhoods across a 160-mile swath that followed Interstate 85. It was an attempt to pack black voters into a single district and give them a chance to elect one of their own to Congress. The Twelfth Congressional District was especially elongated. (A state legislator had quipped, "if you drove down the interstate with both car doors open, you'd kill most of the people in the district.") But in premise and purpose, the twelfth was not unlike numerous other so-called "majority-minority" districts drawn throughout the South in the 1980s to reverse the history of black vote dilution.

Some of these districts reflected states' efforts to comply with the fed-eral Voting Rights Act of 1965, a landmark law that put an end to state literacy tests and other local efforts to keep blacks from the polls. The act barred states from drawing district lines that spread racial minorities among various districts and thereby further reduced their political strength. A 1982 amendment to the act indicated that any voting practice having the effect of discriminating against racial minorities was unlaw-ful, irrespective of the intention of local officials.[30] Much of the South fell under an additional Voting Rights Act provision which subjected the drawing of legislative districts to U.S. Justice Department control.[31]

Then, in 1986, in an opinion by Brennan and over the dissent of O'Connor, the high court suggested, without clearly holding, that the 1982 amendment required states to maximize the number of majority-minority districts they drew. The Court said in that 1986 case, *Thornburg v. Gingles,* that several of North Carolina's state legislative districts im-permissibly diluted the strength of black voters. Brennan wrote that it was enough to show that very few blacks had been elected from those dis-tricts to demonstrate that the system violated the Voting Rights Act.[32]

Now that O'Connor controlled the majority, that emphasis changed. She invoked the Constitution to limit use of the Voting Rights Act as a reason to create "majority minority" districts.

In a new North Carolina case before the justices in 1993, *Shaw v. Reno,* white voters argued that the snakelike Twelfth District violated the Con-stitution's equality guarantee, because it clearly separated voters by race. Justice O'Connor and four of her conservative colleagues agreed, includ-ing Thomas, and ruled for the first time ever that whites could challenge the constitutionality of "bizarrely" shaped redistricting plans that ap-peared to classify voters by race.

O'Connor said such strangely shaped districts reinforced "the percep-tion that members of the same racial group—regardless of their age, ed-ucation, economic status, or the community in which they live—think alike, share the same political interests, and will prefer the same candi-dates at the polls." She then wrote in a rhetorical flourish that the districts bear "an uncomfortable resemblance to political apartheid" because they are based on skin color.[33]

In the end, her opinion set the Court on a course directly opposite

Brennan's by reducing the federal pressure that could be applied to state legislatures to try to maximize the power of African-American voters. Not surprisingly, Brennan and O'Connor had witnessed two versions of state politics. O'Connor was a party loyalist who trusted the state legislative system. As soon as she settled in Phoenix as a young lawyer in the late 1950s, she became active in the Republican Party. She got herself appointed to the state Senate, then ran and won reelection. She worked herself into a position to be part of the team mapping new legislative districts and made sure they benefited her own Republican Party. Years later, she told her fellow justices that any legislator who did not help his or her own party in the redistricting process should be impeached. "Perhaps I am swayed by my own experience as a legislator," she said in one memo, as she argued that courts should allow political—as opposed to racial—gerrymanders.[34]

Brennan, meanwhile, had seen politics at its worst. As *Governing* magazine's Alan Ehrenhalt wrote in an essay analyzing Brennan's record on voting rights cases, Brennan had grown up "in a grimy New Jersey factory town dominated by crooked ward bosses and a greedy patronage system" and, as a state judge, tried "cases involving an even worse political machine than the one from [his] childhood—a machine that rigged elections, shook down taxpayers for financial support and threatened to put its few outspoken critics in jail."[35]

Justice Souter, Brennan's successor, originally had been on O'Connor's side in the 1993 case of *Shaw v. Reno*. But he switched to a dissenting position, saying her opinion reneged on two decades of voting-rights remediation and history. Souter also complained that her "appearances"-based standard was unclear.[36]

Justice White, who as a deputy attorney general in the Kennedy administration had faced down segregationists in the South, wrote the lead dissent in *Shaw v. Reno*. White said "majority minority" districts did not deprive white voters of any rights. He said it was "both a fiction and a departure from settled equal protection principles" to regard the white voters as having a case. He noted that white voters were still the majority in ten of the twelve districts, or 83 percent, even though they constituted 79 percent of the state's voting-age population.

In another complaint that would echo among legal analysts outside the Court, White criticized O'Connor's opinion for setting no clear standards for assessing the constitutionality of voting districts. Her opinion was tied to the unusual shape of the Twelfth District. "By focusing on looks, rather than impact," White wrote, judges would be forced to look at superficialities such as size and shape. Of the majority's overall standard tied to appearances, White wrote, "How it intends to manage this standard, I do not know."[37]

As other voting rights cases came to the Court, O'Connor remained the decisive fifth vote, always offering an open-ended legal rationale and basing her decision on the discrete facts of the case.

White's dissent in the North Carolina redistricting case was his last. He retired after thirty-one years, saying it was time to give someone else a chance.[38] To succeed White, newly elected President Clinton named Ruth Bader Ginsburg in the summer of 1993. A former women's rights legal advocate who had successfully argued five cases before the justices, Ginsburg had been on the U.S. Court of Appeals for the District of Columbia Circuit. Clinton's choice of Ginsburg lifted from O'Connor the burden of representing—in the public's mind—all women.

O'Connor and Ginsburg differed in appearance and personality. O'Connor radiated a large and outgoing manner. Ginsburg was petite and shy, and sometimes had trouble looking people directly in the eye. Behind a pair of oversized glasses, the Brooklyn native stood for an East Coast intellectualism. She had been on the law review at both Harvard and Columbia. The mother of two children, she also had challenged female stereotypes. She did not cook. She recalled reprimanding the principal at her son's school for telephoning her whenever the boy was in trouble. "This child has two parents," she told the principal. "Please alternate calls for conferences." She also told audiences that women would not be liberated until men took equal care of children. "If I had an affirmative action program to design, it would be to give men every incentive to be concerned about the rearing of children."[39]

Despite such differences of style—including Ginsburg's avoidance of O'Connor's aerobics class ("I'm not a morning person")—the two women were natural allies. "I greeted her with enormous pleasure," O'Connor said. "Justice O'Connor is the most helpful big sister anyone could have," Ginsburg remarked.[40]

"If you think I'm glad to have another woman at the Court," O'Connor also told Ginsburg at one point, "you can imagine how glad John is to have Marty." For twelve years, John alone had given lie to the name of a small, elegant dining room at the Court reserved for justices' spouses, the "Ladies' Dining Room." (After O'Connor had joined the Court, a proposal to rename the room, where the wives of the justices traditionally met for lunch several times a year, to the "Spouses' Dining Room," was rejected for reasons of style and tradition.)[41]

In the fall of 1993, soon after she had taken her seat, Ginsburg went to O'Connor for advice about handling her first assignment from Rehnquist. Traditionally, the first opinion for a new justice involves a case that all nine agree on and that can be written up without difficulty. But Ginsburg was assigned to draft the Court's opinion in a case involving the Employee Retirement Income Security Act, a notoriously complex federal law covering worker benefits. The Court divided 6–3. Justice O'Connor was one of the dissenters.

"Sandra, how can he do this to me?" Ginsburg said to O'Connor.

"Ruth, you just do it, and get your opinion in circulation before he makes the next set of assignments," O'Connor said.

Recalling the story years later, Ginsburg said of O'Connor's no-nonsense, no-pity response: "That is so typical Sandra." A few years later, O'Connor would offer Ginsburg advice of the most personal kind. "She was the first person to call me in the hospital," Ginsburg said of her 1999 surgery for colorectal cancer. "She seemed really concerned. She said, 'You're going to get a lot of letters. Do not even try to respond.' "[42]

O'Connor recommended that Ginsburg schedule chemotherapy for Fridays so that she would have the weekend to recover. "Then she said, 'Whatever you do, stay physically active.' " She encouraged Ginsburg to hire a personal trainer. Ginsburg also sought O'Connor's advice when choosing to make her experience surviving cancer public.[43] Justice Ginsburg said that O'Connor had not been naturally inclined to divulge her personal experience but that "she became increasingly aware of how much it would mean to other women."[44]

In many of their terms together, some lawyers addressed Justice Ginsburg as Justice O'Connor. It happened to even the most experienced appellate lawyers. So it had been fortuitous that in 1993, when Ginsburg was sworn in, the National Association of Women Judges presented T-shirts to the two women: "I'm Sandra, not Ruth" and "I'm Ruth, not Sandra."

. . .

Two YEARS LATER, in 1995, O'Connor again took advantage of Justice Thomas's vote and the changed Court. She wrote a decision reversing the Brennan approach in *Metro Broadcasting v. Federal Communications Commission,* which in 1990 upheld a preference program for minority broadcasters. The new dispute involved Adarand Constructors, a guardrail construction company that challenged a U.S. Department of Transportation program favoring firms that awarded subcontracts to minority-owned businesses. Defying Brennan's *Metro Broadcasting* precedent, O'Connor won a bare majority to require the most searching judicial scrutiny for all government policies based on race, even congressionally mandated ones. "[W]henever the government treats any person unequally because of his or her race, that person has suffered an injury that falls squarely within the language and spirit of the Constitution's guarantee of equal protection," she wrote. O'Connor did not go so far as to say that such tough scrutiny would prevent the government from ever using racial classifications. "The unhappy persistence of both the practice and lingering effects of racial discrimination against minority groups in this country is an unfortunate reality, and government is not disqualified from acting to respond to it."[45]

The standard she articulated in *Adarand Constructors v. Pena* erased the distinction between invidious discrimination and benign preferences—"the difference between a 'No Trespassing' sign and a welcome mat," as Justice Stevens wrote. "It would treat a Dixiecrat Senator's decision to vote against Thurgood Marshall's confirmation in order to keep African-Americans off the Supreme Court as on par with President Johnson's evaluation of his nominee's race as a positive factor."[46]

But O'Connor was especially pleased that she turned her dissent from *Metro Broadcasting* into the majority view. Her thoughts were captured—temporarily, it turned out—in her 2003 book *The Majesty of the Law.* After noting that the standards "expressed in my dissent in *Metro Broadcasting* were, in due course, adopted," she added: "I must confess to having hopes that some of my other dissents will one day be similarly vindicated." But while she expressed these sentiments in the galleys sent to reviewers in early 2003, the sentences were omitted in the final version of the book.[47]

• • •

Two weeks after the *Adarand* ruling, on June 25, 1995, retired Chief Justice Warren Burger died. He was 87. "Little did I think in 1979 that I might one day serve as an associate justice," Justice O'Connor said, as she offered a eulogy for the chief justice who had supported her nomination, and she recalled the houseboat vacation she and Burger had shared. Dressed in a navy blue jacket and skirt and surrounded at the front of the National Presbyterian Church in Washington by wreaths of vibrant flowers, O'Connor told the congregation, "I began a friendship with and a respect for Warren Burger there that never dimmed."

She recalled the scene on September 25, 1981, the day she was sworn in. She reminded the church audience, which included every one of the other justices, that Burger had taken her arm and led her down the Court front steps to confront the battery of reporters. She called it an act of kindness. Then, perhaps summoning up the lessons of Professor Rathbun from her Stanford years, and her own ideals, O'Connor said, "I have always believed that one can serve God by caring for our families and others and by serving our community and the nation. Warren Burger did that."[48]

In 1997, two years after Burger's death, Brennan died. He was 91. He had been in poor health and in a nursing home since breaking a hip eight months earlier.[49]

O'Connor did not attend Brennan's funeral mass held at St. Matthew's Cathedral in Washington, DC, on July 29, 1997. Neither did Chief Justice Rehnquist, nor Justices Kennedy or Scalia. When questioned by a *Washington Post* columnist, the Supreme Court's public information office had no explanation for the absences.[50]

For O'Connor, other plans might have intervened. Perhaps she was tired. O'Connor had spent the earlier part of July in Krakow, Poland, at a meeting of the Central and East European Law Initiative. She then traveled to Vienna, Austria, to teach a class. But she was back in the country at the end of July, and attended an American Bar Association conference three days after Brennan's service.

Justice Souter delivered a eulogy for the man whose seat he had taken. "One thing we are not doing here today is saying good-bye to William Brennan, the justice," Souter said. "It is true, the life of the man is over; so is the liberal era when Justice Brennan's voice was the voice of the Supreme Court. But the law as he saw it will transcend his own time, and only the Lord can know when the Court and country will come to final terms with Justice Brennan's reading of the American Constitution. He has left so much to be dealt with."[51]

14

━━◆◆◆◆━━

ABORTION BATTLES CONTINUE

The changes at the Supreme Court in the early 1990s had the potential to eliminate, not simply scale back, what had been declared a woman's constitutional right to end a pregnancy. These changes tested O'Connor's developing legal standard for abortion rights and her strategic position among the nine. William Brennan had retired in 1990 after thirty-four years as a justice, and the following year, Thurgood Marshall, a twenty-four-year veteran, stepped down. President George H. W. Bush had appointed David Souter and Clarence Thomas. During their confirmation hearings, neither appointee had disclosed how he would vote on *Roe v. Wade.* But the tone of the testimony of each was strikingly different.

Souter told the Senate Judiciary Committee of his regard for the Court's 1965 ruling in *Griswold v. Connecticut,* which relied on a privacy right located in the Fourteenth Amendment to protect a married couple's use of contraception. When asked whether he believed procreation was a fundamental right, Souter said, "I would assume that if we are going to have any core concept of marital privacy, that would certainly have to rank at its fundamental heart." He said he understood the anguish of women facing an abortion decision and, in the middle of senators' questions, said he suddenly remembered an experience from twenty-four years earlier. As a Harvard law student, Souter had been a proctor in an undergraduate dormitory. A student and his pregnant girlfriend came to Souter to talk about the woman's desire to "self-abort."

"I spent two hours in a small dormitory bedroom that afternoon," Souter recalled as he answered a question from Ohio Democratic Senator Howard Metzenbaum, "in that room, because that was the most private place we could get so that no one in the next suite of rooms could hear, listening to her and trying to counsel her to approach her problem in a way different from what she was doing, and your question has brought that back to me."[1]

One year later, Thomas's hearings were far more contentious, partly because of his record as an outspoken conservative. His writings and speeches suggested a narrow interpretation of the Constitution, which would lead him to reject a right to abortion. But Thomas was a reluctant witness on substantive areas of the law. He told the committee he had never debated the ruling in *Roe v. Wade* when it came out in 1973. He declined to talk about it with senators, too: "I think it is important to indicate that the area of *Roe v. Wade* is difficult, it is a controversial area. Cases are coming before the Court in many different postures." Thomas said it would undermine his ability to be impartial in those cases if he were to talk about *Roe v. Wade*.[2]

Soon after Thomas was seated, the justices took up a decisive test of *Roe v. Wade*. The case, *Planned Parenthood of Southeastern Pennsylvania v. Casey*, arrived at the Court just as the subject of abortion was escalating in the rhetoric of another presidential election, too. It was spring 1992, and Bush was running for reelection. Arkansas governor Bill Clinton, the presumptive Democratic nominee, was trying to win women's votes by arguing that *Roe v. Wade* hung in the balance. At the same time in the early 1990s, abortion clinics were experiencing increased harassment of employees and patients by the militant antiabortion group Operation Rescue, and, separately, were even being hit on occasion by extremists' firebombs.

Pennsylvania's law required a woman to tell her husband of her intention to obtain an abortion. It imposed a twenty-four-hour waiting period on a woman seeking to have the procedure and required physicians to give her exhaustive information about the fetus and the abortion procedure, to obtain an "informed consent" from her. A district court judge had invalidated the law, but the U.S. Court of Appeals for the Third Circuit reinstated it, relying on—and narrowly interpreting—O'Connor's 1989 opinion in the *Webster* case from Missouri.[3]

On April 22, 1992, when lawyer Kathryn Kolbert stepped to the lectern on behalf of Planned Parenthood and others challenging the Pennsylvania regulations, she stressed the significance of the abortion right in America and of the way the nation had come to count on it. "Whether our Constitution endows government with the power to force a woman to continue or to end a pregnancy against her will is the central question in this case," she said. "Never before has this Court bestowed and taken back a fundamental right that has been part of the settled rights and expectations of literally millions of Americans for nearly two decades."

Kolbert's arguments were sweeping and philosophical. The justices let her speak for several minutes. When Justice O'Connor interrupted her, she said, "Ms. Kolbert, you're arguing the case as though all we have before us is whether to apply *stare decisis* [regard for precedent] and preserve *Roe v. Wade* in all its aspects. Nevertheless, we granted [a hearing] on some specific questions in this case. Do you plan to address any of those in your argument?"

"Your Honor, I do," Kolbert answered, but still wanting to stick to her main point, continued, "however, the central question in the case is, what is the standard that this Court uses to evaluate the restrictions that are at issue, and therefore one cannot . . ."

O'Connor cut her off: "Well, the standard may affect the outcome or it may not, but at bottom we still have to deal with specific issues, and I wondered if you were going to address them."

Kolbert did not digress further. She turned to the Pennsylvania regulation that O'Connor would be most likely to resist: the husband-notification provision.

When it was his turn at the lectern, Pennsylvania attorney general Ernest D. Preate Jr. said all of the state's regulations could be upheld "under the analysis that was applied by this Court in *Webster*." He also told the justices that *"Roe v. Wade* need not be revisited by this Court except to reaffirm that *Roe* did not establish an absolute right to abortion on demand, but rather a limited right subject to reasonable state regulations."

Blackmun bristled at Preate's suggestion that *Roe* could have provided for "abortion on demand" and asked sternly, "Have you read *Roe?*"

"Yes, I have," Preate said.

"Thank you," Blackmun responded and let Preate continue.

When Preate then referred to the provision requiring married women to tell their husbands that they intend to obtain an abortion, O'Connor jumped in. "Now, the provision does not require notification to a father who is not the husband, I take it," she asked.

"That's correct, Justice O'Connor," Preate answered.

". . . or notice if the woman is unmarried?" she added.

"It only applies to married women," Preate acknowledged.

"So what's the interest, to try to preserve the marriage?" O'Connor asked.

"There are several interests," Preate said. "The interest, of course, in protecting the life of the unborn child."

"Well, then," O'Connor asked, "why not require notice to all fathers? It's a curious sort of a provision, isn't it?"

"It is that," Preate admitted, "but the legislature has made the judgment that it wanted its statute to apply in this specific instance because it wanted to further the integrity of marriages."

O'Connor then posed a hypothetical: "Would you say that the state could similarly require a woman to notify anyone with whom she had intercourse that she planned to use some means of birth control after the intercourse that operates, let's say, as an abortifacient [which prevents implantation of a fertilized egg]? Could the state do that? I mean, it would be the same state interest, I suppose."

"The state interest would be the same, but I think that would be problematic. . . ."

"And why would it be problematic, do you think?"

"I think that with regard to applying a statute to all women, that it might create a severe obstacle, an absolute obstacle to their obtaining an abortion."

"Well," O'Connor remarked at one point, clearly suspicious of involving the husband, "we're talking about the provision for notification in this case under the statute to the husband, and I'm just asking whether a different type of state regulation would have to be upheld under your standard."[4]

Two days later, in the justices' private conference, Rehnquist had an easy majority to uphold the Pennsylvania provisions except the spousal notification. How far he could go to restrict *Roe v. Wade* was not clear. Bush appointee Thomas expressed strong anti-*Roe* sentiment, but Bush's other appointee, Souter, did not want to confront it. He said he believed it should be upheld and he wanted to use O'Connor's standard forbidding restrictions that place an "undue burden" on the mother's right to end a pregnancy.

Souter had tipped his hand earlier. In January 1992, when the justices were considering whether to take up *Planned Parenthood v. Casey,* Souter had asked that they focus specifically on the weight of precedent—that is, prior court rulings—in the constitutional right to abortion. Souter, 52 at the time, was the most unassuming of the nine justices. He lived in a sparsely furnished apartment in a Southwest section of Washington, off the beaten path, kept to himself, and eschewed the town's social scene. He preferred a lunch of apple and yogurt at his desk to joining his colleagues around a dining table.

But he and O'Connor knew at the outset that they wanted to separate themselves from Rehnquist and his view that the Court was wrong to have found a "fundamental right" to abortion in 1973. They also were ready to reject the regulation requiring a woman to notify her husband of her intention to obtain an abortion.

Unlike O'Connor and Souter, Kennedy previously had staked out a position strongly against the 1973 landmark, when he signed Rehnquist's opinion in the 1989 *Webster* case from Missouri. Kennedy, a practicing Roman Catholic, even once denounced *Roe* as the "Dred Scott of our time," referring to the 1857 ruling that allowed slavery to continue and helped begin the Civil War.[5] So, a presumption existed that Kennedy would be with Rehnquist, giving the chief justice five votes, even without O'Connor and Souter, to overrule *Roe.*

But at this make-or-break moment, Kennedy concluded that an abortion decision was a personal choice protected by the Constitution's guarantee of privacy. With O'Connor's past writings as a starting point for their rationale, the threesome worked quickly together, dividing up parts of the opinion, and kept their efforts quiet from the other justices to avoid being pressured by either side. They would affirm the essential core of *Roe v. Wade* but discard the trimester analysis and institute a standard prohibiting restrictions that put an "undue burden" on a woman seeking to end a pregnancy. Further, they would try to explain to the American people why, under the Court's traditional regard for precedent, *Roe* should endure. This was an opportunity for O'Connor to refine her approach to abortion rights that she had been developing since the 1983 *Akron* case.

As they were all deep into the writing of their drafts, Kennedy penned a personal note to Blackmun on May 29, 1992. "I need to see you as soon as you have a few free moments. I want to tell you about some developments in *Planned Parenthood v. Casey,* and I think part of what I say should come as welcome news." After Kennedy and Blackmun met on May 30, Blackmun wrote himself a note that said, "The 3 [are] on the case." Among his jotting: "adopt SOC's undue B"—presumably, her "undue burden" standard.[6]

A week later, O'Connor, Kennedy, and Souter circulated a draft opinion to the rest of their colleagues. In their first paragraph, they noted with some exasperation that five times in the last decade the Reagan and Bush administrations had asked that they invalidate *Roe*. "Liberty finds no refuge in a jurisprudence of doubt," their draft declared. The justices went on to describe how, for better or worse, *Roe* was an enduring part of the nation's way of life.[7]

"Your opinion is impressive," Justice Stevens wrote back immediately. "You are to be congratulated on a fine piece of work. I think I understand why you decided to write jointly, and I agree that your decision is a wise one." Stevens had some suggestions for changes but he mainly wanted to encourage their effort. A few days later, Stevens recommended that the trio switch around a few sections of the sixty-page opinion so that the affirmation of *Roe*—with which Stevens and Blackmun agreed, giving them a majority—came first.[8]

"In my view," Stevens told the three justices, "an opinion that begins as an opinion of the Court [that is, a five-member majority] and continues to speak for the Court for twenty-five pages would be far more powerful than one that starts out as a plurality opinion and shifts back and forth between a Court opinion and a plurality opinion."

O'Connor, Kennedy, and Souter agreed to the suggested change.

For Chief Justice Rehnquist, who had been present at the origin of *Roe* and thought he finally was positioned to reverse it, this was very bad news. To make matters worse, law clerks apparently were talking to the media about internal negotiations. *Newsweek* magazine ran a "Periscope" item that said, "With only three weeks left in the Supreme Court term, the pressure is on to reach a decision in *Planned Parenthood v. Casey,* the Pennsylvania case that could reverse the 1973 landmark *Roe v. Wade* decision that legalized abortion. *Newsweek* has learned that the justices have not yet begun the process of circulating opinions to each other for comment and review. But sources say at least three of the nine justices are planning to draft opinions in *Casey.* That suggests the possibility of a murky, perhaps inconclusive, decision. No matter what the outcome, sources at the court expect the decision will be handed down the last day of the term."[9]

Rehnquist sent a note to all the clerks about the piece, which, while not a complete picture, had suggested some of the negotiating underway. "While most of the story deals with matters of common knowledge to anyone who observes the Court," Rehnquist wrote, "part of it does not. The story is attributed to 'sources' and 'clerks.' Each of you is admonished to bear in mind the following portion of the Supreme Court Law Clerk Code of Conduct: 'There should be as little communication as possible between the clerk and representatives of the press.' " For Rehnquist, "as little communication as possible," was a euphemism for no communication at all.[10]

Once the joint opinion by O'Connor, Kennedy, and Souter began to circulate among all the justices, Stevens and Blackmun worried that the alliance might begin to fracture. The liberal justices believed that all three were taking a personal risk breaking from political expectations of their anti-*Roe* sentiment. Kennedy particularly was feeling pressure from more conservative justices, especially Scalia, a fellow Roman Catholic. Kennedy told a reporter for *California Lawyer* magazine, who had prearranged an interview for the morning of June 29: "Sometimes you don't know whether you are Caesar about to cross the Rubicon or Captain Queeg cutting your own tow line."[11] About an hour later, he joined his colleagues on the bench to announce the opinion in *Planned Parenthood v. Casey* and uphold a woman's right to end a pregnancy.

O'Connor spoke first for the trio and announced that they were affirming the essential holding of *Roe v. Wade*. "Some of us as individuals find abortion offensive to our most basic principles or morality, but that cannot control our decision" she said. "Our obligation is to define the liberty of all, not to mandate our own moral code."

Then came Kennedy, who stressed that "at the heart of liberty is the right to define one's own concept of existing, of meaning, of the universe and of the mystery of human life." When it was Souter's turn to speak from the bench, he emphasized his regard for precedent and declared that "an entire generation has come of age" assuming the existence of *Roe v. Wade.* His message, indeed the message of all three justices who had crafted the compromise opinion, was that men and women had been engaging in relationships and making choices in reliance on *Roe v. Wade* and of the availability of abortion. After nearly three decades, it was not time to draw back from *Roe.*

O'Connor's pragmatic rhetoric laced the opinion. The threesome noted that "while [*Roe*] has engendered disapproval, it has not been unworkable," and that "the Court's duty in the present case is clear." More important, she modified her "undue burden" standard, saying, "A finding of an undue burden is a shorthand for the conclusion that a state regulation has the purpose or effect of placing a substantial obstacle in the path of a woman seeking an abortion of a nonviable fetus." Her earlier stance, articulated in the 1980s, would have allowed more state restrictions on abortion. Acknowledging that some of her previous statements had been "inconsistent," she abandoned her earlier references to states' having a "compelling" interest in fetal life that potentially could eclipse the mother's interests.

In the end, the Court reinstated the twenty-four-hour waiting period and mandatory counseling but struck down the spousal-notice provision. To obtain a majority to uphold the restrictions, O'Connor, Kennedy, and Souter were joined by Rehnquist, White, Scalia, and Thomas. To uphold *Roe,* they had the fourth and fifth votes from Blackmun and Stevens.[12]

Blackmun in a concurrence called the joint opinion by O'Connor, Kennedy, and Souter "an act of personal courage and constitutional principle." But he also noted that the margin for abortion rights was a single vote. "I am 83 years old," he said. "I cannot remain on this Court forever, and when I do step down, the confirmation process for my successor well may focus on the issue before us today."[13]

Chief Justice Rehnquist penned a harsh dissenting opinion, asserting that the plurality had rendered *Roe* a "facade," replacing the 1973 standards with a framework "not built to last." "*Roe v. Wade* stands as a sort of judicial Potemkin village," he wrote, "which may be pointed out to passersby as a monument to the importance of adhering to precedent."

The most potent criticism flowed, predictably, from Scalia's pen. He believed the issue should be left to elected officials and the democratic process rather than value judgments of the Court. He mocked the first line of the plurality's opinion—"Liberty finds no refuge in a jurisprudence of doubt"—and asserted that the opinion made little clear.

"There is a poignant aspect to today's opinion," he wrote. "Its length, and what might be called its epic tone, suggest that its authors believe they are bringing to an end a troublesome era in the history of our Nation, and of our Court. 'It is the dimension' of authority, they say, to call the contending sides of national controversy to end their national division by accepting a common mandate rooted in the Constitution." Scalia warned that it would never happen, and concluded: "We should get out of this area, where we have no right to be, and where we do neither ourselves nor the country any good by remaining."

The Court's ruling was attacked by commentators on the right and left—although it appeared the majority of Americans approved. Robert Bork, who five years earlier had been turned down by the Senate for a seat on the high court, wrote in a July 8, 1992, piece for the *New York Times:* "Public discussion of the decision almost completely ignores the Constitution and focuses instead on abortion. Hence, the three who controlled the outcome ... are called by the media 'centrists' and 'moderates.' They may be that on the political spectrum, but on a constitutional spectrum their joint opinion is more properly termed 'radical.' The inescapable fact is that the Constitution contains not one word that can be tortured into the slightest relevance to abortion, one way or the other. . . . Until 1973, the Court was content to let the people and their elected representatives govern, but with *Roe* it usurped their democratic prerogatives."[14] Bork left little doubt that if he had been appointed to the Court rather than Kennedy, *Roe v. Wade* would have been overturned.

Law professors were divided in their assessment of O'Connor's position. Northeastern University law professors Judith Olans Brown, Wendy Parmet, and Mary E. O'Connell wrote in the *Indiana Law Re-*

view: "While the point is unprovable, it seems quite likely that Justice O'Connor, an upper middle class, highly educated, married woman who had experienced gender discrimination, could appreciate the indignity of having to ask her husband for permission to have an abortion. She could much less readily understand the problems poor women face when they must take two days off from work [because of the waiting period requirement] to undergo the procedure."[15] Writing in the *Supreme Court Review,* Professor Kenneth Karst called the opinion in *Planned Parenthood v. Casey* "Justice O'Connor's most important contribution to women's equal citizenship. . . . In setting out the 'undue burden' standard, she modifies what she said in *Akron* . . . substituting a new version considerably more protective of the right of choice."[16]

At the time, the vast middle of America approved of the Court's ruling in *Casey.* Polls showed that 70 percent of those surveyed believed the Court got it about right. As William Schneider wrote in *The Atlantic* magazine four months after the decision, "The debate over abortion seems to have no middle ground—except in public opinion." He noted that while support for abortion rights has edged upward over the past three years, half the country continues to say that abortion should be legal only "under certain circumstances."[17]

For her part, O'Connor was on an airplane soon after the decision was announced. She left for Africa, on a U.S. Information Agency–sponsored trip. She traveled to Kigali, Rwanda, and Nairobi, Kenya, where she spoke to professional and judicial groups in both countries. From Africa, she flew to Salzburg in mid-July for more conferences, and John joined her there.

IT WOULD BE EIGHT years before the Supreme Court revisited the abortion dilemma. Then, too, O'Connor's role as a crucial vote was evident. The case that came to the Court in spring 2000 involved a type of abortion procedure rather than any frontal challenge to *Roe v. Wade.* Bill Clinton, now in the second term of his presidency, had appointed Justices Ruth Bader Ginsburg, in 1993, and Stephen Breyer, in 1994. Both Ginsburg and Breyer had told the Senate Judiciary Committee that they believed in the constitutional right to abortion.

The new dispute *Stenberg v. Carhart* involved a Nebraska state ban on a procedure critics called "partial birth" abortion. The statute, similar to ones in thirty-one states at the time, prohibited a method "in which the person performing the abortion partially delivers vaginally a living unborn child before killing the child and completing the delivery." As the Court held arguments on a rainy April morning, only a handful of demonstrators, not hundreds as on earlier occasions, gathered.

As Nebraska attorney general Donald Stenberg defended the abortion ban, Justice O'Connor told him that the statute appeared to cover not only the relatively rare method of delivering part of the fetus into the birth canal before collapsing its skull, but also the most common form of second trimester abortion known as dilation and extraction, or D&X.

"These are both very gruesome procedures," O'Connor said. She challenged Stenberg's contention that the state was banning only the rarely used abortion method. "It is difficult to read the statute and . . . think so." As was her way, she wanted to reduce the rhetoric. Abortion is gruesome in all situations, she intimated, but maybe in some it is necessary.

There were five votes, including O'Connor's, to strike down the Nebraska statute. Stevens, the most senior justice of the group, assigned the opinion to Breyer, who had developed a good working relationship with O'Connor. Stevens knew Breyer would not overplay his hand and lose O'Connor's crucial vote.

"Millions of Americans believe that life begins at conception, and consequently that an abortion is akin to causing the death of an innocent child; they recoil at the thought that a law would permit it," Breyer began in his opinion for the majority. "Other millions fear that a law that forbids abortion would condemn many American women to lives that lack dignity, depriving them of equal liberty." Breyer said that the Nebraska law could be read as a ban of more than the controversial method of delivering part of the fetus into the birth canal before collapsing its skull. Physicians who use a more common second-trimester procedure "must fear prosecution, conviction and imprisonment." Breyer's opinion, setting a national precedent striking down other state bans on the procedure, was signed by O'Connor, Stevens, Souter, and Ginsburg.[18]

O'Connor wrote a concurring opinion that raised the possibility that states ultimately would be able to craft "partial birth" abortion bans that

could be constitutional. "A ban on partial-birth abortion that only pro-
scribed the D&X [dilation and extraction] method of abortion and that
included an exception for the mother would be constitutional in my
view," she said, laying out how government could draft a maternal health
exception and win her vote.

Dissenting Justice Thomas, joined by Rehnquist and Scalia, said the
majority's ruling was "indefensible" and amounted to an endorsement of
"infanticide." Kennedy, who had provided the fifth vote to uphold abortion rights in 1992, also dissented, separating himself from former partners O'Connor and Souter. He said that states should be free to outlaw
the "abhorrent" procedure that had been banned in Nebraska. Kennedy
expressed bitterness and a sense of betrayal about how the majority was
using principles derived from the *Casey* opinion, which he had signed, to
protect the so-called "partial birth" procedure. He asserted that the joint
opinion from *Casey* was "premised on the states having an important
constitutional role in defining their interests in the abortion debate."
Kennedy said the majority should have acknowledged Nebraska's "concern for the life of the unborn and for the partially born."

The most memorable objection again came from Scalia: "The notion
that the Constitution . . . prohibits the states from simply banning this
visibly brutal means of eliminating our half-born posterity is quite simply
absurd. . . . While I am in a I-told-you-so mood, I must recall my be-
musement, in *Casey,* at the joint opinion's expressed belief that *Roe v.
Wade* had 'call[ed] the contending sides of a national controversy to end
their national division. . . . ' "

As Scalia voiced his objections, a few protesters gathered in another
morning of drizzle outside the Court, carrying placards of dismembered
fetuses and quoting Scripture—testifying to the fact that the national debate over abortion would continue.[19]

Sandra and John O'Connor relax in an apartment in Frankfurt, Germany, in the mid-1950s, when John was a lawyer in the U.S. Army and Sandra worked as a civilian attorney for the government. *(Courtesy Arizona Historical Society Museum at Papago Park)*

Sandra and John pose with her parents, Ada Mae and Harry Day. *(Courtesy Arizona Historical Society Museum at Papago Park)*

Sandra Day *(front row, fourth from right)* stands with the 1952 staff of the *Stanford Law Review*. *(Collection of the Supreme Court of the United States, courtesy of Stanford University)*

O'Connor is sworn in as an Arizona State senator on October 31, 1969. She was appointed to fill the unexpired term of a woman who took a position in the Nixon administration. In the 1970 elections, O'Connor then campaigned and won the seat. *(The Arizona Republic)*

Sandra, John, and their three sons *(from top to bottom),* Scott, Brian, and Jay, in a publicity photograph from 1969. *(Collection of the Supreme Court of the United States)*

Arizona Trial Judge Sandra O'Connor and Chief Justice Warren Burger vacation on a houseboat at Lake Powell, August 1979. The two met on the trip arranged by a mutual friend. *(Collection of the Supreme Court of the United States, photograph by John Driggs)*

John O'Connor helps his wife with her black judicial robe, December 5, 1979, after her appointment to the Arizona Court of Appeals. Governor Bruce Babbitt named O'Connor to the position. *(The Arizona Republic)*

President Reagan's historic announcement on July 7, 1981, that he was nominating Sandra Day O'Connor to the Supreme Court was grist for editorial cartoonists. This Herblock cartoon appeared in the *Washington Post* on the following day. *("Well, It's About Time"* © 1981 by Herblock *in the* Washington Post*)*

Ronald Reagan hosts a reception for Sandra Day O'Connor on
July 15, 1981, when she is in Washington preparing for her Senate
confirmation hearings. Here she chats with the president and Attorney
General William French Smith. *(Courtesy Ronald Reagan Library)*

White House portrait, July 1981.
(Courtesy Ronald Reagan Library)

Arizona Senator Barry Goldwater sits with O'Connor before formally introducing her to the Senate Judiciary Committee on her first day of hearings, September 9, 1981. *(Courtesy Arizona Historical Foundation Photograph Collection)*

Chief Justice Warren Burger administers the constitutional oath of office to Sandra Day O'Connor, September 25, 1981, as John O'Connor looks on. The constitutional oath is required of all federal employees. On the same day, O'Connor takes the judicial oath in a ceremony in a courtroom where cameras are not allowed. *(Courtesy Ronald Reagan Library)*

Newly sworn in, Justice Sandra Day O'Connor stands with her Supreme
Court colleagues on the day she takes the oath of office. *From left:*
Harry A. Blackmun, Thurgood Marshall, William J. Brennan Jr.,
Warren Burger, O'Connor, Byron R. White, Lewis F. Powell Jr.,
William Rehnquist, John Paul Stevens. *(Courtesy Ronald Reagan Library)*

Sandra, at a gala dinner in her honor in Phoenix on November 26, 1981.
The event was one of many in a state celebration dubbed "Sandra Day
O'Connor Day." *(The Arizona Republic)*

Sandra and John O'Connor, with First Lady Barbara Bush and
President George H. W. Bush, at a White House reception,
February 1, 1989. *(Collection of the Supreme Court of the United States,
photograph by the White House)*

Justice O'Connor sits with Justice Ruth Bader Ginsburg in the U.S.
Capitol's Statuary Hall, March 2001. Ginsburg, who was sworn in
in 1993, is the High Court's second woman to be appointed justice.
(David Hume Kennerly/Getty Images)

Justice O'Connor talks with her law clerks outside her chambers, June 2002, as the annual term is ending. *(David Hume Kennerly/Getty Images)*

February 13, 2003, at the dedication of the Sandra Day O'Connor High School, in Glendale, Arizona. *(The Arizona Republic)*

15

SCALIA V. O'CONNOR

Looking unusually relaxed, Justice O'Connor sat in a large overstuffed chair before an audience of lawyers in Coronado, California, talking about the collegial—and not so collegial—sides of the Supreme Court. Her audience devoured her stories, including one about the time Justice Blackmun briefly filled in as chief justice and suggested shutting down the opinion-writing and taking up square dancing. O'Connor said she wholeheartedly endorsed the square-dancing idea. As she answered questions from the audience this August 1994, she chatted casually about other Court rituals. When she was asked about civility among judges, O'Connor first recited the childhood saying, "Sticks and stones will break my bones, but words will never hurt me." But then she added somberly, "That probably isn't true."[1]

Justice O'Connor had become a regular target of criticism from analysts outside the Court and even from her brethren within. As her position of influence was widely accepted, it also was increasingly scrutinized. In 1993, freelance journalist Howard Kohn described O'Connor in a profile for the *Los Angeles Times* as "arguably, the most powerful woman in the nation" and wisely observed, "When she is on the high bench, you can see the indelible cool, but underneath, you suspect, there must be fire."[2] Retired justice Lewis Powell reinforced the prevailing wisdom in a personal note to her and her husband, John, in the fall of

1993: "I agree with the view now frequently expressed that Sandra sits at the 'center' of the Supreme Court and is the Court's most influential member."[3]

As a result of her obviously dominant position, law professors and legal commentators more and more dissected her record. How was she affecting the law in America? Overall, her record was not criticized on ideological grounds, as was the case for conservatives Scalia and Thomas and for liberals Brennan and Marshall. Critics bemoaned, instead, O'Connor's incremental approach. They said her decisions lacked clarity and were unpredictable. More significantly, the split-the-difference method that helped her control the outcome of a case made it difficult— sometimes extraordinarily so—for lower-court judges attempting to apply an O'Connor decision to similar cases.

Inside the Court, no one was more at odds with her than Justice Scalia. His comment in a 1989 abortion case from Missouri, that her rationale "cannot be taken seriously," was broadly quoted. But there were many other instances of his derision. He complained in one case about an ap-proach that shunned "clear rules that might avoid litigation" and said in another that she offered "a standard so devoid of content that it produces rather than eliminates uncertainty in this field."[4]

"I don't think a judge is supposed to come up with the best result," Jus-tice Scalia said in an interview. "He's supposed to come up with the result that the law demands. Almost always he's dealing with a text and almost always his job is to give that text the fairest, most reasonable interpreta-tion. Only in that way is he being faithful to the democratic experiment. Sometimes you reach results that are not good results. That's because sometimes laws that are adopted are not good laws."[5]

Increasingly, observers of the Court focused on the contrasting ap-proaches of O'Connor and Scalia. As O'Connor was drawing more aca-demic scrutiny, Scalia was achieving celebrity status on campuses for being decisive and definitive. In approach to the law and style, they were opposites. Scalia had a loud, dominating presence that contrasted with O'Connor's sense of decorum. In a 1993 profile for *Playboy* magazine, writer Joe Morgenstern captured how Scalia could fill the courtroom: "If mind were muscle and Court sessions were televised, Scalia would be the Arnold Schwarzenegger of American jurisprudence. When he listens to hapless litigants, he tilts his head at a show-me angle or taps his fingers on the desk in front of him as if he were playing the piano, which he enjoys doing when off the bench. When he speaks, he lunges forward with a jabbing forefinger to emphasize key words. Justice Scalia is the Court's self-appointed prosecutor, interrogator, elucidator or inquisitor—depending on who's catching his flak."[6]

It was not just lawyers at the lectern who caught his flak. He took shots at O'Connor and other justices, sometimes jumping in during their line of questioning to ask whether any of it was relevant. In a 1993 speech before a Washington, DC, audience, he justified his tactics: "where we see an idea that deserves clunking over the head, we clunk it over the head. Bad ideas should be shown for what they are."[7]

Scalia's comments got under O'Connor's skin, but her rearing on the Lazy B served her well. For the most part, she could take it—or at least appear to take it. "Well, it's better than a punch in the nose," she said when one of her clerks brought her a draft of a Scalia opinion concurring in her bottom-line judgment but offering a competing legal rationale. Most times, Scalia's disparagement did not stop her. She won the votes of enough of her colleagues. She was the majority-maker.

When O'Connor lost to Scalia, it stung. In 1990, Scalia pulled out a narrow majority to abandon a strict legal standard regarding the free exercise of religion. It was a case from Oregon that allowed states to broadly prosecute the sacramental use of peyote, a hallucinogenic drug. The situation involved two members of an American Indian church who were fired from their job at a private drug-rehabilitation center because they had ingested ceremonial peyote. They were then denied state unemployment benefits, they sued the state of Oregon alleging a violation of their free exercise of religion. O'Connor agreed that the men could be denied the unemployment benefits because of their use of controlled substances, but she wanted to evaluate Oregon's law under a test that required that a state prove it has a "compelling interest" in enforcing a statute that infringed on religious freedom. She believed Scalia had departed from well-settled principles regarding individual religious liberty.[8]

The new standard Scalia articulated for general laws that affected religious practices was significant, because many laws that end up impinging on religion were written to apply to everyone and were not intended to interfere with religious exercise. For example, a local ordinance prohibiting the consumption of alcohol could incidentally prohibit a

Catholic priest from using wine in communion, or a Jewish family from drinking wine at a seder dinner.

The morning that Scalia announced the ruling in *Employment Division v. Smith,* O'Connor slipped a note to Justice Blackmun on the bench: "Harry, the Court took the wrong turn today in the free exercise case in my view. It pains me."[9]

Scalia, the only child of a father who was a professor of Romance languages and a mother who taught elementary school, grew up in the tight ethnic neighborhoods of New Jersey and Queens, New York. In a world far from O'Connor's cherished West, Scalia traveled daily by subway to a Catholic preparatory school, then attended the Jesuit-run Georgetown University in Washington, DC. He graduated first in his class at Georgetown University and then earned a Harvard law degree in 1960, magna cum laude.

Scalia's early legal career was varied. Unlike O'Connor, who was an outsider to the world of the corporate law firm, Scalia immediately won a series of high-status jobs. He worked first for the law firm of Jones, Day, Reavis and Pogue in Cleveland, and then became a law professor at the University of Virginia. He joined the Nixon administration in 1971 as general counsel of the White House Office of Telecommunications Policy. In 1974, Richard Nixon appointed Scalia head of the little known but prestigious Office of Legal Counsel in the Justice Department, coincidentally the job Rehnquist had held before being named to the Supreme Court. Scalia returned to academic life in 1976, mostly teaching at the University of Chicago, and built a reputation as a powerfully articulate conservative thinker. Scalia worked the inside game of law and politics as O'Connor had worked it from the outside, breaking in as a civic volunteer and unpaid party loyalist.

In 1982, President Ronald Reagan appointed Scalia to the U.S. Court of Appeals for the District of Columbia Circuit. When Reagan elevated him to the Supreme Court in 1986, some of Scalia's fellow judges, as well as legal analysts who had followed his career, thought he could become the conservative version of Justice Brennan. But rather than brokering compromises that benefited conservatives, Scalia thwarted consensus. He was a stickler for the nuances of every legal rationale and even individual footnotes. The nit-picky memos he fired off to other chambers became known as "Nino-grams."[10]

But Scalia's wit and way with words drew admiration. He alternately quoted William Shakespeare and Cole Porter in his opinions. His rhetoric was fervent and colorful, standing out in the unemotional dry world of legal writing. He developed a cult following among law students, particularly conservatives who were developing a strong presence on the nation's campuses. Once, while he was greeting Louisiana State University law students after a speech in the early 1990s, a student approached Scalia and said, "I've named my pet fish after you."

"Oh, you've named him 'Nino,'" the justice said. "No," the student said, "I've named him 'Justice Scalia.'" A professor who overheard the conversation later asked the student whether he had other fish named after other justices. "No," he replied. "Justice Scalia ate all the others."[12]

Scalia delighted in keeping track of grammatical errors made by his colleagues and others. In 1991, Scalia urged Blackmun to join him in this sport. Blackmun was already doing this in the privacy of his own chambers with draft documents and other correspondence. Blackmun could hardly read anything without circling incorrect grammar and misspellings. Even the "thank you" notes Blackmun received, which remained in his file after his death, were marked with corrections.

Scalia's version of the exercise went further. He called his one-man enterprise "The Chancellor's English Society" and joked that the mission was "to identify and stamp out illiteracies and barbaric neologisms in legal writing—or at least to commiserate about them." When Blackmun had written to Scalia about a few of his own pet language peeves, Scalia responded: "I am glad that 'cite to' has struck someone else as wrong. Drives me crazy. I am with you on 'parameter,' which is usually employed imprecisely, and always unimaginatively. 'Viable' is trite-speak for 'practical' or 'workable.' You have not 'lost the battle' on that one; those with taste never use it, except in its literal medical context. I would sooner be watching a rock video than referring to a 'viable option.' . . ."[13]

The Senate Judiciary Committee happened to be holding hearings for Clarence Thomas around the time that Scalia invited Blackmun into his "society," and when Blackmun wrote back about other language errors, he added as a postscript: "I undertook an occasional glance at the [Clarence] Thomas hearings. To my consternation, no fewer than three United States Senators misused 'parameter.' . . . I still have a case of the shakes."[14]

Unlike Blackmun, Scalia put his taunts—substantive and linguistic—into his opinions. "I join the opinion of the Court except that portion which takes seriously, and thus encourages in the future, an argument that should be laughed out of Court," he wrote at one point.[15] When O'Connor wrote the opinion for the Court upholding an Erie, Pennsylvania, ban on nude dancing a few years later, he criticized the reasoning (with his usual wit) as offering not even a "fig leaf" of precedent and "performing a neat trick" in reaching its conclusion.[16]

THE SUBSTANTIVE VIEWS of O'Connor and Scalia clashed directly on the constitutional rules for the separation of church and state, particularly in a 1995 case arising from a Ku Klux Klan challenge to Ohio state officials. The case of *Capitol Square Review Board v. Pinette* offered a matchup of the two justices' respective positions, hers open-ended, his definitive. It also showed how O'Connor could control an area of the law that had very real consequences for cities and state governments nationwide.

The dispute had begun in December 1993 as the holiday season rolled around. Civic groups began seeking space for their festive displays on the ten-acre plaza on the Capitol grounds in Columbus, Ohio. The Capitol Square Review Board gave permission to state officials to put up the state's customary Christmas tree. The board also approved a rabbi's application for a menorah. But the board turned down a request from the Ohio Ku Klux Klan to place a large Latin cross on the plaza. The board said that allowing the Christian cross would be a violation of the requisite constitutional separation of church and state.

Vincent Pinette, then president of the Ohio KKK, sued the Capitol Square Review Board, accusing state officials of violating the KKK's free-speech rights under the First Amendment. Lower courts agreed with the Klan, saying the state had no legitimate grounds to deny its permit when it was open to the other displays. The U.S. Court of Appeals for the Sixth Circuit rejected state officials' argument that they could refuse the Klan's cross because allowing it on Capitol grounds would violate the First Amendment's guarantee that government make no law "respecting an establishment of religion." The appeals court said the board was not really trying to forbid a religious symbol but rather what many perceived as a symbol of bigotry.

"Some speech may be distasteful, unpopular, and outright offensive," the appeals court said, as it ruled that the state board violated the free-speech rights of the Klan, "but the protection found in the First Amendment does not depend upon popular opinion."[17] (The Klan put up its cross on December 21, 1993, but it was immediately torn down by vandals.)[18]

The case came to the justices as standards for religion in public life were in flux. Beginning in the 1940s, the Court had made clear a preference for minimal involvement of government with religion, whether it be aid to church schools or religious symbols on public property. But conservatives strongly disagreed with such a high "wall" of separation between church and state. When O'Connor joined the Court, the modern test for determining whether a government action violated the First Amendment's Establishment Clause dated to a 1971 ruling in *Lemon v. Kurtzman.* That case dictated that any constitutionally permissible mixing of church and state meet three criteria. The government action had to have a secular purpose. It could not advance or inhibit religion. And it could not foster excessive "entanglement" with religion.

Beginning in 1984, that complicated standard was modified—largely through O'Connor's articulation—so that the critical question in cases involving religious displays came down to whether a "reasonable observer" would believe government was endorsing religion. In the 1984 case of *Lynch v. Donnelly,* city officials in Pawtucket, Rhode Island, wanted to include a crèche in their annual holiday display. O'Connor looked at the context to see what the city would "communicate" by displaying the crèche along with purely secular symbols, such as a Christmas tree, and found that the government would not appear to be endorsing Christian beliefs but celebrating a secular public holiday.[19] The idea was that the mingling of secular symbols (plastic reindeer, candy canes, etc.) with the crèche diluted any religious message. Five years later, in 1989, the Court ruled that a menorah displayed with a Christmas tree could remain, but that a crèche standing alone had to go, based generally on an "endorsement" test.[20]

The appeal in the KKK case was argued at the Supreme Court on

April 26, 1995. Michael Renner, representing the board, stepped to the lectern first. He asserted that a cross standing against the backdrop of a state capitol sent a message of government support for that cross.

"Ohio suggests that this Court adopt a workable rule that any purely religious display which is unattended and positioned at the very seat of government should be considered as a violation of the Establishment Clause," Renner said. He acknowledged that there was a disclaimer at the site, alerting visitors that the exhibit was not sponsored by the state. But, Renner said, that was not effective in severing a connection to the state.

"I just think your argument is so far-fetched," O'Connor said, showing her hand. "Here is this thing with a sign that says this isn't government-sponsored."

Then, on behalf of Pinette and other Klansmen, Benson Wolman said, "[T]he state has permitted a variety of displays. . . . Suddenly it chooses to say my client's symbol shall not be there, and it relies upon its claim of Establishment Clause." His point: state officials simply did not want the KKK presence on state property and were using the constitutional separation of church and state as pretext.

Justice Clarence Thomas, who rarely spoke during oral arguments, suddenly joined in, questioning Wolman about the symbolism of the Klan cross.

"You say that this is a religious symbol. What is the religion of the Klan?" Thomas asked.

"The Klan members hold themselves out in this record as Christians," Wolman said.

"What does a burning cross symbolize?" Thomas then asked.

"A burning cross, I believe, would symbolize the general orientation of the Ku Klux Klan against racial minorities, not just you . . . [also] ethnic minorities, myself and others, a whole variety of purposes," Wolman answered.

"But that message doesn't implicate the Establishment Clause," Thomas said, referring to the church-state test. ". . . [W]e're shoehorning a political case into the religious component of the First Amendment."

"We believe the state has done just that," Wolman said.[21]

The justices came down 7–2 against the board's refusal to allow the Ku

Klux Klan to display the cross. Only Justices Stevens and Ginsburg believed that the large cross near the Ohio government flags appeared to be government support for religion. Thomas was with the majority. But he said the religious component of the cross was minimal. He considered the cross a symbol of hate, and the erection of the cross a political act, not Christian one.[22]

Chief Justice Rehnquist assigned the Court's opinion to Scalia, although it was clear from the start that Scalia would not be able to write the legal reasoning for a majority. Scalia believed that private religious speech was protected by the First Amendment's free speech clause, simply because it was speech. "[I]n Anglo-American history, at least, government suppression of speech has so commonly been directed precisely at religious speech that a free-speech clause without religion would be Hamlet without the prince," Scalia wrote. "Accordingly, we have not excluded from free-speech protections religious proselytizing, or even acts of worship."

O'Connor would not join that rationale, and she persuaded Justices Souter and Breyer to sign on to her concurring opinion. She also drew support from Stevens and Ginsburg for her "endorsement" test, although once they applied the O'Connor standard, they said Ohio's allowing the cross constituted a government endorsement of religion.

In her opinion, joined in part by Stevens, Souter, Ginsburg, and Breyer, O'Connor wrote, "Today's proponents of the endorsement test all agree that we should attribute to the observer knowledge that the cross is a religious symbol, that Capitol Square is owned by the State, and that the large building nearby is the seat of the state government." She then concluded—and this is where Stevens and Ginsburg broke off—"the reasonable observer would view the Klan's cross display fully aware that Capitol Square is a public space in which a multiplicity of groups, both secular and religious, engage in expressive conduct."

O'Connor acknowledged that her standard required difficult line-drawing, but she said such a cautious approach was the only way to handle the Constitution's requisite separation of church and state. Scalia responded that "the endorsement test does not supply an appropriate standard for the inquiry before us. It supplies no standard whatsoever." And he explained why: "The lower federal courts that the [O'Connor] concurrence identifies as having applied the endorsement test in precisely

the context before us today . . . have reached precisely differing results—
which is what led the Court to take this case." Scalia then observed that
"if further proof of the invited chaos is required," one need only look at
the way Justice O'Connor reaches one result using the endorsement test
and Justices Stevens and Ginsburg reach another. "It is irresponsible to
make the Nation's legislators walk this minefield," he wrote.[23]

O'Connor's position had the advantage of ensuring that there would
be no blanket prohibition, or allowance, of government hosted religious
symbols. But, as Scalia observed, the test was highly subjective. Can it
ever be predicted, before a situation is tested, what a reasonable observer
would find to be a symbolic endorsement of religion by government?

THROUGHOUT THE LEGAL COMMUNITY, it was an enduring refrain:
the terrain O'Connor controlled was not predictable. "By her refusal to
commit herself to consistent principles," George Washington University
professor and *New Republic* columnist Jeffrey Rosen wrote in a *New York
Times* magazine article in 2001, "O'Connor forces the Court and those
who follow it to engage in a guessing game about her wishes in case after
case. Each of her decisions is a ticket for one train only." [24]

But Rosen also had an apt reason for O'Connor's methods: "It is that
she approaches her job less like a typical Justice than like the state legislator she once was," he wrote. "O'Connor, who prefers vague standards to
clear rules, does not derive her opinions from consistent principles that
guide her from case to case. Her pragmatic approach allows her to remain not only at the center of the Court but also at the center of American
politics."

On the magazine cover, the editors used a pop art cartoon picture of
O'Connor's face. O'Connor's son Scott wrote to the magazine's editors:
"The artists over at Marvel or DC Comics could have drawn a better like-
ness of the Justice than the one on your cover. The mouth is all wrong.
Mom deserves better, especially with Jeffrey Rosen touting her as the next
Chief." (Rosen had written that O'Connor could be chosen to succeed
Rehnquist, an idea that O'Connor scoffed at, saying she was too old to be
chosen.[25])

O'Connor had no lack of critics. In the conservative *National Review,*
Ramesh Ponnuru wrote in 2003, "Because she announces no clear princi-

ples, everyone, lower federal courts included, is left guessing what the outcome of the next case will be. Her decisions invite new cases, in which she can refine her tests further. Her approach, in other words, amounts to the assumption of the power to issue arbitrary vetoes." In the same vein, University of Georgia law professor Eric J. Segall said that O'Connor's "reluctance to articulate rules governing cases other than the one at hand as well as her inconsistent treatment of legal doctrine do not provide enough stability, predictability and transparency to differentiate legal rules from personal preferences."[26]

Some academics found it difficult to talk of Scalia and O'Connor together, as if he were an intellectual powerhouse and she were a mere swing vote. That echoed the pattern that had been established in accounts of her subtle rivalry with Brennan. The men were regarded as having more brainpower and direction. O'Connor was seen as controlling by default, a sort of "least common denominator" jurisprudence.[27] But that was the product of her overall approach. She wanted the law to develop incrementally, which did not make her a champion to those who had a strong ideological orientation.

O'Connor had her admirers, however. Not so coincidentally, those associated with centrist Lewis Powell and advocates of judicial "minimalism" were at the forefront. "She tries, first, to do justice on the facts of a particular case. Then she links the results in the case to general principles," said Powell biographer John Jeffries, a University of Virginia law professor. "That's a very different approach from someone who starts off with ideological principles. It also is more in the common-law tradition, and I think Americans generally have more confidence in judges who do not reach too broadly."[28] The University of Chicago's Cass Sunstein defended the intellectual validity of O'Connor's methods in his writings on the benefit of a reserved approach to judging. In his book *One Case at a Time,* Sunstein described O'Connor as seeking "standards" as opposed to "rules," a familiar legal distinction. With a standard, Sunstein wrote, a case is decided in its specific context. "A standard is a good way to keep things open for the future," he wrote. Sunstein elaborated later that the "minimalism" embraced by O'Connor could foster democracy, "not only in the sense that it leaves issues open for democratic deliberation, but also and more fundamentally in the sense that it promotes reason-giving and ensures that certain important decisions are made by democratically accountable actors." By that, Sunstein meant elected officials who had to answer to the people, not justices appointed for life.[29]

O'Connor, to be sure, altered the usual standard by which justices were assessed. She could not be measured in terms of a large constitutional vision. Her approach sowed confusion, too. But she made things happen. She built coalitions. She tried for consensus. She never took a cheap shot at a colleague. She also worked to neutralize tensions at a time of increased polarization in Washington.

In the mid-1990s, Congress was entering a new era of partisan gridlock. The 1994 elections brought an end to forty years of Democratic control of the House of Representatives and witnessed the conservative takeover led by Georgia Republican Newt Gingrich and several other freshmen intent on paring down government welfare programs and reducing the federal budget. In the executive branch, where Bill Clinton held the White House and had been elected to a second term, his affair with intern Monica Lewinsky, First Lady Hillary Clinton's Whitewater land dealings, and the independent counsel probe by Ken Starr dominated the news in the nation's capital during the late 1990s. Amid the violent swings that were marking national politics, O'Connor forced the Supreme Court to move in slow increments.

O'Connor's fellow justices described her as a pragmatist who kept an eye on the world beyond Washington. Justice Breyer said she understood the institutional role of the Court, and he attributed some of her approach to her legislative background. "It's political not in the sense of Democrat and Republican. It's political in the sense of the governing role of the courts, particularly the Supreme Court. It matters not just what the substantive rule of the decision is, but how it's phrased, whether you use examples. All that matters in the way in which a judgment is received. She tries to think through the consequences of saying less or saying more. And if there are great unknowns out there, she does not believe you should go further than you have to go."[30]

"Her method is to calm things down, let things cool off for a while," said Justice Thomas, who was known for his boldly conservative writing. "I'm way over here," he said gesturing for effect to his right. "But she's, 'Let's modulate.' "[31]

Her colleagues also said that they believed there were no ill feelings between her and Scalia, despite regular reports to the contrary.[32] "I think everybody respects Nino's wonderful writing ability and his style and all the rest," Justice Stevens said, when asked about the relationship between O'Connor and Scalia. "But everybody on the Court from time to time has thought he was unwise to take such an extreme position, both in tone and in position. She probably feels the same way."[33]

O'Connor and Scalia were antagonists on the law. But they were not personal enemies in the mode of Hugo Black (who served 1937–1971) and Felix Frankurter (who served 1939–1962), whose enmity was legendary. "I thought Felix was going to hit me today, he got so mad," Black once said after a heated discussion.[34]

Justice Scalia said in an interview, "Sandra may not have liked an occasional barb in one of my opinions, but I considered her a good friend and I think she considered me a good friend." Scalia recalled meeting O'Connor for the first time when they traveled together on an Anglo-American judicial exchange to London. It was in the mid-1980s, when he was still an appeals court judge. She struck him as friendly and adventuresome, although he got a dose of her on-the-dot style. "There was a garden party. The Queen came around, and you had a chance to speak to her, if she spoke to you. . . . When we got off the bus, Sandra had said we meet back here at ten after whatever time it was. And as I and two of the other delegates approached the bus, just a minute or two late, we see the bus pulling away." Scalia ran after the bus, waving his coat, but to no avail. "By god, I learned my lesson," he said. "Don't mess with Sandra."[35]

O'Connor could give back to Scalia almost as good as he gave. In one 1993 case, she wrote Scalia a note that began, "I think that your fine opinion should be amended slightly so as to clarify . . ." She then went on with several changes that prompted Blackmun to jot on her draft that she was "feeding his stuff back to him!"[36]

O'Connor refrained from criticizing Scalia in any public way. "She never puts people down. She is never acerbic," Justice Ginsburg said. "Our opinions might be described as bland and boring but we both stay away from zingers in our writing." Ginsburg and Scalia had served together on the District of Columbia Circuit and were longtime friends. They and their spouses spent New Year's Eve together each year. Ginsburg acknowledged that Scalia had a way of setting the justices on edge:

"I love him. But sometimes I'd like to strangle him. Still, more than any of my colleagues, he has the ability to make me smile, even laugh, because of his engaging wit."[37]

Whatever O'Connor thought of Scalia, she, more often than not, had the advantage of getting what she wanted out of a case. Scalia, on the other hand, often lost cases that were deeply important to him. At the end of the 1995–1996 term, for example, he dissented in several high-profile disputes, including one that protected homosexuals from discrimination, *Romer v. Evans*,[38] and one ensuring that the state-funded Virginia Military Institute did not exclude women students, *United States v. Virginia*.[39] Scalia accused the Court majority of taking sides in the "culture wars." Neither of those cases, however, was a particularly close call. Scalia was the only one who dissented in the VMI dispute,[40] and the *Romer* case was decided by a 6–3 vote, with Scalia in dissent joined by Rehnquist and Thomas. In yet another case at the end of that 1995–1996 term, when Scalia dissented from a decision that said the Constitution protects public contractors from patronage firings, he wrote, joined by Thomas: "The court must be living in another world. Day by day, case by case, it is busy designing a Constitution for a country I do not recognize."[41]

In a personal note to Blackmun, on July 2, 1996, Scalia said that he was "more discouraged this year than I have been at the end of any of my previous nine terms up here." Scalia, who had turned 60 that spring, added, "I am beginning to repeat myself, and I don't see much use in it any more."[42] But Scalia stayed and continued to fire his grapeshot at O'Connor. He criticized her for what he believed was damaging ambiguity and a constant desire to "have it both ways."[43]

As the years went on, Scalia had only more reason for frustration. O'Connor's deciding vote and rationale continued to control church-state disputes, affirmative action, abortion rights, and the respective allocation of power between the federal government and the states.

In that last area, involving the relative lines of authority between the federal government and the states, Scalia was largely with O'Connor. They both favored diminished federal authority and greater state sovereignty than the Court had ensured in previous decades. But it was O'Connor's rationale that helped make the historic federalism shift happen. She articulated her ideal during her first term in *FERC v. Mississippi*, when she wrote in dissent:"State legislative and administrative bodies are not field offices of the national bureaucracy. Nor are they think tanks to which Congress may assign problems for extended study. Instead, each state is a sovereign within its own domain, governing its citizens and providing for their general welfare." Then, in *New York v. United States,* she won a majority to void a key part of a federal law requiring states to clean up their low-level radioactive waste. The Court ruled in 1992 that Congress improperly sought to "commandeer" state legislatures to enact regulations to dispose of the waste. That ruling enhanced state protection from the federal government under the Tenth Amendment.[44]

Four years later, the Court struck down the Gun Free School Zones Act as an invalid exercise of Congress's power to regulate interstate commerce. The decision in *United States v. Lopez* accelerated the majority's effort to curb the power of Washington in favor of the states. That opinion was written by Chief Justice Rehnquist, and it immediately recalled the dissenting statements he and O'Connor wrote in the 1985 *Garcia v. San Antonio Metropolitan Transit Authority.* Then they had warned that a change in Court membership could return power to the states.[45]

For about a decade, a five justice majority, of Kennedy, Thomas, Rehnquist, O'Connor, and Scalia, curtailed federal powers across the board. In 2000, they invalidated a portion of the Violence Against Women Act allowing victims of gender-based violence to win money damages in civil litigation. Some women's groups thought that the case of *United States v. Morrison* might cause O'Connor to extract herself from the federalism revolution.[46] The law at issue was intended to help survivors of rape and domestic violence, and the case was brought by a Virginia Tech student who claimed she had been raped by two football players. But, in an opinion written by Rehnquist, joined by O'Connor, the Court said Congress lacked the authority—under its interstate commerce power or on other grounds—to federalize remedies for private local violence against women around the country in such legislation.[47]

The consistency of the conservative fivesome began to wane in 2003, when the Court first voted to allow lawsuits against state employers under the federal Family and Medical Leave Act, which guaranteed employees twelve weeks off to care for a newborn or sick relative. The Court the following year permitted the federal Americans with Disabilities Act to be invoked against states and counties that did not make their court-houses accessible to the handicapped.[48] In both of those cases, O'Connor was with the majority to endorse the federal legislation.

But in 2005 she was in dissent, as a majority led by liberal Justice Stevens rejected federalism arguments and ruled that the U.S. govern-ment may enforce its antidrug laws in states that attempted to permit the medical use of marijuana. (The case was brought by two California women suffering from serious medical conditions, who said marijuana eased their pain and allowed them to function on a daily basis.) The Court said that Congress's power to regulate interstate commerce over-rode California's Compassionate Use Act, which had been adopted by voters in a ballot initiative and reinforced through legislation, and which authorized marijuana use for medicinal purposes. In a strong dissent, O'Connor wrote, "[T]he government has made no showing in fact that the possession and use of homegrown marijuana for medical purposes, in California or elsewhere, has a substantial effect on interstate commerce." She said the Court should have followed *Lopez* and *Morrison*—which curtailed federal involvement in state affairs. Scalia and Kennedy, who previously had been consistent members of the majority trying to curb Congress, joined Stevens's judgment.[49]

O'Connor suggested in her dissenting opinion that they had betrayed the federalism principles invoked over the past decade. "If I were a Cali-fornia citizen, I would not have voted for the medical marijuana ballot initiative; if I were a California legislator, I would not have supported the Compassionate Use Act. But whatever the wisdom of California's exper-iment with medical marijuana, the federalism principles that have driven our Commerce Clause cases require that room for experiment be protected in this case." It was a singular loss in an area that she had other-wise made her own.

O'CONNOR, FOR the most part, had mastered the Court. But she was beginning to feel her years. In 1996, at age 66, she was forced to give up one of her greatest athletic passions. Skiing had been part of family vaca-tions since she and John first traveled in Europe during his army duty. But at Sun Valley, Idaho, as she descended the intermediate-level Blue Grouse run, she fell and fractured her right shoulder.

O'Connor still golfed, and she sought out the best courses. She went fly-fishing whenever possible, and worked to get better at it. Roy Herberger, president of Arizona-based Thunderbird, The American Graduate School of International Management, and a longtime friend of O'Connor, recalled being on a plane and noticing a woman up a row and across the aisle, casting with an abbreviated rod and reel. "I thought, 'What in the world is that woman doing?' " Herberger got up from his seat and discovered it was Justice O'Connor casting with a mock fishing reel. "In between reading briefs, she was working on another skill to be more competitive," he said.[50]

A few years later, O'Connor faced another personal challenge. On a visit to Phoenix, John collapsed while at lunch with friends and was rushed to the hospital. It turned out that John's heart had stopped and he required a pacemaker. Something else began happening. John was unusually forgetful. The justice first became aware of it in small ways, charming even. He liked to tell jokes, a trait his wife especially appreciated. "When John would stand up and tell a joke," recalled Justice Kennedy, "Sandra couldn't take her eyes off of him. Her eyes would sparkle. Even if she heard the joke before, she would laugh."[51]

But one day, in the middle of a joke, John forgot a punch line. Wasn't that strange, he told his wife. O'Connor repeated what seemed merely a silly story to her friends. Only in retrospect would it become clear that her husband's forgetfulness was ushering in a new period of their life together.

LEWIS POWELL DIED in 1998. He had been in poor health and living in Richmond. But his presence in the world had been a comfort to O'Connor. "No one did more than Lewis Powell to help get me settled as a new justice," she said during a eulogy. "He found us a place to live. He allowed me to hire one of his two secretaries as my chambers secretary and said it was like cutting off his right arm. Most important, he was willing to talk about cases and issues. His door was always open. I miss those visits and those discussions, even today."[52]

O'Connor referred to the fact that the tall and agile Powell was a superb dancer. "I had the privilege of dancing with him several times," she told the Richmond church congregation that included all of the justices

and retired Justice White. Holding back her emotions, O'Connor concluded, "Lewis Powell: We love you and we always will."

Her relationship with Powell had been one of a kind. He had been
there at the right moment for her. Circulating in the same upper-class social set, they were able to bond despite their gender differences and his
old-school ways. She scoffed at his description of himself as only a "footnote" in history, telling him: "you have been one of the great justices of
this century and certainly the best loved." [53]

"They listened to one another. They talked to one another. They
didn't try to steamroll one another," recalled J. Harvie Wilkinson, a U.S.
appeals court judge who began his legal career as a law clerk to Powell.
"They were engaged in a search for what was the right thing to do under
the law." [54] Powell's mentoring and collegiality had been of critical importance as she began to assert herself in the mid-1980s and as she
wielded more influence in the 1990s.

IN THE EARLY twenty-first century, it had become a truism among legal
analysts that the Court, for better or worse, was definitely O'Connor's.
The *New York Times Magazine* cover story by Jeffrey Rosen in 2001 called
her "the most powerful woman in America." [55]

But there was one major area of the law in which O'Connor did not
prevail, and it involved the role of judges and juries in criminal sentencing. In a series of cases that began in June 2000, a narrow majority that included Scalia—along with Thomas and Court liberals Ginsburg,
Stevens, and Souter—limited judges' authority under laws that tried to
regularize criminal sentencing. It began with a little-noticed case from
New Jersey. Charles Apprendi, who was white, pleaded guilty in 1995 to
firing several bullets into a neighboring black family's home. The maximum sentence for the firearms offense was ten years. But the judge, relying on New Jersey's hate-crime law, determined that Apprendi was
motivated by racial bias, and added two more years to the maximum
firearms penalty. He sentenced Apprendi to twelve years.

Apprendi appealed the enhanced sentence, saying the judge's determination of racial bias violated his right to have a jury determine if all the
facts of his case were proven beyond a reasonable doubt. The New Jersey
Supreme Court upheld Apprendi's sentence and the "hate crime" en-

hancement. The U.S. Supreme Court reversed, agreeing with Apprendi that the New Jersey law unconstitutionally gave the judge the power to increase the sentence. The majority said any fact that increases the penalty for a crime beyond the prescribed statutory maximum must be submitted to a jury and proved beyond a reasonable doubt.[56] The justices said the Sixth Amendment's right to a jury barred judges from doing the kind of fact-finding that occurred in Apprendi's case.

O'Connor was among the four dissenters and the most outraged. She predicted—accurately, it would turn out—that the decision would be a "watershed change" in criminal sentencing. She said the decision would invalidate sentencing reform in federal and state systems, which sought to equalize sentences based on objective factors. "In one bold stroke the Court today casts aside our traditional cautious approach and instead embraces a universal and seemingly bright-line rule" to forbid legislative initiatives that had put solely into the hands of judges factual issues that could enhance a sentence.[57]

O'Connor's concern arose from the fact that about twenty-five years earlier, Congress and state legislatures had begun enacting sentencing reforms to end major disparities in prison time between similarly situated defendants. These systems generally limited the sentences judges could invoke, but allowed them to raise or lower a sentence based on certain set factors. She now feared a return to the earlier system of great disparity in sentences, with juries and judges leveling widely varying punishments in similar cases.

O'Connor was so distressed about the ruling that a month later, in July 2000, when she went to England for an American Bar Association conference, she brought up the case in a speech she gave to kick off the event. On the rolling meadows of Runnymede, where the Magna Carta had been signed, O'Connor digressed from her talk about the common heritage of British and American law to say the Supreme Court majority made a grave mistake in its ruling in the *Apprendi* case. The juxtaposition was jarring: it was an upbeat, ceremonial occasion, and here she was, invoking one of her losses.[58]

OVER THE NEXT FIVE years at the Court, the same five-justice majority—without O'Connor—reinforced the jury rule in criminal sentencing disputes. In a 2004 case, Scalia wrote the opinion striking down many state rules that set standard prison terms for various crimes but directed judges to make findings about facts (for example, did the crime involve guns or drugs?) that could increase the sentence. As it had in *Apprendi v. New Jersey,* the same majority said that the Sixth Amendment right to a jury trial necessarily required juries, not judges, to determine whether a crime involved elements necessitating a longer sentence.[59]

In an angry dissent from the bench, O'Connor said, "What I have feared most has now come to pass. Over twenty years of sentencing reform are all but lost, and tens of thousands of criminal judgments are in jeopardy." She predicted that the U.S. Sentencing Guidelines, established two decades earlier, would fall next. She was right. No one on the Court budged. The five-justice majority of both liberals (Stevens, Souter, Ginsburg) and conservatives (Scalia and Thomas) held together in subsequent cases testing the *Apprendi v. New Jersey* premise. In the end, O'Connor realized that this area would not be hers. In March 2005, when the Court yet again emphasized its jury rule and said that judges could not even engage in fact-finding to determine any prior offenses that might affect a defendant's sentence, O'Connor effectively gave up.[60] Her dissenting opinion was terse. She said the Court's ruling made "little sense."

But even for the competitor on the Court, there was a time to accept that she could not prevail. O'Connor declared: "It is a battle I have lost."[61]

16

---•—◦×◦—•---

OPEN FILES

Before she joined the Supreme Court, Sandra Day O'Connor was sympathetic to the justices who were angered by the sensational book *The Brethren*. "It's not easy being #1," she had written as she commiserated with Chief Justice Warren Burger's administrative assistant in December 1979 about the revealing and unflattering portrayal of Burger.[1] *The Brethren* provided a behind-the-scenes look at how the justices resolved disputes on abortion, capital punishment, and school desegregation. By gaining the confidences of dozens of law clerks and even some justices, authors Bob Woodward and Scott Armstrong presented a tale that went beyond the dry side of the law and focused on personal rivalries and internal tensions.[2] At the Court, the justices worried, as Lewis Powell put it, about "the effect on the public of a book that holds the Court up to ridicule and suspicion."[3]

Just over a decade later, O'Connor was a Court veteran worried about how her own work might be portrayed in public. In late 1990, she discovered that recently retired Justice William Brennan was allowing researchers to view his private files of cases and correspondence. Even before his retirement, Brennan had given select law professors this access. The availability of Brennan's files to certain scholars resulted in some of the leading academic works about the Warren and Burger Courts.[4]

But now, O'Connor learned, Brennan's biographer Stephen Wermiel, a *Wall Street Journal* reporter, was reading all of Brennan's case files. Wermiel had casually mentioned his access when he visited O'Connor in her chambers to begin interviewing her about Brennan. He did not think his comments about Brennan's papers would rouse O'Connor, because other books already had relied on them.[5]

O'Connor, however, immediately told Chief Justice Rehnquist that she was concerned confidential information would be revealed in a way that could damage the Court. Since becoming a justice, O'Connor had managed her public image carefully. She allowed few interviews. She did not meet with reporters in her chambers, as some of the other justices did regularly. She did not open her files to researchers. She gave public speeches, but mostly in well-managed, nonconfrontational settings. She certainly did not want additional exposure through the files of another justice. And her views were not unique.

The institution's trademark was secrecy. The justices entered the building through an underground garage and took a private elevator to their chambers. They decided cases behind closed doors. No television or photography was allowed in the courtroom. While the justices' final decisions were laid out in black and white, the way those rulings were crafted traditionally was a secret. No great pressure was put on the Court by the legal establishment and press corps to be more open.

In a separate vein, O'Connor believed it was important to be able to work out judicial positions in private, free of fears that the deliberative process would be revealed later. If the many steps she took in the resolution of a case were disclosed, she reasoned, it could limit her freedom of discussion.

Soon after discovering Brennan's arrangement with Wermiel, O'Connor and Rehnquist met with Brennan in the new, smaller chambers he was assigned as a retired justice, one floor up from the rest of the justices. Brennan was still feeling the effects of the stroke five months earlier that had prompted his retirement. He was tired and sometimes confused. "His mental acuity was far from 100 percent," recalled Wermiel, who was working closely with the justice for his book. "There were times when he was clear and well focused. There were other times when he was talking about World War II as if it was going on now."[6]

O'Connor and Rehnquist urged Brennan not to give his files to Wermiel or other researchers. O'Connor, particularly, believed that any correspondence she had sent to Brennan should be considered hers, not his. It was an awkward meeting among the three justices. Brennan lacked his usual confidence, and he let O'Connor and Rehnquist do most of the talking. A few days later, on December 19, 1990, Brennan wrote to all of his colleagues: "Sandra and the Chief have expressed to me the concern—shared, they tell me, by others of you—that researchers who examine my official papers thereby gain access to memoranda written to me by other Justices. They have suggested that, to avoid embarrassment to any of our colleagues, I should not grant access to files that may include any written material from Justices who are still sitting on the Court."[7]

That condition would have meant that Brennan could not reveal materials dating to 1962, the year White, longest-tenured on the Rehnquist Court, had joined the bench. But several justices who had served with Brennan since 1956 and overlapping White already had made their papers public, including former chief justice Earl Warren. Further, retired justice Lewis Powell, a former colleague of most of the justices who were sitting in 1990, had turned his materials over to biographer John Jeffries, a University of Virginia law professor and former Powell law clerk. When Jeffries was finished with the files, Powell specified that the archive be made available to researchers at the Washington and Lee University Law School.[8]

The proposal by O'Connor and Rehnquist was not embraced by all of their colleagues. Some thought the demands too strict. Justice White believed decisions related to personal papers should be up to individual justices. Marshall and Blackmun, who were considering eventually making their papers fully public at the Library of Congress, refused to join O'Connor and Rehnquist. Still, Brennan was loyal to the institution. And he did not want to alienate any of his colleagues. In the end, he allowed Wermiel the access already promised, but he said he would not permit later researchers to see case materials he gave to the Library of Congress for any terms after 1986, the year Rehnquist had become chief justice.

Brennan's compromise turned out to be a greater concession to O'Connor and Rehnquist than the approach decided upon by Justices Marshall and Blackmun in later years. They opened their papers wholesale, and—unlike Brennan's estate, which limited use to specially selected researchers—allowed the public full access.

Marshall's papers became available at the Library of Congress in early

1993, shortly after his death. His colleagues, apparently unaware of what he was planning, did nothing ahead of time to stop him. But once the news of the availability of his files broke, the controversy over Marshall's papers consumed the Court for weeks and was another major irritant to O'Connor.

The *Washington Post* discovered the documents before any other news organization and used them in a four-part series published in May 1993. On one hand, the series made the justices look conscientious: "The exchanges are serious, sometimes scholarly, occasionally brash and personalized, but generally well-reasoned and most often cast in understated, genteel language." Yet, the news stories revealed internal deliberations from Marshall's tenure (1967–1991) that the justices believed should remain secret. One of the *Washington Post* stories detailed O'Connor's evolving opinions in the pivotal 1989 abortion case, *Webster v. Reproductive Health Services.*[9]

Rehnquist drafted a letter to Library of Congress director James Billington as soon as the *Post* series began: "I speak for all of the active Justices of the Court when I say that we are appalled by the Library's decision to open to the public Justice Thurgood Marshall's papers. . . . Most members of the Court recognize that after the passage of a certain amount of time, our papers should be available for historical research. But to release Justice Marshall's papers dealing with deliberations which occurred as recently as two terms ago is something quite different. Unless there is some presently unknown basis for the Library's action, we now question whether the Library is a fit repository for any of our papers."

Rehnquist circulated the letter to the other justices and said he wanted all of them to sign it so that the point would be made as forcefully as possible. O'Connor generally agreed and said, "Perhaps the final sentence could state that the failure of the Library to consult with and to consider all the ramifications and effects of granting such an early release of confidential materials may discourage future grants of judicial papers to the Library of Congress."[10]

Separately, Justice Anthony Kennedy wondered whether the Library really was at fault. "After our meeting this morning," he told Rehnquist in a memo, "there was some confirmation that Thurgood may have told the Library representatives that after his death he had no particular instructions to give." Justice White wrote that he had discovered that "three persons from the Library had met with Thurgood and that Thurgood clearly said he wanted his papers to be released immediately after his death." He told Rehnquist he thought the chief justice's letter was "unduly rough" and said he would not sign it.[11] In the end, the letter Rehnquist sent rebuked the Library of Congress for using "bad judgment" in making public Marshall's files. Rehnquist was forced to say he was speaking for a "majority of the active Justices" rather than a unanimous Court.[12]

More than a decade later, in 2004, when Blackmun's private internal memoranda were made public, it was revealed that O'Connor had taken the lead during the uproar over the Marshall files to try to keep Court correspondence private. The Blackmun archive showed that in June 1993 O'Connor had circulated a proposed policy dealing with future release of justices' papers. Her stated concern was that justices' loosely formed thoughts or tentative votes would be revealed. "In order to participate in the full work of the Court during the course of each term," she had written, "Justices must exchange with each other frank and candid statements of their views with respect to legal issues. Often these views by necessity are tentative. This is so because of the press of time and because a free and open exchange of tentative views is itself part of the creative and disciplined process by which Justices shape their understanding of the law. A system that encourages tentative or exploratory statement is essential to the judicial process."

She suggested they all agree that sitting justices never release papers, and that retired justices wait a minimum of ten years before allowing access to materials. From Blackmun's record of votes in the matter, five other justices joined O'Connor: Rehnquist, Kennedy, Souter, Thomas, and Ginsburg. On the other side were Blackmun, Stevens, and Scalia. In the end, Chief Justice Rehnquist was loath to impose the rule without unanimity.[13]

Bernard Schwartz, a University of Tulsa law professor whom Brennan had granted the use of his papers and who had followed the dispute over the Marshall archive, wrote in *Decision: How the Supreme Court Decides Cases* that after the Marshall papers incident, O'Connor told him in a letter that she had "removed a number of items in [her] files." Schwartz also reported that O'Connor had told a Drake University law faculty luncheon that, because of the controversy over the Marshall papers' release, other justices, too, "stripped" their files of some materials.[14]

The voluminous files of Blackmun, who served 1970–1994 and died in 1999, were much more extensive than Marshall's or Brennan's. Blackmun, who began keeping a diary as a young boy, had saved virtually everything he had ever written or ever received from the other justices. When O'Connor passed him a note on the bench one day, telling him his hearing aid was emitting a loud sound and asking if he could turn it down, Blackmun filed away the note.[15] He saved all the memos his clerks had written, many of which commented on the handiwork of other justices. For example, one of his clerks thought O'Connor's draft dissent in the *Metro Broadcasting* affirmative action case was "rambling and disorganized."[16] Other notes contained in the public file were more biting, such as one memo suggesting that Rehnquist did not deserve to be known by his title "chief justice," because of his position against abortion rights.[17]

In 2004, a few days after Blackmun's files became public at the Library of Congress, as he had arranged, O'Connor told a New York audience that the opening of the papers was "unfortunate." Other justices revealed privately that they felt Blackmun had betrayed the institution. Several justices, including O'Connor, said it would be a very long time before another justice's files were made public.[18]

17

APPEARANCES COUNT

Before the 2000 virtual tie election in Florida, which involved Texas governor George W. Bush and Vice President Al Gore, the idea of a modern presidential campaign being decided by the Supreme Court of the United States was unthinkable. The struggle that dominated the news for five weeks after the November 7 election was better suited to Hollywood than the American political system. Few who had closely followed the Rehnquist Court's minimalist tendencies and deference to states believed that the Court would intervene to put an end to Florida's ballot recounts and seesawing vote tallies. In fact, some justices said as much. Immediately after the November 7 election, when neither Republican Bush nor Democrat Gore could be declared president, Justice O'Connor rebuked her brother, Alan, for jauntily predicting that the Florida matter would end up in her court. "Oh no, it could never go to the Supreme Court. That's a state matter," O'Connor said a few days after the election. At a dinner O'Connor prepared for Alan and about a dozen other visiting Arizonans at her Chevy Chase home, she was just as firm in her conviction. "It's a mess and they need to straighten it out," she said. Alan recalled that his sister's tone was one of "general annoyance" that state officials had not resolved the emerging ballot discrepancies.[1]

But on December 11, improbable as it once had seemed, the Supreme Court was the scene for oral arguments between lawyers for Bush and for

Gore. O'Connor and Anthony Kennedy, the usual swing votes, received the greatest media attention. At stake were Florida's decisive twenty-five presidential electors. Since Election Day, vote tallies had fluctuated between the Texas governor, whose father had been president in 1989–1993, and the vice president, who was trying to succeed two-term president Bill Clinton. Clinton had beaten the first president Bush, and the relationship between the competing heirs was bitter and, at times, petty. After midnight, when the television networks had declared Bush the winner, Gore called him to concede. But then, about an hour later, when the networks were pulling back and saying Florida was too close to call, Gore telephoned Bush again.

"Let me make sure I understand," Bush reportedly told Gore. "You are calling back to retract your concession?"

"Well you don't have to be snippy about it," Gore retorted.[2]

Later in the day on November 8, the Florida Division of Elections reported that Bush had received 2,909,135 votes and Gore 2,907,351, a margin of 1,784 for Bush.[3] Because that margin of victory was less than "one-half of a percent . . . of the votes cast," an automatic machine recount was conducted under state law. The result showed Bush still winning the race but by a diminished margin. Gore then sought hand recounts, as was his right under Florida law, limiting the request to four counties where Democratic voters complained most about ballot problems.[4] One example was Palm Beach County's "butterfly ballot," which listed candidates in two columns and put the voting holes between the two. As a result, some Democratic voters said they mistakenly had voted for independent candidate Pat Buchanan, the conservative commentator and former Reagan administration official, rather than Gore. "My guess is I probably got some votes down there that really did not belong to me," Buchanan said on NBC's *Today* show.[5]

The Florida election controversy first came to the Supreme Court in late November, as a result of Gore's request for recounts in certain counties. That *Bush v. Palm Beach County Canvassing Board* dispute centered on the deadline for local canvassing boards to submit their returns to the secretary of state. The secretary, Katherine Harris, refused to waive a November 14 deadline imposed by statute. Gore and county officials challenged the hard rule, and the Florida Supreme Court subsequently set the deadline at November 26. Bush then appealed to the U.S.

Supreme Court. In the interim, on November 26, the Florida Elections Canvassing Commission certified all the results of the election, even though the manual recounts in various counties were not completed. The commission declared Bush the winner by 537 votes.[6]

On December 4, the U.S. Supreme Court unanimously rejected the Florida Supreme Court decision finding flexibility in the original November 14 certification deadline. The justices observed, "As a general rule, this Court defers to a state court's interpretation of a state statute. But in the case of a law enacted by a state legislature applicable . . . to the selection of Presidential electors, the legislature is not acting solely under the authority given it by the people of the State, but by virtue of a direct grant of authority made under Article II."[7] (The U.S. Constitution's Article II, which would remain a point of contention throughout all the litigation, dictated that presidential electors were to be appointed by each state "in such manner as the legislature" directed.) That decision in *Bush v. Palm Beach County Canvassing Board* was a signal that the justices would not favor changes in state rules to accommodate continuing recounts.

Gore proceeded to launch a series of legal moves, trying to keep the manual counts going, and a lawsuit that would become *Bush v. Gore* quickly ascended to the Florida Supreme Court in Tallahassee. Gore forces were pushing for every vote to be counted in the specified counties, but the Bush team insisted there had been a count and a recount and that the election should be considered over. The Florida Supreme Court agreed with Gore that counts should continue. Its decision came on December 8, one month and one day after the nation went to the polls. By a 4–3 vote, the Florida Supreme Court said the Canvassing Commission's certification was flawed, partly because of Miami-Dade County's failure to tabulate by hand nine thousand ballots on which the machines had failed to detect any vote for president, known as an "undervote." The Florida Court ordered a hand recount in dozens of counties, including Miami-Dade. To many Republicans, the ruling flouted state law giving the commission the power to certify results.

Bush lawyers immediately appealed to the justices, and before Florida counties had completed one full day of recounts, the U.S. Supreme Court halted their effort and announced it would hear oral arguments in two days. The drama of that midafternoon order on Saturday, December 9, can hardly be overstated. It constituted a sudden end to recounts that were Al Gore's best hope for reversing the state certification. The high court's action froze the review of thousands of ballots in dozens of Florida counties and left them to an uncertain fate. Local election officials and judges were weary and perplexed over what to do. In Leon County, where some five thousand of nine thousand ballots remained to be recounted, armed sheriff's deputies put boxes of ballots into a high-security van normally used for transporting prisoners.[8]

As with the Florida Supreme Court, the high court action on December 9 was taken by one vote. The courts were as closely divided as the nation. The justices who ordered the Florida recounts stopped were Chief Justice Rehnquist and Justices O'Connor, Scalia, Kennedy, and Thomas. These were the justices on the ideological and political right, all appointed by Republican presidents.

Scalia took the unusual step of commenting in a concurring statement on the two key parts of the standard test for issuing a "stay" of a lower court order—whether the appealing party was likely to prevail and whether he would suffer "irreparable harm" if the justices did not intervene. "It suffices to say that the issuance of the stay suggests that a majority of the Court, while not deciding the issues presented, believe that [Bush] has a substantial probability of success," Scalia wrote. He pointed to the fact that one of the principal assertions in Bush's appeal was that the votes ordered to be counted were not "legally cast votes." Scalia declared, "The counting of votes that are of questionable legality does in my view threaten irreparable harm to [Bush] and to the country, by casting a cloud upon what he claims to be the legitimacy of his election."[9]

It was a striking opinion, suggesting that the "cloud" of initially counted but later invalidated votes would cause Bush irreparable harm. Dissenting were the liberal justices: Stevens, Souter, Ginsburg, and Breyer. "Counting every legally cast vote cannot constitute irreparable harm," they wrote in a statement that had a tone of weariness compared with the force of Scalia's declaration.

The justices typically were divided on questions of states' rights and the authority of state courts. But here, the five in the majority were the five who usually wanted the federal government out of state affairs and who routinely deferred to state-court interpretations of its laws. For their part, the four in dissent appeared to be suggesting a state autonomy they were not known for defending in federalism cases.

That dichotomy added to the politically charged atmosphere of the dispute, which played out under the scrutiny of twenty-four-hour television and radio coverage and Internet commentary. On the day of the oral arguments, television satellite trucks ringed the marble building. Inside the courtroom on December 11, spectator seats were packed with teams of lawyers associated with each campaign, along with members of the candidates' families. The daughters of Bush vice-presidential running mate, Dick Cheney—Mary Cheney and Elizabeth Cheney Perry—were there, as were three of Gore's four children, Karenna, Kristin, and Albert III. When the justices entered the courtroom, everyone rose, according to custom. As the nine seated themselves at evenly spaced intervals along the bench, there was a palpable sense of tension. The legal questions they faced were whether the Florida court's ruling violated a constitutional mandate giving legislatures authority for the appointment of presidential electors and whether the Florida court's recount plan, which allowed standards for counting to vary county-by-county, breached due process and equal protection of the law.

When Gore's lawyer, David Boies, was at the lectern, O'Connor made clear her displeasure with the Florida court's decision ordering manual recounts and its interpretation of state law. O'Connor strongly suggested that she believed the Florida court failed to follow the Florida legislature's statutory enactments.

As Boies defended the Florida court's intervention, she said, "You are responding as though there were no special burden to show some deference to legislative choices. . . . [I]n the context of selection of presidential electors, isn't there a big red flag up there [to state courts]: 'Watch out'?" She plainly believed that the Florida Supreme Court had no business intervening with the legislatively authorized commission.[10]

"I think there is, in a sense, Your Honor, and I think the Florida Supreme Court was grappling with it," Boies answered.

Then, on the question of what standards the ballot reviewers were supposed to use in deciding what each ballot meant, O'Connor expressed impatience with voters who apparently had trouble filling out ballots. "Well, why isn't the standard the one that voters are instructed to follow, for goodness sakes? I mean, it couldn't be clearer. I mean, why don't we go to that standard?" The question was typical O'Connor: sharp and demanding. Why can't everyone just follow the directions?

A frustrated Boies wanted to answer, "For goodness sakes, Justice O'Connor. Haven't you read anything we've written or heard anything we've said?"[11] He did not, of course. Rather, Boies said, "Well, Your Honor, because in Florida law ... where a voter's intent can be discerned, even if they don't do what they're told, the votes are supposed to be counted." He tried to explain the state's interest in trying to figure out how people actually wanted their votes cast.

As soon as the arguments were over, Boies's words and those of all the other lawyers and justices were broadcast nationwide. In an unprecedented move, the Supreme Court had allowed an immediate release of the oral argument tape for distribution. As a result, there was more public attention to the case of *Bush v. Gore,* as it developed before the justices, than to any other case in history.

After nearly twenty years on the Court, O'Connor had built a reputation as the justice controlling a divided bench. In doing so, she had been aided by one of her most distinctive qualities: She was a politician. She had stuffed envelopes for Barry Goldwater's Senate reelection campaign in 1958. She had held just about every leadership position in the local GOP before becoming an Arizona state senator in 1969. She was elected Republican majority leader in the state Senate. She was cochairman of Richard Nixon's 1972 reelection campaign in Arizona. Even after she became a state judge, she continued to stay in touch with Republican leaders and seriously considered running for Arizona governor. Her political experience was especially striking when compared to the rest of the justices, most of whom had absolutely no experience in elective politics.

O'Connor's partisan ties could easily be considered old news. But an incident at a friend's election-night party deepened O'Connor's reputation as an active Republican partisan in some quarters. As first reported by *Newsweek* and the *Wall Street Journal,* Justice O'Connor became visibly upset when, shortly before eight p.m., CBS anchor Dan Rather said Florida had gone to Gore. (In the next few hours, it would become clear that the critical state was up for grabs and that neither Gore nor Bush could claim it.) "This is terrible," O'Connor said when it looked as if Florida was decisively Gore's. She left the room in apparent disgust. Her husband, John, told the others in the room that his wife was concerned because the couple wanted to retire, and she preferred that a Republican president name her successor.[12]

O'Connor privately disputed the story, saying she was angry that the network had called the election while some people on the West Coast were still casting ballots. Only she would know what she meant, but the notion that she was agitated by the possibility of a Democrat in the White House was retold in all the major newspapers. A separate report by Jeffrey Toobin in his 2001 book *Too Close to Call* added to the view of O'Connor as a Republican loyalist: "[T]he day after the Supreme Court's first opinion on the election, O'Connor and her husband had attended a party. . . . When the subject of the election controversy came up, Justice O'Connor was livid. 'You just don't know what those Gore people have been doing,' she said. 'They went into a nursing home and registered people that they shouldn't have. It was outrageous.' It was unclear where the Justice had picked up this unproven accusation, which had circulated only in the more eccentric right-wing outlets, but O'Connor recounted the story with fervor."[13]

Irrespective of her off-bench comments, O'Connor's questions signaled in many ways that she believed the Florida court had badly erred. For his part, Kennedy expressed concerns about the ambiguous and conflicting standards among Florida recount procedures. At one point during the December 11 arguments, he asked Boies, "so . . . even in one county, it could vary from table to table, 'I'm counting these ballots, you're counting this one?'" Kennedy (and many in the audience) seemed surprised by Boies's answer that that would indeed be the case. But Kennedy did not fully tip his hand, and asked tough questions of both sides.

Kennedy was known for being indecisive. Yet it turned out that Kennedy was never really ready to switch sides. None of the justices were. According to law clerks interviewed later, and subsequent stories that revisited the controversy, all nine stuck with their preliminary votes.[14] The hard part was not the bottom-line vote, it was settling on the governing rationale. Two questions had to be answered: Did the recounting in Florida, ordered by the state's highest court, violate the Constitution— either its Article II guarantee or equal protection and due process principles. If the justices said yes to either claim, they needed to address whether any kind of recounts could continue.

In a moment of incongruity, just after oral arguments, as the justices struggled with the case, Court employees began decorating a twenty-five-foot Christmas tree in the building's Great Hall. With Christmas carols playing on a portable recorder, workers lavishly covered the Wisconsin blue spruce with colored lights and tinsel. The joviality offered a strange juxtaposition to the angst in some of the chambers as the justices and their clerks tried to write opinions. Meanwhile, in the ground-floor press room, hundreds of reporters crammed into a space usually used by about two dozen. In a number of languages, they spoke anxiously into cell phones. The whole postelection episode soon began its thirty-seventh day, as the calendar turned over to December 12. Everyone waited, as the wrangling continued upstairs.

The majority was clearly suspicious of the Florida Supreme Court's allowing the recounts to continue even after the certification. But under normal circumstances, the majority would be reluctant to second-guess a state supreme court. One of the most powerful rules of constitutional federalism is that interpretation of the laws of a state is left to its own high court. Further, the justices knew that their decision—effectively, picking the next president of the United States—would be scrutinized by the public and press and be seen as a precedent that could cast a shadow over future elections.

Shortly after ten p.m., on December 12, the justices ruled 5–4 that the recounts could not go forward. In a joint but unsigned opinion, the majority reversed the Florida Supreme Court's ruling that had allowed a review of the so-called undervotes, those ballots on which votes for other offices were registered but not for that of president. The five justices who had shut down the recounts—Rehnquist, O'Connor, Scalia, Kennedy, and Thomas—declared that the county-by-county variations allowed by the Florida court for reviewing ballots, together with its acceptance of partial counts in one county and not others, violated constitutional guarantees of equal protection and due process.

The opinion was labeled a "per curiam," which meant "by the Court," and did not identify any justice as its author. The "per curiam" designation was typically reserved for a case in which there was little disagreement and the law straightforward. But here, it was just the opposite.

The five justices in the majority believed that the court-ordered recounts violated the Constitution, because county recount procedures varied too widely to be fair, and time had run out to institute appropriate standards. "When a Court orders a statewide remedy," the per curiam opinion said, "there must be at least some assurance that the rudimentary requirements of equal treatment and fundamental fairness are satisfied." Justices Souter and Breyer implicitly endorsed that view by saying in their dissenting opinion that there could be a violation of constitutional equality standards if votes were allowed to be counted with "after the fact" standards. The danger was that identical ballots would be treated differently.

The real disagreement in *Bush v. Gore* was over what to do. The five conservatives said it was too late to continue the counting. The four dissenters (Souter and Breyer, joined by Stevens and Ginsburg) wanted to send the case back to Florida courts to decide whether the counting could be resumed with set standards or whether a December 12 deadline would preclude such action. Under federal law, December 12 was the "safe harbor" deadline that automatically protected a state's presidential electors from challenge by Congress. There was much debate over the importance of the December 12 date, and even if courts had not acted by December 12, many legal analysts said it was unlikely that Congress would have intervened immediately.

The five-justice majority hung much of its decision on that December 12 deadline: "That date is upon us, and there is no recount procedure in place under the State Supreme Court's order that comports with minimal constitutional standards. . . . [I]t is evident that any recount seeking to meet the Dec. 12 date will be unconstitutional. . . ."

The majority acknowledged that normally disputes over the selection of a president were political questions, not judicial matters, but the justices said it sometimes "becomes our unsought responsibility to resolve the federal and constitutional issues the judicial system has been forced to confront." In one final twist, the Court acknowledged that it had not committed itself to the principles of *Bush v. Gore* beyond the case: "Our consideration is limited to the present circumstances, for the problem of equal protection in election processes generally presents many complexities." That was a clear signal that the justices had acted under such time pressure and with enough uncertainty that they were quite unsure what, if any, meaning the decision should have in future cases.[15]

How could the five justices who had most consistently favored states' rights and advocated judicial restraint—O'Connor most certainly at the lead—suddenly throw out a decision by a state's highest court and intervene to decide the momentous question of who should be the next president of the United States? That's what the dissenters wanted to know. "Rarely has this Court rejected outright an interpretation of state law by a state high court," Justice Ginsburg observed in her dissenting statement signed by Stevens, Souter, and Breyer. "The extraordinary setting of this case has obscured the ordinary principle that dictates its proper resolution: Federal Courts defer to state high Courts' interpretations of their state's own law. This principle reflects the core of federalism, on which all agree."

Justice Stevens, who at 80 was the eldest member of the Court, wrote, "Although we may never know with complete certainty the identity of the winner of this year's Presidential election, the identity of the loser is perfectly clear. It is the nation's confidence in the judge as an impartial guardian of the rule of law."

The majority's opinion opened the justices up to charges of partisan politicking. As expected, commentators split largely along ideological lines in their assessments of the Court's action. Those who agreed with the ruling said the justices rightly overturned a Florida court that had tread on the legislative domain. "The Tallahassee majority ordered revised tallies from three heavily Democratic counties included in Florida's running total, though none of these numbers had ever been properly certified by the state," declared *The Weekly Standard,* a conservative magazine. "Results that *had* already been properly certified in Florida's sixty-four other counties, the state Supreme Court now pronounced presumptively invalid, subject to a manual review of the 'undervote' in each." In that vein, Federal appeals court judge and prolific legal commentator Richard Posner later argued that the Florida Supreme Court erred by interfering with the state election officials and permitting the manual recounts. Adopting a pragmatic approach, he said the Supreme Court's action favoring Bush headed off a constitutional crisis.

Meanwhile, *The Nation,* a liberal periodical, asserted, "The Supreme Court decision effectively handing the presidency to George W. Bush reveals the intensely partisan nature of the Court's current majority. The Court, to be sure, has always been political, but rarely as blatantly as today. Nor are there many precedents for Justices trampling on their own previous convictions to reach a predetermined conclusion."[16]

As often happens, critics made their complaints known loudly. The justices were bombarded with thousands of letters from angry Americans. Many messages to the justices were sarcastic and nasty. O'Connor received one letter with a drawing of a skull and cross bones.[17] Dissatisfied law professors asked, "What will I tell my students?" Yale University law professor Akhil Amar answered in an opinion piece in the *Los Angeles Times:* "It will be my painful duty to say, 'Put not your trust in judges.' "[18]

"The problem with *Bush v. Gore,* I suspect, was the case was too salient an example of judicial misbehavior for many legal academics to swallow," Professor Jack M. Balkin wrote in the *Yale Law Journal.* "It was no isolated fender bender in which a local judge helped out the son of a former law partner. Rather, the case decided the outcome of a Presidential election and may well have determined who would sit on the Supreme Court and the lower federal Courts for decades to come. Moreover, unlike the judge deciding the case of a fender bender in some obscure venue, the Court could not have failed to recognize that all eyes were upon it. That the conservative Justices acted as they did suggested that their partisanship was so thorough and pervasive that it blinded them to their own biases."[19]

This is what was so striking for those who had studied O'Connor. She was a woman for whom appearances mattered, in the law and in personal gestures. She had continually shown an awareness of the public response to the Court as an institution. In her opinions, she typically explained why the Court ruled as it did. A prime example was the 1992 ruling she forged with Kennedy and Souter that upheld abortion rights. She explained that although the justices might not agree with *Roe v. Wade,* people had lived with it, reordered their lives around it. Now, in the most controversial case of her tenure, she said nothing. She explained nothing. Just when the public might have wanted to be reassured, she walked silently off the stage.

O'Connor let the mixed signals just sit out there. What motivated this former state court judge whose one law review article before joining the Supreme Court had emphasized how demoralizing it is for state-court judges to be second-guessed by federal judges? Many critics questioned her motives, of course. But it was also natural to question why she would not have written an opinion addressing some of the obvious issues or added her usually unifying voice.

She was plainly vexed by all the talk about whether a ballot chad was hanging or dimpled, and her irritation with the Florida courts was clear at the outset. But a substantial number of ballots had to be read through hand counts, because of malfunctioning voting machines. To those who wanted the recounts to continue, a manual recount was the only way to determine voters' intentions in the democratic process. (Since the 2000 election, punch-card voting has been abandoned by many jurisdictions.[20])

Was her decision ideological, political, or simply a matter of believing that the Court was needed to settle the unsettled election and resolve an urgent constitutional question? It is impossible to know without O'Connor herself stepping in to reveal her personal motivations.

"I think there simply is no 'Truth of the Matter' to be unearthed," wrote Harvard law professor Laurence H. Tribe, who represented Gore during the case. "It . . . makes little sense to talk as though we could, even in principle, know whether partisan considerations really provided the final motivation for the majority's actions in *Bush v. Gore*. . . . [I]t must also be kept in mind that, when talking not of something relatively straight-forward like bribery, but of something as complex and elusive as partisan bias, the danger is great that the bias will be as much in the eye of the accuser as in the heart of the accused."[21]

"There was a great deal of criticism," O'Connor acknowledged a year later. "It was a difficult case. It's too bad that it came up . . . We don't enjoy being thrust into the middle of political controversy."[22]

In the end, irrespective of O'Connor's reason for her action, the vote in the historic case became part of her legacy in the mind of the body politic. Her Court—and it repeatedly had been called the O'Connor Court— had stridden into the most extraordinary electoral crisis in a century and resolved the matter with one decisive ruling.

Later in December 2000, O'Connor and her husband, John, returned to Arizona for the Christmas holiday. The justice sought out rest and re- laxation, which for her included several rounds of golf. It is instructive to recall O'Connor's approach to the game upon learning to play in her early forties. She took lessons at the Paradise Valley Country Club, working with a pro and hitting buckets of balls on the driving range for at least two years until she was satisfied with her game. Only then did she play against her male colleagues in Arizona.[23]

Now, in this post–*Bush v. Gore* period, when all the major newspapers and broadcasters were focused on the fallout from the Court's ruling and she was accused of pure partisan politicking, was her game affected? As agitated as she was, did she hit it in the trees, a sand-trap, a water hazard? No. On the eighth hole at the Paradise Valley Country Club, O'Connor hit a hole in one. The first of her life. A scream of glee rang out across the greens.[24] She pumped her fist in the air. Competitor to the core.

Once back in Washington, O'Connor spent the early months of 2001 trying to mend relations inside the Court. She stayed in close contact with Justice Breyer, President Clinton's 1994 appointee to succeed Harry Blackmun, and worked to ease relations among disillusioned liberal clerks. After a few months, O'Connor tried to make light of the situation. At a benefit dinner and mock trial of Shakespeare's King Lear held at the Court in May 2001, O'Connor teased as she was announcing the verdict that "it was suggested that we [turn over] the case to the Florida Supreme Court." *Bush v. Gore* hung in the air.[25]

ABOUT THIS TIME, O'Connor began edging more toward the center of the Court in a series of cases that drew great public attention. It was a trend observed through the years by many commentators, and now it was difficult to assess whether this was a response to the public fallout from *Bush v. Gore* or a continuation of the natural evolution of her approach. One of O'Connor's law clerks from the 1980s said the ascent of Bush, a conservative, to the White House on its own might have drawn her leftward. "She tends to be a reaction-formation type of person. She does not want the institutions of government to swing too far right or too far left," he said.

The shift was slight but real, and the pattern was borne out by high-profile cases, as well as broader statistics that showed her increasingly voting with Justices Stevens, Souter, Ginsburg, and Breyer.[26]

In the spring of 2001, for example, O'Connor voted for the first time to uphold the drawing of a heavily black congressional district intended to enhance the political power of racial minorities in North Carolina.[27] In the past, O'Connor had been the fifth vote against so-called majority-

minority districts that were strangely configured, stating, "reapportionment is one area in which appearances do matter." Later, O'Connor was
with the same five-justice majority to strike down heavy minority-
packed districts from Texas and Georgia. But now, in 2001, she gave the
usual dissenters (Stevens, Souter, Ginsburg, and Breyer) a majority to
permit a North Carolina district that had been at the Court three times
before in various permutations.

She did not write an opinion. Rather, she joined an opinion for the
Court penned by Breyer that relied heavily on O'Connor's words from
past rulings. "Race in this case closely correlates with political behavior,"
he wrote, adopting arguments from North Carolina officials that politicians who drew the map were trying to protect an incumbent and shore
up party strength rather than merely to segregate voters by race. Equally
important, Breyer offered a more expansive interpretation of *Shaw v.
Reno* than legal analysts had thought possible. Breyer's opinion for the
Court said that when race correlates highly with political affiliation, the
white voters have to show at least that the legislature could have achieved
its political objectives in ways that would have ended up with greater
racial balance. This put more of a burden on whites than had O'Connor's
original 1993 *Shaw v. Reno* decision. As a practical matter, the Breyer
opinion demonstrated that districts consolidating blacks or Hispanics
could be constitutional.[28]

The North Carolina case was representative of the bond O'Connor
was forming with Breyer, who had similar pragmatic tendencies and also
a political streak. Breyer was born and reared in San Francisco, the oldest
of two sons. His father was a lawyer for the city public-school system; his
mother was active in community affairs and Democratic politics. Like
O'Connor, he graduated from Stanford University with a bachelor's degree. Breyer went to Harvard Law School. He became a Supreme Court
law clerk to Justice Arthur Goldberg, then a U.S. Justice Department an-
titrust attorney and Harvard law professor.

Breyer gravitated to politics and became counsel to the Senate Judiciary Committee. He was instrumental in negotiating legislation to
deregulate the airlines and in developing the groundwork for an over-
haul of criminal sentencing laws. A chief aide to Massachusetts Democratic senator Edward Kennedy, Breyer nonetheless built enduring
relations with Republicans, which helped him win easy bipartisan confir-

mation by the Senate in 1994. When President Clinton introduced him in the Rose Garden that summer, Breyer said—in words that could have been O'Connor's—that the law should bring people "together in a way that is more harmonious, that is better so that they can work productively together."[29]

O'Connor and Breyer found their relationship mutually beneficial. Breyer was a determined junior justice, always looking for ways to have more influence among the nine. For O'Connor, Breyer was a bridge to the liberal wing and a partner in the view that the law was best defined in increments. They were pragmatists. Furthermore, Breyer was respectful and deferential to O'Connor in opinions even when he disagreed with her. In that way, he was the opposite of the sharp-tongued Scalia.

At a black-tie dinner at the University Club in Washington in February 2001, Breyer was called upon to introduce O'Connor, who was the keynote speaker. He did it in a pinch. The event's organizers actually did not know until cocktails were underway that Justice Scalia, who was supposed to make the introduction, was not available. Because of a missed communication, he had never officially been invited. Breyer happened to be in the audience, and the master of ceremonies sheepishly asked him to fill in. When Breyer rose on O'Connor's behalf, he called her "a colleague and a friend." Breyer told of their travels together. He recounted how attending judicial conferences with O'Connor had taken him around the world, from Frankfurt to Paris and beyond. "Yes," Breyer said, relating a remark from a mutual friend: "You can't go wrong following Justice O'Connor."[30]

In time, all nine justices moved past the internal tensions created by the decision in *Bush v. Gore.* The terrorist attacks of September 11, 2001, brought them together, as they did other officials in Washington normally in conflict. Coincidentally, on September 11, O'Connor and Breyer were together in India at a judicial conference. It took them several difficult days to get back to the United States, returning by way of a succession of cargo and commercial airplanes.[31]

In the summer of 2001, O'Connor used the occasion of a speech to the Minnesota Women Lawyers Association to reveal new thinking on the death penalty. This view of the issue stood in contrast to her rhetoric from the 1980s, when she often stressed that reexamining convictions or sentences had a societal cost, including that the guilty could go free. "If statistics are any indication," she now said, "the system may well be allowing some innocent defendants to be executed." She said that in 2000, six death-row inmates had been exonerated and released, and that since 1973 some ninety inmates had been set free. "After twenty years on the high court, I have to acknowledge that serious questions are being raised about whether the death penalty is being fairly administered in this country," she said, revealing again how much she kept an eye toward public opinion and national trends. Most immediately on the front pages those days were stories of inmates who had been exonerated through DNA testing and tales of incompetent lawyers who had been appointed to represent capital defendants.

O'Connor noted that since she joined the Court, the number of death-row inmates had more than quadrupled, to nearly four thousand. "Unfortunately, as the rate of executions [has] increased, problems in the way [in] which the death penalty has been administered have become more apparent," she said. O'Connor specifically pointed to defendants' problems getting experienced defense attorneys. In the news around that time were stories about sleeping lawyers, drunken lawyers, and those who simply took the ready money as public defenders and offered a lazy defense. "Perhaps it's time to look at minimum standards for appointed counsel in death cases and adequate compensation for appointed counsel when they are used," she said.[32]

For most of her tenure, O'Connor had been firmly in support of capital punishment. She had authored opinions that eliminated routes of appeal and made it difficult for death-row prisoners to claim that their lawyers were ineffective. Nothing in her then-twenty-year record suggested that she was backing away from the belief that the death penalty was constitutional. Rather, it seemed that she was telling states that if they wanted to continue invoking the ultimate punishment, they needed to correct the flaws in their systems, specifically to ensure that capital defendants were adequately represented.

Two years after the Minneapolis speech, O'Connor applied this sentiment in the case of a Maryland man convicted of murdering a 77-year-old woman. His defense lawyers had decided not to pursue or introduce evidence of his abused childhood. The possible mitigating evidence might have convinced a jury to give him life in prison rather than death, O'Connor noted. Her decision in the case of Kevin Wiggins marked only the second time that the Court had found defense counsel in a capital case inadequate and it signaled to lower courts that it was time to bring more scrutiny to court-appointed lawyers in such cases. In a similar move two years later, O'Connor was the swing vote to order a new trial for a Pennsylvania man, Ronald Rompilla, whose court-appointed lawyers failed to examine the record of his prior conviction for rape even after prosecutors said they would introduce the conviction as an aggravating factor. That record contained evidence of a traumatic childhood and mental health problems that might have caused a jury to sentence Rompilla to life in prison rather than death.[33]

In a 2002 death penalty case, *Atkins v. Virginia,* which directly addressed the question of who could be subjected to the ultimate punishment, O'Connor reversed a previous stance and voted to ban capital punishment for mentally retarded defendants. She joined an opinion by Justice Stevens saying the execution of mentally retarded criminals violated the Constitution's ban on cruel and unusual punishment. What made the difference for O'Connor, who wrote an opinion in 1989 allowing the death penalty for the retarded, was the number of states that had changed position on the issue. In 1989, sixteen states banned it, but the number had grown to thirty in 2002. As ever, O'Connor was watching and listening to the people. Stevens's majority opinion also pointed to polling data that showed the public generally opposed to the use of the death penalty for retarded defendants. Stevens said the retarded have limited judgment, so they could not act with the same moral culpability as other criminals and could not help their defense counsel put on the best case.[34]

The following year, O'Connor joined with liberals Stevens, Souter, Ginsburg, and Breyer in one of the most controversial disputes of the day. In *Grutter v. Bollinger* and *Gratz v. Bollinger,* the question was whether colleges and universities should be allowed to use a student's race as a factor in admissions. The cases arose as affirmative action was showing surprising resilience, despite years of assault by politicians and conservative-led drives to vote it down in the polls. The enduring use of affirmative action was exactly the kind of trend O'Connor would have noticed.

It had been a quarter-century since the Supreme Court examined campus affirmative action in the case of *Regents of the University of California v. Bakke*. For O'Connor, revisiting *Bakke* brought into play her evolving approach to legal dilemmas, her eye for the needs of the nation, and her relationship with Lewis Powell, who wrote the controlling opinion in *Bakke*.

The University of Michigan cases began in 1997, when three white students filed lawsuits alleging that Michigan's dual-track admissions systems for whites and for selected racial minorities violated the Fourteenth Amendment's guarantee of equal protection under the law. Jennifer Gratz and Patrick Hamacher had been denied admission to the undergraduate program, which used a system automatically assigning more points to minority applicants. Separately, Barbara Grutter had been turned down by the law school, which, within a more individualized screening system applied a "plus" factor for minority applicants. All three students believed that the credentials of black students who had been admitted were weaker than theirs.

The university countered that a diverse student body was integral to a high-quality education, relying on the opinion in *Bakke* written by Powell, who had cast the deciding vote in the 5–4 case. It insisted that the minority students admitted were part of a pool of generally qualified students. It argued that without specifically favoring racial minorities it could not enroll the requisite "critical mass" of minorities. If the law school had not given minorities a boost, for example, the University of Michigan said they would have made up only 4 percent, instead of 14.5 percent, of its incoming class of 350 students in 2000.[35]

As lawyers on both sides of the separate law school and undergraduate cases prepared their arguments, they focused on O'Connor, invoking her past statements to their respective advantage. In 1986, she had suggested that diversity may justify campus affirmative action when she wrote, relying on Powell's *Bakke* opinion, that "a state interest in the promotion of racial diversity has been found sufficiently 'compelling,' at least in the context of higher education." But she had also, in the area of racial redistricting, written: "Classifications based on race carry a danger of stigmatic harm. Unless they are reserved for remedial settings, they may in fact promote notions of racial inferiority and lead to politics of racial hostility."[36]

In the end, when the Court ruled on June 23, 2003, O'Connor again carved a middle option that defined the center in a highly polarized debate. Casting the critical fifth vote and writing the opinion for the Court, O'Connor stressed the importance of campuses' being open to all races, as well as the ability of colleges and universities to provide diverse, well-trained graduates for business, the military, and other American institutions.

With her husband, John, sitting in a special reserved section of the courtroom, and numerous law clerks crowded into the alcoves, the first woman justice spoke in a clear, forceful voice about how diversity promotes learning. "The path to leadership must be visibly open," she said, as she read parts of the decision in the law-school case brought by Barbara Grutter.

"Effective participation by members of all racial and ethnic groups in the civic life of our nation is essential if the dream of one nation, indivisible, is to be realized," she elaborated in her written opinion for the Court. "Moreover, universities, and in particular, law schools, represent the training ground for a large number of our Nation's leaders. Individuals with law degrees occupy roughly half the state governorships, more than half the seats in the United States Senate, and more than a third of the seats in the United States House of Representatives."[37] Education had liberated O'Connor. As much as she hated being sent away to El Paso, the Radford School had paved the way for her admittance to Stanford, which then set the course of her adult life.

Sixty-five leading U.S. businesses had sided with Michigan, emphasizing their interest in a diverse, well-trained workforce in the global economy through a "friend of the Court" brief. A distinguished group of former high-ranking military officers similarly had backed Michigan, saying "the military cannot achieve an officer corps that is both highly qualified and racially diverse unless the service academies and the ROTC use limited race-conscious recruiting and admissions policies." O'Connor referred to those briefs in her decision. "These benefits [flowing from a diverse student body] are not theoretical but real, as major American businesses have made clear that the skills needed in today's increasingly global marketplace can only be developed through exposure to widely diverse people, cultures, ideas, and viewpoints."[38]

Justice Thomas, who, along with Rehnquist, Scalia, and Kennedy, was in the minority, penned a personal dissent that began with an 1865 passage from Frederick Douglass that said, in part, "What I ask for the Negro is not benevolence, not pity, not sympathy, but simply *justice.*" Thomas said Michigan's double standard giving blacks a boost was unconstitutional and, turning the tables, declared, "No one would argue that a university could set up a lower general admission standard and then impose heightened requirements only on black applicants."

O'Connor's decision upheld the Michigan law school program, which considered the race of an applicant along with several other characteristics. But she also indicated the limits of her endorsement of affirmative action. She stated that such policies likely would not be needed in twenty-five years. Separately, in the dispute over the undergraduate admissions system, she made clear her view that schools could not blindly give minority students extra points guaranteeing their acceptance. Schools must individually assess applicants' backgrounds and records, she wrote. That position caused her to join Rehnquist and the three other conservative justices in an opinion striking down the Michigan undergraduate admissions program, which automatically gave a twenty-point bonus to racial minorities. Breyer joined the judgment against the undergraduate admissions policy but did not sign Rehnquist's opinion.[39]

For more than a decade, conservative activists had been working to bring a new case to the high court to reverse *Bakke* and to end racial preferences in admissions. They had had mixed rulings in lower courts, and a resolution by the Supreme Court had been eagerly awaited. Unlike the cases of the 1980s and 1990s involving racial policies in the workplace or government contracting, the Michigan dispute cut to the heart of the American belief that education is a ticket to success. That made the difference for O'Connor.

In the University of Michigan case, O'Connor believed that the Court should assert itself as an actor more than an arbiter. Just as she supported the Court's forceful intervention in *Bush v. Gore* because she believed lower courts and legislators had failed to ensure an orderly outcome, she embraced the Court's prominence in the great public debate over affirmative action. Amid an ideological battle, and as lower-court judges were conflicted over how to rule, she offered a pragmatic compromise. She gave college administrators room to devise their own policies within certain strictures—and, at least temporarily, defused the issue in the courts.

Also in 2003, O'Connor effectively retreated from *Bowers v. Hardwick,* a 1986 Court opinion she had signed allowing states to outlaw consensual sexual relations between gay people. In the new case, she said states no longer could outlaw homosexual sodomy. The controlling Court opinion in *Lawrence v. Texas* was written by Kennedy, who found that a Texas statute prohibiting the activity violated due process because of the fundamental character of such sexual choices. Kennedy's decision for five justices overruled *Bowers v. Hardwick*. In a concurring statement, O'Connor declined to join the majority's outright reversal of the 1986 decision, but she found separate equality grounds for striking down the Texas criminal prohibition: "Texas' sodomy law brands all homosexuals as criminals, thereby making it more difficult for homosexuals to be treated in the same manner as everyone else. . . . A law branding one class of persons as criminal solely based on the state's moral disapproval of that class and the conduct associated with that class runs contrary to the values of the Constitution and the Equal Protection Clause under any standard of review."[40]

O'Connor was unwilling to acknowledge any error in her 1986 vote in *Bowers,* nor to join the majority's view emphasizing privacy in the bedroom for consenting adults. But, as she had in a 1996 gay-rights case from Colorado, *Romer v. Evans,* she separated herself from Rehnquist, Scalia, and Thomas by voting to ensure that states could not pass laws based on their moral disapproval of gay men and lesbians.

AROUND THIS TIME, Justice O'Connor also told the world more about herself and her family, with her memoir, *Lazy B,* published by Random House in 2002. Two years earlier, she had telephoned her brother in Tucson: "Alan, I think we should do a book together." Her brother recalled, "She said, you know, ever since I went on the Court, people have asked me how somebody from a rural, humble background—and being a woman—could achieve [a position on the Supreme Court].' She said this book will be the answer to that."[41]

The book was written in the voice of O'Connor, but brother and sister worked on it together, dividing up chapters, telling about their parents and the cowboys who worked the ranch. *Lazy B* was a best-seller. But some critics longed for more substance. Its "revelations about how the land, people and values shaped Sandra Day O'Connor are as skimpy as the region's rainfall," Carol Doup Muller wrote for the *Christian Science Monitor.* Linda Greenhouse of the *New York Times* noted in a book review that *Lazy B* "makes no explicit attempt to reconcile the two Sandra Day O'Connors"—the girl who endured many hardships in the West and the one who is the central player on the Court.[42]

Asked what she hoped readers would take away from the book, Justice O'Connor said, "An appreciation for the qualities of the life that existed [on the ranch]. The harshness of it, but the beauty of it. And the notion that people can take care of the land in that harsh setting and even improve it a bit." She and her brother, Alan, traveled to several book signings and lectures. "We do a real good ham-and-egg," Alan said. "She's the draw but we do a good job together. When we were at Harvard, the only thing she said ahead of time was 'Do you want to go first, or should I go first?' And I said, 'I think I should lead off because you're the home-run hitter.' She said, 'OK, you start.' But when we got on stage, she just got up and went to work."[43]

ONE LAST ISSUE LINGERED from the 2000 election—one that pertained to Sandra Day O'Connor not so much as justice, but as wife. The reports about John's comments at the election-night party regarding his wife's desire to retire while a Republican was in the White House drew concern from friends. He had seemed uncharacteristically indiscreet. What only family knew at the time and what close friends later learned was that John, then 70, had been diagnosed with Alzheimer's disease. Some of O'Connor's friends wondered, in hindsight, whether the comments by the usually circumspect John were one of the first public signs of his illness.

Awareness of John's situation slowly seeped out into the wider circle of the O'Connors' friends and acquaintances. O'Connor resorted to her most practical self, bringing John with her to her chambers as she worked and to public appearances, always keeping him in her sight.

But even with her great skill at managing difficult situations, there must have been an emotional toll. Justice O'Connor's mother, Ada Mae, had also suffered from the mentally degenerative disease. The great love of her life was now faltering in the ways typical of Alzheimer's patients, requiring his wife to usher him through the routines of their lives. John sometimes would forget what to do with a tennis racquet, a golf club, even a fork at dinner. But then, as often happens with Alzheimer's patients, he would have moments of lucidity, and friends would see "the old John."

In public, Justice O'Connor did not reveal the sadness and regret that others felt when they saw John sitting passively or acting confused—wondering whether he should stay seated as she rose to greet someone or perform an obligation. People who had long known O'Connor felt the grief of the situation, but noticed, too, that she acted as if nothing was amiss. She did what she had to do: kept track of John and fulfilled her official duties without missing a beat. The woman who had survived the physical and emotional isolation of Harry Day's ranch, had broken barriers in the male-dominated worlds of politics and the law, and had overcome breast cancer now added the personal achievement of not being undone by the slow disappearance of the old John.

"Work is her refuge," one justice said in an interview. Another justice, when asked how O'Connor managed in the face of so many personal and professional demands, answered in a way that captured the core of O'Connor: "She just does."

18

❖

MOVING FORWARD

At the Washington National Cathedral's Easter service in spring 2005, Justice O'Connor was dressed in a deep-purple suit emblematic of the holiday. Accompanied by her husband and friends, she arrived about an hour early for the eleven a.m. service. As she circulated among the other early arrivals, John sat quietly in a reserved front section of the nave. She was in her element, briefly visiting with friends and greeting others who recognized her. The previous day, she had celebrated her seventy-fifth birthday. Outside the vaulted cathedral on this March 27, it was overcast and drizzly. But inside, O'Connor, with her white hair luminous under the lights, appeared in a splendid mood.

On occasions such as this, John still accompanied her. His Alzheimer's made him confused and disoriented, but with guidance he could still manage well enough in public. They were all getting older. Her friend, Bill Rehnquist, 80, had been diagnosed with thyroid cancer and was undergoing chemotherapy treatment. A tracheotomy tube had been inserted to help him breathe more easily. He had missed four months of oral arguments. But just before Easter, Rehnquist had returned to the bench. In his fashion, he was soldiering on, as was Justice O'Connor. Drawing on old strengths, she held her losses at bay.

The previous summer, O'Connor's sixth grandchild had been born. "Let's be thankful for blessings large and small," she wrote in the family's

2004 Christmas card adorned with a picture of Dylan, the infant son of Jay and his wife, Heather. In years past, John had created their Christmas cards, such as one with playful pictures of his head and hers pasted into vintage vehicles.

Since her early days in Washington, the National Cathedral had been woven into O'Connor's life. She had become a reader of the scripture lessons, most often at services in the cathedral's small Bethlehem Chapel. Less than a year earlier, she had read at the cathedral funeral service for Ronald Reagan, the president who had brought her to Washington. Reciting the words from John Winthrop's 1630 sermon of "a city upon a hill," O'Connor had said: "Make others' conditions our own; rejoice together, mourn together, labor and suffer together, always having before our eyes our commission and community in the work, as members of the same body."[1]

THE WEEKS FOLLOWING the Easter service were difficult, as the work of the 2004–2005 Supreme Court term came to an end and Rehnquist's health seemed to decline. She and Rehnquist had traveled the same path, from Stanford to Phoenix to Washington and the Supreme Court. Not weighed down by the baggage of his gender, Rehnquist had it easier. But here they both were, a mission shared, for nearly a quarter-century. In their later years on the bench, they had sat next to each other, at times whispering during oral arguments. Her seat directly to Rehnquist's left was a result of her seniority, second only to John Paul Stevens, who sat on Rehnquist's right. It was a good arrangement for two old friends who enjoyed sharing private remarks.

Asked whether she and Rehnquist ever had discussed how surprising it was that they had ended up together on the Supreme Court, O'Connor was dismissive. "No," she said. "It just happened. That's the way it is."[2] The truth of how this happened was much more complex than that Western matter-of-factness she put forward. But somehow it served her—perhaps enabled her ambition and success—to talk as if things just happened.[3]

As was the case with Harry Day on the Lazy B, work had always been at the center of O'Connor's life—no less now, in her elderly years, than in her youth. On the brink of marking a quarter-century on the Court,

O'Connor was acutely aware of the legacy she would leave. "Being a member of the Court is a little like walking through fresh concrete," she said in spring 2005. "We look back and see those opinions that we've written and they sort of harden after us."[4]

In the week after Easter, she delivered an opinion that broadly interpreted a 1972 law intended to end sex discrimination in high schools and colleges. She was, as usual, the fifth vote. But her opinion was not usual. Its breadth and boldness reflected, perhaps, the personal connection she might have felt to the case. Since its passage more than three decades earlier, the law known as Title IX had provided young women with more opportunities to participate in school sports and other programs.

Roderick Jackson, a girls' basketball coach in Birmingham, Alabama, had lost his coaching job after he complained that his team had to use athletic equipment and facilities inferior to those of the boys' basketball team. Jackson had sued under Title IX of the Education Amendments of 1972, which prohibited sex bias at high schools and colleges receiving federal funds. But lower-court judges had ruled against Jackson, saying Title IX did not give a whistleblower a right to sue for retaliation. Although some other lower courts had ruled the opposite way, the rejection of Jackson's claim was plausible because Title IX's terms did not explicitly mention retaliation, whereas Title VII of the 1964 Civil Rights Act did.[5]

In her written opinion, O'Connor said teachers and coaches who faced retribution could sue for money damages under Title IX. "Retaliation against a person because that person has complained of sex discrimination is another form of intentional sex discrimination," O'Connor wrote. As a practical matter, she emphasized, the congressional goal of preventing and redressing discrimination "would be difficult, if not impossible, to achieve if persons who complain about sex discrimination did not have effective protection against retaliation."

Coaches such as Jackson are often in the best position to protect the rights of their students, O'Connor said. They are able to identify discrimination and bring it to the attention of school administrators.[6]

The opinion in *Jackson v. Birmingham Board of Education* flowed from positions set forth in other Title IX cases, including one in 1999 arising from a poignant set of facts involving indifference on the part of a school toward a girl's plight. That case, *Davis v. Monroe County Board of Edu-*

cation, elicited sharper rhetoric from O'Connor, who wrote for the majority.

When LaShonda Davis was in fifth grade, in Forsyth, Georgia, a boy in her class sexually taunted her week after week. LaShonda's mother complained to school officials, but they did nothing to stop the boy. So she sued under Title IX, claiming that the school should be financially responsible for the harm caused by the peer torment. The legal question became whether public schools could be forced to pay damages for failing to stop student sexual harassment. When oral arguments began, all eyes naturally were on O'Connor, and she was the first to ask questions. "I'm sure that schoolchildren nationwide tease each other, and little boys tease little girls ... throughout their years in school," she said skeptically of the Davis position. "Is every one of these incidents going to lead to some kind of lawsuit?"[7]

But in the end, just as later happened in *Jackson v. Birmingham Board of Education,* it was O'Connor who provided the crucial fifth vote and wrote the opinion favoring the victim of discrimination. She said that public schools could be forced to pay damages for failing to stop student sexual harassment. At the heart of her opinion was a recognition that sometimes peer harassment is so severe that it prevents a student from learning. In a dissent joined by Rehnquist, Scalia, and Thomas, Justice Kennedy said that O'Connor was ignoring the facts of school life and inviting federal interference in local matters, promising many lawsuits that "will impose serious financial burdens on local school districts, the taxpayers who support them and the children they serve." From the bench, on the day she announced the opinion in LaShonda Davis's case, O'Connor observed tersely that Kennedy had claimed the Court's ruling would teach "little Johnny a perverse lesson in federalism." No, she rejoined, the decision makes sure "that little Mary may attend class."[8] Justice O'Connor, the first woman on the Court, was boldly and broadly challenging gender injustices.

EARLY IN THE TWENTY-FIRST CENTURY, O'Connor was taking stock beyond her opinions. She had continued to write books looking back on her life. She gathered and published a compilation of her writings and speeches called *The Majesty of the Law: Reflections of a Supreme*

Court Justice and, separately, was preparing a children's book about her favorite horse, Chico, from the Lazy B.[9] "I just thought it was better now than a few years from now, to spell out some of the concepts I've accumulated," she said after she finished *Majesty of the Law*. She insisted that she did not have what she called "the obituary syndrome"—an attempt to chronicle a career that might be ending. But it was clear that she wanted to have a strong say in how she was judged and to preserve her life story for the future.[10]

The *Majesty of the Law* was an amalgam of speeches she had given, letters she had received, and occasional fresh thoughts. It was as if she wanted to lay down certain markers. Reviews were lukewarm. "At its best," wrote the *Financial Times,* "the book is like the Justice herself: commonsensical rather than deep. But too often it is neither. It offers rare glimpses of the homespun wisdom of this most down-to-earth of jurists. But they are just that: rare."[11] In a *New York Times* book review, University of Chicago law professor Dennis Hutchinson wrote that *Majesty of the Law* offered "potted histories of the Court," "dutiful memorials to former colleagues," yet "an occasional glimpse into the steely judge behind the muted prose."[12]

When *Majesty* was published, O'Connor conducted various promotional interviews with newspapers and radio and television networks, as she had with the publication of the *Lazy B*. These events gave reporters a chance to ask her about divisive cases, such as *Bush v. Gore*. But her answers were pat and boiled down to her usual "Yes, the cases are difficult but we do our best." And she continued to reject questions about her role as a swing-vote justice. "I think it's ridiculous because all nine people have to cast a vote and there's no way to single out one as more significant than another," she said. "It doesn't work that way."[13]

Purely coincidentally, but fitting for a justice who was stepping back and reviewing her years in the law, O'Connor happened to encounter for the first time since her 1981 confirmation a Phoenix woman who had vigorously opposed her appointment. Carolyn Gerster, an antiabortion activist, had told the Senate Judiciary Committee that Reagan had been misled, that O'Connor had favored abortion rights. Gerster told the committee that speaking out against a Phoenix notable had alienated her from the community but the issue compelled her to come forward. Now, in late 2003, they ended up, each with her family, at the Paradise Valley

Country Club. Without acknowledging the other, each woman attended to her family. Then, as they both were leaving, O'Connor approached Gerster and said hello. They talked for a few minutes. The subject of the conversation? Their grandchildren.[14]

MOVING THROUGH HER EARLY SEVENTIES, O'Connor stepped up her work on the international legal scene. "There will never be another time in history when such a huge part of the world all of a sudden was trying to form nation states and to develop institutions and . . . a free-market environment," she said in an interview.[15] As part of President Bush's effort to generate democratic structures of government in the Persian Gulf, he asked O'Connor to represent the United States at an Arab Judicial Forum in Manama, Bahrain, in 2003. There, she spoke about the importance of an independent judiciary. "When the power to make laws is separated from the power to interpret and apply them, the very foundation of the rule of law—that controversies are adjudicated on the basis of previously established rules—is strengthened."[16]

After the forum, O'Connor took questions from reporters. She was asked about legal changes "related to human rights and the improvement of judiciary systems" in Arab countries. She responded, "I always enjoy visiting with judges from other nations. We have a lot of common interests. We end up having to resolve many similar problems. We're all concerned about what are the best ethical standards for judges. How do we enforce them? How should judges be selected? How long should they serve? Should there be a term of years or something longer? These are common issues of interest to all of us."[17] Her responses, polite but predictable, were not illuminating. But she was there. Her presence alone made a case for herself and for all women. "Women must show *their* public face," she wrote in *The Majesty of the Law.* "We must help to work out our own community problems. We must insist on having equal voices and equal responsibilities. . . . In large part, success depends on changing minds at home, in the streets, and at the workplace—not just in legislatures and the courts. Each and every one of us has an important role to play in completing that task."[18] O'Connor's presence in international legal circles also reflected her sense of the perspectives beyond American borders. This view showed itself in her reliance on foreign legal materials in a number of cases in her last years, among them decisions about capital punishment.[19]

In 2004, the high court ruled on the first cases testing President Bush's antiterrorist legal strategy. After hijackers crashed airplanes into New York City's World Trade Center towers, the Pentagon in suburban Virginia, and a field in Pennsylvania, the United States had invaded Afghanistan to destroy the base of terrorist leader Osama bin Laden and his Al Qaeda network. The Bush administration claimed that the president had sweeping power to imprison indefinitely anyone picked up in the war zone in connection with those or other military activities and to designate those individuals "enemy combatants."[20]

O'Connor took a leading role as the Court struck down the policies that allowed such detainees to be held, without hearings, in U.S. military prisons. In *Hamdi v. Rumsfeld* she wrote the opinion favoring Yaser Esam Hamdi, who was born in Louisiana, grew up in Saudi Arabia, and was captured with Taliban fighters in Afghanistan in late 2001. Hamdi had been designated an enemy combatant by President Bush and held incommunicado in a military brig in Charleston, South Carolina.[21]

Rejecting the Bush administration's arguments that detainees' cases should be kept out of the courts, she said that even in wartime, the Constitution "assuredly envisions a role for all three branches when individual liberties are at stake." She wrote that a U.S. citizen held as an enemy combatant has a right to due process of law, to be told the charges against him, and to be able to have his claim of innocence heard by a neutral judge or military tribunal. "History and common sense teach us that an unchecked system of detention carries the potential to become a means for oppression and abuse."[22] These were strong words of principle, asserting the power of the courts. But, as usual, O'Connor left many questions unanswered and many avenues open. It was not clear even a year after the rulings what precise constitutional limits constrained the administration in its handling of the detainees from the wars in Afghanistan and Iraq.

O'CONNOR'S PLACE in the social milieu of the Court remained important to the other justices. That was seen in April 2005, as she joined Scalia and Breyer in a "constitutional conversation" at the National Archives.[23] The evening was more revealing of their individual personalities and the culture of the Court than of their substantive views. As the three justices sat in casual armchairs on the stage of the auditorium, O'Connor and Scalia played off each other, like a familiar pair of spouses or siblings. They finished each other's sentences—but probably not the way the other wanted them finished.

At one point, Scalia talked about the integrity of the Constitution and how its validity rests with the text rather than the Court.

"Even the most fundamental thing as to whether women could have the vote in 1920, somebody didn't come to the Court and say, you know, we have an equal protection clause—"

"Well, they did," O'Connor tartly rejoined, "but it was rejected."

And so it went through the evening, as they each amended or embroidered the other's comments.

Scalia and O'Connor both chided Breyer when he talked about still being the junior justice after more than a decade and the last to have his say as they conducted the initial round of votes in conference.

Scalia: "He has the best seat, as much as he complains about being the junior justice. When it goes around the table and it's four to four, you know, they're all—"

O'Connor: "He gets to decide!"

In response to a question about the ban on cameras in their courtroom, Breyer invoked a refrain common among the justices, that they fear a disruption of their proceedings, and that each of them believes they are trustees of the institution, safeguarding its reputation and tradition. Even the symbols of the Court reflect the slow deliberative process, O'Connor added. She observed that in the courtyards, there are several lanterns. At their base are tortoises, "because they move slowly, and that's what we do."

Throughout her tenure, O'Connor promoted civility among the justices, even as she was ever the competitor. Justice Thomas recalled in an interview that O'Connor strove for many years to persuade all of them to eat lunch together after the justices' daily oral arguments, rather than each returning to their individual chambers to eat alone or work on cases. Thomas said he resisted her entreaties when he joined the Court in 1991. "I was not inclined to do so. I was really tired. I wanted to get my work done. We had mail piled up. I wanted to spend time with my law clerks. But she kept insisting that I join [the budding group] for lunch. 'Clarence, you should join us for lunch now.' " Thomas said he eventually did. Then, after Ginsburg and Breyer came on the Court in 1993 and 1994, respectively, and as O'Connor persisted, all nine began dining together. "Now, you have a group of people who really enjoy each other's company," said Thomas. "And I think it's because of Justice O'Connor's insistence."[24]

O'CONNOR ARRIVED in Washington knowing how to count votes. The divided Court—and divided, polarized nation—played to her strength as a consensus builder and gave her a way to be "constructive," as she might say. Once she found the middle, she never left it. She developed an incremental approach, taking her cues from the country and pushing it ever so slightly. She would neither drive the culture of the nation, nor seriously upset it.

O'Connor brushed off questions about her own influence. "There's only nine of us, so everyone has a very key vote," she said. "It's not a question about gaining power or influence. We try to persuade by the strength of the argument in a particular case."[25]

She declined to acknowledge her decisive presence. But that was part of her way. She shaped the law with her Western pragmatism, her feel for the American center—and a shrewd but quiet negotiating skill. She remained a complex figure: the savvy politician, a mother of three sons, a breast cancer survivor, and a wife to a man who gave up much of his own career for hers and with whom she had shared life's vicissitudes. She cast herself as merely "the right person, at the right time, in the right place. . . . In short, one must be lucky." It was a remark that evoked Brooklyn Dodgers general manager Branch Rickey's adage: "Luck is the residue of design."[26]

At the end of one interview, she paused at the entryway of her expansive suite and pointed to one of her favorite pictures from the day she was sworn in, September 25, 1981. In it, she stands, smiling broadly, with the eight men whom she joined. "There are only three of us left," she said at the time, referring to herself, Rehnquist, and Stevens. "It's so different now. As Justice [Byron] White used to say, when you change one justice, you change the whole Court."[27]

Her appointment, more than most, transformed it.

EPILOGUE

Sandra Day O'Connor announced her retirement from the Supreme Court on July 1, 2005. She had been on the bench a year short of a quarter century and seemed in her prime. Ordinary Americans had no inkling that she was contemplating retirement; neither did her colleagues on the Supreme Court.[1]

"I was surprised," Justice Antonin Scalia said. "I think I heard it on the radio on the way into chambers."[2] O'Connor's announcement came as the media focused on Chief Justice William Rehnquist, who had been coping with thyroid cancer since the previous October. He had undergone a tracheotomy to make it easier to breathe but still spoke haltingly and with obvious difficulty. If anyone appeared ready to retire it was the 80-year-old Chief Justice. But, as the term ended in late June, Rehnquist decided to stay as long as his health allowed.[3]

Justice O'Connor said through the Court's public information office that she wanted to spend more time with her husband John. It was a small acknowledgement that her husband of 53 years was ill. She never used the word Alzheimer's, but what had been recognized in Washington legal circles quickly found its way into national news reports. Senator Arlen Specter, a Republican from Pennsylvania and chairman of the Senate Judiciary Committee, said at a press conference on July 1 that it was "well known" that John suffered from Alzheimer's Disease.[4]

There was some symmetry in Justice O'Connor's retiring because of her husband. Twenty-four years earlier, John had compromised on his legal career when the couple moved to Washington. He had relinquished an impressive partnership at a Phoenix law firm, and the positions he took in Washington never offered the professional opportunities he had enjoyed in Arizona.[5]

Some feminists reacted to O'Connor's retirement as if it were a betrayal of their cause. But O'Connor had never quite fit the image of a modern feminist.[6] As far back as 1982, Stanford University law professor Barbara Babcock had disparaged O'Connor's public statement that working women should put their families first. Babcock believed the assertion was preposterous because so many accomplished women lawyers of the day had succeeded by making career, not family, their priority. If O'Connor had been speaking of her own family life in 1982, she was carrying it out in the most consequential way in 2005.[7]

Justice O'Connor, on whose vote the Court pivoted in so many legal disputes, was certainly aware that her departure could affect the law in America. President George W. Bush had vowed to name someone in the mode of Justices Scalia and Thomas when a vacancy came open. Indeed, after Bush nominated John Roberts to succeed O'Connor, Justice Scalia observed that, "I may get a colleague whose philosophy is more congenial to mine." But, he added, "I don't think I'll get a colleague who could be any more pleasant or amiable and intent on keeping a good attitude at the Court."[8] In a great many ways, her absence would make a difference.

O'Connor, for her part, did not dwell on what might have been. In mid-July she flew to Istanbul for a legal conference. As she had done when faced with other life challenges—her breast cancer, the death of her parents, the sale of the Lazy B—she plunged ahead. With her usual matter-of-factness, she asked her audiences to move on, too.

Her first public appearance in the United States after her retirement announcement was in Spokane, Washington, on July 21, at the annual meeting of the 9th U.S. Circuit Court of Appeals. Responding to questions, she praised Ronald Reagan for upholding his promise to appoint a woman. Asked about highlights from her years at the Court, she was reluctant to single out cases. "I don't know what opinions that I've written are going to have lasting significance," she said. But then she added. "In terms of the terrorist threats that we face today, I was privileged to write in the [Yaser Esam] Hamdi case, in ways that may point a useful direction." The Court ruled that an American citizen captured by the U.S. military on the battlefield in Afghanistan and held as an enemy combatant was entitled to a hearing to challenge the claims against him. "It is during our most challenging and uncertain moments that our nation's commitment to due process is most severely tested," O'Connor wrote, "and it is in those times that we must preserve our commitment at home to the principles for which we fight abroad."[9]

In Spokane, she concluded with a favorite poem.[10] It was addressed to individuals who might believe they can never be replaced, or as O'Connor recited, those with an ego "in bloom" who believe they are "the best qualified in the room."

> *"Take a bucket, fill it with water,*
> *Put your hand in, up to the wrist*
> *Pull it out, and the hole that's remaining*
> *Is a measure of how you'll be missed."*

O'Connor's audience began applauding, but she held up her hand and firmly told them that she was not done.

> *"The moral in this quaint example*
> *Is do just the best that you can,*
> *Be proud of yourself, but remember,*
> *There is no indispensable . . .* (O'Connor paused just a second) *. . . woman."*

They all laughed. Sandra Day O'Connor left the stage smiling.

SIXTEEN YEARS EARLIER, as O'Connor was dealing with the shock of a breast cancer diagnosis and several difficult cases, she wrote her colleagues a note that began, "The unexpected has become the order of the day." That refrain suited the events of early September 2005 as the nation reeled from the devastation of Hurricane Katrina. Rehnquist, who had told O'Connor he expected to begin the new term on the first Monday of October, died on the night of September 3. Two days later, President Bush withdrew the nomination of John Roberts for O'Connor's impending vacancy. He wanted Roberts to take the chief justice's position instead. President Bush suggested that he would not have to act immediately to fill O'Connor's seat because, in announcing her retirement, she had said that she would stay on the bench until her successor was confirmed.

On September 6, pallbearers carried Rehnquist's flag-draped casket up the marble steps of the Supreme Court, between two lines of justices and other dignitaries. An indelible image from the scene was O'Connor's tear-streaked face. Her longtime friend was gone. The sadness of her visage was captured on the front pages of the nation's newspapers the next morning. But by then, the day of Rehnquist's funeral service, O'Connor had turned to the task at hand. She would lead off the tributes to the chief justice at the historic St. Matthew's Cathedral. When it was time, once again, for O'Connor to take the stage, she was ready. The choir had barely finished the last note of its preceding piece, "Faith of Our Fathers," when she was on her feet. Beneath the vaulted ceiling and vibrant mosaics, she walked purposefully to the lectern. Her remarks were upbeat, not heartrending. With warmth and humor she recounted their many decades together, highlighting Rehnquist's brilliant but unpretentious side. "The chief was a betting man," she concluded. "I think the chief bet he could live out another term despite his illness. He lost that bet, as did all of us, but he won all the prizes for a life well lived."

Then, at the end of the day, after a hearse had carried Rehnquist's casket to Arlington National Cemetery, Sandra Day O'Connor returned to the Court to continue the work that was hers.

ACKNOWLEDGMENTS

This book benefits from the guidance and support of many professional colleagues, friends, and family. Four talented people were with me from the beginning, unstinting in their encouragement and generous with their time: Lou Cannon, Pam Fessler, Phyllis Richman, and Roberto Suro. With their deep experience as authors and their diverse views, they were a constant source of advice on Justice O'Connor's trajectory in American law and politics. All of them offered support that went far beyond the call of friendship. Lou, with his expertise as Ronald Reagan's biographer, rendered early guidance on my outline and sent comments from California right up to publication. No one could have sought a better counselor. In the final months of this project, many veteran writers and editors offered helpful suggestions on the manuscript: Douglas Armstrong, Richard Carelli, Alan Ehrenhalt, David Maraniss, Robin Meszoly and Phillippa Strum.

Throughout my research, this book also benefited from the work of my fellow reporters on the Supreme Court beat, past and present. One person deserves to be singled out: Fred Barbash, who covered the Court for The Washington Post at the time of the O'Connor nomination. He was my editor in the 1990s, and his talent for making esoteric subjects accessible remains my model. In the same vein, Elder Witt, my co-author on Supreme Court reference books through Congressional Quarterly, was an invaluable source of wisdom.

Several libraries and archives, as cited in my note on sources, were the foundation for this biography. The Arizona State Library's archives division at the state capitol offered a trove of well-organized documents from Senator O'Connor's legislative years. Three other collections merit special mention for the many hours I logged in their files and the assistance of their archivists over many months: John Jacob at the Powell Archives at Washington and Lee University; the innumerable professionals at the Library of Congress, where the papers of Justices William Brennan, Harry Blackmun and Thurgood Marshall are housed; and Donna Colletta and her colleagues at the Arizona Republic newspaper library. The devotion of these men and women to the historical record is inspiring. I have special gratitude toward the executors of the Brennan estate who gave me access to files not generally open to the public. These materials, as well as conversations with Brennan biographer Stephen Wermiel, were invaluable in my understanding of the relationship between Justice O'Connor and Justice Brennan at a crucial time in their tenure. At the Supreme Court, Kathy Arberg, and the public information staff, and Steve Petteway, Court photographer, met my many queries with speed and unfailing professionalism.

Seven of Justice O'Connor's eight colleagues broke from their usual aversion to the press to sit for interviews, which significantly augmented my understanding of Justice O'Connor. Countless family and friends of hers went out of their way to help, but two made a noteworthy contribution: O'Connor's brother, Alan Day, and her son, Jay O'Connor. They clarified many points of family history and enhanced my understanding of the woman beneath the black robe.

Two lawyers who argue often before the justices rendered incalculable assistance. Duke University law professor Erwin Chemerinsky offered thoughtful guidance for distilling the intricacies of the law. And in an act of supreme generosity, Richard Taranto, a former law clerk to O'Connor, lent his keen insight and legal precision to the manuscript. If mistakes remain, they are mine alone.

Two institutions provided grants that helped with research and travel. The Woodrow Wilson International Center for Scholars, under the leadership of the Honorable Lee Hamilton, twice awarded me in-residence scholarships. While at the Wilson Center, I was aided by research assistants Gavin Fields and Christopher Laskowski. Stanford University's Hoover Institution offered me fellowships to conduct research at the campus that made such a difference in Sandra Day O'Connor's life.

At USA Today, my wise editor David Lindsey was unfailingly supportive of this book. Its completion is owed to his indulgence of my leaves of absence. I am also indebted to Washington Bureau Chief Susan Page and my colleagues who were enthusiastic about this project from the start. Reporter Richard Willing was generous in filling in for me on the Supreme Court beat and then relinquishing a gem of an assignment when I returned. My deep appreciation extends to Editor Ken Paulson, Executive Editor John Hillkirk, and Managing Editor for News Editor Carol Stevens, under whose leadership I was able to step away from daily journalism and engage in deeper research on the Supreme Court.

At the Ecco imprint of HarperCollins, Dan Halpern and Gheña Glijansky provided first-rate editorial guidance. When they decided to accelerate production of this book because of Justice O'Connor's announced retirement, they worked overtime to keep the quality high. Gheña deserves special praise for handling with such skill and enthusiasm—and late hours—a project she inherited only in its final months when my first editor Julia Serebrinsky went on maternity leave (with twins!). My agent David Black had the very smart instinct two years ago that Ecco would be the perfect house for this project, and he was right. David also offered crucial advice when I was drafting the proposal, which, in a testament to his thinking, ended up executed almost exactly as we envisioned it—except for the small detail of a retirement.

I tried not to let this book dominate my household and relations with my family. I failed. My parents, Mary Jane and Vince Biskupic, were thoroughly supportive and offered their expertise on the law and language. My eight younger siblings were encouraging at every stage. In a class of her own was my sister-in-law, Cary Biskupic, a law librarian who flew to Washington and worked around the clock with me to double-check more than a thousand end-notes that had to be completed immediately when the production schedule changed. No one could have asked for a smarter, more cheerful partner.

My husband, Clay Lewis, and daughter Elizabeth remained founts of enthusiasm through my months of distraction. Clay, an author and former English professor, read the manuscript and helped with the narrative. Elizabeth offered the sage advice that could only come from a middle-schooler: "Please don't make it like books that people use only to look up things. Make it interesting." To the two most interesting, wonderful individuals, Clay and Elizabeth, this book is dedicated.

AUTHOR'S NOTE AND
INFORMATION ON SOURCES

This book is the product of more than two hundred interviews and my reading of thousands of once-private Supreme Court documents. All but one of Justice O'Connor's eight present colleagues on the Supreme Court sat for interviews, and I have conducted many interviews with her brother and sister, sons, friends, and former colleagues. I have been to the Lazy B ranch.

Justice O'Connor declined several written requests to meet with me for this book. On earlier occasions, in 2002 and 2003, however, I interviewed her in her chambers. I have made plentiful use of those transcripts and my records from sixteen years as a Supreme Court correspondent. Since the 1988–1989 term, I have covered Justice O'Connor on a regular basis, for *Congressional Quarterly,* the *Washington Post,* and *USA Today.* My colleagues at other news organizations have been generous with their insights, as have many of Justice O'Connor's former law clerks.

But the most fruitful source has been the correspondence contained in files at the Arizona Capitol, where she was a state senator; at the Ronald Reagan Library, documenting her 1981 nomination; and in the archives of her former Supreme Court colleagues, Justices William J. Brennan Jr., Thurgood Marshall, Harry A. Blackmun, and Lewis F. Powell Jr. These papers have allowed me to see Sandra Day O'Connor as she expressed herself in private and on her less guarded days.

After the publication of the *Lazy B* memoir, I asked Justice O'Connor how writing a personal history had changed her. "I don't think this changed me," she said somewhat impatiently. "I tried to remember my life, to put it down on paper. I spend my life putting things on paper." When her second book, a collection of her views of the law, was published, I observed that she did not reveal her feelings about breaking down barriers as the first woman justice. "I'm more of a doer," she said. "There's not a lot of introspection at the Lazy B or in my life generally."

Mindful of such resistance, I have tried nonetheless to understand this important woman's motivations. This book is not intended to be a comprehensive review of all of her decisions. My emphasis is her ascension in the legislative and judicial realms. Justice O'Connor's final legacy will only be understood with time.

NOTES

PROLOGUE

1. William French Smith, "History of the Nomination of Justice Sandra Day O'Connor," January 7, 1985, Ronald Reagan Library; William French Smith, *Law and Justice in the Reagan Administration: The Memoir of an Attorney General* (Stanford, California: Hoover Institution Press, 1991), pp. 62–69; author's interviews with Fred Fielding, Ken Starr, Edwin Meese.

2. David S. Broder, "Reagan Wounded by Assailant's Bullet; Prognosis is 'Excellent'; 3 Others Shot," *Washington Post,* March 31, 1981; Terence Hunt, "President Wounded in Assassination Attempt," Associated Press, March 30, 1981.

3. Smith, *Law and Justice,* p. 65.

4. Author's interview with John Driggs.

5. Steven R. Weisman, "Stewart Will Quit High Court July 3; Reasons Not Given," *New York Times,* June 19, 1981; Kevin M. Costelloe, "A Judge Is a Judge Is a Judge, Says Stewart," Associated Press, June 19, 1981.

6. Author's interview with F. Henry Habicht.

7. Nofziger to Reagan, June 22, 1981, Ronald Reagan Library.

8. Author's interviews with Ken Starr and Edwin Meese.

9. "Candidates Hail Turnout of 200 at Camelback High," *Arizona Republic,* September 30, 1970; "Variety of Styles," *Arizona Republic,* November 8, 1977; Sarah Auffret, "Looking Good," *Arizona Republic,* November 27, 1979.

10. Jeffrey P. Haney, "O'Connor Enthralls Y. Crowd," *Deseret News,* September 27, 2002.

11. Author's interview with Ken Starr.

12. Smith, *Law and Justice,* p. 67.

13. Ibid.

14. Author's interview with Reagan administration official on background; Sandra Day O'Connor, *The Majesty of the Law: Reflections of a Supreme Court Justice* (New York: Random House, 2003), p. 198.

15. Smith, *Law and Justice,* p. 68; author's interview with Fred Fielding.

1. PIONEER ROOTS

1. Sandra Day O'Connor and H. Alan Day, *Lazy B* (New York: Random House, 2002), p. 95. Harry had been in Tucson on business when Sandra was born. He came to El Paso, stayed one night, and then returned to the Lazy B.

2.   Harry Day to Ada Mae Day, September 17, 1928, Day family papers, Arizona Historical Society.

3.   Thomas E. Sheridan, *Arizona: A History* (Tucson, Arizona: University of Arizona Press, 1995), p. 126; Marshall Trimble, *Arizona: A Cavalcade of History* (Tucson, Arizona: Rio Nuevo Publishers, 2003), p. 162.

4.   O'Connor, *Lazy B,* p. ix; Peter Huber, *Sandra Day O'Connor* (New York: Chelsea House, 1990), p. 21.

5.   Found by author in Day family papers, Arizona Historical Society.

6.   Author's interview with Alan Day.

7.   Alice Day to Harry Day, May 23, 1925, Day family papers, Arizona Historical Society.

8.   Alice Day to Harry Day, August 1, 1925, Day family papers, Arizona Historical Society.

9.   Courtland Day to Harry Day, September 12, 1927. On letterhead titled H.C. Day and Son, Stock Growers. Day family papers, Arizona Historical Society.

10.   O'Connor wrote in *Lazy B* that her parents were married by a justice of the peace; papers in the family archive refer to marriage by a Presbyterian minister.

11.   Harry Day to Eleanor Day, September 19, 1927, Day family papers, Arizona Historical Society.

12.   O'Connor, *Lazy B,* p. 94.

13.   David M. Kennedy, *Freedom From Fear: The American People in Depression and War, 1929–1945* (New York: Oxford University Press, 1999) p. 85.

14.   Harry Day to Eleanor Day, October 26, 1958, Day family papers, Arizona Historical Society.

15.   "Coast Cattle Market Slow"; John P. Boughan, "Wheat Prices Fail to Hold," *Tucson Daily Citizen,* March 26, 1930; "Unemployment in March Improves," *Arizona Daily Star,* March 26, 1930; Kirke Simpson, "Washington Bystander," *Arizona Daily Star,* March 26, 1930.

16.   "Justice Taft Dies," *Tucson Daily Citizen,* March 9, 1930.

17.   O'Connor, *Lazy B,* p. 25.

18.   Ibid; author's interview with Alan Day. Some legal documents remain in the Day family papers.

19.   O'Connor, *Lazy B,* p. 37.

20.   Author's interview with Alan Day.

21.   O'Connor, *Lazy B,* p. 43.

22.   Author's interview with Alan Day.

23.   Wallace Stegner, *Angle of Repose* (New York: Penguin Books, 1992), p. 134.

24.   Harry Day to Courtland Day, May 18, 1936, Day family papers, Arizona Historical Society.

25.   Author's interview with Alan Day.

26.   *Lochner v. People of State of New York,* 198 U.S. 45 (1905).

27.   *Railroad Retirement Board v. Alton Railroad Co.,* 295 U.S. 330 (1935); *A.L.A. Schechter Poultry Corp. v. United States,* 295 U.S. 495 (1935).

28.   William E. Leuchtenburg, *The Supreme Court Reborn: The Constitutional Revolution in the Age of Roosevelt* (New York: Oxford University Press, 1995) p. 90.

29.   Joan Biskupic and Elder Witt, *"Congressional Quarterly's Guide to the Supreme Court*

(Washington, DC: Congressional Quarterly, 1997), vol 1., p. 249. The Four Horsemen: Willis Van Devanter, James C. McReynolds, George Sutherland, and Pierce Butler.

30. Leuchtenburg, *Supreme Court Reborn,* p. 108.

31. Ted Morgan, *FDR: A Biography* (New York: Simon and Schuster, 1985), p. 471.

32. *West Coast Hotel Co. v. Parrish,* 300 U.S. 379 (1937).

33. Sandra O'Connor's interview with the Phoenix History Project.

34. Author's interviews with Alan Day, Jay O'Connor, Sandra Day O'Connor.

35. O'Connor, *Lazy B,* p. xi. The nicknames came from younger sister Ann's attempts to spell. She began calling her dad D-A and her mother M-O.

36. Ibid, p. 115.

37. Sandra O'Connor's interview with the Phoenix History Project.

38. Author's interviews with Molly Joyce (Flournoy's daughter) and Ann Day.

39. Author's interview with Molly Joyce, who also provided written comments about Sandra and Flournoy's childhood to the author.

40. Mamie Wilkey to Sandra and Flournoy, undated, Day family papers, Arizona Historical Society.

41. O'Connor, *Lazy B,* p. 41.

42. Michael Pollack, "A Gallery of Memories," *New York Times,* January 7, 1996.

43. "People in the News," Associated Press, May 13, 1987.

44. Author's interview with Ann Day.

45. Author's interview with Alan Day.

46. Alan and Ann overcame their bumpy childhoods. Ann earned bachelor's and master's degrees in education from Arizona State University and the University of Arizona, respectively; she was elected to the Arizona State Senate and, later, the Pima County Board of Supervisors. Alan earned a bachelor's degree in business administration from the University of Arizona and ran the Lazy B for three decades. When the ranch was sold, he became an investor in other property.

47. O'Connor, *Lazy B,* p. 117–118.

48. Nomination of Sandra Day O'Connor, Senate Judiciary Committee Hearing, September 9–11, 1981.

49. Author's interview with Alan Day.

50. Ibid.; O'Connor, *Lazy B,* pp. 240–243.

51. O'Connor, *Lazy B,* pp. 29–30.

52. Ibid., p. 29.

53. Author's interview with Alan Day.

54. Ibid.

55. Author's interview with Ann Day.

56. Author's interview with Alan Day.

57. Laura Krugman Ray, "Justices at Home: Three Supreme Court Memoirs," *Michigan Law Review* (2003), vol. 101, p. 2103.

2. "THE RULES OF THE GAME"

1. Author's interview with Alan Day.

2. *Stanford Daily,* September 23, 1946, and September 25, 1946.

3. Author's interview with Diane Cooley.

4. Stanford Quad Yearbook, 1950, p. 143.

5.　Sandra Day O'Connor and H. Alan Day, *Lazy B* (New York: Random House, 2002), p. 283.

6.　"Harry Rathbun, law professor, Founder of Creative Initiative Foundation and Beyond War, dies at 93," Business Wire, September 30, 1987; "Harry Rathbun: Co-Founded Beyond War Peace Movement," *Los Angeles Times,* October 1, 1987; Michael Taylor, "Emilia Lindeman Rathbun—innovative community activist," *San Francisco Chronicle,* October 15, 2004.

7.　After Sandra left campus, Rathbun founded the Beyond War Peace Movement and established the Creative Initiative, which focused on an individual's role on earth.

8.　Harry J. Rathbun, *The Anglo-American Legal System* (Stanford, California: Stanford University Press, 1941), p. iii.

9.　Author's interview with Sandra Day O'Connor.

10.　O'Connor, *Lazy B,* p. 283.

11.　Rathbun, *Anglo-American Legal System,* p. iv.

12.　"Times to Remember: Voices of Stanford Law," 1995 (VHS). Provided to author by Stanford Law School.

13.　Author's interview with Fred Steiner, who also provided a written reminiscence to the author.

14.　Author's interview with Sandra Day O'Connor.

15.　Author's interview with Fred Steiner.

16.　Author's interview with Diane Cooley.

17.　Author's interview with Jay O'Connor.

18.　"Times to Remember: Voices of Stanford Law."

19.　Author's interview with Jay O'Connor.

20.　Ibid.

21.　O'Connor, *Lazy B,* p. 285.

22.　"Engagement of Miss Day, John Jay O'Connor Announced," *El Paso Times,* October 8, 1952.

23.　"Weddings," *Lordsburg Liberal,* December 26, 1952.

24.　"Was O'Connor No. 3? School Now Not Sure," United Press International, July 13, 1981. Some reports at the time of her appointment said that she graduated third in her class, but Stanford officials later cleared the record and said rankings other than first in the class were not tracked. Additionally, a June 13, 1981, memo prepared by the White House Press Office noted "there were no actual rankings made of the class."

25.　O'Connor has said this on multiple occasions, including on June 11, 2004, when she obtained a Lifetime Achievement award from the State Bar Association of Arizona.

26.　By the time she came to the Supreme Court, John and Sandra O'Connor's financial disclosure forms showed that they had more than a million dollars in assets—making her the richest justice at the time.

27.　Dickson Hartwell, "Sandra: Feminity and Fact-Power Characterize Arizona's Pretty State Senator," *Phoenix Magazine,* February 1971.

28.　Sandra O'Connor's interview with the Phoenix History Project.

29.　Zachary A. Smith, *Politics and Public Policy in Arizona* (Westport, Connecticut: Praeger Publishers, 1996), p. 4.

30.　Thomas E. Sheridan, *Arizona: A History* (Tucson, Arizona: The University of Arizona Press, 1995), p. 281.

31.　Author's interview with Jay O'Connor.

32. Pat Smith, "Magazine Cupid for Lawyer Couple," *Arizona Republic,* September 27, 1957.

33. Sandra O'Connor's interview with the Phoenix History Project.

34. "Tobin, O'Connor Open Law Office in Maryvale," *Weekly Gazette,* April 1, 1958; author's interview with Tom Tobin.

35. Sandra O'Connor's interview with the Phoenix History Project.

36. Author's interview with Tom Tobin.

37. Sandra O'Connor's interview with the Phoenix History Project.

38. Sandra Day O'Connor, "Remarks to Associated Women Students at A.S.U.," May 1970.

39. Author's interview with John and Gail Driggs.

40. Election Poster, Phoenix Rotary Club, Day family papers, Arizona Historical Society.

41. Smith, *Politics and Public Policy in Arizona,* pp. 11–12.

42. Marshall Trimble, *Arizona: A Cavalcade of History* (Tucson, Arizona: Rio Nuevo Publishers, 2003), pp. 272–73.

43. Bradford Luckingham, *Phoenix: The History of a Southwestern Metropolis* (Tucson, Arizona: The University of Arizona Press, 1989), pp. 168–169, 175.

44. Robert Alan Goldberg, *Barry Goldwater* (New Haven, Connecticut: Yale University Press, 1995), p. 88. Goldberg also wrote, "In one instance, Phoenix attorney and Young Republican William Rehnquist was ordered away from a polling place when he demanded that African-Americans read from the Constitution before being allowed to mark their ballots." This widely asserted claim, disputed by Rehnquist, would become a subject of his Supreme Court confirmation screening in 1971 and 1986.

45. *Colegrove v. Green,* 328 U.S. 549 (1946).

46. *Baker v. Carr,* 369 U.S. 186 (1962); *Reynolds v. Sims,* 377 U.S. 533 (1964).

47. Trimble, *Arizona: A Cavalcade of History,* p. 273.

48. "O'Connor Recalls First Impression with Goldwater," *Arizona Republic,* December 3, 1986.

49. Goldberg, *Barry Goldwater,* p. 133.

50. From a speech at Madison Square Garden, May 12, 1964 (facts on file, May 21–27, 1964).

51. Sandra O'Connor's interview with the Phoenix History Project.

52. Ibid.

53. Ibid.

54. Author's interview with Jay O'Connor.

55. Sandra O'Connor's interview with the Phoenix History Project.

56. Ibid.

57. O'Connor, "Remarks to Associated Women Students at A.S.U.," legislator's papers, Arizona State Library, Archives and Public Records."

58. Sandra Day O'Connor, *The Majesty of the Law: Reflections of a Supreme Court Justice* (New York: Random House, 2003), pp. 200–201.

3. A SUPREME COURT OPENING

1. Author's interview with John Driggs (former mayor); "39 Appointed to New Unit," *Arizona Republic,* September 29, 1971; "39 Appointed to historical commission," *Phoenix Gazette,* September 29, 1971.

2. Bernie Wynn, "Equality Redistricting Plan Acceptable to Senate GOP," *Arizona Republic,* October 6, 1971; Lois Boyles, "Legislature Expects to Finish Work Today," *Phoenix Gazette,* October 21, 1971; Bernie Wynn, "Legislature Set to Adjourn This Afternoon," *Arizona Republic,* October 22, 1971. "Figures Tell Redistricting Story," *Arizona Republic* editorial, October 24, 1971. "Any political party worth the name would be foolish to do otherwise," the *Arizona Republic* intoned in the editorial after Democrats complained that the GOP-dominated legislature's maps were politically inspired.

3. Sandra Day O'Connor, "Remarks to Associated Women Students at A.S.U.," May 1970.

4. "Family Rose to Occasion for Sandra," *Phoenix Gazette,* March 26, 1970.

5. Author's interview with John Driggs.

6. The amendment would not be sent to the states for another year, but was already the subject of controversy in the states.

7. Senator Sandra Day O'Connor, legislator's papers, Arizona State Library, Archives and Public Records.

8. Dickson Hartwell, "Sandra: Femininity and Fact-Power Characterize Arizona's Pretty State Senator," *Phoenix Magazine,* February 1971.

9. Author's interview with John Driggs.

10. Nixon tapes, No. 580–13.

11. Ibid.

12. Nixon tapes, No. 11–1.

13. Nixon tapes, No. 12–15.

14. Ibid.

15. "Rehnquist Appointment: Setback Claimed for Civil Rights," *Phoenix Gazette,* October 22, 1971.

16. *Congressional Quarterly Almanac,* 1971, vol. 27, p. 852.

17. "Comments of William Rehnquist at the Public Hearing on the Public Accommodations Ordinance Proposed for the City of Phoenix," June 15, 1964.

18. "Minister, Wife Swear Rehnquist Harassed Voters," *Phoenix Gazette,* November 25, 1971; Arthur S. Miller, "Study of William Rehnquist Reveals Series of Paradoxical Qualities," *Arizona Republic,* November 9, 1971.

19. "Rehnquist Appointment," *Phoenix Gazette.*

20. Author's interview with Cloves Campbell; Cloves C. Campbell Sr., *I Refused to Leave the 'Hood* (Phoenix, Arizona: Cloves C. Campbell Sr., 2002).

21. Author's interview with Cloves Campbell.

22. "Rehnquist Appointment," *Phoenix Gazette.*

23. Leon Friedman, "He Was a Very Elusive Target," *New York Times,* December 12, 1971.

24. O'Connor to Rehnquist, October 26, 1971, legislator's papers, Arizona State Library, Archives and Public Records.

25. Eugene Pulliam, "Will the Federal Bureaucracy Destroy Individual Freedom in America?" *Arizona Republic,* October 24, 1971; "Final Story: The Pulliam Era Ends," *Arizona Republic,* July 2, 2000.

26. Found by author in Day family papers, Arizona Historical Society.

27. O'Connor to Pulliam, October 27, 1971, legislator's papers, Arizona State Library, Archives and Public Records.

28. "Extract from Speech Oct. 28, 1971, by Senator O'Connor to Camelback Kiwanis Club," legislator's papers, Arizona State Library, Archives and Public Records.

29. O'Connor to Rehnquist, October 29, 1971, legislator's papers, Arizona State Library, Archives and Public Records.

30. O'Connor to Holcomb, November 9, 1971, legislator's papers, Arizona State Library, Archives and Public Records.

31. Rehnquist to John and Sandra O'Connor, November 10, 1971, legislator's papers, Arizona State Library, Archives and Public Records.

32. "Woman Director: Mrs. O'Connor Is Bank's First," *Arizona Republic,* January 24, 1971.

33. O'Connor to Rehnquist, November 11, 1971, legislator's papers, Arizona State Library, Archives and Public Records.

34. *Congressional Quarterly Almanac,* 1971, p. 855.

35. "Rehnquist Refutes Dems on Harassing Voters," United Press International, November 21, 1971; Ben Cole, "Views Changed on Rights Law, Rehnquist Says," *Arizona Republic,* November 4, 1971.

36. "Supreme Court: Memo From Rehnquist," *Newsweek,* December 13, 1971. (The issue was available on newsstands a week earlier than its publication date.)

37. Rehnquist wrote to Senator Eastland that the memo was "not an accurate statement of my own view at the time." For a detailed discussion of the controversy, see Richard Kluger, *Simple Justice* (New York: Alfred A. Knopf, 1975, 2004), pp. 607–615.

38. Friedman, "Elusive Target."

39. Goldwater to Rehnquist, December 11, 1971, papers of Barry Goldwater, Arizona Historical Foundation, Arizona State University.

40. O'Connor to Hazeltine, January 11, 1972, legislator's papers, Arizona State Library, Archives and Public Records.

41. O'Connor to Mrs. John H. (Cynthia) Hall, January 13, 1972, legislator's papers, Arizona State Library, Archives and Public Records.

42. John W. Dean, *The Rehnquist Choice* (New York: Touchstone, 2002), p. 285.

43. Ralph Dunagin, *Orlando Sentinel* cartoon, November 10, 1971.

4. "NEVER ONE OF THE BOYS"

1. Margaret Thomas, "Valleyites Welcome Summer with Square Dancing Party," *Arizona Republic,* June 12, 1972.

2. Margaret Thomas, "Bridge Over the River," *Arizona Republic,* February 2, 1972.

3. Author's interview with Sharon Rockefeller. Rockefeller is the daughter of Illinois Senator Charles Percy and the wife of West Virginia Senator John J. Rockefeller IV. She became president and CEO of WETA, the public television station in Washington, D.C.

4. "Woman-Work Bill Passes Senate by Single Vote," *Phoenix Gazette,* February 27, 1970.

5. "1972 Phoenix Man & Woman of the Year," Phoenix Advertising Club, Inc., 24th Annual Awards Banquet, February 7, 1973, legislator's papers, Arizona State Library, Archives and Public Records.

6. Harry Day to Eleanor Day, October 26, 1985, Day family papers, Arizona Historical Society.

7. Author's interview with Sam Mardian.

8. Author's interview with Thomas C. Reed.

9. O'Connor to Reed, June 15, 1972, legislator's papers, Arizona State Library, Archives and Public Records.

10. O'Connor to Goldwater, August 29, 1972, legislator's papers, Arizona State Library, Archives and Public Records.

11. Jerry Kammer, *The Second Long Walk: The Navajo-Hopi Land Dispute* (Albuquerque, New Mexico: University of New Mexico Press, 1980), pp. 98–99.

12. Ibid.

13. O'Connor to Zelman, November 3, 1972, legislator's papers, Arizona State Library, Archives and Public Records.

14. Goldwater to O'Connor, September 9, 1972, legislator's papers, Arizona State Library, Archives and Public Records.

15. O'Connor to Goldwater, September 18, 1972, legislator's papers, Arizona State Library, Archives and Public Records.

16. *Congressional Quarterly Almanac,* 1972, vol. 28, p. 1013. Nixon won all eleven states of the old Confederacy and all the border states.

17. Ibid., p. 1014, Of major party vote: Nixon won 67 percent; Mc Govern, 33 percent.

18. Reed to Armstrong, October 27, 1972, legislator's papers, Arizona State Library, Archives and Public Records.

19. Author's interview with Thomas Reed.

20. Don Bolles, "Akers Named House Speaker; Sen. O'Connor Gets Key Role," *Arizona Republic,* November 9, 1972.

21. Bernie Wynn, "A Woman May Lead Arizona Senate GOP," *Arizona Republic,* July 21, 1972.

22. Ibid.

23. Bernie Wynn, "House GOP Can Boast of Its Leaders," *Arizona Republic,* November 12, 1972.

24. Theodore A. Rushton, "State Senate Majority Leader: Mrs. O'Connor Meets Challenge of a Tough Job, *Tucson Daily Citizen,* March 16, 1973. See also Howard E. Boice Jr., "Floor Debate Tests Senate Majority Chief," *Arizona Republic,* February 5, 1973.

25. Thomas E. Sheridan, *Arizona: A History* (Tucson, Arizona: The University of Arizona Press, 1995), pp. 317–53; Marshall Trimble, *Arizona: A Calvalcade of History* (Tucson, Arizona: Rio Nuevo Publishers, 2003), pp. 268–289.

26. *Roe v. Wade,* 410 U.S. 113 (1973).

27. Author's interview with Carolyn Gerster (National Right to Life Committee).

28. "Senate Rules Next: Committee Moves on Abortion Bill," *Phoenix Gazette,* April 29, 1970; Howard E. Boice Jr., "Abortion Bill Clears Senate Judiciary Panel, *Arizona Republic,* April 30, 1970.

29. "3 Catholic Bishops Issue Statement Calling Abortion Bill 'Moral Evil,' " *Arizona Republic,* February 23, 1970.

30. "Clergymen Seek Open Hearings on Abortion Bill," *Arizona Republic,* March 25, 1970; Howard E. Boice Jr., "Abortion Reform Fails to Clear Rules Unit," *Arizona Republic,* May 1, 1970.

31. "Memorial Advanced by Panel," *Phoenix Gazette,* April 22, 1974.

32. "Curb On Abortion Added to UA Bill," *Phoenix Gazette,* April 3, 1994; "Abortion Ban, VA Stadium Bill signed," *Phoenix Gazette,* May 16, 1974.

33. *Congressional Quarterly Almanac,* 1972, vol. 28, pp. 199–202.

34. Goldwater to O'Connor, April 10, 1972, legislator's papers, Arizona State Library, Archives and Public Records.

35. "Women Defend Goldwater on Insulting Quip," *Arizona Republic,* August 15, 1974.

36. "Senate Maneuvers into Equal Rights Debate," *Phoenix Gazette,* March 24, 1972.

37. "Variety of Styles," *Arizona Republic,* November 8, 1977.

38. Paul Schatt, "Seesawing Senators Spell Death to Equal Rights Bill," *Arizona Republic,* March 6, 1973.

39. "Women Stage Capitol Rally, Protest Rights Amendment," *Phoenix Gazette,* February 4, 1974; Ginger Hutton, "At the Capitol: Opposing ERA Forces Continue to Clash," *Arizona Republic,* February 8, 1974.

40. O'Connor's form response to inquiries from constituents concerning ERA, February 18, 1974, legislator's papers, Arizona State Library, Archives and Public Records.

41. "Equal Rights Referendum Held Illegal," *Phoenix Gazette,* March 20, 1974; "Statewide Vote Ruled Out on Equal Rights Proposal," *Arizona Republic,* March 21, 1974.

42. "Equal Rights Bill Rejected in Senate," *Arizona Republic,* April 2, 1974. The House Judiciary Committee had similarly rejected the measure.

43. Janet Sanford, "ERA: Is the Battle Lost?" *Phoenix Gazette,* February 12, 1974.

44. Cottin Pogrebin, " 'Dragon Lady' or 'Compassionate'?—Words from Her Friends and Colleagues," *Ms.,* October 1981.

45. Peter Huber, *Sandra Day O'Connor* (New York: Chelsea House, 1990), p. 40.

46. Author's interview with Diane Cooley.

47. Author's interviews with Jay O'Connor and Brian O'Connor.

48. As an adult, Brian would continue his pattern of adventure and, in 2003, climb Mount Everest.

49. Dorothy Goebel, "Doling Out Dollars . . . How Much Allowance?" *Phoenix Gazette,* June 5, 1974.

50. Sandra Day O'Connor, *The Majesty of the Law: Reflections of a Supreme Court Justice* (New York: Random House, 2003), p. 200.

51. Harry Day to Sandra Day O'Connor, February 9, 1972, Day family papers, Arizona Historical Society.

52. Ibid.

53. See, for example, Harry Day to Mamie Wilkey, February 25, 1958, Day family papers, Arizona Historical Society.

54. "Mrs. O'Connor Won't Seek Return to State Senate," *Phoenix Gazette,* April 24, 1974.

55. Howard Kohn, "Front and Center; On a Changing Supreme Court, Sandra Day O'Connor Has Emerged as a New Power, Especially on the Issue That Will Not Go Away: Abortion," *Los Angeles Times Magazine,* April 18, 1993.

56. Bob Woodward and Carl Bernstein, *The Final Days* (New York: Simon & Schuster, 1987), pp. 147–149.

57. Author's interviews with Jay O'Connor and Brian O'Connor.

58. Robert Alan Goldberg, *Barry Goldwater* (New Haven, Connecticut: Yale University Press, 1995).

59. Author's interview with John Driggs.

60. Ed Magnuson, "Aftermath of a Burglary: What Happened to the Cast of a Political Drama," *Time,* June 14, 1982.

61. "Sandra O'Connor to Run for New Superior Court," *Phoenix Gazette,* May 23, 1974.

62. John Kolbe, "Court Race Turns into a Scorcher," *Phoenix Gazette,* September 4, 1974.

63. Ibid.

64. Campaign literature, Day family papers, Arizona Historical Society.

65. Anthony Sommer, "O'Connor, McDonald Oust 2 Incumbent Judges," *Phoenix Gazette,* September 11, 1974.

66. Linda Kauss, "A Day in Court With Judge Sandra O'Connor," *Phoenix Gazette,* September 18, 1975.

67. Edythe Jensen, "Tearful Scene in Courtroom: Realtor, Mother of Two Given Prison Term on Check Forgeries," *Phoenix Gazette,* August 2, 1978.

68. Huber, *Sandra Day O'Connor,* p. 46.

69. John Kolbe, "Pressured by GOP: Judge O'Connor Urged to Run for Governor," *Phoenix Gazette,* March 30, 1978; John Kolbe, "Republicans Have Their Backs to the Wall," *Phoenix Gazette,* April 3, 1978.

70. John Kolbe, "State GOP Searching for that 'Right Someone,' " *Phoenix Gazette,* September 8, 1977; Bernie Wynn, "Sandra O'Connor to run for Governor—with 3 IFs," *Arizona Republic,* March 31, 1978.

71. "New GOP Leadership." *Arizona Republic,* September 27, 1978; Bernie Wynn, "GOP Chief Denies Seeking to Stop Judge's Candidacy," *Arizona Republic,* April 4, 1978.

72. John Kolbe, "State GOP is Humpty Dumpty Case," *Phoenix Gazette,* July 27, 1978.

73. John Kolbe, "O'Connor Rejects Governor's Race," *Phoenix Gazette,* April 4, 1978.

74. John Kolbe, "O'Connor's Decision Still Reverberating in GOP," *Phoenix Gazette,* April 17, 1978.

75. Author's interview with John Driggs.

76. Author's interview with Gail Driggs.

77. Author's interviews with John Driggs, Gail Driggs, and Mark Cannon.

78. Author's interview with Bruce Babbitt; Edythe Jensen, "Judge O'Connor on the Move Again," *Phoenix Gazette,* November 30, 1979.

79. Author's interview with John Driggs.

80. O'Connor to Cannon, December 9, 1979, transcribed by Cannon and provided to author.

5. REAGAN'S CHOICE

1. Wesley G. Pippert, "Carter Concentrates on Industrial States," United Press International, October 11, 1980; Martin Shram and David S. Broder, "Reagan's Gears Locked as President Pulls Even," *Washington Post,* October 17, 1980.

2. Author's interview with Stuart Spencer.

3. Ibid. Fallout from Reagan's opposition to the ERA was bringing picketers to his rallies.

4. News release, October 14, 1980, Ronald Reagan Library.

5. Lou Cannon, "Reagan Pledges He Would Name a Woman to the Supreme Court," *New York Times,* October 15, 1980.

6. Steven R. Weisman, "President Sees Politics in Reagan Vow to Put Woman on High Court, *New York Times,* October 16, 1980.

7. Edward Walsh, "Education Nominee Told Her Chances for Supreme Court Not Precluded," *Washington Post,* October 31, 1979. After Hufstedler was appointed, President Carter named Mary Schroeder, then an Arizona appellate court jurist, to the Ninth Circuit. O'Connor was appointed to the Schroeder vacancy by Governor Babbitt.

8. Hedrick Smith, "Carter and Reagan Voicing Confidence on Debate Showing," *New York Times,* October 30, 1980; "General News" poll report, United Press International, October 31, 1980.

9. Ed Magnuson, "The Brethren's First Sister: A Supreme Court Nominee—and a Triumph for Common Sense," *Time,* July 20, 1981.

10. Author's interview with Fred Fielding.

11. Annenberg to Deaver, January 22, 1981, Ronald Reagan Library.

12. Nixon tapes, No. 580–13.

13. Author's interview with Fred Fielding.

14. Author's interview with Mark Cannon.

15. Transcript, interview of Sandra Day O'Connor for KAET *Horizon* television program, November 27, 2002.

16. Author's interviews with Dennis DeConcini and Kevin Costelloe.

17. Author's interview with Dennis DeConcini.

18. Author's interview with F. Henry Habicht.

19. Ford to Reagan, June 25, 1981, Ronald Reagan Library.

20. William French Smith, *Law and Justice in the Reagan Administration: The Memoirs of an Attorney General* (Stanford, California: Hoover Institution Press, 1991), p. 70.

21. Smith, *Law and Justice,* p. 70.

22. Borcherdt to Fielding, June 26, 1981, Ronald Reagan Library.

23. Author's interview with Ken Starr.

24. Author's interview with Edwin Meese.

25. KAET interview.

26. Smith died in 1990, and Reagan died in 2004 after a long struggle with Alzheimer's disease. Neither was able to be interviewed about how Reagan might have first received O'Connor's name.

27. Author's interview with Robert McConnell.

28. The next morning's *Washington Post* quoted officials saying O'Connor was the leading candidate on a short list, most of them women, for Stewart's seat.

29. There were many superficial similarities between the two women. Gerster was born in 1929, one year before O'Connor. Gerster entered the University of Oregon at about age 16 and graduated from its medical school at age 21. After internships and residency programs, Gerster joined the army to see Europe. She met her husband, a German, in Frankfurt. They eventually returned to Phoenix, believing it would be a good place to start a joint practice and raise a family. They had five boys.

30. Author's interview with Carolyn Gerster.

31. "Abortion Group Backs Reagan for President," Associated Press, January 20, 1980; author's interview with Carolyn Gerster.

32. Uhlmann to Meese, July 6, 1981, Ronald Reagan Library.

33. Voluminous correspondence expressing concerns about or opposition to O'Connor's appointment, Ronald Reagan Library.

34. Burger would change his vote, but not yet.

35. Fielding to Baker, July 6, 1981, Ronald Reagan Library.

36. Daily Diary of President Ronald Reagan, July 6, 1981, Ronald Reagan Library.

37. Author's interview with Sandra Day O'Connor.

38. "Remarks Announcing the Intention to Nominate Sandra Day O'Connor to Be an

Associate Justice of the Supreme Court of the United States," available through the University of Texas electronic archive, http://www.reagan.utexas.edu/resource/speeches/1981/70781a.htm.

39. "Honored by Post, Nominee Declares," *New York Times,* July 8, 1981; "Woman Named to Supreme Court Shows Off Family at News Conference," Associated Press, July 8, 1981.

40. B. Drummond Ayres Jr., " 'A Reputation for Excelling': Sandra Day O'Connor," *New York Times,* July 8, 1981.

41. Magnuson, "Brethren's First Sister."

42. KAET interview.

43. Sandra Day O'Connor and H. Alan Day, *Lazy B* (New York: Random House, 2002), p. 299.

44. Sam Negri, "Rancher Reflects on Early Years of Girl who Became a Judge," *Arizona Republic,* July 16, 1981.

45. Sandra Day O'Connor, *The Majesty of the Law: Reflections of a Supreme Court Justice* (New York: Random House, 2003), p. xv.

46. *The Nation* editorial reprinted in "For the Record," *Washington Post,* September 18, 1981; See also, Kevin Phillips, "O'Connor Choice New Double Standard," *El Paso Times,* July 20, 1981.

47. "O'Connor Is Endorsed by American Bar Panel," *Baltimore Sun,* September 9, 1981.

48. Author's interview with Mark Cannon.

49. Author's interview with Ken Starr.

50. Roland Evans and Robert Novak, "Why Did He Choose Her?" *Washington Post,* July 10, 1981.

51. Author's interview with Robert McConnell.

52. Magnuson, "Brethren's First Sister."

53. Friedersdorf to Reagan, July 8, 1981, Ronald Reagan Library.

54. White House Memorandum, undated, Ronald Reagan Library.

55. Mary McGrory, "An Honorable Choice," *Universal Press.* McGrory's column was syndicated through Universal Press. The *Washington Star* ceased publishing in August 1981, and McGrory's work began appearing in the *Washington Post.* "Announcement," *Washington Post,* August 8, 1981.

56. Fortas had received, and held for a number of months, a $20,000 honorarium for becoming a consultant to a charitable foundation headed by a former client. The payment was returned when the man was subsequently indicted. Hedrick Smith, "Reagan's Court Choice: A Deft Maneuver," *New York Times,* July 9, 1981.

57. Bill Peterson, "For Reagan and the New Right, the Honeymoon Is Over," *Washington Post,* July 12, 1981; Evans and Novak, "Why Did He Choose Her?" *Washington Post,* July 10, 1981.

58. Author's interview with Alan Day.

59. O'Connor, *The Majesty of the Law,* p. 198.

60. Powell's handwritten note to secretary, July 27, 1981, Lewis F. Powell Jr. Archives, Washington and Lee University.

61. Author's interview with Robert McConnell.

62. Ibid.

63. Friedersdorf to Baker, July 14, 1981, Ronald Reagan Library.

64. Author's interview with Robert McConnell.

65. Friedersdorf to Baker, Meese, Deaver, and Fielding, July 14, 1981, Ronald Reagan Library.

66. O'Connor, *The Majesty of the Law,* p. xii. .

67. Nomination of Sandra Day O'Connor, Senate Judiciary Committee Hearings, September 9–11, 1981. U.S. Government Printing Office, Washington, D.C., 1982. All subsequent quotations from hearings taken from GPO transcript.

68. Ellen Debenport, "Falwell Surprised at O'Connor's Conservatism," United Press International, September 14, 1981.

69. Ibid. Kevin Costelloe, "Biden to O'Connor: Speak Out, Don't Be Intimidated," Associated Press, September 10, 1981; Fred Barbash, "Judge O'Connor's Bravura Stirs a Throb in Conservative Hearts," *Washington Post,* September 13, 1981.

70. O'Connor, *The Majesty of the Law,* p. xii.

71. Reagan to D'Amato, September 15, 1981, Ronald Reagan Library.

72. Friedersdorf and Moore to Reagan, September 16, 1981, Ronald Reagan Library.

73. Fred Barbash, "O'Connor Confirmed as First Woman on Supreme Court," *Washington Post,* September 22, 1981.

6. THE MARBLE PALACE

1. Fred Barbash, "O'Connor Takes Oath as Justice," *Washington Post,* September 26, 1981; Robert Sangeorge, "A Woman in John Marshall's Chair," United Press International, September 25, 1981.

2. Powell's letter to his family, September 23, 1981; Powell's letter to Stewart, July 7, 1981, Lewis F. Powell Jr. Archives, Washington and Lee University.

3. Blackmun to Burger, November 17, 1980; Powell to Burger, November 17, 1980, Lewis F. Powell Jr. Archives, Washington and Lee University.

4. Burger to all justices, November 20, 1980, Lewis F. Powell Jr. Archives, .Washington and Lee University.

5. Sandra Day O'Connor and H. Alan Day, *Lazy B* (New York: Random House, 2002), p. x.

6. Richard Carelli, "Back to Work for Justice O'Connor," Associated Press, September 26, 1981.

7. Author's interviews with Ann Day and Alan Day.

8. Bill Roeder, "Sandra O'Connor's 'Mini-Inaugural,' " *Newsweek,* September 28, 1981.

9. "Back in Arizona," *Phoenix Gazette,* September 23, 1981.

10. O'Connor to Reagan, October 13, 1981, Ronald Reagan Library.

11. Pam Hait, "Sandra Day O'Connor Warm, Witty and Wise," *Ladies' Home Journal,* April 1982, vol. 99, no. 4, p. 40.

12. Author's interview with Ruth McGregor.

13. Ibid.

14. Original letter Blackmun to Powell, annotations on the letter were made by Powell and from Burger, August 12, 1931, Archive of Lewis F. Powell Jr., Washington and Lee University.

15. Author's interview with John Paul Stevens.

16. "Supreme Court Visitors' Theater Film Dialogue and Narration—As Edited," York Associates Television, Inc., December 1, 1996; for overview of how the Supreme Court works, see Joan Biskupic, "The Court of Last Resort: The 'Supremes' Are America's Ultimate Arbiters," *Washington Post,* October 9, 1996.

17.　Powell to Stewart and Rehnquist, July 13, 1978, Lewis F. Powell Jr. Archives, Washington and Lee University; David J. Garrow, "The Supreme Court and *The Brethren*," *Constitutional Commentary,* 2001, vol. 18, no. 2.

18.　Bob Woodward and Scott Armstrong, *The Brethren: Inside the Supreme Court* (New York: Simon and Schuster, 1979), p. 315.

19.　Rehnquist to Powell, January 18, 1985, Lewis F. Powell Jr. Archives, Washington and Lee University.

20.　Now the William Mitchell College of Law.

21.　Joan Biskupic, "Brennan Tribute Marks Opening of Study Center; Law School Facility to Stress Jurist's Coalition-Building Style," *Washington Post,* May 9, 1995.

22.　Joan Biskupic, "Justice Brennan, Voice of Court's Social Revolution, Dies," *Washington Post,* July 25, 1997.

23.　Brennan's note to all justices, September 10, 1979, papers of Harry A. Blackmun, Library of Congress.

24.　See Dennis J. Hutchinson, *The Man Who Once Was Whizzer White* (New York: The Free Press, 1998).

25.　"Sightings 'Round the City," *Washington Post,* December 28, 1981. Powell often quipped that he, not White, had been the first to dance with O'Connor.

26.　Juan Williams, *Thurgood Marshall: American Revolutionary* (New York: Random House, 1998), p. 375.

27.　Linda Greenhouse, *Becoming Justice Blackmun: Harry Blackmun's Supreme Court Journey* (New York: Times Books, 2005).

28.　Blackmun to Wong, September 11, 1981; Wong to Blackmun, September 11, 1981; Blackmun to Wong again, September 11, 1981, papers of Harry A Blackmun, Library of Congress.

29.　Confirmed by a justice with knowledge of the conversation.

30.　Powell to all justices, December 31, 1979, Lewis F. Powell Jr. Archives, Washington and Lee University.

31.　Recounted by Public Information Officer Toni House in her speeches. See "A Funny Thing Happened on the Way to the Bench," speech to National Conference of Court Public Information Officers, December 2, 1992. Provided to author by Court's Public Information Office.

32.　Rehnquist to Burger, July 2, 1981, Lewis F. Powell Jr. Archives, Washington and Lee University.

33.　Hait, "Sandra Day O'Connor."

34.　Linda Greenhouse, "The Supreme Court; Justice O'Connor Is Mostly With the Majority," *New York Times,* January 29, 1982.

35.　Powell's letter to his children, October 24, 1981, Lewis F. Powell Jr. Archives, Washington and Lee University.

36.　Aric Press and Diane Camper, "The Court's New Tough Guy," *Newsweek,* June 21, 1982.

37.　Lois Romano, "Justice on the Party Circuit; Sandra Day O'Connor Holds Court with the Capital's Elite," *Washington Post,* May 4, 1983.

38.　Hait, "Sandra Day O'Connor."

39.　It fell to lower-court judges to resolve initially any subsequent questions over whether ostensibly similar practices or policies could be distinguished under the Supreme Court precedent.

40. O'Connor to Burger in *Fair Assessment v. McNary,* October 19, 1980, Lewis F. Powell Jr. Archives, Washington and Lee University.

41. *FERC v. Mississippi,* 456 U.S. 742 (1982).

42. Sandra Day O'Connor, "Trends in the Relationship Between the Federal and State Courts from the Perspective of a State Judge," *William and Mary Law Review,* 1981, vol. 22, p. 802.

43. Kevin Costelloe, "Washington Deadline," Associated Press, November 2, 1981.

44. Powell to Rehnquist, April 3, 1981, Lewis F. Powell Jr. Archives, Washington and Lee University.

45. Lundy said that he had been denied the constitutional right to confront all the witnesses against him because the trial judge had limited his lawyer's questioning of the rape victim; that he had been denied a fair trial because of various statements made by the prosecutor; and that the trial judge had issued an erroneous instruction about the presumptive truth of witnesses.

46. Stevens to O'Connor, November 24, 1981; Blackmun to O'Connor, November 24, 1981, Lewis F. Powell Jr. Archives, Washington and Lee University.

47. *Fay v. Noia,* 372 U.S. 391 (1963); Brennan to O'Connor, November 25, 1981, Lewis F. Powell Jr. Archives, Washington and Lee University.

48. Rehnquist to O'Connor, November 25, 1981, Lewis F. Powell Jr. Archives, Washington and Lee University.

49. "Domestic News," United Press International, November 25, 1981.

50. Richard A. Cordray and James T. Vradelis, "The Emerging Jurisprudence of Justice O'Connor," *University of Chicago Law Review,* 1985, vol. 52, p. 389.

51. *Engle v. Isaac,* 456 U.S. 107 (1982).

52. Powell to law clerk, undated, Lewis F. Powell Jr. Archives, Washinton and Lee University.

53. *Engle v. Isaac.*

54. Stephen Wermiel, "Low-Roading on the High Court," *Wall Street Journal,* September 13, 1982.

55. O'Connor to all justices, December 14, 1981, Lewis F. Powell Jr. Archives, Washington and Lee University.

56. Burger to O'Connor, December 15, 1981; Rehnquist to Burger, December 15, 1981; Powell to Burger, December 15, 1981; Stevens to Burger, December 18, 1981, Lewis F. Powell Jr. Archives, Washington and Lee University.

57. Brennan to Burger, December 16, 1981, Lewis F. Powell Jr. Archives, Washington and Lee University.

58. David Bird and Dorothy J. Gaiter, "Notes on People; Despite Criticism, Nancy Reagan Ranks No. 1," *New York Times,* December 24, 1981; Steven R. Weisman, "Reagan Plays Golf Before Big Party," *New York Times,* January 1, 1982.

59. Lawrence K. Altman, "Justice Rehnquist Back at Work After Treatment for Drug Reaction," *New York Times,* January 12, 1982.

60. Facts of case drawn from *Plyler v. Doe,* 457 U.S. 202 (1982); chronology of Brennan's actions drawn from internal memos in the case contained in the papers of William J. Brennan Jr., Library of Congress; Lewis F. Powell Jr. Archives, Washington and Lee University; papers of Thurgood Marshall, Library of Congress; papers of Harry A. Blackmun, Library of Congress.

61. Author's interview with Richard Fallon.

62. *San Antonio Independent School District v. Rodriguez,* 411 U.S. 1 (1973).

63. Brennan to Powell, January 25, 1982, Lewis F. Powell Jr. Archives, Washington and Lee University.

64. Example of Burger effort to dissuade Powell from Brennan position, Burger to Powell, April 9, 1982, "I am profoundly troubled by the developments in this case and of course will not join it as it stands. What limiting principle can confine this massive expansion of the Fourteenth Amendment . . ." Lewis F. Powell Jr. Archives, Washington and Lee University.

65. *Plyler v. Doe,* 457 U.S. 202 (1982).

66. *Nixon v. Fitzgerald,* 457 U.S. 731 (1982); Burger to Powell, date June 15, 1982, Lewis F. Powell Jr. Archives, Washington and Lee.

67. Powell to O'Connor; O'Connor to Powell, March 10, 1982, Lewis F. Powell Jr. Archives, Washington and Lee University.

68. Rehnquist to Marshall, June 7, 1982, papers of Thurgood Marshall, Library of Congress.

69. Marshall to all of the justices, June 18, 1982, papers of Thurgood Marshall, Library of Congress.

70. *Ford Motor Co. v. EEOC,* 458 U.S. 219 (1982).

71. Author interview with Ruth McGregor.

72. *FERC v. Mississippi,* 456 U.S. 742 (1982).

73. Powell to O'Connor, May 20, 1982; O'Connor draft to all justices, May 26, 1982; Blackmun to White, June 21, 1982; Powell to O'Connor, June 22, 1982, Lewis F. Powell Jr. Archives, Washington and Lee University.

74. O'Connor to Powell, June 23, 1982, Lewis F. Powell Jr. Archives, Washington and Lee University; *Enmund v. Florida,* 458 U.S. 782 (1982).

75. Five years later, O'Connor was in the majority in a decision that allowed an accomplice to be executed. *Tison v. Arizona,* 481 U.S. 137 (1987).

76. Kenneth L. Karst, "Justice O'Connor and the Substance of Equal Citizenship," *Supreme Court Review 2003,* p. 357.

7. THE GENDER TRAP

1. Author's interview with Hunter Gholson.

2. Transcript of oral argument in *Mississippi University for Women v. Hogan.*

3. O'Connor to Powell, February 1982, Lewis F. Powell Jr. Archives, Washington and Lee University.

4. Reginald Stuart, "Mississippi College Enrolls First Man," *New York Times,* August 30, 1981.

5. Wilbur O. Colom, "The Trials of a Mississippi Lawyer," *New York Times,* May 15, 1983.

6. 646 F.2d 1116 (1981); 653 F.2d 222 (1981).

7. Stuart, "Mississippi College Enrolls First Man."

8. Kathy Sawyer, "Women's Ranks Are Growing in Many Job Areas; Women's Ranks Growing in Many Traditionally Male Occupations," *Washington Post,* August 24, 1981.

9. *Craig v. Boren,* 429 U.S. 190 (1976).

10. Amicus brief from American Civil Liberties Union, *Craig v. Boren,* Case No. 75–628.

11. With that ruling, the justices crafted a rule of heightened judicial scrutiny for gender

discrimination—a test stricter than the rational-basis test applied to most government policies but not as strict as judicial review for race discrimination.

12. Sandra O'Connor interview with the Phoenix History Project.

13. Author's interview with Hunter Gholson.

14. Colom, "Trials of a Mississippi Lawyer."

15. Ibid.

16. Amicus brief from the National Women's Law Center and others in *Mississippi University for Women v. Hogan,* Case No. 81–406.

17. Sandra O'Connor interview with the Phoenix History Project.

18. Notes of Justices Powell, Brennan, and Blackmun, March 24, 1982, Lewis F. Powell Jr. Archives, Washington and Lee University; papers of William J. Brennan Jr. and Harry A. Blackmun, Library of Congress.

19. Donnie Radcliffe, "Heeere's Nancy!: First Lady Steals Show at Annual Gridiron Dinner," *Washington Post,* March 29, 1982; Allan Cromley, "Gridiron Song and Dance Finely Tuned for Notable Washington Audience," *Sunday Oklahoman,* March 28, 1982.

20. Susan Estrich, *Sex and Power* (New York: Riverhead Books, 2000), p. 50. Some said it was because his secretary (who later became his wife) liked to be the only woman in the office.

21. Stephen Wermiel, "Low-Roading on the High Court," *Wall Street Journal,* September 13, 1982.

22. Fred Barbash, "Blackmun Discusses His Court; In Rare TV Interview, He Talks of Justices, Stresses," *Washington Post,* December 5, 1982.

23. O'Connor to Blackmun, July 1, 1982, papers of Harry A. Blackmun, Library of Congress.

24. Mary Lynn Kotz, "The Verdict," *ARTnews,* October 1999.

25. Pam Hait, "Sandra Day O'Connor Warm, Witty and Wise," *Ladies' Home Journal,* April 1982, vol. 99, no. 4, p. 40.

26. Author's interview with Scott Bales.

27. Author's interview with Glen Nager.

28. Amicus brief from MUW Alumnae Association in *Mississippi University for Women v. Hogan,* Case No. 81–406.

29. Author's interview with Barbara Babcock.

30. Powell memorandum for file, June 7, 1982, Lewis F. Powell Jr. Archives, Washington and Lee University.

31. One of his clerks at the time, Richard Fallon, recalled him pointing to a law clerk's casual attire one Saturday and saying, "Are those what they call 'blue jeans'?" Richard H. Fallon Jr., "A Tribute to Justice Lewis F. Powell, Jr.," *Harvard Law Review,* 1987, vol. 101, p. 399.

32. "What Individuals Can Do," *Christian Science Monitor,* July 16, 1982.

33. *Mississippi University for Women v. Hogan,* 458 U.S. 718 (1982).

34. "Nurses and Needlework," *Washington Post,* July 5, 1982.

35. Author's interview with Ruth Bader Ginsburg.

36. Colom, "Trials of a Mississippi Lawyer."

37. *City of Akron v. Akron Center for Reproductive Health,* 462 U.S. 416 (1983).

38. *Roe v. Wade,* 410 U.S. 113 (1973).

39. Transcript of oral argument in *City of Akron.* For account of pure drama in the

courtroom, see Fred Barbash, "Justices, in Fervent Debate, Tackle Abortion Issue Again," *Washington Post,* December 1, 1982.

40. O'Connor to Powell, March 7, 1983, Lewis F. Powell Jr. Archives, Washington and Lee University.

41. O'Connor to Powell, May 4, 1983, Lewis F. Powell Jr. Archives, Washington and Lee University.

42. O'Connor drafts in *City of Akron,* first draft, May 5, 1983; second draft, May 10, 1983; third draft, June 13, 1983, Lewis F. Powell Jr. Archives, Washington and Lee University.

43. This language remained in the final opinion.

44. *City of Akron v. Akron Center For Reproductive Health.*

45. Uhlmann to Harper, June 15, 1983, Ronald Reagan Library; Linda Greenhouse, "High Court Clears Up Any Doubts on Abortion," *New York Times,* June 19, 1983.

46. Fred Barbarsh, "Supreme Court Reaffirms 1973 Abortion Decision," *Washington Post,* June 13, 1983.

47. O'Connor to Powell, June 17, 1983, Lewis F. Powell Jr. Archives, Washington and Lee University.

48. Law clerk to Blackmun, May 12, 1983, papers of Harry A. Blackmun, Library of Congress.

49. John A. Jenkins, "Perchance to Dream," *New York Times Magazine,* February 20, 1983.

50. Burger to all justices, White to Burger, and Stevens to Burger, September 28, 1983; Rehnquist to Burger, Brennan to Burger, White to Burger, and O'Connor to Burger, September 29, 1983, Lewis F. Powell Jr. Archives, Washington and Lee University.

51. "In the Name of the Law: Legal ABC's," *New York Times,* September 29, 1983; "High Court's '9 Men' Were a Surprise to One," *New York Times,* October 12, 1983.

52. David Margolick, "Women's Bar Award to Justice O'Connor Comes Under Attack," *New York Times,* May 9, 1984.

53. Sandra Day O'Connor and H. Alan Day, *Lazy B* (New York: Random House, 2002), p. 298.

54. Author's interviews with Alan Day and Glen Nager.

55. Harry Day to Sandra Day O'Connor, June 22, 1970, Day family papers, Arizona Historical Society.

56. O'Connor, *Lazy B,* pp. 301–2.

8. ASCENDING THE BENCH

1. Rehnquist to Powell, January 18, 1985, Lewis F. Powell Jr. Archives, Washington and Lee University.

2. Rehnquist to Powell, March 25, 1985, Lewis F. Powell Jr. Archives, Washington and Lee University.

3. O'Connor to Powell, January 24, 1985, Lewis F. Powell Jr. Archives, Washington and Lee University.

4. Elizabeth Kastor, "The Inaugural Weekend; for Women Only," *Washington Post,* January 21, 1985.

5. Jane Mayer and Doyle McManus, *Landslide: The Unmaking of the President, 1984–1988* (Boston, Massachusetts: Houghton Mifflin, 1988), p. 47.

6. Fred Barbash and Al Kamen, "Third Justice Speaks Out; Blackmun Says 'Weary' Court Is Moving Right," *Washington Post,* September 20, 1984.

7. David Lauter, "Justices Turn to Speechmaking During Recess," *National Law Journal,* November 5, 1984; Fred Barbash, "Justices Making Their Frustrations Public," *Washington Post,* September 23, 1984; Stuart Taylor, "Justice Stevens Is Sharply Critical of Supreme Court Conservatives," *New York Times,* August 5, 1984.

8. "And Now, the Arizona Twins; Justice O'Connor Teams Up With Court Conservative Rehnquist," *Time,* April 19, 1982.

9. Blackmun to Powell, January 30, 1987, Lewis F. Powell Jr. Archives, Washington and Lee University.

10. Blackmun to O'Connor; O'Connor to Blackmun, May 9, 1984; papers of Harry A. Blackmun, Library of Congress.

11. O'Connor to Blackmun, December 13, 1985; Blackmun to O'Connor, O'Connor to Blackmun, December 17, 1985, papers of Harry A. Blackmun, Library of Congress.

12. Facts of case drawn from *Patton v. Yount,* 467 U.S. 1025 (1984).

13. O'Connor to Powell, March 2, 1984, Lewis F. Powell Jr. Archives, Washington and Lee University.

14. Ibid.

15. Powell to law clerk, March 6, 1984, Lewis F. Powell Jr. Archives, Washington and Lee University.

16. *Patton v. Yount.*

17. Facts drawn from *Dun & Bradstreet v. Greenmoss Builders,* 472 U.S. 749 (1985).

18. *New York Times Co. v. Sullivan,* 376 U.S. 254 (1964).

19. Specifically *Gertz v. Robert Welch,* 418 U.S. 323 (1974).

20. O'Connor to Burger, March 28, 1984, Lewis F. Powell Jr. Archives, Washington and Lee University.

21. Powell to law clerk, June 30, 1984, Lewis F. Powell Jr. Archives, Washington and Lee University.

22. O'Connor to Powell, January 22, 1985, Lewis F. Powell Jr. Archives, Washington and Lee University.

23. Law clerk to Powell, January 24, 1985, Lewis F. Powell Jr. Archives, Washington and Lee University; author's interview with law clerk Daniel Ortiz.

24. O'Connor to Powell, February 11, 1985, Lewis F. Powell Jr. Archives, Washington and Lee University.

25. Pepperdine Alumni Quarterly Report, papers of Harry A. Blackmun, Library of Congress.

26. Pam Hait, "Sandra Day O'Connor Warm, Witty and Wise," *Ladies' Home Journal,* April 1982, vol. 99, no. 4, p. 40; author's interviews with former law clerks.

27. Joan S. Marie, "Her Honor: The Rancher's Daughter," *Saturday Evening Post,* September 1985, p. 42. A notice about the morning classes was circulated to all incoming clerks, saying: "The class is a nice way to loosen up . . ." July 18, 1985, papers of William J. Brennan Jr., Library of Congress.

28. Lois Romano, "Grilled on the Gridiron: It Was *Baker v. Ferraro,* but Reagan Got the Rough Ride," *Washington Post,* March 25, 1985.

29. Lee Comegys, "Artful Conversation," United Press International, November 9, 1984.

30. Elizabeth Kastor, "John Riggins' Big Sleep: He Came, He Jawed, He Conked Out," *Washington Post,* February 1, 1985.

31. Richard Carelli, "Washington Dateline," Associated Press, August 14, 1985.

32. Show #12, NFL Films Presents, 2004 (VHS).

33. O'Connor to Powell, February 19, 1985, Lewis F. Powell Jr. Archives, Washington and Lee University.

34. Brennan to all justices; Stevens to Brennan, March 21, 1985, papers of William J. Brennan Jr., Library of Congress.

35. *New York Times v. Sullivan.*

36. *Dun & Bradstreet v. Greenmoss Builders.*

37. *Garcia v. San Antonio Metropolitan Transit Authority,* 469 U.S. 528 (1985).

38. Powell's conference notes, October 3, 1984, Lewis F. Powell Jr. Archives, Washington and Lee University. Also papers of Harry A. Blackmun, William J. Brennan, and Thurgood Marshall, Library of Congress.

39. *FERC v. Mississippi,* 456 U.S. 742 (1982).

40. Blackmun to all justices, June 11, 1984, Lewis F. Powell Jr. Archives, Washington and Lee University. For discussion of law clerk's role in Blackmun decision, see Linda Greenhouse, *Becoming Justice Blackmun: Harry Blackmun's Supreme Court Journey* (New York: Times Books, 2005), p. 148.

41. *Ibid.* Powell wrote "Wow" on his copy of Blackmun's note.

42. O'Connor to all justices, June 11, 1984, Lewis F. Powell Jr. Archives, Washington and Lee University.

43. Blackmun to Brennan, June 11, 1985, papers of Harry A. Blackmun, Library of Congress.

44. Stevens to Burger, June 12, 1984, Lewis F. Powell Jr. Archives, Washington and Lee University.

45. Burger to Rehnquist, October 5, 1984, Lewis F. Powell Jr. Archives, Washington and Lee University.

46. *National League of Cities v. Usery,* 426 U.S. 833 (1976).

47. Powell to O'Connor, December 26, 1984, Lewis F. Powell Jr. Archives, Washington and Lee University.

48. *Garcia v. San Antonio Metropolitan Transit Authority.*

49. Buchanan to Regan, July 10, 1985, Ronald Reagan Library.

50. *Lynch v. Donnelly.* 465 U.S. 668 (1984).

51. Facts drawn from *Wygant v. Jackson Board of Education,* 476 U.S. 267 (1986).

52. Sandra Day O'Connor, "A Tribute to Justice Thurgood Marshall: Thurgood Marshall: The Influence of a Raconteur," *Stanford Law Review,* 1992, vol. 44, p. 1217.

53. Powell's conference notes, November 8, 1985, Lewis F. Powell Jr. Archives, Washington and Lee University; Brennan's conference notes, November 8, 1985, papers of William J. Brennan Jr., Library of Congress.

54. Blackmun's conference notes, November 8, 1985, papers of Harry A. Blackmun, Library of Congress; author's interviews with former law clerks.

55. Brennan to Marshall, Blackmun, and Stevens, November 20, 1985, papers of Thurgood Marshall, Library of Congress.

56. Beverly B. Cook, "Justice Sandra Day O'Connor: Transition to a Republican Court Agenda," in *The Burger Court: Political and Judicial Profiles,* eds., Charles M. Lamb and Stephen C Halpern (Urbana: University of Illinois Press, 1991), p. 240.

57.   O'Connor to Powell, December 19, 1985, Lewis F. Powell Jr. Archives, Washington and Lee University.

58.   Brennan to Marshall, February 6, 1986, papers of Thurgood Marshall, Library of Congress.

59.   Powell to O'Connor, March 19, 1986; Powell to O'Connor, April 7, 1986, Lewis F. Powell Jr. Archives, Washington and Lee University.

60.   *Wygant v. Jackson Board of Education.*

61.   Stuart Taylor Jr., "High Court Bars a Layoff Method Favoring Blacks," *New York Times,* May 20, 1986; Al Kamen, "High Court Ruling Signals Support for Affirmative Action," *Washington Post,* May 20, 1986.

62.   Author's interview with Sandra Day O'Connor.

63.   Evan Thomas, "Reagan's Mr. Right; Rehnquist Is Picked for the Court's Top Job," *Time,* June 30, 1986.

64.   Linda Greenhouse, "Senate, 65 to 33, Votes to Confirm Rehnquist as 16th Chief Justice," *New York Times,* September 18, 1986.

65.   George Lardner Jr. and Al Kamen, "Rehnquist Hearings Leave Questions of Veracity," *Washington Post,* August 10, 1986.

66.   John C. Jeffries Jr., *Justice Lewis F. Powell, Jr.* (New York: Charles Scribner's Sons, 1994), p. 534.

67.   Ibid., p. 535.

68.   Jack Nelson, "Democrats Take the Election Prize: A 55–45 Majority in Senate," *Los Angeles Times,* November 6, 1986.

69.   Helen Dewar and Spencer Rich, "GOP's Class of '80 Runs Into Trouble 2nd Time Around," *Washington Post,* November 5, 1986.

70.   O'Connor to Rehnquist, Powell, and Stevens, undated, Lewis F. Powell Jr. Archives, Washington and Lee University. In addition to betting on Denton over Shelby, O'Connor bet badly on Republican Mark Andrews over Democrat Kent Conrad in North Dakota and Republican Jim Abdnor over Democrat Tom Daschle in South Dakota.

71.   John C. Metaxas, "Penn Protest," *National Law Journal,* December 15, 1986.

72.   Jeffrey T. Leeds, "A Life on the Court," *New York Times Magazine,* October 5, 1986.

73.   There were five other votes on his side this time, not just four, as was the situation in the 1982 case of nursing student Joe Hogan, *Mississippi University for Women v. Hogan,* when Brennan had assigned the case to O'Connor.

74.   O'Connor to Brennan, January 8, 1987, papers of William J. Brennan Jr., Library of Congress; *Johnson v. Transportation Agency,* 480 U.S. 616 (1987).

75.   *Newsweek,* April 6, 1987.

76.   Linda Greenhouse, "The Law: At the Bar; Name-Calling in the Supreme Court: When the Justices Vent Their Spleen, Is There a Social Cost?" *New York Times,* July 28, 1989.

77.   "Appointment to Court (for Family Records)," August 27, 1981, Lewis F. Powell Jr. Archives, Washington and Lee University.

78.   O'Connor to Powell, June 26, 1987, Lewis F. Powell Jr. Archives, Washington and Lee University.

9. "THE TRANSITORY NATURE OF LIFE"

1.   Richard Carelli, "Kennedy May Hold Decisive Vote as Supreme Court Opens New Term," Associated Press, October 1, 1988.

2. The first instance of Powell using the "nine law firms" expression appears to be September 23, 1976, in a speech to the Richmond Chamber of Commerce. Note to author from Powell Archivist John Jacob, December 8, 2004.

3. "Bork's Path: Nomination, Rejection, Resignation," Associated Press, January 14, 1988.

4. David G. Savage and David Lauter, "Burger Testifies at Hearing That He Favors Bork; If Nominee 'Is Not in the Mainstream, Neither Am I," *Los Angeles Times,* September 24, 1987. Former chief justice Burger was the only justice who formally testified for Bork; Justice Stevens and White made public statements praising the nominee.

5. "Confidential—Nomination of Judge Robert Bork," October 14, 1987, Lewis F. Powell Jr. Archives, Washington and Lee University.

6. Reagan had never officially nominated Ginsburg, but his aides had announced his intention. James Gerstenzang and Karen Tumulty, "Ginsburg Withdraws, Citing Furor Over Use of Marijuana," *Los Angeles Times,* November 8, 1987.

7. The justices sit by alternating seniority. Newest justice, Antonin Scalia, was on the far right of the bench. The far left seat, next to O'Connor, was empty until Kennedy was confirmed.

8. "Supreme Court Justice Felt Hounded by Media," Associated Press, September 16, 1988.

9. O'Connor to Powell, August 23, 1988, Lewis F. Powell Jr. Archives, Washington and Lee University.

10. Rehnquist to all justices, October 18, 1988, papers of Harry A. Blackmun, Library of Congress.

11. Rehnquist to all justices, October 28, 1988, papers of Harry A. Blackmun, Library of Congress.

12. Speech to the National Coalition for Cancer Survivorship, November 3, 1994 (VHS). O'Connor spoke publicly about her cancer for the first time.

13. Ibid.; author's interviews with Alan Day, Ann Day, Jay O'Connor, and Nancy Ignatius.

14. Cancer Survivorship speech.

15. Author's interview with Jay O'Connor.

16. Ibid.

17. "Justice O'Connor Visits W&L," *Washington & Lee Law News,* November 10, 1988.

18. "O'Connor Back at Court After Surgery," *Los Angeles Times,* November 1, 1988.

19. O'Connor to all sitting justices, Burger, and Powell, October 21, 1988, Lewis F. Powell Jr. Archives, Washington and Lee University.

20. James H. Rubin, "O'Connor in Good Condition Following Cancer Surgery," Associated Press, October 24, 1988.

21. "O'Connor to Join Bryan, Cave and Return to Phoenix," *PR Newswire,* October 28, 1988. The announcement said John O'Connor would be in Phoenix "a minimum of two weeks a month."

22. David G. Savage, "High Court's O'Connor Has Breast Surgery," *Los Angeles Times,* October 22, 1988; report repeated in James H. Rubin, "O'Connor in Good Condition Following Cancer Surgery," Associated Press, October 24, 1988.

23. Cancer Survivorship speech.

24. Author's interview with Nancy Ignatius.

25. Al Kamen and Marjorie Williams, "Woman of the Hour," *Washington Post Magazine,* June 11, 1989.

26. O'Connor to Powell, October 28, 1988, Lewis F. Powell Jr. Archives, Washington and Lee University.

27. Cancer Survivorship speech.

28. Ibid.

29. Ibid.

30. Author's interview with John Paul Stevens.

31. Author's interview with Jay O'Connor.

32. Author's interview with Nancy Ignatius.

33. Author's interview with Ruth McGregor.

34. Author's interview with former clerk on background.

35. The Supreme Court itself said her "aggressiveness apparently spilled over into abrasiveness." *Pricewaterhouse v. Hopkins,* 490 U.S. 228 (1989).

36. Brief from respondent Hopkins in *Pricewaterhouse v. Hopkins,* Case No. 87–1167.

37. Brief from petitioner Pricewaterhouse in *Pricewaterhouse v. Hopkins,* Case No. 87–1167.

38. *Pricewaterhouse v. Hopkins.*

39. Amicus brief from the American Psychological Association in *Pricewaterhouse v. Hopkins,* Case No. 87–1167.

40. Amicus brief from NOW Legal Defense and Education Fund and other organizations in *Pricewaterhouse v. Hopkins,* Case No. 87–1167.

41. Transcript of oral argument in *Pricewaterhouse v. Hopkins.*

42. "Gallbladder Operation Performed on Brennan," *New York Times,* December 13, 1988.

43. O'Connor to Brennan, December 13, 1988, papers of Thurgood Marshall, Library of Congress.

44. Brennan to O'Connor, December 14, 1988, papers of Thurgood Marshall, Library of Congress.

45. O'Connor to Brennan, December 16, 1988; Brennan to O'Connor, January 6, 1989, papers of Thurgood Marshall, Library of Congress.

46. O'Connor to Brennan, January 10, 1989, papers of Thurgood Marshall, Library of Congress.

47. *Pricewaterhouse v. Hopkins.*

48. *Hopkins v. Pricewaterhouse,* 920 F.2d 967 (D.C. Circuit, 1990).

49. See for example, *Wards Cove Packing Co. v. Atonio,* 490 U.S. 642 (1989) and *Patterson v. McLean Credit Union,* 485 U.S. 617 (1989).

50. *Wards Cove Packing Co. v. Atonio.*

51. The Civil Rights Act of 1991.

52. *Congressional Quarterly Almanac,* 1989, pp. 314–319; Linda Greenhouse, "The Year the Court Turned to the Right," *New York Times,* July 7, 1989; see also David Savage, *Turning Right: The Making of the Rehnquist Supreme Court* (New York: John Wiley, 1993).

10. STILL IN THE GAME

1. Speech to the National Coalition for Cancer Survivorship, November 3, 1994 (VHS).

2. Robin Toner, "Hailed by Big Crowds, Dukakis Foresees an Upset," and E.J. Dionne

Jr., "Yes, Late Voter Swings Do Happen, But Underdogs Can't Count on Them," *New York Times,* November 5, 1988; Ben Bradlee Jr., "Dukakis Shifts Plans to Chase Hints of Momentum," *Boston Globe,* November 7, 1988.

3. Rehnquist to Stevens, O'Connor, Kennedy, and Powell, November 14, 1988, Lewis F. Powell Jr. Archives, Washington and Lee University. For an explanation of how winnings and losses are calculated, see Forrest Maltzman, Lee Sigelman, and Paul J. Wahlbeck, "Supreme Court Justices Really Do Follow the Election Returns," *PS Online,* October 2004.

4. Author's interview with Antonin Scalia.

5. O'Connor to Rehnquist, January 22, 1987, Lewis F. Powell Jr. Archives, Washington and Lee University. See also photo in *Washington Post,* January 23, 1987.

6. Cancer Survivorship speech.

7. "Change in O'Connor's Appearance Noted," United Press International, November 28, 1988.

8. Phil McCombs, Jim Naughton, Charles Trueheart, Kara Swisher, and Sarah Booth Conroy, "The Fetes Accompli!: From George to Georgette, A Night on the Town," *Washington Post,* January 22, 1989.

9. This point was made in Edward Lazarus, *Closed Chambers: The First Eyewitness Account of the Epic Struggles Inside the Supreme Court* (New York: Times Books, 1998).

10. *Penry v. Lynaugh,* 492 U.S. 302 (1989); O'Connor to Rehnquist, January 13, 1989, papers of Thurgood Marshall, Library of Congress.

11. Ike Flores, "Ted Bundy Was Competent at 1980 Murder Trial, Judge Rules," Associated Press, December 17, 1987; "A List of Women Ted Bundy Has Confessed to Killing," Associated Press, January 25, 1989.

12. Under U.S. Supreme Court practice, it takes four votes to grant a petition for review, but five votes to grant a stay of execution. "Florida High Court Refuses to Put Off Bundy Execution," *New York Times,* January 21, 1989.

13. Facts drawn from *Teague v. Lane,* 489 U.S. 288 (1989).

14. Ibid. The standard O'Connor adopted had not been urged by the main parties in the case, but rather by the conservative Criminal Justice Legal Foundation, based in Sacramento, in an amicus curiae brief.

15. Stevens to O'Connor, November 29, 1988, papers of Thurgood Marshall, Library of Congress.

16. *Teague v. Lane.* In cases after *Teague,* a majority adopted her approach.

17. *DeShaney v. Winnebago County,* 489 U.S. 189 (1989).

18. Susan Bandes, "Taking Justice to Its Logical Extreme: A Comment on *Teague v. Lane,*" *Southern California Law Review,* 1993, vol. 66, p. 2453.

19. Barry Friedman, "Habeas and Hubris," *Vanderbilt Law Review,* 1992, vol. 45, p. 797.

20. *Richmond v. J.A. Croson Co.* 488 U.S. 469 (1989).

21. Transcript of oral argument in *Richmond v. J. A. Croson Co.*

22. *Richmond v. Croson.* Parts of O'Connor's opinion addressing doctrinal issues garnered fewer votes; Scalia wanted to go further in rejecting affirmative action and separately agreed to strict scrutiny but did not join that portion of her opinion.

23. "30 Percent Solution," *Richmond Times-Dispatch,* January 24, 1989; Tom Wicker, "In the Nation: Hype and Reality," *New York Times,* January 27, 1989.

24. "Bush Sees Kemp Sworn In," *Washington Post,* February 14, 1989.

25. "Remarks of President Bush at the Swearing-In Ceremony of Clayton Yeutter," White House transcript, February 16, 1989.

26. Author's interview with Sam Mardian.

27. Al Kamen, "2 Experts Fault O'Connor for Letter; Justice Said to Misquote Court Rulings on Christianity of U.S.," *Washington Post,* March 15, 1989.

28. Ibid. Bruce Fein, who had been an associate deputy attorney general in the Reagan administration, said it was "improper" for O'Connor to write a letter that could be seen as compromising her impartiality on a religious freedom question. He said she should not have "gratuitously intruded herself into the political process. . . ."

29. Alan M. Dershowitz, "Justice O'Connor's Second Indiscretion," *New York Times,* April 2, 1989.

30. Al Kamen, "O'Connor Regrets Letter Was Used for Politics," *Washington Post,* March 16, 1989.

31. Al Kamen, "Justice O'Connor to Brief GOP Donors at High Court; ABA Code Bars Speeches to Political Groups," *Washington Post,* May 1, 1987.

32. Edwin M. Yoder Jr., "Justice O'Connor's Unfortunate Letter," *Washington Post,* March 19, 1989.

33. Kamen, "2 Experts Fault O'Connor for Letter."

34. "The 'Christian Nation' Controversy," *American Lawyer,* June 1989.

35. O'Connor to Brennan, June 6, 1989; Brennan to Rehnquist, June 28, 1989, papers of Harry A. Blackmun, Library of Congress.

36. *Allegheny County v. Greater Pittsburgh ACLU,* 492 U.S. 573 (1989).

37. *Penry v. Lynaugh* 492 U.S. 302 (1989). The only state of those using capital punishment at the time banning the execution of the mentally retarded was Georgia, although O'Connor also noted that Maryland had enacted a similar statute set to take effect on July 1, 1989. Thirteen years after *Penry,* the Court reversed its position, *Atkins v. Virginia.*

38. *Stanford v. Kentucky,* 492 U.S. 361 (1989). Sixteen years later, the Court reversed its position, *Roper v. Simmons.*

39. *Wyoming v. United States,* 492 U.S. 406 (1989). Brennan's draft dissents, first draft, June 20, 1989; second draft, June 23, 1989, papers of Thurgood Marshall, Library of Congress.

40. O'Connor to all justices, June 22, 1989, papers of Thurgood Marshall, Library of Congress.

41. *Cruzan v. Missouri Department of Health,* 497 U.S. 261 (1990).

42. *Washington v. Glucksburg,* 521 U.S. 702 (1997).

11. SHIFTING GROUND ON ABORTION

1. *Thornburgh v. American College of Obstetricians and Gynecologists,* 476 U.S. 747, (1986).

2. O'Connor's draft in *Thornburgh v. American College of Obstetricians and Gynecologists,* May 6, 1986, papers of Harry A. Blackmun, Library of Congress.

3. With each abortion case over the past decade and a half, the majority committed to abortion rights had decreased. In 1983 *(Akron v. Akron Center for Reproductive Health),* the majority slipped to 6–3, with new justice O'Connor joining Rehnquist and White. Then, in 1986 *(Thornburgh),* the majority was 5–4. Chief Justice Burger switched sides and joined the dissent.

4. *Thornburgh v. American College of Obstetricians and Gynecologists.*

5.   "Justice Fears for Roe Ruling," *New York Times,* September 14, 1988.

6.   Bork's chief Senate critic, Massachusetts Democrat Edward M. Kennedy, claimed that if the conservative appeals-court judge were approved, women with unwanted pregnancies would be relegated to back alleys. Moderate Republicans, such as Arlen Specter of Pennsylvania, who voted against Bork, said they believed he would undermine the constitutional right to privacy. Senator Bob Packwood, a Republican from Oregon, who also had voted against Bork, described the abortion issue as "more divisive than Vietnam."

7.   Nomination of Sandra Day O'Connor, Senate Judiciary Committee Hearing, September 9–11, 1981, p. 126.

8.   *Akron v. Akron Center for Reproductive Health,* 462 U.S. 416 (1983).

9.   Ibid.

10.   Laura Sessions, Ann Devroy, "Bush Cites Abortion 'Tragedy' In Call to 67,000 Protestors; Demonstrations Held at D.C. Clinics," *Washington Post,* January 24, 1989.

11.   Amicus brief of the United States in *Webster v. Reproductive Health Services,* Case No. 88–605.

12.   The previous record for amicus curiae briefs—fifty-eight—was set in the 1978 case *Regents of the University of California v. Bakke,* which first upheld affirmative action on college campuses.

13.   "Mail on Abortion Deluges Court," Associated Press, April 19, 1989.

14.   George Hackett and Ann McDaniel, "All Eyes on Justice O'Connor," *Newsweek,* May 1, 1989; "NOW Leader Sees Big Turnout at Abortion Rights March," *New York Times,* April 8, 1989.

15.   Robin Toner, "Right to Abortion Draws Thousands to Capital Rally," *New York Times,* April 10, 1989.

16.   Transcript of oral argument in *Webster v. Reproductive Health Services.*

17.   Blackmun's conference notes, April 28, 1989, papers of Harry A. Blackmun, Library of Congress.

18.   Lazarus to Blackmun, May 1, 1989, papers of Harry A. Blackmun, Library of Congress.

19.   Al Kamen and Marjorie Williams, "Woman of the Hour," *Washington Post,* June 11, 1989.

20.   Edward Lazarus, *Closed Chambers: The First Eyewitness Account of the Epic Struggles Inside the Supreme Court* (New York: Times Books, 1998), p. 384.

21.   Amicus Brief of Women Who Have Had Abortions and Friends of Amici Curiae in *Webster v. Reproductive Health Services,* Case No. 88–605.

22.   Sandra Day O'Connor, *The Majesty of the Law* (New York: Random House, 2003), p. 195.

23.   Nomination of Sandra Day O'Connor, p. 98.

24.   Sandra Day O'Connor and H. Alan Day, *Lazy B* (New York: Random House, 2002), p. 142.

25.   Al Kamen, "Justice O'Connor 'Just Fine,' " *Washington Post,* May 3, 1989.

26.   Rehnquist to all justices, May 25, 1986, papers of Thurgood Marshall and papers of Harry A. Blackmun, Library of Congress.

27.   Stevens to Rehnquist, May 30, 1989, Blackmun draft in *Webster* case, June 21, 1989, papers of Harry A. Blackmun, Library of Congress.

28.   For example, Bernard Schwartz, *Decision: How the Supreme Court Decides Cases* (New York: Oxford University Press, 1996), pp. 23–29.

29. Lazarus, *Closed Chambers,* p. 263. Clerks "were divided between two well-entrenched and hostile camps. Across the room, we glared at each other, eyes hooded with distrust or outright contempt."

30. *Texas v. Johnson,* 491 U.S. 397 (1989). The split was not the familiar one between conservatives and liberals. In the majority were Brennan, Marshall, Blackmun, Scalia, and Kennedy. Dissenting were Rehnquist, White, Stevens, and O'Connor.

31. *Congressional Quarterly Almanac,* 1989, p. 308.

32. Lazarus to Blackmun, June 22, 1989, papers of Harry A. Blackmun, Library of Congress.

33. *Webster v. Reproductive Health Services,* 492 U.S. 490 (1989).

34. Powell to O'Connor, July 10, 1989, Lewis F. Powell Jr. Archives, Washington and Lee University.

35. Al Kamen, "Supreme Court Restricts Right to Abortion, Giving States Wide Latitude for Regulation; 5–4 Ruling Stops Short of Overturning 'Roe,'" *Washington Post,* July 4, 1989. Travel documented in O'Connor 1990 Financial Disclosure Report, Administrative Office of the U.S. Courts.

36. Author's interview with John Paul Stevens.

37. Author's interview with Ruth Bader Ginsburg.

38. *Congressional Quarterly Almanac,* 1990, p. 529.

39. Susan R. Estrich and Kathleen M. Sullivan, "Colloquy: *Webster v. Reproductive Health Services;* Abortion Politics: Writing for an Audience of One," *University of Pennsylvania Law Review,* vol. 138, p. 119 (1989).

40. Roland Evans and Robert Novak, "O'Connor Facing Supreme Court Squeeze on Abortion Issue," *Bergen Record,* July 26, 1989.

41. Powell to O'Connor, July 10, 1989, Lewis F. Powell Jr. Archives, Washington and Lee University.

12. END OF AN ERA

1. Author's interview with Marci Hamilton.

2. Christopher Connell, "Raisa Gorbachev Visiting White House Twice Today," Associated Press, May 31, 1990.

3. "O'Connor Puts Rumors to Rest," *New York Times,* June 25, 1990.

4. Brennan to Stevens, March 22, 1990, papers of Harry A. Blackmun, Library of Congress.

5. *Hodgson v. Minnesota,* 497 U.S. 417 (1990). Elsewhere in the opinion, she joined the four conservative justices to rule that Minnesota's alternative provision, requiring parental notice unless the minor appeared before a judge prior to obtaining an abortion, could stand. In earlier cases, the Court had ruled that minors must have access to a judicial-bypass procedure when parental consent is required for an abortion, but it had never answered the question for parental notification laws.

6. Author's interview with John Paul Stevens.

7. Brennan to Marshall, June 7, 1990, papers of Thurgood Marshall, Library of Congress.

8. *Pennsylvania v. Muniz,* 496 U.S. 582 (1990).

9. *Miranda v. Arizona,* 384 U.S. 436 (1966). The right flows from the guarantee of the Constitution's Fifth Amendment: No "person . . . shall be compelled in any criminal case to be a witness against himself."

10. Brennan to Marshall, June 7, 1990, papers of Thurgood Marshall, Library of Congress.

11. Brennan to Marshall, June 13, 1990, papers of Thurgood Marshall, Library of Congress.

12. Cases allowing exceptions to *Miranda* protections include *Oregon v. Elstad,* 470 U.S. 298 (1985) and *Moran v. Burbine,* 475 U.S. 412 (1986); denying an exception *New York v. Quarles,* 467 U.S. 649 (1984).

13. Lynn Rosellini, "The Most Powerful Liberal in America," *U.S. News & World Report,* January 8, 1990.

14. *Butler v. McKellar,* 494 U.S. 407 (1990); *Lewis v. Jeffers,* 497 U.S. 764 (1990), *Saffle v. Parks,* 494 U.S. 484 (1990); *Sawyer v. Smith,* 497 U.S. 227 (1990).

15. *Congressional Quarterly Almanac,* 1990, vol. 46, pp. 487–488.

16. Speech to Attorney General's Crime Summit, March 4, 1991, Lewis F. Powell Jr. Archives, Washington and Lee University.

17. *Butler v. McKellar.*

18. *Lewis v. Jeffers.*

19. Blackmun's draft in *Lewis v. Jeffers,* June 13, 1990, papers of Harry A. Blackmun, Library of Congress.

20. Stevens to Blackmun, June 15, 1990, papers of Harry A. Blackmun, Library of Congress.

21. *Coleman v. Thompson,* 501 U.S. 722 (1991).

22. "Federalism, Despoiled," *New York Times,* June 27, 1991.

23. David Reed, "Virginia Executes Man Whose Claims Gained Widespread Attention," Associated Press, May 21, 1992.

24. Speech to the National Coalition for Cancer Survivorship, November 3, 1994 (VHS).

25. *Metro Broadcasting, Inc. v. FCC,* 497 U.S. 547 (1990).

26. Ibid.

27. Brennan to President G. H. W. Bush, July 20, 1990, papers of Harry A. Blackmun, Library of Congress.

28. *Cooper v. Aaron,* 358 U.S. 1 (1958); *Baker v. Carr,* 369 U.S. 186 (1962); *New York Times v. Sullivan,* 376 U.S. 254 (1954); *Fay v. Noia,* 372 U.S. 391 (1963).

29. Joan Biskupic, "The Rehnquist Court: They Want to Be Known as Jurists, Not Activists," *Washington Post,* January 9, 2000.

30. Richard A. Posner, "In Memoriam: William J. Brennan, Jr.," *Harvard Law Review,* 1997, vol. 111, p. 9.

31. Wong to all justices, August 9, 1990, Lewis F. Powell Jr. Archives, Washington and Lee University.

13. FINDING NEW BEARINGS

1. Sandra Day O'Connor and H. Alan Day, *Lazy B* (New York: Random House, 2002), p. 311.

2. Blackmun to O'Connor, October 14, 1994, papers of Harry A. Blackmun, Library of Congress.

3. O'Connor to Blackmun, October 17, 1994; papers of Harry A. Blackmun, Library of Congress.

4. *Congressional Quarterly Almanac,* 1990, vol. 46, pp. 508–515.

5. Pam Hait, "Sandra Day O'Connor Warm, Witty and Wise," *Ladies' Home Journal,* April 1982, vol. 99, No. 4, p. 40.

6. Invitation for May 13, 1992, papers of Harry A. Blackmun, Library of Congress.

7. *Barnes v. Glen Theatre,* 501 U.S. 560 (1991).

8. *City of Erie v. Pap's A. M. Kandyland,* 529 U.S. 277 (2000).

9. Alexander Whol, "Whose Court Is It?: Conservatives in Search of Their Own Brennan," *ABA Journal,* 1992, vol. 78, p. 40.

10. Joan Biskupic, "Voicing Supreme Dissent: Rare, Loud and Clear," *Washington Post,* July 5, 1999; Al Kamen, "Court Upholds Independent Counsel Law," *Washington Post,* June 30, 1988.

11. *Morrison v. Olson,* 487 U.S. 654 (1988).

12. O'Connor to Powell, March 6, 1991, Lewis F. Powell Jr. Archives, Washington and Lee University. No one in the press apparently recognized that was her first such move, but the fact was memorialized in a personal note she sent to retired Justice Powell.

13. *Pacific Mutual Life Insurance Co. v. Haslip,* 499 U.S. 1 (1991).

14. Ibid.

15. *BMW of North America, Inc. v. Gore,* 517 U.S. 559 (1996); *State Farm Mutual Insurance Co. v. Campbell,* 538 U.S. 408 (2003)

16. Juan Williams, *Thurgood Marshall: American Revolutionary* (New York: Random House, 1998), p. 391.

17. Ruth Marcus, "Plain-Spoken Marshall Spars With Reporters," *Washington Post,* June 29, 1991.

18. *Payne v. Tennessee,* 501 U.S. 808 (1991).

19. Effectively reversing *Booth v. Maryland,* 482 U.S. 496 (1987); *South Carolina v. Gathers,* 490 U.S. 805 (1989).

20. Author's interview with Charles Blanchard.

21. Sandra Day O'Connor, "A Tribute to Justice Thurgood Marshall: Thurgood Marshall: The Influence of a Raconteur," *Stanford Law Review,* 1992, vol. 44, p. 1217.

22. *Richmond v. J. A. Croson Co.,* 488 U.S. 469 (1989).

23. Joan Biskupic, "Thomas is Bolder, Confident—Outside the Court," *USA Today,* January 31, 2001; Joel Engelhardt, "Justice Talks of Morals and Battles of the Soul," *Palm Beach Post,* February 2, 1998.

24. *Congressional Quarterly Almanac,* 1991, vol. 47, p. 227.

25. Thomas had been head of the civil rights office at Department of Education before becoming chairman of the EEOC.

26. Jane Mayer and Jill Abramson, *Strange Justice: The Selling of Clarence Thomas* (New York: Houghton Mifflin Co.) 1994, p. 349.

27. *Wright v. West,* 505 U.S. 277 (1992). Blackmun's handwritten conference notes, March 27, 1992; Thomas draft in *Wright,* May 26, 1992; O'Connor draft in *Wright,* June 2, 1992, papers of Harry A. Blackmun, Library of Congress.

28. Blackmun to O'Connor, June 8, 1992, papers of Harry A. Blackmun, Library of Congress.

29. Author's interview with Clarence Thomas.

30. The amendment was a response to the Court's ruling in *Mobile v. Bolden,* 466 U.S. 55 (1980), narrowing the 1965 Act.

31. See Joan Biskupic and Elder Witt, *Congressional Quarterly's Guide to the Supreme Court* (Washington, DC: Congressional Quarterly 1997), vol. 1, pp. 514–517.

32. *Thornburg v. Gingles,* 478 U.S. 30 (1986).

33. *Shaw v. Reno,* 509 U.S. 630 (1993).

34. O'Connor to Powell, June 9, 1986, Lewis F. Powell Jr. Archives, Washington and Lee University; *Davis v. Bandemer,* 478 U.S. (1986).

35. Alan Ehrenhalt, "The Court That Forgot About Politics," *Governing Magazine,* December 1994.

36. Blackmun's handwritten conference notes, April 23, 1993; law clerk to Blackmun, June 25, 1993; papers of Harry A. Blackmun, Library of Congress.

37. *Shaw v. Reno.*

38. Byron White had announced his retirement earlier, March 19, 1993.

39. Joan Biskupic, "High Court's Justice With a Cause; Bench Position Amplifies Ginsburg's Lifelong Feminist Message," *Washington Post,* April 17, 1995.

40. Joan Biskupic, "Female Justices Attest to Fraternity on Bench; O'Connor and Ginsburg, in Separate Speeches, Discuss Personal Aspects of Supreme Court Life," *Washington Post,* August 21, 1994.

41. Fred J. Maroon, *The Supreme Court of the United States* (Washington, DC: Lickle Publishing in cooperation with The Supreme Court Historical Society, 1996), p. 79.

42. Author's interview with Ruth Bader Ginsburg.

43. "Remarks for Washington Hospital Center Dinner," October 17, 2001. Provided to author by Court's Public Information Office.

44. Author's interview with Ruth Bader Ginsburg.

45. *Adarand Constructors, Inc. v. Pena,* 515 U.S. 200 (1995).

46. Ibid.

47. Change brought to author's attention by David Garrow, April 11, 2003.

48. Funeral proceedings were taped by C-Span and reviewed by the author.

49. Joan Biskupic, " 'The Biggest Heart in the Building': Colleagues and Friends Remember Force of His Opinions, Persuasiveness, Good Humor and Charisma," *Washington Post,* July 25, 1997.

50. Al Kamen, "In the Loop," *Washington Post,* August 1, 1997, and August 4, 1997.

51. Joan Biskupic and Saundra Torry, "Rites Celebrate Justice Brennan's Enduring Legacy," *Washington Post,* July 30, 1997; David H. Souter, "In Memoriam: William J. Brennan, Jr.," *Harvard Law Review,* 1997, vol. 111, p. 1.

14. ABORTION BATTLES CONTINUE

1. *Congressional Quarterly Almanac,* 1990, p. 513.

2. *Congressional Quarterly Almanac,* 1991, p. 278.

3. 947 F.2d 682 (1991). Reference to O'Connor's opinion in *Webster.*

4. Transcript of oral argument in *Planned Parenthood of Southeastern Pennsylvania v. Casey.*

5. David G. Savage, "The Rescue of *Roe vs. Wade;* How a Dramatic Change of Heart By a Supreme Court Justice Affirmed the Right to Abortion—Just When the Issue Seemed Headed for Certain Defeat," *Los Angeles Times,* December 13, 1992.

6. Kennedy to Blackmun, May 29, 1992; Blackmun note for his files, May 30, 1992, papers of Harry A. Blackmun, Library of Congress.

7. First draft circulated by O'Connor, Kennedy, and Souter, June 3, 1992, papers of Harry A. Blackmun, Library of Congress.

8. Stevens to O'Connor, Kennedy, and Souter, June 3, 1992, papers of Harry A. Blackmun, Library of Congress.

9. "Muddled on Abortion," *Newsweek,* June 15, 1992.

10. Rehnquist note to law clerks, June 10, 1992, papers of Harry A. Blackmun, Library of Congress.

11. Richard C. Reuben, "Man in the Middle," *California Lawyer,* October 1992, vol. 12, no. 10, p. 34.

12. *Planned Parenthood of Southeastern Pennsylvania v. Casey,* 505 U.S. 833 (1992).

13. Blackmun's concurrence in *Casey* also was unique in asserting that state restrictions on abortion would be prohibited by the constitutional guarantee of equality for women.

14. Robert H. Bork, "Again, a Struggle for the Soul of the Court," *New York Times,* July 8, 1992.

15. Judith Olans Brown, Wendy E. Parmet, and Mary E. O'Connell, "The Rugged Feminisim of Sandra Day O'Connor," *Indiana Law Review,* 1999, vol. 32, p. 1219.

16. Kenneth L. Karst, "Justice O'Connor and the Substance of Equal Citizenship," *Supreme Court Review 2003,* p. 357.

17. William Schneider, "The Battle for Saliency: The Abortion Issue in This Election Campaign," *The Atlantic,* October 1992.

18. *Stenberg v. Carhart,* 530 U.S. 914 (2000). For account of oral argument see Joan Biskupic, "Abortion Argued at High Court; Partial Birth Law Prompts Skepticism," *Washington Post,* April 26, 2000.

19. Joan Biskupic, "Abortion Debate Will Continue to Rage Despite Ruling, Need to Speak Out Is Strong," *USA Today,* June 29, 2000.

15. SCALIA V. O'CONNOR

1. Joan Biskupic, "Female Justices Attest to Fraternity on Bench; O'Connor and Ginsburg, in Separate Speeches, Discuss Personal Aspects of Supreme Court Life," *Washington Post,* August 21, 1994.

2. Howard Kohn, "Front and Center; on a Changing Supreme Court, Sandra Day O'Connor Has Emerged as a New Power, Especially on the Issue That Will Not Go Away: Abortion," *Los Angeles Times Magazine,* April 18, 1993.

3. Powell to Sandra and John O'Connor, January 4, 1993, Lewis F. Powell Jr. Archives, Washington and Lee University.

4. *Devlin v. Scardelletti,* 536 U.S. 1; *O'Connor v. Ortega,* 480 U.S. 709 (1987).

5. Author's interview with Antonin Scalia.

6. Joe Morgenstern, "Scalia the Terrible: Supreme Court Justice Antonin Scalia," *Playboy,* July 1993; see also Joan Biskupic, "In Terms of Moral Indignation, Scalia Is a Majority of One," *Washington Post,* June 30, 1996; Joan Biskupic, "Nothing Subtle About Scalia," *Washington Post,* February 18, 1997.

7. Joan Biskupic, " 'All Friends' On Court, Scalia Says," *Washington Post,* March 27, 1993.

8. *Employment Division, Department of Human Resources of Oregon v. Smith,* 494 U.S. 872 (1990). For consequence of decision, see, for example, Michael McConnell, "Free Exercise Revisionism and the *Smith* Decision," *University of Chicago Law Review,* vol. 57, p. 1109.

9. O'Connor to Blackmun, April 17, 1990, papers of Harry A. Blackmun, Library of Congress.

10. Ethan Bronner, "Combative Justice Scalia Moves Into Ascendancy," *Boston Globe,* April 29, 1990.

12. Joan Biskupic, "No Shades of Gray for Scalia," *USA Today,* September 18, 2002.

13. Scalia to Blackmun, August 31, 1991, papers of Harry A. Blackmun, Library of Congress.

14. Blackmun to Scalia, September 18, 1991, papers of Harry A. Blackmun, Library of Congress.

15. *United States v. Estate of Romani,* 523 U.S. 517 (1998).

16. *City of Erie v. Pap's A. M. Kandyland,* 599 U.S. 277 (2000).

17. *Pinette v. Capitol Square Review Board,* 30 F.3d 675 (1994).

18. Joan Biskupic, "Klansmen's Cross Comes to Court," *Washington Post,* April 23, 1995.

19. *Lynch v. Donnelly,* 465 U.S. 668 (1984).

20. *Allegheny County v. American Civil Liberties Union,* 492 U.S. 573 (1989).

21. Transcript of oral argument in *Capitol Square Review Board v. Pinette.*

22. Thomas wrote a separate opinion to this effect.

23. *Capital Square Review Board v. Pinette,* 515 U.S. 753 (1995).

24. Jeffrey Rosen, "A Majority of One," *New York Times Magazine,* June 3, 2001.

25. Scott H. O'Connor letter to the *New York Times,* printed in the magazine under the title "A Majority of One," June 24, 2001; author's interview with Sandra Day O'Connor.

26. Ramesh Ponnuru, "Sandra's Day: Why the Rehnquist Court Has Been the O'Connor Court, and How to Replace Her (Should It Come to That)," National Review, June 30, 2003; Author's interview with Eric Segall, author of work in progress *Justice O'Connor and the Rule of Law.*

27. Stephen Wermiel, "The Jurisprudence of Justice Sandra Day O'Connor: A Dual Role," *Women's Rights Law Reporter,* Summer/Fall 1991, 13 Women's Rts L. Rep. 129.

28. Author's interview with John C. Jeffries Jr.

29. Cass R. Sunstein, *One Case at a Time* (Cambridge, Massachusetts: Harvard University Press, 2001), pp. 41–42.

30. Author's interview with Stephen Breyer.

31. Author's interview with Clarence Thomas.

32. Margaret Talbot, "Supreme Confidence: The Jurisprudence of Justice Antonin Scalia," *New Yorker,* March 28, 2005.

33. Author's interview with John Paul Stevens.

34. Bernard Schwartz, *Super Chief: Earl Warren and His Supreme Court* (New York: New York University Press, 1983), p. 35.

35. Author's interview with Antonin Scalia.

36. *St. Mary's Honor Center v. Hicks,* 509 U.S. 502 (1993); O'Connor to Scalia with copies to other justices, June 23, 1993, papers of Harry A. Blackmun, Library of Congress.

37. Author's interview with Ruth Bader Ginsburg.

38. *Romer v. Evans,* 517 U.S. 620 (1996).

39. *United States v. Virginia,* 518 U.S. 515 (1996).

40. Clarence Thomas recused himself from the VMI case. His son was a cadet at the school.

41. *O'Hare Truck Service, Inc. v. City of Northlake,* 518 U.S. 712 (1996).

42. Scalia to Blackmun, July 2, 1996, papers of Harry A. Blackmun, Library of Congress.

43. Most recently in *Roper v. Simmons,* Docket No. 03–633 (2005).

44. *FERC v. Mississippi,* 456 U.S. 742 (1982); *New York v. United States,* 505 U.S. 144 (1992).

45. *United States v. Lopez,* 514 U.S. 549 (1995). See also Joan Biskupic, "High Court Rulings Bring Federal-State Power Balance to Forefront," *Washington Post,* May 25, 1995.

46. Joan Biskupic, "Dispute May Test Power of Congress; Court to Review Law on Gender Violence," *Washington Post,* September 29, 1999.

47. *United States v. Morrison,* 529 U.S. 598 (2000).

48. *Nevada Department of Human Resources v. Hibbs,* 538 U.S. 721 (2003); *Tennessee v. Lane,* 541 U.S. 509 (2004).

49. *Gonzales v. Raich,* No. 03–1454 (2005).

50. Author's interview with Roy Herberger.

51. Author's interview with Anthony Kennedy.

52. Eulogy for Lewis Powell, August 31, 1998. C-Span videotape of event viewed by author.

53. O'Connor to Powell, June 26, 1987, Lewis F. Powell Jr. Archives, Washington and Lee University.

54. Author's interview with J. Harvie Wilkinson.

55. Jeffrey Rosen, "A Majority of One," *New York Times Magazine,* June 3, 2001; Ramesh Ponnuru, "Sandra's Day: Why the Rehnquist Court Has Been the O'Connor Court, and How to Replace Her (Should It Come to That)," *National Review,* June 30, 2003.

56. Unless, of course, the defendant has submitted a guilty plea.

57. *Apprendi v. New Jersey,* 530 U.S. 466 (2000).

58. Author attended O'Connor Runnymede Speech, July 15, 2000.

59. *Blakely v. Washington,* 541 U.S._ (2004).

60. O'Connor did not read a dissent from the bench this time. She was not even in Court that day. No oral arguments were scheduled, and she already was out of town on another commitment.

61. *Shepard v. United States,* 125 S.C.T. 1254 (2005).

16. OPEN FILES

1. O'Connor to Mark Cannon, December 9, 1979; typed copy of handwritten letter provided to author by Cannon.

2. Bob Woodward and Scott Armstrong, *The Brethren: Inside the Supreme Court* (New York: Simon and Schuster, 1979).

3. Powell to his law clerks, January 16, 1980, Lewis F. Powell Jr. Archives, Washington and Lee University.

4. For example, Bernard Schwartz, *The Ascent of Pragmatism: The Burger Court in Action* (Reading, Massachusetts: Addison-Wesley, 1990).

5. Author's interview with Stephen Wermiel.

6. Ibid.

7. Brennan to all justices, December 19, 1990, papers of Harry A. Blackmun, Library of Congress.

8. John C. Jeffries Jr., *Justice Lewis F. Powell, Jr.* (New York: Charles Scribner's Sons,

1994); author's interview with John Jeffries. The Powell archives, located in Lexington, Virginia, were generally not mined by researchers and journalists as were the justices' papers at the Library of Congress.

9. Benjamin Weiser and Joan Biskupic, "Secrets of the High Court; Papers Afford a Rare Glimpse of Justices' Deliberations," *Washington Post,* May 23, 1994; Benjamin Weiser and Bob Woodward, "Roe's Eleventh-Hour Reprieve," *Washington Post,* May 23, 1993.

10. Rehnquist to all justices, May 24, 1993; O'Connor to Rehnquist, May 25, 1993, papers of Harry A. Blackmun, Library of Congress.

11. Kennedy to Rehnquist; White to Rehnquist, May 24, 1993, papers of Harry A. Blackmun, Library of Congress.

12. Joan Biskupic, "Chief Justice Castigates Library; Rehnquist Calls Opening Marshall Files 'Bad Judgment,' " *Washington Post,* May 26, 1993.

13. O'Connor draft Statement of Understanding About Release of Court Working Papers, June 17, 1993; Blackmun's handwritten notes recording outcome of conference meeting and "CJ loath to go on 6–3 vote," June 28, 1993, papers of Harry A. Blackmun, Library of Congress.

14. Bernard Schwartz, *Decision: How the Supreme Court Decides Cases* (New York: Oxford University Press, 1996), p. x.

15. O'Connor to Blackmun, asking him to adjust his hearing aid, November 1992, Papers of Harry A. Blackmun, Library of Congress.

16. Law clerk to Blackmun, June 15, 1990, papers of Harry A. Blackmun, Library of Congress.

17. Law clerk to Blackmun, June 26, 1992, papers of Harry A. Blackmun, Library of Congress.

18. Frank Eltman, "Justice O'Connor Calls Release of Blackmun Papers 'Unfortunate'," Associated Press, March 9, 2004. At a July 21, 2005, appearance in Spokane, Washington, O'Connor said her Court papers would not become public while justices with whom she had served were still on the Court.

17. APPEARANCES COUNT

1. Author's interview with Alan Day.

2. "Thirty-Seven Days: A Special Report," *Los Angeles Times,* December 17, 2000.

3. Florida Division of Elections figures cited in *Bush v. Gore,* 531 U.S. 98 (2000) and *Bush v. Palm Beach County Canvassing Board,* 531 U.S. 70 (2000).

4. Broward, Miami-Dade, Palm Beach and Volusia Counties.

5. Transcript of the *Today* show, NBC News, November 9, 2000.

6. Mike Williams, "Florida Names Bush Winner as He Asks Gore to Halt Fight," *Atlanta Journal and Constitution,* November 27, 2000.

7. *Bush v. Palm Beach County Canvassing Board.*

8. Terence Hunt, "U.S. Supreme Court Halts Recount; Arguments Scheduled for Monday," Associated Press, December 10, 2000; Mark Z. Barabak and Richard A. Serrano, "Divided 5–4, U.S. Supreme Court Orders Halt to Florida Recounts," *Los Angeles Times,* December 10, 2000.

9. *Bush v. Gore.*

10. Transcript of oral argument in *Bush v. Gore,* available on Supreme Court Web site, www.supremecourtus.gov.

11. David Boies, *Courting Justice* (New York: Hyperion, 2004), p. 445.

12. Evan Thomas and Michael Isikoff, "The Truth Behind the Pillars," *Newsweek*, December 25, 2000. A similar story also was reported by the *Wall Street Journal*.

13. Jeffrey Toobin, *Too Close to Call: The Thirty-Six Day Battle to Decide the 2000 Election* (New York: Random House, 2001), pp. 248–249.

14. Author interviewed law clerks and justices in the aftermath of the case; other reporters followed up with investigative stories, including David Margolick, Evgenia Peretz, and Michael Shnayerson, "The Path to Florida," *Vanity Fair*, October 2004.

15. *Bush v. Gore.*

16. David Tell, "The Bush Victory," *The Weekly Standard*, December 25, 2000. Richard Posner, *Breaking the Deadlock: The 2000 Election, the Constitution, and the Courts* (Princeton, New Jersey: Princeton University Press, 2001); "Partisanship Rules," *The Nation*, January 1, 2001.

17. Joan Biskupic, "Election Still Splits Court," *USA Today*, January 22, 2001.

18. Akhil Reed Amar, "Should We Trust Judges?" *Los Angeles Times*, December 17, 2000.

19. Jack M. Balkin, *"Bush v. Gore* and the Boundary Between Law and Politics," *Yale Law Journal*, 2001, vol. 110, p. 1407.

20. Jim Drinkard, "Special Report: Remember Chads? They've Hung Around," July 13, 2004, *USA Today*.

21. Laurence H. Tribe, "The Supreme Court 2000 Term, Comment: *Bush v. Gore* and Its Disguises: Freeing *Bush v. Gore* from Its Hall of Mirrors," *Harvard Law Review*, 2001, vol. 115, p. 170.

22. Transcript of *Dateline*, NBC News, January 25, 2002.

23. Al Kamen and Marjorie Williams, "Woman of the Hour," *Washington Post Magazine*, June 11, 1989.

24. Author's interview with Roy Herberger.

25. Joan Biskupic, "Election Still Splits Court," *USA Today*, January 22, 2001; Joan Biskupic, "Florida Recount Dominated High Court's Term," *USA Today*, June 29, 2001.

26. Joan Biskupic, "O'Connor Not Confined by Conservatism," *USA Today*, June 24, 2004; see also Alan M. Dershowitz, "Curious Fallout From *Bush v. Gore*," *New York Times*, July 4, 2001; Stuart Taylor Jr., "Veering Left: The Art of Judicial Evolution," *National Journal*, July 5, 2003.

27. *Hunt v. Cromartie*, retitled *Easley v. Cromartie* for the official reports, 532 U.S. 234 (2001).

28. Ibid.

29. Transcript of Clinton and Breyer news conference, *Federal News Service*, May 16, 1994.

30. Joan Biskupic, "Unlikely Alliance Keeps Court Centered," *USA Today*, June 21, 2001.

31. Author's interview with Stephen Breyer.

32. Maria Elena Baca, "Sandra Day O'Connor Speaks in Minneapolis," *Minneapolis Star Tribune*, July 3, 2001.

33. *Wiggins v. Smith*, 539 U.S. 510 (2003). A state court had found that in not vigorously pursuing mitigating evidence, defense lawyers had permissibly made "a deliberate, tactical decision to concentrate their effort at convincing the jury that Wiggins was not directly responsible for the murder." A federal trial court ruled that such a "tactical decision" can only

be deemed "reasonable" if it is based on information the attorney had after conducting a reasonable investigation. The federal appellate court disagreed, reinstating the sentence; *Rompilla v. Beard,* Docket No. 5462 (2005).

34. *Atkins v. Virginia,* 536 U.S. 304 (2002). The court noted that in 1989, only sixteen states had banned the execution of the retarded: The fourteen states that rejected capital punishment completely and just two others. The court said that was not evidence of a national consensus.

35. Facts drawn from *Grutter v. Bollinger,* 539 U.S. 306 (2003); *Gratz v. Bollinger,* 539 U.S. 244 (2003).

36. *Wygant v. Jackson Board of Education,* 476 U.S. 267 (1986); *Richmond v. J. A. Croson Co.,* 488 U.S. 469 (1989).

37. *Grutter v. Bollinger.*

38. Ibid.

39. Ibid.

40. *Lawrence v. Texas,* 539 U.S. 558 (2003).

41. Author's interview with Alan Day.

42. Carol Doup Muller, "The Honorable Cowgirl," *Christian Science Monitor,* January 17, 2002; Linda Greenhouse, "Happy Trails," *New York Times Book Review,* February 3, 2002.

43. Author's interview with Alan Day.

18. MOVING FORWARD

1. Program, Reagan funeral service, June 11, 2004.

2. Author's interview with Sandra Day O'Connor.

3. Sandra Day O'Connor and H. Alan Day, *Lazy B* (New York: Random House, 2002), p. 318. The last line of the book is: "But, as with life and death on the Lazy B, that's the way it is."

4. Transcript of "Constitutional Conversation Hosted by the National Constitution Center, the National Archives and the Aspen Institute," *Federal News Service,* April 22, 2005. Author was in attendance.

5. Facts drawn from *Jackson v. Birmingham Board of Education,* Docket No. 02–1672 (2005).

6. Ibid. Her opinion, joined by Justices Stevens, Souter, Breyer, and Ginsburg, reinstated Jackson's lawsuit.

7. Transcript of oral argument in *Davis v. Monroe County Board of Education,* 529 U.S. 629 (1999).

8. Ibid. As a result of the decision, school districts nationwide established new policies for taking harassment reports and acting on them.

9. "Balancing the Scales of Justice; Sandra Day O'Connor, the First Woman of the Supreme Court, Has the Last Word" (interview with *KidsPost*), *Washington Post,* March 24, 2005. The book about her horse was published in late August 2005.

10. Author's interview with Sandra Day O'Connor; Joan Biskupic, "O'Connor Pauses to Reflect on 'The Majesty of the Law,'" *USA Today,* April 9, 2003.

11. Patti Waldmeir, "A Legal History Maker Reserves Judgment," *Financial Times,* May 9, 2003.

12. Dennis Hutchinson, "Bench Press," *New York Times Book Review,* June 29, 2003.

13.   Transcript of *All Things Considered,* National Public Radio, May 14, 2003.

14.   Author's interview with Carolyn Gerster.

15.   Author's interview with Sandra Day O'Connor.

16.   Transcript of "Remarks by Sandra Day O'Connor, Associate Justice, Supreme Court of the United States," at the Arab Judicial Forum, September 15–17, 2003. Available at www.arabjudicialforum.org/ajf_oconnor_remarks.html.

17.   Transcript of press availability at the Arab Judicial Forum, United States Consulate, September 17, 2003.

18.   Sandra Day O'Connor, *The Majesty of the Law: Reflections of a Supreme Court Justice* (New York: Random House, 2003), p. 201.

19.   *Atkins v. Virginia,* 536 U.S. 304 (2002); *Roper v. Simmons,* Docket No. 03–633 (2005).

20.   A year later, the United States, with massive air strikes and troops on the ground, drove Saddam Hussein from power in Iraq and established a large-scale military presence there that was continuing as of the writing of this book.

21.   *Hamdi v. Rumsfeld,* 124 S.C.T. 2633 (2004). A second major case at this time was brought by detainees captured during U.S. military actions in Afghanistan and elsewhere and housed at a U.S. naval base in Guantanamo Bay, Cuba. None of the men were charged or had access to lawyers or a hearing. The families of twelve Kuwaiti and two Australian prisoners challenged the legality of the detentions in U.S. Courts. The justices, with O'Connor in the majority, rejected the administration's claim that United States Courts lacked jurisdiction because the claims were coming from foreigners imprisoned off American soil. *Rasul v. Bush,* Docket No. 03–334 (2004).

22.   *Hamdi v. Rumsfeld.*

23.   "Constitutional Conversation" transcript.

24.   Author's interview with Clarence Thomas.

25.   Author's interview with Sandra Day O'Connor.

26.   Henry J. Abraham, *Justices, Presidents and Senators: A History of U.S. Supreme Court Appointments From Washington to Clinton* (Lanham, Maryland: Rowman and Littlefield, 1999), p. 286; John J. Monteleone, ed., *Branch Rickey's Little Blue Book* (New York: Macmillan, 1995).

27.   Author's interview with Sandra Day O'Connor.

EPILOGUE

1.   A Court messenger deliver O'Connor's retirement letter to President Bush on the morning of July 1, 2005.

2.   Author's interview with Antonin Scalia.

3.   Two weeks later, on July 14, Rehnquist issued a public statement saying, "I will continue to perform my duties as Chief Justice as long as my health permits."

4.   Press Conference of Arlen Specter, Senate Radio and TV Gallery, Federal News Service transcript, July 1, 2005.

5.   Joan Biskupic, "O'Connor's Final Decision Puts Family First," USA Today, July 5, 2005.

6.   Hanna Rosin, "Feminists on O'Connor: A Mixed Verdict," The Washington Post, July 3, 2005.

7.   Author's interview with Barbara Babcock. Previously cited in Chapter 7.

8.   Author's interview with Antonin Scalia. President Bush announced on September 5, 2005, that he was withdrawing Roberts's nomination for O'Connor's seat and choosing him to succeed Rehnquist.

9.   Hamdi v. Rumsfeld, 124 S.C.T. 2633 (2004).

10.   O'Connor referred to the poem as having been written by an Anonymous poet, and news sources reported it as such. Titled "Indispensable Man," the poem was written by Saxon White Kessinger in 1959 and first published in 1966.

SELECTED BIBLIOGRAPHY

ARCHIVES

Harry A. Blackmun papers, Library of Congress

William J. Brennan Jr. papers, Library of Congress

Day family papers, Arizona Historical Society

Barry Goldwater papers, Arizona Historical Foundation, Arizona State University

Thurgood Marshall papers, Library of Congress

Richard Nixon tapes, National Archives and Records Administration

Senator Sandra Day O'Connor papers, Arizona State Library, Archives and Public Records

Phoenix History Project, Arizona Historical Society

Lewis F. Powell Jr. Archives, Washington and Lee University

Ronald Reagan Library

NEWSPAPERS, MAGAZINES, AND JOURNALS

ABA Journal, American Lawyer, Arizona Daily Star, Arizona Republic, Associated Press, The Atlantic, Baltimore Sun, Congressional Quarterly, El Paso Times, Governing Magazine, Ladies' Home Journal, Los Angeles Times, The Nation, National Law Journal, New Republic, New York Times, New Yorker, Newsweek, Phoenix Gazette, Phoenix Magazine, Saturday Evening Post, Stanford Daily, Time, Tucson Daily Citizen, Washington Post, Washington Star, USA Today, U.S. News & World Report

LAW REVIEWS

University of Chicago Law Review, Constitutional Commentary, Harvard Law Review, Indiana Law Review, Michigan Law Review, Pennsylvania Law Review, Southern California Law Review, Stanford Law Review, Supreme Court Review,

Vanderbilt Law Review, Virginia Law Review, William and Mary Law Review, Women's Rights Law Reporter, Yale Law Journal

BOOKS

Abraham, Henry J. *Justices, Presidents and Senators, Revised: A History of U.S. Supreme Court Appointments from Washington to Clinton.* Lanham, Maryland: Rowman and Littlefield, 1999.

Biskupic, Joan and Witt, Elder. *Guide to the U.S. Supreme Court.* Washington, DC: Congressional Quarterly, 1997.

Blasi, Vincent, ed. *The Burger Court: The Counter-Revolution That Wasn't.* New Haven, Connecticut: Yale University Press, 1983.

Brownlee, W. Elliot, and Graham, Hugh Davis, eds., *The Reagan Presidency: Pragmatic Conservatism and Its Legacies.* Lawrence, Kansas: University Press of Kansas, 2003.

Cannon, Lou. *President Reagan: Role of a Lifetime.* New York: Simon & Schuster, 1991.

Craig, Barbara Hinkson, and O'Brien, David M. *Abortion and American Politics.* Chatham, New Jersey: Chatham House, 1993.

Davis, Sue. *Justice Rehnquist and the Constitution.* Princeton, New Jersey: Princeton University Press, 1989.

Dean, John W. *The Rehnquist Choice.* New York: Touchstone, 2002.

Epstein, Lee, and Knight, Jack. *The Choices Justices Make.* Washington, DC. Congressional Quarterly, 1998.

Estrich, Susan. *Sex and Power.* New York: Riverhead Books, 2000.

Fallon, Richard H. *Implementing the Constitution.* Cambridge, Massachusetts: Harvard University, 2001.

Foskett, Ken. *Judging Thomas: The Life and Times of Clarence Thomas.* New York: William Morrow, 2004.

Friedman, Leon, and Israel, Fred L., eds. *The Justices of the United States Supreme Court.* New York: Chelsea House, 1997.

Gabor, Andrea. *Einstein's Wife: Work and Marriage in the Lives of Five Great Twentieth-Century Women.* New York: Viking, 1995.

Garrow, David J. *Liberty and Sexuality: The Right of Privacy and the Making of Roe v. Wade.* New York: Macmillan, 1994.

Goldberg, Robert Alan. *Barry Goldwater.* New Haven, Connecticut: Yale University Press, 1995.

Greenhouse, Linda. *Becoming Justice Blackmun: Harry Blackmun's Supreme Court Journey.* New York: Times Books, 2005.

Huber, Peter. *Sandra Day O'Connor.* New York: Chelsea House, 1990.

Hutchinson, Dennis J. *The Man Who Once Was Whizzer White: Portrait of Justice*

Byron R. White. New York: The Free Press, 1998.

Jeffries, John C. Jr. *Justice Lewis F. Powell, Jr. and the Era of Judicial Balance*. New York: Scribner, 1994.

Kammer, Jerry. *The Second Long Walk: The Navajo-Hopi Land Dispute*. Albuquerque, New Mexico: University of New Mexico Press, 1980.

Kennedy, David M. *Freedom From Fear: The American People in Depression and War, 1929–1945*. New York: Oxford University Press, 1999.

Kluger, Richard. *Simple Justice*. New York: Vintage Books, 1975.

Lazarus, Edward. *Closed Chambers: The First Eyewitness Account of the Epic Struggles Inside the Supreme Court*. New York: Times Books, 1998.

Leuchtenburg, William E. *The Supreme Court Reborn: The Constitutional Revolution in the Age of Roosevelt*. New York: Oxford University Press, 1995.

Luckingham, Bradford. *Phoenix: The History of a Southwestern Metropolis*. Tucson, Arizona: The University of Arizona Press, 1989.

Maroon, Fred J. *The Supreme Court of the United States*. Washington, DC: Lickle Publishing with The Supreme Court Historical Society, 2002.

Maveety, Nancy. *Justice Sandra Day O'Connor: Strategist on the Supreme Court*. Lanham, Maryland: Rowman & Littlefield, 1996.

Mayer, Jane, and Abramson, Jill. *Strange Justice: The Selling of Clarence Thomas*. New York: Houghton Mifflin, 1994.

Mayer, Jane, and McManus, Doyle. *Landslide: The Unmaking of the President, 1984–1988*. Boston, Massachusetts: Houghton Mifflin, 1988.

McCloskey, Robert G. *The American Supreme Court*. Chicago: The University of Chicago Press, 2005. Fourth ed. Revised by Sanford Levinson.

Morgan, Ted. *FDR: A Biography*. New York: Simon & Schuster, 1985.

O'Connor, Sandra Day. *The Majesty of the Law: Reflections of a Supreme Court Justice*. New York: Random House, 2003.

O'Connor, Sandra Day and Day, H. Alan. *Lazy B*. New York: Random House, 2002.

Posner, Richard A. *Breaking the Deadlock: The 2000 Election, the Constitution, and the Courts*. Princeton, New Jersey: Princeton University Press, 2001.

Rakove, Jack N. *The Unfinished Election of 2000: Leading Scholars Examine America's Strangest Election*. New York: Basic Books, 2001.

Rathbun, Harry J. *The Anglo-American Legal System*. Stanford, California: Stanford University Press, 1941.

Rehnquist, William H. *The Supreme Court*. New York: Knopf, 2001.

Savage, David. *Turning Right: The Making of the Rehnquist Supreme Court*. New York: John Wiley, 1993.

Schwartz, Bernard. *The Ascent of Pragmatism: The Burger Court in Action*. Reading, Massachusetts: Addison-Wesley, 1990.

Schwartz, Bernard. *Decision: How the Supreme Court Decides Cases.* New York: Oxford University Press, 1996.

Schwartz, Bernard. *Super Chief: Earl Warren and His Supreme Court, a Judicial Biography.* New York: New York University Press, 1983.

Schwartz, Herman. *The Burger Years: Rights and Wrongs in the Supreme Court 1969–1986.* New York: Viking, 1987.

Simon, James F. *The Center Holds: The Power Struggle Inside the Rehnquist Court.* New York: Simon & Schuster, 1995.

Sheridan, Thomas E. *Arizona: A History.* Tucson, Arizona: University of Arizona Press, 1995.

Smith, William French. *Law and Justice in the Reagan Administration: The Memoir of an Attorney General.* Stanford, California: Hoover Institution Press, 1991.

Smith, Zachary A. *Politics and Public Policy in Arizona.* Westport, Connecticut: Praeger Publishers, 1996.

Stegner, Wallace. *Angle of Repose.* New York: Penguin Books, 1992.

Stohr, Greg. *A Black and White Case: How Affirmative Action Survived Its Greatest Legal Challenge.* Princeton, New Jersey: Bloomberg Press, 2004.

Sunstein, Cass R. *One Case at a Time: Judicial Minimalism on the Supreme Court.* Cambridge, Massachusetts: Harvard University Press, 2001.

Toobin, Jeffrey. *Too Close to Call: The Thirty-Six Day Battle to Decide the 2000 Election.* New York: Random House, 2001.

Trimble, Marshall. *Arizona: A Cavalcade of History.* Tucson, Arizona: Rio Nuevo Publishers, 2003.

Tushnet, Mark. *A Court Divided: The Rehnquist Court and the Future of Constitutional Law.* New York: W. W. Norton, 2005.

Tushnet, Mark. *Making Constitutional Law: Thurgood Marshall and the Supreme Court, 1961–1991.* New York: Oxford University Press, 1997.

Van Sickel, Robert W. *Not a Particularly Different Voice: The Jurisprudence of Sandra Day O'Connor.* New York: Peter Lang, 1998.

Williams, Juan. *Thurgood Marshall: American Revolutionary.* New York: Random House, 1998.

Woodward, Bob, and Armstrong, Scott. *The Brethren.* New York: Simon & Schuster, 1979.

Woodward, Bob, and Bernstein, Carl. *The Final Days.* New York: Simon & Schuster, 1987.

INDEX